D1602767

OURS,
YOURS,
MINE

OURS, YOURS, MINE

Mutuality and the Emergence of the Separate Self

Anni Bergman, Ph.D.
in collaboration with Maria F. Fahey

JASON ARONSON INC.
Northvale, New Jersey
London

This book was set in 10 pt. New Century Schoolbook.

10 9 8 7 6 5 4 3 2 1

Library of Congress Cataloging-in-Publication Data

Bergman, Anni, 1919–
    Ours, yours, mine : mutuality and the emergence of the separate self / Anni Bergman.
        p. cm.
    Includes bibliographical references and index.
    ISBN 1-56821-374-3
    1. Separation-individuation. 2. Self in children. 3 Child psychotherapy. 4. Psychoses in children—Treatment. I.Title.
    [DNLM: 1. Individuation—in infancy & childhood collected works.
    2. Personality Development—in infancy & childhood collected works.
    3. Mother–Child Relations collected works. 4. Psychotic Disorders—in infancy & childhood collected works. 5. Psychotic Disorders—therapy collected works. WS 105.5.P3 B499o 1998]
    RJ507. S46B47 1998
    155. 4—dc21
    DNLM/DLC
    for Library of Congress   98–21039

Printed in the United States of America on acid-free paper. For information and catalog write to Jason Aronson Inc., 230 Livingston Street, Northvale, New Jersey 07647. Or visit our website: http://www.aronson.com

for

Kostia, Libby, and Sam

Tobi, Nancy, Patrick, and Macky

Contents

II. Facilitating the Separation-Individuation Process in the Clinical Situation

Acknowledgments

The papers in this collection, written during a span of almost thirty years, can hardly be called *mine*: representing the work of many, they really are *ours*.

My assistant for over ten years, Maria Fahey, who is also my friend, editor, co-thinker, and recent co-author, is the one who has made the book happen. Without her devoted, painstaking, and creative work, these collected papers could not have become a book. The project began when Michael Moskowitz, former publisher at Aronson, asked me if I would be willing to do a volume of my papers. Michael and Sally Moskowitz, who were among my first students, have become colleagues on whose support and encouragement I rely. I am grateful to Michael for having encouraged me to do the book, and I treasure having him and Sally as colleagues and friends.

The central theme of the book is the separation-individuation process as I have been privileged to observe it in both normal and pathological development. I shall never forget how thrilled I was when Margaret Mahler accepted me onto her research team, even though my formal education as a psychoanalyst and researcher had not yet begun. I shall always be grateful for the opportunity she provided, and for the privilege to think with her about the meanings we could infer from what we saw and heard as mothers and babies interacted with each other in the playspace in which the research occurred.

It was my further privilege to become a therapist of autistic and psychotic children and their mothers. I am deeply grateful to the parents of my child patients who entrusted their children to me, and I am grateful to the children who allowed me to help them in their painful growing-up processes.

I continue to hold my exceptional colleagues from the Mahler Research group in the highest regard. I am particularly grateful to Manny Furer, who was my supervisor during the long treatment of a child who did not talk for many years. He shared my passion for trying to get into her world and make sense of it, and he provided the theoretical underpinnings that made my understanding possible. Without Manny's help, I would not have been able to persist in my conviction that she was talking to us, long before she could use words. I was also supervised by Herman Roiphe, whose intense dedication to psychoanalytic ideas I very much admired.

Fred Pine, our research psychoanalyst, could always find ways to create clarity, to make meaning out of chaos. I always loved to hear his mind work. John McDevitt's longterm commitment to the research and its subjects made the follow-up studies possible. Through our long years of work, his reliability and availability have been without match.

I would also like to acknowledge the help I received from the Research Training Programme of the International Psychoanalytic Association, where I presented follow-up material from the original Separation-Individuation research. In particular, I would like to thank Peter Fonagy and Robert Emde, who discussed my work and provided encouragement, support, and valuable suggestions.

My work in the field of psychoanalysis and observational research began at the time my older son left home to go to college, and this book will be published when my oldest grandson is about to graduate. My family's love and encouragement have been a constant support. I thank my children and grandchildren for being there: my love for them has sustained me through difficult times. My husband, Peter, was always supportive of my work and patient with the demands it made on my time. I am sad that he cannot be here for the publication of this book, which I know would have given him great pleasure and made him very proud.

My brother, Arnold Rink, and his wife Ada have been a strong and loving connection to my family of origin and have helped me in more ways than I can say. Not only have they recognized and appreciated my work, but they have always provided wonderful times and places to be together. I am happy that their grandson, Ronald, who is completing his Ph.D. in psychology at the University of Padua, will be using some of the separation-individuation data in his dissertation. My brother and his family live in Italy—a country I love—and it is especially meaningful to me that my dear friend, Renata Gaddini, who feels like family, made available an exquisite place in Capri for me and Maria to work on this book in the inspiring atmosphere of Villa Quattro Venti. We cannot thank her enough.

My work has grown richer through my contact with colleagues all over the world who have invited me to present and teach separation-individuation theory and at whose homes I have stayed. The opportunities to present my work at many institutes and universities in many countries has been truly generative. In this regard I wish to give particular thanks to Fifi Piene, who in 1978 was the first to invite me to present my work in Norway, and to Tellervo Keaenanen, my very appreciative and appreciated host in Finland. I am also particularly grateful to my friend and colleague, Adriana Lis, Professor at the University of Padua, where I have had the privilege to teach many times. I have particularly appreciated the valuable comments Adriana has made on my papers in progress.

It has always been very important to me to do my work as part of a group. In the 1970s I was invited to become a faculty member of the clinical psychology program at the City University of New York, which became a supportive and intellectually stimulating home base for over twenty years. Together with Gilbert Voyat and Linda Gunsberg, I started the City University Child Center, an unusual project described in Chapter 15 of this book. The many students and faculty involved were unequaled in their creativity and enthusiasm, and many became friends, collaborators, and co-authors. I would like to give special mention to Arnold Wilson, first a therapeutic companion, later a co-teacher and co-author. He has always generously lent his scholarly thinking. In particular, I want to thank Steven Ellman and Lawrence Gould, who provided support and love, even in difficult times. I admire Steve's wonderful mind and his dedication to psychoanalytic scholarship, and I appreciate Larry for his creative ways of thinking and his warmth. They both remain extraordinarily special to me.

Before ending I would like to express gratitude to my analyst, Werner Nathan, who was instrumental in my own psychological birth. I know he too would be happy about this book.

—Anni Bergman
February 1999

Introduction

In 1959 I joined two research projects under the direction of Margaret Mahler: the study of the separation-individuation process and the study of infantile psychosis. The goal of the separation-individuation research was to observe and understand how a child's separate self develops out of the matrix of the mother–child dual unity. The goal of the infantile psychosis study was to understand better and to learn how to treat mother–child couples for whom the separation-individuation process had not unfolded on its own. The children who came to the center for treatment were unable to use their mothers to facilitate their participation in the world as separate human beings. Thus, the developmental process that unfolds naturally in most children—the very process that was being observed and documented in the separation-individuation research—could only proceed with the utmost difficulty for the children who needed treatment. The observations of normal development and the progression of the developmental process were key in my understanding of psychotic children and in my ability to help them develop and change. In turn, what I learned from the children I treated by way of participating in their distorted and painful psychological births helped me to understand some of the challenges all mother–child couples face in the process of a child's achievement of separateness and autonomy.

This book is based on my work on understanding the beginnings of the sense of self and its development through the life cycle. The papers collected here, drawn from four decades of work and written during the last two decades, discuss various facets and applications of my research and clinical work. While I am presenting the papers in two main sections—"Separation-Individuation Theory" and "Facilitating the Separation-Individuation Process in the Clinical Situation"—there is a great deal of overlap, as the papers themselves reflect how the theoretical understandings gained in my research on development processes and my clinical work have informed each other. Thus, many theoretical papers are illustrated with clinical vignettes, and many clinical papers are built on separation-individuation and other developmental theories.

The papers collected here are drawn largely from my involvement in longitudinal work—both from long-term therapy and from the original and follow-up research on separation-individuation. I have returned to the development of individuals' lives at various points in their life cycles and have studied, learned, and written about them at various points in mine. Because each paper has a particular idea that grew from my study at that time, I have decided to leave the papers largely intact, even though this results in some repetition of case material through this volume.

The focus of the separation-individuation research was not the effect of the separation *from* mother but rather the development of the separate self *in the presence of* mother. A central theme of this book is how the achievement of mutuality and separateness coincides: separateness is always dependent on being in relationship to an other, and mutuality is always dependent on the ability to recognize the other as separate. While the original research (Mahler et al. 1975) may have overemphasized the achievement of separateness, it is important to remember that the research design was to observe the mother–child couple and the evolving relationship between them. The use of participant-observers, who formed relationships with both the children and the mothers, further recognized that the most meaningful observations occur in the context of a relationship—as they do in the analytic situation.

The idea of the couple has been central in my observations and in my clinical work. My analytic work began with the the treatment of psychotic children using the tripartite treatment design, the premise of which is that psychotic children have not formed enough of a separate self to be treated alone and that it is important to see them in therapy together with their primary caretakers. The therapist is to be a catalyst for a viable child–mother relationship while at the same time the therapist is to establish a unique relationship with both the child and the mother. The work with the psychotic child–mother couple was designed to promote a mutual relationship from which the child could separate and individuate; only then could a psychotic child be treated separately. This kind of work with mother–child couples has since become an accepted way of treating infants and toddlers with adjustment difficulties and delays.

The design of the original separation-individuation research left ample space for researchers to use their own selves in the investigations. Observers spent four mornings per week with the children and their mothers in an unstructured setting. While it was the multiple observations of many different observers that eventually resulted in the articulation of separation-individuation theory, the setting was such that each participant-observer could use his or her own creativity, curiosity, and particular background as a basis for asking questions and seeking answers. Several questions seem always to have captured my interest: Where does the essential part of the self originate and how does this essential self survive traumatic experience, undergo transformation, and continue through the life cycle? What interferes with expressing and using the essential self? How are play and creativity, beginning in a child's earliest relationships, used to express the essential self and facilitate development?

I began my research and clinical work at the Masters Children's Center, which provided me with a thorough grounding in psychoanalytic theory and the evolving conceptualizations of the separation-individuation process. The observational research on separation-individuation beginning in the sixth month of life was well on its way when the revolutionary work of infant researchers starting at birth began to throw such extraordinary light on the infant's earliest ca-

pacity to relate to others and to develop agency. The work of
Brazelton, Sander, Emde, Stern, Beebe, and Trevarthen has inspired
me to expand the knowledge I had gained from my observations in
the separation-individuation research. In addition, I am interested
in how the phenomena observed in the 1960s in a relatively small
group of middle-class mothers, who for the most part did not work
outside the home and were in fairly stable marriages, can be applied
to the vast world with all its variations and permutations of family
life. The intensive study of a group of mother–child couples in the
first three years of life and the ongoing follow up continues to provide data valuable to the understanding and further investigation of
developmental processes and their applications to the therapeutic
situation.

The intimate knowledge of the phenomena of separation-individuation during infancy and toddlerhood is constantly alive in my mind
as I work with adult patients. Contemporary Freudian psychoanalysts have become increasingly interested in understanding the psychoanalytic process in the interplay of transference and countertransference enactments in the analyst–patient couple, an interest that
has developed along with the burgeoning knowledge of the nature of
the mother–infant couple during the first three years of life. The task
of using insights gained from observational studies of infant–mother
couples in understanding what transpires between the analyst and
the patient is not a simple one because there is the danger of drawing behavioral analogies that leave out the complexities of the adult
personality. Nonetheless, I believe that thorough and detailed knowledge of early developmental processes enhances the psychoanalytic
process and makes the preverbal period of development accessible in
the analytic situation.

While at one time it was assumed that the therapeutic object relationship was of importance in the treatment of borderline or severely
narcissistic character pathology, it is now more generally accepted
that even for patients with less serious pathology an understanding
and reworking of the early mother–child relationship is an important
part of the work of analysis. Modell (1990) says that "[f]or some patients, the therapeutic setting may be their first opportunity to be a
child" (p. 147). I would specify that, for some patients, the therapeutic
setting may be an opportunity to be a child at a particular stage of

early childhood—or even infancy. Varying degrees of difficulties and deficiencies in a particular stage of the mother–child relationship can be worked through in the analytic setting. An important avenue to understanding a patient's reworking of preverbal issues is the first-hand observation of mother–child interaction during the nonverbal period, with the task of constructing meaning from these observations.

I have found that separation-individuation phenomena observed and described in the original separation-individuation research reoccur in the analysis of patients whose separation-individuation process was curtailed by the unavailability of an adequately attuned mother. An emotionally attuned analyst who has learned from observing mother–child couples to understand the nonverbal enactment of interpersonal and intrapsychic phenomena can be more aware of the repetition of these phenomena in the analytic setting and can facilitate the process of making conscious the unconscious reenactments.

In the analytic process the relationship of analyst and analysand promotes the patient's sense of herself as a separate individual with a capacity to experience and be in charge of her own life while being intimately connected to significant others. The fear that self-realization will not be welcomed or even tolerated by the mother is a common one and goes far beyond the fear generated through oedipal rivalry, though there is, of course, always an interplay between conflicts on various levels.

Separation-individuation theory describes the process of developing self and object representations in the course of the first three years of life. Originally the separation-individuation process was seen as one in which the lion's share of adaptation had to be achieved by the child because the mother was already an individual with limited capacity for change or adaptation. The original research insufficiently took into account how each particular child influenced the development of her mother's sense of self, not only because of the individual temperament each child brings into the world but—perhaps even more significantly—because of the way each child has unique meaning for the mother. Each child reawakens in the mother particular aspects of her own early relationships, which in turn influence her way of being a mother to that particular child and her way of coauthoring the story of that particular child's life. Just as developmental theorists observe the development of the mother–child couple, contemporary analysts think of the analytic process as a more active exchange between two individuals, rather than a process in which it is only one, namely the analysand, who has a significant emotional experience resulting in growth and individuation.

Having studied and observed first hand the detailed phenomena of the separation-individuation process, especially during practicing and rapprochement, has helped me to become intuitively available to patients who have profound unresolved separation-individuation problems. The nature of the disturbance in the earliest relationship influences the nature of the analytic transference. For example, at the beginning of her analysis, one adult patient needed me to be a nonintrusive, emotionally available, and benign presence who could enjoy her explorations of the world and of herself. It was only after I had gained her trust as the good mother of the practicing child who was eager to accept the treasures of her dreams without analyzing them that eventually she could begin to experience and work through the rapprochement conflicts. Another patient often wanted me just to be there and listen to her, but my sense was not that she needed me for refueling, but rather that she needed me to give her permission to express her needs without being shamed, punished, or deprived. For this patient, I needed to be the rapprochement mother who could withstand her ambivalence and her rage without retaliating. The object relationship to an analyst who is affectively attuned and sensitive to developmental processes helps analysands reach a higher stage of self-realization as well as a more developed capacity for intimate relatedness. While cases involving unresolved separation-individuation issues are very different in presenting problems and in the way the analytic process unfolds, they have in common that the patient's sense of a separate self is very fragile and the ability to relate to a separate other is impaired. An analyst's ability to understand and respond to the particular developmental needs of the analysand gives the analyst the patience and hope to endure feeling not-good-enough and to avoid projecting that feeling onto the analysand. In this way patients who seem to be unanalyzable can go through the long and difficult process that is required to repair deficits arising from early emotional unavailability and incompatibility in the mother–child relationship. These patients come to analysis without a stable representation of what Stern has described as "self-with-mother." The hope in this kind of treatment is that the patient is able to build a stable representation of self-with-analyst, which will help the patient become available for other intimate object relationships.

The first section of this book, a collection of theoretical papers that grew out of my participation in separation-individuation research, begins with an introductory chapter on separation-individuation theory and is followed by a series of papers that elaborate on a particular aspect of the process. These papers, presented here in roughly the order in which they were written, show the development of my interests in particular aspects of the separation-individuation process. "From Mother to the World Outside: The Use of Space during the Separation-Individuation Process" traces the way in which toddlers create transitional spaces that allow them to stay connected to mother as they separate from her. Through a discussion of the importance of and use by the child of possessions, "Ours, Yours, Mine" shows how a sense of "mine" and "yours" grows out of an earlier sense of "ours." This sense of "ours" is influenced by the gender of a child and the mother's feelings about it. An early discussion, "Speculations on the Development of Gender Role Characteristics," is followed by "Considerations about the Development of the Girl during the Separation-Individuation Process," which illustrates the special struggles of the girl separating from mother and achieving her own separate female identity. Written with Arnold Wilson, "Thoughts about Stages on the Way to Empathy and the Capacity for Concern" shows how the road to mature empathy does not follow a straight path but has particular characteristics and vicissitudes in each subphase of the separation-individuation process. In this paper, the relevance of the development of empathy to the treatment of adult patients is illustrated by two clinical vignettes. "The Mother's Experience during the Earliest Phases of Infant Development" describes what I have called "regression in the service of the baby" in the earliest phase of motherhood and the difficulties some mothers have entering this state with a particular child. It also shows how a mother's ability to emerge from this early maternal preoccupation (Winnicott) is necessary when her infant begins to show ever-greater interest in the outside world and needs the availability of the mother in new ways. The early feeling of oneness with mother is revived in early rapprochement when toddlers love to share their new discoveries with mother. In "On the Development of Female Identity: Issues of Mother–Daughter Interaction during the Separation-Individuation Process," I discuss how early rapprochement has been observed to be particularly pleasurable for the girl. How this longing for closeness to mother can last into adulthood is illustrated through a clinical vignette of an adult woman in psychoanalysis whose rapprochement crisis seems never to have been sufficiently resolved. Coauthored with Ilene Lefcourt, "Self–Other Action Play: A Window into the Representational World of the Infant" describes the games characteristic of each separation-individuation subphase and how these mother–infant games serve to promote the child's formation and integration of self and object representations. It also shows how play in each subphase helps the child master the inevitable conflicts and losses. The section of the book on the process of separation-individuation ends with three papers coauthored with Maria Fahey based on the most recent observations of some of the original subjects who are now adults. Because of the extensive observational data of the preverbal period, the adult follow-up study has offered a rare opportunity to see how elements of the unremembered preverbal past remain significant in adult life. These three papers represent a modest attempt to find connections between what we observed in the subjects' earliest relationship and their adult life choices, conflicts, and fulfillments. "Two Women and Their Mothers: On the Internalization and Development of Mother–Daughter Relationships" traces how a mother's earliest representations of a daughter influence the separation-individuation process and the unfolding of each daughter's life as a woman. "Autonomy and the Need for the Caretaking Other" continues the theme of a mother's representation of a particular child and illustrates how the mother and child together develop and elaborate this representation and how the representation influences adult life. "Love, Admiration, and Identification" explores how the subtle differences in two mothers' representations of a wished-for and cherished baby girl seem to have affected the ways in which the subphases of separation-individuation were navigated and experienced and how the specific representation continues to inform the adult woman's sense of herself.

There has always been a part of me that refuses to believe that there are indeed people in this world who have no sense of self. This belief has given me the patience and endurance to work in long-term treatment with autistic and psychotic children and with adults with severe narcissistic problems. In such cases I have always thought of myself as the necessary other—an other who is needed by every individual to develop his or her own separate self.

The process of becoming this necessary other for a severely disturbed patient requires intensive treatment and the availability of a support team for the child, the family, and the therapist. I found the intensive therapeutic work at the Center needed to be supplemented by therapeutic companions who could facilitate the child's transition into the outside world and lighten the burden for the parents. For myself as therapist, the opportunity to have my work acknowledged and reflected upon by others, namely colleagues and supervisors, was indispensable. The work that was done at the Masters Children's Center would not have been possible without the environment that was provided: individual supervision of each case, informal discussions among colleagues, and formal presentations at case conferences all contributed to counteract the inevitable loneliness, doubts, and discouragement that go along with this work, but also provided the opportunity to share the excitement of facilitating change, which needs to be confirmed and acknowledged by another who is not directly involved in the process. I have found that treating disturbed children in private practice is helped considerably by building a support system.

The second part of this book begins with two case studies, "From Psychological Birth to Motherhood: the Treatment of an Autistic Child with Follow-up into Her Adult Life as a Mother" and "I and You: The Separation-Individuation Process in the Treatment of a Symbiotic-Psychotic Child with Follow-up." Following these longitudinal case studies is a paper describing my work as codirector of a therapeutic treatment center at the City University of New York, which I cofounded with Gilbert Voyat and Linda Gunsberg in 1976. This center served an inner-city population where children were seen in a day-long therapeutic program. What distinguished this center from other programs of its kind was that each child was seen at least twice weekly by clinical psychology student therapists who were beginning their training and who were open to ideas about building the sense of self in psychoanalytically oriented therapy. Twice weekly therapy could be helpful to these children because it occurred in the context of a center where student therapists were adequately supported by each other and by supervisors and where children were additionally supported by a therapeutic classroom and therapeutic companions, all of whom studied and were committed to contemporary psychoanalytic theories of the self. "Using Insights from Observational Research of Mothers and Babies in the Therapy of Preschool Children" describes the object relational treatment approach and the university setting of the center. The three elements of the therapeutic program—the design of the classroom, individual psychoanalytically oriented therapy, and role of therapeutic companions—are discussed in detail with clinical cases and vignettes. "The Oral Deadlock: Treatment of a Psychotic Child," coauthored with Michael Schwartzman, Phyllis Sloate, and Arnold Wilson, describes a team intervention made at the point of what seemed to be a hopeless impasse in the treatment of a symbiotic-psychotic child. Coauthored with Arnold Wilson, "A Model for the Day Treatment of Severely Disturbed Children" describes the treatment of a 6-year-old boy and shows how the neurobiological aspects of developmental delays and their treatment were integrated into the overall treatment approach. "To Be or Not to Be Separate" describes how understanding play characteristic of each separation-individuation subphase can facilitate the separation-individuation process in the treatment of developmentally delayed children.

This collection of papers reflects the interplay of elements that have furthered my research on developmental processes and my practice of treating children with developmental difficulties. Observations have led to the formulation of theories, and theories have helped focus observations. Exaggerated developmental difficulties have illuminated normal developmental processes, and the understanding of normal developmental processes has been useful in helping patients overcome obstacles to their development. My work has given me the opportunity to be involved intimately in the developmental processes of individuals starting with their earliest relationships and continuing into their adult relationships, including parenthood. The search for continuity and meaning, shared in therapy with patients and in research with collaborators, has been most essential to my own work.

I

Separation-Individuation Theory— Then and Now

1

Separation-Individuation Theory and Ongoing Research

Introduction

In 1982, Margaret Mahler (1983) gave a paper at the first World Congress on Infant Psychiatry at the end of which she paraphrased the prologue to *Thus Spoke Zarathustra*, "I say unto you: you must still have chaos in yourself to be able to give birth to a dancing star" (p. 6). She went on to say, "I, the researcher of development of infants from four to thirty-six months of age, feel I have a most propitious chaos in my mind right now while trying to integrate the rich and most interesting 'knowledge explosion' with the separation-individuation process" (Mahler 1983, p. 6). The "knowledge explosion" of which Mahler spoke then, namely the observations of infant researchers, has grown for fifteen years further. At the centenary celebration of her birth, a congress was held in her native town, Sopron, where researchers from Europe had the opportunity to question some of the separation-individuation concepts as well as to express their appreciation for the rich contributions separation-individuation observations and theory have made to psychoanalysis.

In this chapter I will describe the history and development of the original separation-individuation research from its beginnings in 1959 through the present adult follow-up study. I hope to be able to give you a glimpse of the original study as well as my own responses to the important critiques of the theory as it was originally formulated.

Margaret Mahler always emphasized that her original background as a pediatrician sparked her passionate interest in the human infant's early development. In her memoirs she says, "For me . . . the general problem of identity, and especially the way in which one arrives at a sense of self, has always been primary" (Stepansky 1988, pp. 136–137). Originally she perceived that the human infant's development begins from a state of nonresponsiveness to the outside world—*the normal autistic phase*—and proceeds through a phase of nondifferentiation from the mothering partner—*the symbiotic phase*—to the ultimate realization of self as separate and autonomous. In her memoirs Mahler refers to a presentation she gave together with Bert Gosliner in 1954 to the New York Psychoanalytic Society, in which she described an adolescent patient, a ticquer, who was enmeshed in a symbiotic, parasitic relationship with his mother (Stepansky 1988). Using this case as a pathological example, Mahler and Gosliner then described a process by which the normal baby establishes a viable identity. In the discussion of this paper Anna-Marie Weil suggested that this process be named *separation-individuation*.

A few years later Mahler decided to apply for research funds to do an observational study of the separation-individuation process in normal mothers and their infants. She originally hypothesized that this process took place during the second year of life and began her research by studying a group of 1-year-olds and their mothers. Soon after the observational research began, however, she realized that by the age of 1 children were already in the midst of this process. From then on, mother–child pairs were studied beginning at 6 months, which was hypothesized to be the height of the symbiotic phase and the beginning of separation-individuation. The fact that siblings of the original research subjects began to enter the project provided the opportunity to observe infants beginning at birth, but formal observations of the first five months were never made. This decision was influenced by Mahler's conviction that the infant before separation existed as part of a dual unity and that it would not be possible to draw inferences from observational data to the internal life of the baby before the beginning of separation-individuation.

Though she did not observe newborn infants herself, Mahler was enormously interested in and excited by the work of infant researchers and eventually had regular meetings with Daniel Stern and T. Berry Brazelton. She was an avid reader of the early work done by infant psychiatrists, and she attended and participated in the First Congress of the World Association of Infant Psychiatry and Allied Disciplines, held in Portugal. Mahler also admired the new film technology that enabled infant researchers to observe mother–infant interactions not visible to the naked eye, but she felt that there was an important difference between observations in the laboratory and observations in naturalistic settings. Let me insert here an observation of my own in regard to the difference between observations in the laboratory and observations in a naturalistic setting. I believe that the observations done by infant researchers in the laboratory with modern film technology enabling us to study interactions frame by frame have sensitized us to such an extent that we now notice extremely subtle interactions in naturalistic settings that earlier on we would have missed.

Eventually Mahler came to realize that her earliest observations of what she had perceived to be an autistic phase were probably limited to the period of the first few weeks of the infant's life and that even then the normal infant was never completely unaware of its surroundings. A reformulation of what she still called the autistic phase exists as her introduction to the film *On the Phenomena Indicative of the Emergence of a Sense of Self* (1982), in which she speaks of the autistic phase as the one in which the newborn has to adjust to extrauterine existence to find a niche in the external world. She describes how the newborn has to achieve physiological homeostasis, that is, adequate inner regulation in synchrony with the vocal and gestural rhythms of the caregiver, and how each infant is an active partner in the early dialogue. Those of us who were close colleagues of Mahler know that she eventually gave up the idea of the normal autistic phase (personal communication 1983).

At the time the separation-individuation research began, drawing inferences about mental life from observing nonverbal and even early verbal interactions was not generally accepted by psychoanalysts, who believed that only the psychoanalytic situation itself could provide access to the inner world. Thus, Mahler's choice of a naturalistic observational research study was revolutionary. The research on separation-individuation had the goal of understanding an intrapsychic process: observed behaviors were the base for making inferences. A research situation was created in which the spontaneous day-to-day interactions of mother and child could be observed in a natural playground-like setting. A large playroom with many attractive and colorful toys contained a small area arranged as a sitting room for mothers in which they could chat, sip coffee, or read—and from which they had full view of and free access to their children. As soon as the children were mobile they tended to move back and forth freely between the toy area and the mothers' sitting area. At least two participant-observers were always present to join in conversation with the mothers and play with the children.

The conceptualization of the subphases grew out of repeated observations and out of the cross-sectional methodology of the research. The observational data accumulated during the seven years of the original study are voluminous: they were collected by a team of participant and nonparticipant observers as well as by senior clinicians who also conducted regular interviews with the mothers. Thus, for any given day a mother–child pair attended the center, there may be pages of observations done by as many as four different observers. Because psychoanalysis tends toward intensive, long-term, one-to-one observation in the psychoanalytic setting, earlier psychoanalytic developmental research had tended toward case studies rather than cross-case comparisons. What was unique about the separation-individuation research was the combination of longitudinal observations of the developmental period from 6 months to 3 years of each of the subjects, along with the case to case comparison of the subjects. It was this methodology that led to the conceptualization of regularly occurring patterns that were eventually articulated as the subphases of the separation-individuation process. For example, when at first a young toddler was observed playing contentedly at some distance from mother, it was interpreted as particular independence on the part of this child. It was only when this behavior was seen again and again in children of similar ages that a practicing subphase could begin to be described and conceptualized. Similarly, when at first intense separation reactions were observed in a 15-month-old boy, it was thought that these separation reactions were specific to this child and his mother. Again, when separation reactions during that particular age period were observed in other children, the rapprochement subphase could begin to be conceptualized and described. Interestingly, those children in whom phase-specific behaviors were somewhat exaggerated facilitated the recognition of similar, less pronounced behaviors in other children. It was only during later stages of the research, when the subphase sequences had been described, that these stages served as a reference point for research and that it became the further goal to confirm or contradict the early observations and formulations.

The Separation-Individuation Process

Symbiosis (4 to 6 months)

Mahler described symbiosis based on theoretical conceptualizations of early development rather than observation. Thus, a dichotomy exists between conceptualizations of the separation-individuation process, which have a solid base in actual mother–infant observations, and descriptions of symbiosis, which are based on metapsychological formulations. Mahler states that symbiosis:

> describes that state of undifferentiation, of fusion with mother, in which the "I" is not yet differentiated from the "not-I" and in which inside and outside are only gradually coming to be sensed as different. Any unpleasurable perception, external or internal, is projected beyond the common boundary of the symbiotic *milieu interieur* which includes the mother partner's gestalt during ministrations. Only transiently . . . does the young infant seem to take in stimuli from beyond the symbiotic milieu. The primordial energy reservoir that is vested in the undifferentiated "ego-id" seems to contain an undifferentiated mixture of libido and aggression. The libidinal cathexis vested in the symbiotic orbit replaces the inborn instinctual stimulus barrier and protects the rudimentary ego from premature phase-unspecific strain, from stress traumata.
>
> The essential feature of symbiosis is hallucinatory or delusional somatopsychic omnipotent fusion with the representation of the mother and, in particular, the delusion of a common boundary be-

tween two physically separate individuals. [Mahler et al. 1975, pp. 44–45]

Later Mahler continues:

> The infant's inner sensations form the core of the self. They seem to remain the central crystallization point of the feeling of self around which a sense of identity will become established. . . . Within this symbiotic common orbit the two partners or poles of the dyad may be regarded as polarizing the organizational and structuring processes. The structures that derived from this double frame of reference represent a framework to which all experiences have to be related before there are clear and whole representations of the self and the object world. [Mahler et al. 1975, p. 47]

After several pages of describing symbiosis in these metapsychological terms, Mahler refers to the mothering partner's holding behavior as the symbiotic organizer—"the midwife of individuation of psychological birth" (Mahler et al. 1975, p. 47). Through my own naturalistic observations of individual mother–infant pairs, I have come to regard the period of symbiosis as a time during which the mother relinquishes some of her own well-established ego functions and boundaries in the process of caring for her very young infant. I have called this process "regression in the service of the baby" (Bergman 1985). Winnicott (1956b) has referred to this state in the mother as *primary maternal preoccupation*. More recently, Daniel Stern (1995) has described the special state of the mother with her newborn in his book, *The Motherhood Constellation*. What Mahler saw as the merger of the baby with the mother, described more recently by Fred Pine (1994) as "moments of merger," is observable, I feel, in the mother as she cares for her infant, with whom she feels a very powerful union. Mothers have described their experience during this period of symbiosis with the infant as one in which they lose their usual way of being in the world (Bergman 1985). They have eloquently articulated something like a symbiotic state in themselves that parallels the state that has been postulated in the baby. The attunement of the mother with the baby and the baby's emergent capacities to attune with the mother are the basis of their intimate relationship, the feeling of oneness, and the mutual sensitivity to each other's states and moods, which we called symbiosis.

Mahler believed that vestiges of the symbiotic phase remain throughout the entire life cycle and described different patterns of holding behaviors in different mothers, showing the influence of such holding behaviors on the infant. For example, the baby of a mother who appeared to breastfeed because it was convenient and because it made her feel successful, rather than because it promoted closeness, was unsmiling for a long time, and when she finally began to smile her smile was rather unspecific well into a time when one would have expected a specific smiling response.

While Mahler sometimes described symbiosis in an abstract, metapsychological manner, she also realized the importance of the intense experience between mother and baby during that period as forming the bedrock for psychological birth. Infant researchers had observed how infants were from the beginning responsive to the world around them and uniquely responsive to their caretakers. These findings raised significant questions about the theory of a normal autistic and symbiotic phase. The film, *On the Phenomena Indicative of the Emergence of a Sense of Self*, was an attempt to come to terms with the differences between Mahler's theory of that time, namely that separation-individuation was preceded by an undifferentiated period, and the findings of infant researchers who had begun to question her concept of the normal autistic and symbiotic phases.

The confusion, of which Mahler herself speaks, is apparent in her introduction to this film in which she says that while infants are outwardly attentive and responsive during the first weeks of life, they are more attuned to sensations from within their bodies than to sensations from the outside world. Mahler describes the increased attention to the outside world that was observed to begin at around 5 months as the emergence from a state of relative nondifferentiation of self from other. While Mahler felt this development to be another birth—thus the name hatching—she also was aware of the importance of mother–infant interactions earlier on: she describes the intricacies of mutual cuing at 2–3 months and describes symbiosis as a "wordless dialogue" between mother and infant.

It was Mahler's intent to study the development of the sense of self starting from the important developmental shift that initiated the process she called *psychological birth*. This major developmental shift has been described by other infant researchers. For example, Louis

Sander (1983) distinguishes a phase of initial regulation during the first three months from reciprocal exchange beginning in the fourth month. Stern (1985) distinguishes the *core self* from the *emergent self*. While he sees the core self beginning at 2–3 months and thinks of the infant from that point on as possessing an integrated sense of self, it is important to take note of the fact that he too describes a crucial psychological transition distinct from birth.

The First Subphase: Differentiation (6 to 9 months)

At the age of around 5 months, which is considered the height of symbiosis, it can be regularly observed that the infant no longer focuses primarily on the mother's face even while nursing and being held in her arms. Babies now begin to look around once their hunger is stilled. They may look at their hands; they may turn away from mother to look around at objects in the immediate environment. Distance perception develops and it is typical for an infant beginning at this age to scan the environment and then look back to mother. This process of looking from mother to the outside and back, of increasing ability to focus on things outside of the symbiotic orbit, was named *hatching*. The fully hatched baby, between 8 and 10 months, has attained a new sense of alertness, can sit up freely, and grasp what he or she wants. During this process of hatching several phenomena are of particular importance.

As the infant begins to hatch—to differentiate—one of the most important phenomena observed was *customs inspection*, a term borrowed from the work of Sylvia Brody (Brody and Axelrod 1970). This term refers to the way an infant will examine both tactilely and visually the faces of observers who are relatively unfamiliar. This examination of the nonmother's face, which is usually done in a sober and thoughtful mood, is very different from the joyful way in which the baby is likely to stroke or pat the mother's face. It is clear that the baby at this point is familiar with mother and reacts to her as uniquely different from the world of nonmother in which the baby begins to be intensely interested, exploring it with curiosity.

Another pattern that develops during this period is checking back to mother. The baby begins visually to compare mother and other, the familiar with the unfamiliar. During this process of comparing mother with the stranger, the phenomenon of *stranger anxiety* develops. However, stranger anxiety is a term coined at a time when it was believed that until about 6 months babies were not yet able to distinguish mother as unique. More recent observations have shown that the unique attachment to mother is present almost from the very beginning. The reaction to strangers, which does not always lead to stranger anxiety, is a process that is not contingent on nonrecognition of mother as different from others: rather it is a process that results from the burgeoning ability to take in the outside world, to comprehend it as being different from mother, and to react to it in a variety of different ways. The term *stranger curiosity* was coined during observations of hatching infants responding to observers and comparing these responses to their ways of being with mother. Thus stranger anxiety covers a wide variety of reactions ranging from curiosity and slight wariness to apprehension, anxiety, and distress. In *The Psychological Birth of the Human Infant* two children of the same mother were compared with each other (Mahler et al. 1975). The older one, Peter, at 7 to 8 months reacted to strangers briefly with curiosity and quickly with apprehension, anxiety, and crying. By contrast, Linda examined strangers with pleasure and curiosity and did not display marked stranger anxiety at any age. These comparative observations demonstrated the important differences between the specific outcome of interactions between Peter and his mother, which were often tense and unpredictable, and those of Linda, whose interactions with mother were mostly pleasurable and harmonious. From these and other observations it was concluded that in children for whom the symbiotic phase had been characterized by pleasure, curiosity about the stranger dominated over anxiety, whereas in children in whom the symbiotic phase was less pleasurable and harmonious, wariness and anxiety predominated in the relationship to the stranger during the period of hatching.

Another important phenomenon of the differentiation subphase is the child's interest in and play with objects that belong to mother, such as her jewelry, keys, eye glasses, or contents of her pocketbook. This play initiated by the baby is usually responded to and elaborated on by the mother. These objects seem to be of special interest and value to the baby because they are perceived as being part of mother, yet can be removed and thus become part of the baby and then can again be returned to mother. This back-and-forth movement between mother and baby is an important early game of interaction between them. Another mother–infant game that begins during this period of differentiation is the universal game of peek-a-boo, usually initiated at first by mother and later taken over and elaborated by the child.

During the period of differentiation, between 5 and 9 months, most babies begin some form of independent locomotion. They at first turn over and then begin to pull themselves along the floor. However, they do not yet seem quite aware that they are separating, that is, moving away, from mother, and mostly the preferred place for them is to be near mother, often at mother's feet or on her lap with their face turned away from her. They also begin to be interested in making things happen, such as switching on and off lights, and banging, dropping, and throwing objects.

It is likely that the timing of the hatching process is closely interwoven with the quality of the mother–child relationship. Thus, it was observed that in cases in which the symbiotic period of dual unity had been delayed or disturbed, the process of differentiation seems to have been delayed or premature. For example, one little girl whose mother had responded to her mechanically, without much warmth, did not seem to mold well, to become a "quasi-part of her mother" (Mahler et al. 1975, p. 58). She smiled indiscriminately, and at an age when other children started to take a more active part in approach and distancing behaviors she turned back to her own body and indulged in prolonged rocking. Thus, the differentiation process was delayed. Another child whose mother was depressed during his early infancy was late in recognizing mother as a special person. The specific smiling response was delayed, and he was late in using the visual modality, which is the first instrument to allow active distancing. Though he was late, he did not show the bland mechanical quality characteristic of the little girl. It was thought that his late hatching was adaptive. He seemed to know finally when he was ready to hatch. By contrast, a child who had a close but uncomfortable early relationship with his mother began to hatch early. He rapidly moved into the phase of differentiation as if to extricate himself from the uncomfortable symbiosis. This was the child who developed intense stranger anxiety, which seems to have been one of his early defensive patterns.

It seemed as if the unsatisfactory symbiotic phase had prevented him from developing a reservoir of basic trust because he had to extricate himself from mother by separating early. He did so before he was truly ready and thus was easily overwhelmed by anxiety and distress.

Those children who had an unusually difficult time with separation from mother tended later on to have histories of unusually early awareness of the outside world. It seems that the earliest differentiation patterns set in motion patterns of personality organization that influence the further development of the separation-individuation process. It was the finding of separation-individuation observations that those infants whose mothers enjoyed the symbiotic phase without too much conflict seemed to start at the average time to show signs of active differentiation by beginning to distance from the mother's body. Where there was ambivalence or too much intrusiveness on the mother's part, differentiation showed disturbances of various degrees and forms.

I have described how the detailed observations of the separation-individuation process allowed the observers to refine conceptualizations of stranger anxiety showing that what had been thought of as stranger anxiety in reality encompassed a wide range of reactions vis-à-vis the stranger (Mahler et al. 1975). A similar refinement took place in the observation of separation anxiety. It was learned that separation reactions changed during the course of the subphases. They are subphase specific, while of course they vary from child to child at any given time in development, and are closely connected to the vicissitudes of the mother–child relationship. The child during differentiation usually reacts to the mother's temporary absence not with open distress or crying but with a general lowering of mood. This lowering of mood was given the name *low-keyedness*, which was compared to conservation withdrawal in monkeys. The hypothesis was developed that this observed lowering of mood had the purpose of holding on, that is, conserving the image of mother while she was not present. If a child in the state of low-keyedness was suddenly intruded upon by an observer who might be attempting to comfort the child or cheer him or her up, the child often responded by breaking into inconsolable crying. The intrusion of the observer seemed to force the child to become acutely aware that mother was absent.

The Second Subphase: Practicing (9 to 15 months)

Early Practicing (9 to 12 months)

The practicing subphase, lasting from about 10 to 15 months, was conceptualized in two parts: the early practicing subphase from about 9 to 12 months and the practicing subphase proper from 12 to 15 months.

The practicing subphase begins with the development of independent locomotion. The ability actively to separate in space from the caretaking mother allows the baby to begin to explore the world beyond her in a much more active way. The passionate interest and investment in the mother now seems to spill over onto inanimate objects, which infants begin to explore actively, investigating their taste and texture with their mouths and hands. The maturation of locomotor and other functions brings with it an enormous expansion of the infant's world. There is more to see; there is more to touch; there is more to do. The excitement produced by the ability to propel oneself and to choose what to investigate at times seems to take precedence over the excitement in mother. However, especially during the beginning of the practicing subphase, an invisible bond seems to exist between infant and mother that unites them even when they are physically separate from one another and not in visual contact.

The mood during the practicing subphase is generally one of elation. There is a relative lessening of attention to mother, who during this particular period often seems to be used like an inanimate object to climb and step on, in order to enhance the infant's capacity for exploration. The rapidly expanding motor capacity is a special source of pleasure. Crawling, standing, coasting, and eventually walking and climbing seem to be the sources for the mood of elation. If we can think of symbiosis as the first blissful stage in human development, we can think of the practicing subphase as the second blissful period. The mastery of locomotion brings with it an enormous increment of energy and pleasure. The narcissistic investment in the body and in mastery and exploration brings about a temporary lessening in the investment in the mother, who can now be taken for granted. This slight lessening in investment in the mother also appears to protect the baby from the full realization of his or her separateness. A feeling of omnipotence fuels what seems to be a silent assumption that mother will always be there when needed. The young toddler who might get tired practicing will look back to mother or go to her briefly for what has been called *emotional refueling*. Even the briefest contact with mother reenergizes the practicing child and allows him or her to continue with the activities of practicing and exploring.

The advent of the ability to move independently, to practice and to explore, had an especially good effect on those children who had an intense but uncomfortable symbiotic relationship. This may well have been due also to the fact that, for the mother of such a child, disengagement and beginning independence come as a relief if earlier they were unable to relieve their infant's distress. These mothers and children had not been able to enjoy close physical contact, but could enjoy each other better now from a somewhat greater distance. As mothers became more relaxed and reassured, they also became better able to comfort and reassure their babies. On the other hand, some mothers who had enjoyed the symbiotic closeness did not take well to the transition period of practicing. Once their children left the maternal orbit, they wished for them to be grown up quickly. Interestingly, these children found it more difficult to grow up and were often demanding of closeness. In one extreme case of this sort, in which a mother seemed to be able to accept her child only as a symbiotic part of herself and actively interfered with his attempts to move away, the surprising observation was made that once he could move away, he seemed to lose contact with his mother when he was at a distance from her. This is in contrast to a child whose mother enjoyed closeness but did not impede the little girl's forays into the outside world. This child was able to maintain closeness with her mother from a distance. She was reassured by looking at her mother or hearing her voice. Another child, on the other hand, whose mother was not able to provide consistent emotional availability, developed normally in regard to her emerging ego functions, but it seemed that her struggle to get her mother's attention sapped her of the energy with which to invest the other-than-mother world, her own autonomous ego functions, and her own body. During the early practicing subphase she was often seen sitting at her mother's feet, apparently waiting for the bits of attention that her mother was able to provide.

She could only explore the outside world briefly; the elation and enthusiasm we saw in the other children was missing for her. Pleasure in the exercise of her autonomous functions could never take
precedence over the need to stay connected to mother, so that she
could never ignore her mother temporarily and fully extend herself
to the exploration of the world.

The optimal distance during the early practicing subphase allows
the moving child freedom and opportunity for exploration at some
physical distance from mother. The mother herself is needed as a
stable point, a home base to fulfill the need for refueling through
physical contact or even looking at mother or hearing her voice. The
mother is also needed to supply enough closeness so that the child
can use her energies for exploration and to permit the child enough
freedom from her own needs for closeness so as not to impede the
growing ability both to be away from mother and remain in contact
with her. If a mother becomes ambivalent toward the child as soon
as the child is able to move away, which interferes with her ability
to be empathically available, it was noticed that the child had difficulty functioning at a distance. It is as if the mother–child relationship during the early practicing subphase sets the tone for the further
process of separation and individuation. During the early practicing
subphase it is especially important that the distance be created at
the child's initiative rather than the mother's. When the child leaves
the mother's lap, distance modalities become important and reassuring. When the mother is not there, so that the child cannot use these
distance modalities to stay in contact, the mood of elation is no longer
fully present. Children were often seen staring sadly at mother's
empty chair or at the door through which she left when she went
out for an interview with one of the observers. Thus, relative obliviousness of mother gives way to increased awareness of separation if
the mother is not present or not emotionally available.

Practicing Subphase Proper (12 to 15 months)

The practicing subphase proper begins with the advent of upright
locomotion. This is the beginning of "the love affair with the world"
(Greenacre 1957). "The toddler takes the greatest step in human
individuation. He walks freely with upright posture. Thus the plane

of his vision changes; from an entirely new vantage point he finds unexpected and changing perspectives, pleasures, and frustrations" (Mahler et al. 1975, pp. 70–71). During this time, from about 12 to 16 months, libidinal cathexis shifts even more to the outside world and the growing autonomous ego functions, and the child seems at times almost intoxicated with himself and his world. This is the peak of narcissism and infantile omnipotence. It is characteristic at this time that children are relatively impervious to knocks and falls and other frustrations. Substitute familiar adults seem to be much more easily accepted than they were before. The elation characteristic of this time may be fueled, in addition, with a sense of elated escape from engulfment by the mother of symbiosis. A characteristic game is running away from mother, apparently with the purpose of being swooped up by her. This is a game of mastery and reassurance that demonstrates to the escaping toddler that mother wants to catch him and swoop him up in her arms.[1] During this period the child makes great strides in asserting his individuality. It seems that here is the first great step toward identity formation. Some mothers become poignantly aware that this is the time during which they have to begin to renounce possession of their infant's body because the infant's ability to run away dramatizes what has been happening for a while. One mother said, "When he runs away from me in the park and I have to carry that heavy little body back home, I tell myself 'You better enjoy this—it won't last long. You won't be carrying him in your arms much longer'" (Mahler et al. 1975, p. 72).

It was noticed in the separation-individuation study that frequently the first steps that the child takes without holding on are taken not toward mother but away from her, and by some children the steps are taken in mother's absence. Often mothers seem to react to their children's first independent steps by giving them a gentle push. This gentle push seems to have a facilitating effect, and if it is altogether absent the child's ability for pleasure in individuation may suffer. This big step into the outside world often seems to create a

---

1. Allan Schore (1994) has emphasized the psychobiological significance of the hyperarousal of the sympathetic nervous system that occurs during the practicing subphase and the enduring attachment bonds formed to the primary caregiver during this period.

sense of anxiety in mothers, as if at this point they begin to wonder whether their child will make it in the world. It was noticed that mothers became more interested in, but sometimes also more critical of, their children's functioning. They began to compare notes and to worry if their child was "behind." Upright locomotion almost seems to become a kind of metaphor for being able to make it in the world, which entails an inherent contradiction between the symbol of walking as the ability to make it and the reality of the child who still needs, and will for a long time need, the parent's care and protection.

Some typical play activities of the practicing period proper can also be understood in terms of the toddler's need to separate and explore and the simultaneous need to remain connected to mother. For example, junior toddlers love to walk around with a pull toy behind them. One could speculate about what goes on in the mind of the child at this time. Does the child think, "I am Mommy with a pull toy baby who goes everywhere with me"? Or, "I am Baby and have a Mommy pull toy who will go wherever I go"? One might ask similar questions about riding on kiddie cars and tricycles, which begin to be favorite activities. Does the child feel strong and powerful like mother or father riding in his or her own car? Or does the child now have a pretend parent always available on whom to ride? In the playroom observations, where these toys have to be shared, it was observed that these riding toys were passionately coveted and considered by the toddler to be his own even when he temporarily dismounted. In a way they seem to fulfill for the child what at this point is needed from the parent, namely, to be there and support the child in independent exploration without making demands. These toys seem to confirm the internal state of magical connection while separating, which is so essential during the practicing period.

The Third Subphase: Rapprochement (15 to 24 months)

Early Rapprochement (15 to 18 months)

Around the age of 15 to 16 months, when most toddlers are quite secure in their walking, running, climbing, and ability to play happily at a distance from mother, an interesting shift was noticed in the observational nursery. Whereas earlier it had been observed that the children's locomotor capacities took them away from their mothers, now almost suddenly their directions changed and they began to move toward mother. The toddler of this age seems to rediscover the mother from whom he or she has distanced during the practicing subphase. This rediscovery of mother is joyous and toddlers approach their mothers frequently, rarely with empty hands. They now love to bring things to mother, to bring objects from the outside world and put them into mother's lap. The size of the object brought back to mother can vary from the little crumb of cookie picked up from the floor to the big riding toy that the toddler can hardly carry. Interestingly, how mother receives these objects at first seems of little consequence to the toddler. If mother's lap is occupied, possibly by a baby sibling, the object might be deposited near mother on a chair or on an observer's lap. Thus, we observed that the activity itself was the driving force, which was not easily discouraged even by a mother who showed no interest in her toddler's gifts. The relative obliviousness to mother's presence that was characteristic of the practicing subphase, during early rapprochement gives way to the need to share with her and the almost constant concern with her whereabouts. The growing awareness of separateness brings with it growing awareness of and need for mother. It also brings with it the dawning realization for the child of his relative smallness and at times the inability to engage mother as he or she might wish to. This is a serious blow to the toddler's feeling of omnipotence, which is at its height during the practicing subphase. Thus, the toddler of this age is much more vulnerable and demanding. No longer is he oblivious to knocks and falls and frustrations as he was in the practicing subphase; he now experiences these as very painful and wishes the mother to undo them. Rather than being able to undo the frustrations that the toddler encounters, mothers often have to add to them. Routine requirements of child care, such as feeding and dressing, can now be experienced by toddlers as an insult to their desire to be omnipotently capable and independent, and it requires utmost patience and tact on the part of the mother to help the child comply with the necessary requirements. Toddlers of this age give their mothers very mixed messages. They want to be close and yet they reject mother's attempt to take care of them. Mothers are puzzled because the child, who during the practicing subphase appeared so independent, now is often demand-

ing, sometimes clinging, requiring mother's presence and attentive-
ness. It is not unusual for a toddler to want to follow mother wherever she goes. This behavior was named *shadowing mother*, in contrast to the equally typical tendency of the toddler to suddenly dart
away and expect mother to be there to catch him and sweep him up
in her arms.

Incompatibilities and misunderstandings between mother and child
can be observed in normal toddlers and their mothers because these
are specific to the contradictions inherent in the rapprochement
subphase. Some mothers find it difficult to accept the child's demanding behaviors. Others find it difficult to tolerate gradual separation.
It is not unusual for mothers at this time to separate abruptly and
suddenly from their toddlers, for example, taking a new job or becoming pregnant.

While toddlers of this age are extremely demanding, they also
begin to develop empathy for their mothers if they have been treated
with care and consideration. Recently a mother of an 18-month-old
toddler reported to me that on a particular day when she was very
depressed and preoccupied, she had been impatient and inattentive
to her toddler's needs and desires. She felt that her little girl understood that she was not able to be responsive and stopped making
demands upon her. The child was serious but did not seem to be upset.
She played by herself and was able to wait for her mother to be again
available to her.

The Rapprochement Crisis (18 to 24 months)

Individuation proceeds very rapidly during the rapprochement
subphase and the child exercises it to the limit. Yet at the same time
the ever-growing awareness of separateness and vulnerability often
leads the toddler to become not only demanding but coercive. The combination of the many contradictory behaviors typical of this subphase
has been called the *rapprochement crisis*. It is during this time when
the toddler most needs the mother's emotional availability that many
mothers find it difficult to cope and become demanding of the toddler in turn. No matter how insistently the toddler tries to coerce the
mother to act as if she were still part of him, the two can no longer
function as a dual unit. Only slowly can the toddler begin to accept

the fact that mother has separate interests and wishes. Verbal communication becomes increasingly important as mutual preverbal empathy between the mother–child pair no longer suffices. More and more the child is able to express his or her own desires and at times insist upon those with great passion. It becomes clear to mothers at this time that it is impossible, as well as undesirable, to fulfill the child's desire to be always at the center of the mother's world, but most toddlers do not easily relinquish the delusion of their own grandeur and omnipotence. Thus, dramatic fights and temper tantrums are characteristic of the rapprochement crisis. If, however, the mother is able to remain quietly available and share her toddler's adventures playfully, their relationship can progress and the mother's emotional participation and availability can facilitate the rich unfolding of the toddler's thought processes, language, curiosity, reality testing, and coping behaviors. Toddlers of this age often seem miraculous in their abilities of comprehension and expressiveness. It is important that the mother be able to enjoy the unfolding of her child's constantly growing desire to comprehend the world and master the skills needed to live in it. The shared moments of mother's understanding and acknowledging the child's burning desire to be present in the mother's mind help to bridge the gap of separateness. I believe that Peter Fonagy (Fonagy and Target 1998) describes this process when he talks about the dialectical theory of self development, which assumes that the psychological self develops through perception of this self in another person's mind. At the Mahler centenary meeting, György Gergely (1997) questioned the validity of the concept of the rapprochement crisis, which, according to him, is not present in toddlers who have developed secure attachments. I would agree that the intensity and duration of the conflicts observed in the original separation-individuation research is probably very much related to security of attachment; I also believe that the conflicts I have described are developmental in origin and are pathological only when they become extreme or are not resolved. However, I believe it would be very worthwhile to examine specifically the connection between secure attachment and rapprochement conflicts.

Toward the end of the rapprochement subphase, beginning role play was observed. Mother is asked to be fairly passive and allow herself to be used to meet the needs of the toddler's unfolding inner life. For example, a common script enacted by children of this age requires mother to cry when toddler leaves, or to cry when she has been hurt. A little boy of 20 months bites his mother playfully and wants her to pretend to cry. He then runs and brings her his blanket, the beloved transitional object, to comfort her. He shifts from being the playful biting or the aggressive hurtful baby to being the comforting parent. Another child tells mother to cry as she plays that she is going to work. She quickly returns and comforts her crying mother as she has been comforted by her. Another favorite game of this period is for toddler to run away and be caught, and also for mother to run away and for toddler to catch her. The ability to play these games, that is, to put oneself in the role of the other, reveals self and object representations on the way to object constancy as well as early identification with mother and the working through of issues and conflicts related to aggression and separation. McDevitt (1997) has shown how conflict and compromise formation begins at this point.

The observation of the anatomical difference for many toddlers also begins in the rapprochement subphase. We observed that girls became aware of the anatomical difference earlier than boys, and occasionally this awareness caused them great pain and anxiety. Galenson and Roiphe (1976) have further examined the beginnings of anatomical difference in their own research. Extreme reactions to the observation of boys' genitals seemed to be connected to difficulties in the mother–child relationship. One girl had an extreme reaction at a time when her father was absent for an extended period and her mother had become depressed. In another case mother was relatively emotionally unavailable and very preoccupied with herself. When her little girl became aware of anatomical difference, she became severely constipated and showed excessive separation reactions. It was the observation of these more extreme reactions that sensitized us to how toddlers of that age become aware of and react to the anatomical difference.

Throughout the rapprochement period, the child rapidly develops the capacity to observe the world as outside of himself and needs the mother's availability to make sense of this separateness and help to integrate the puzzling.

Intense affects resulting in temper tantrums are typical of the rapprochement period, which can be confusing to both the child and the mother. The child's understanding of language develops much more rapidly than the ability to speak, which can be another source of frustration in the mother–child relationship. The mother has to help the child understand not only the world outside but also the child's own often intense affects. It is hard for the mother to appreciate and respond to the complexity of the toddler's rapidly developing internal world. In cases where the attachment to the mother is not secure, the toddler's reactions to separations can be especially puzzling. For example, a child who has been angry with the mother at the point of separation might long for her while she is away and yet upon her return cling to an observer she had rejected while mother was gone. We observed that frequently the first words one insecurely attached little girl said to her returning mother was a demand. This rapprochement period toddler split her object world into good and bad, and the good object was always absent, that is, unavailable. She did not succeed in attaining a unified object representation or in reconciling the good and bad qualities of the love object. At the same time her own self-representation and self-esteem suffered. Here we saw the beginnings of internalization and character formation and the development of traits that significantly influenced further development. With further development one would expect the intensity of the rapprochement crisis to wane, but an insecure attachment of this period is likely to influence the further development of the child and her later choice of love objects.

The resolution of the rapprochement crisis requires for the child the renunciation of omnipotence that blossoms during the practicing subphase, the period during which mother is still experienced as part of the self and exploration of the world outside flourishes. For the mother, the resolution requires renunciation of the child as part of herself. Both mother and child have to allow for each other's separateness. The gradual renunciation of omnipotence during the rapprochement period requires a process of mourning that I believe is similar to the description in Kleinian theory of reaching the depressive position. Steiner (1992) has described reaching the depressive position.

A critical point in the depressive position arises when the task of relininquishing control over the object has to be faced. The earlier trend, which aims at possessing the object and denying reality, has

to be reversed if the depressive position is to be worked though, and
the object is to be allowed its independence.

Freud's (1957) insight about mourning, namely that it cannot take
place without a satisfying relationship, is significant here. Where the
mother–child relationship has been relatively stable and satisfying,
we expect that mourning can occur, rapprochement conflicts will be
resolved, and the child will be able to be on the way to object constancy.

*The Fourth Subphase: The Beginnings of Emotional Object
Constancy and Consolidation of Individuality (24 to 30
months)*

The achievement of affective object constancy depends upon the
gradual internalization of a constant, positively cathected, inner image
of the mother. This makes it possible for the child to function separately and at a distance from mother despite moderate degrees of longing for her. The cognitive achievement of object permanence is a part
of the child's ability to function separately as it enables the child to
keep mother's image in mind, accept that she can be elsewhere, and
be reassured by knowing her whereabouts. The slow establishment
of emotional object constancy is a complex and multidetermined process that rests on trust and confidence in the love object. If the ambivalence toward the mother is too great, a positive image of her
cannot be sustained.

The continuing development of language and symbolic play helps
the child master separateness and separation. As self and object representations become more firmly established the child is better able
to enact needs, impulses, and conflicts through role play. Role play
begins to include characters from the outside world; it is no longer
limited to role exchange between mother and child. This kind of play
rests on a self firmly and flexibly enough established to be able to
put itself in the place of the other—a hallmark in the establishment
of emotional object constancy. The child is able to extend to the widening world characteristics of the self and significant others, as well
as aspects of their relationships. Role play reinforces connections with
emotionally significant others as well as separation from them be-

cause each role enactment embodies a crucial aspect of the self and the other.

During the second half of the third year the child is securely enough connected to the object world to be able to maintain emotional equilibrium in the face of the mother's absence or minor frustrations. The basis for this growing stability and quality of the inner representation is the actual mother–child relationship as it unfolds in the day-to-day interaction between mother and child during the entire separation-individuation period. This relative stability, however, is not permanent and can easily be threatened by new storms arising either from the vicissitudes of further development or traumatic events in the child's life. Nevertheless, by the third year there is in the life of each child a particular constellation that has grown out of the unique way each mother–child pair has navigated the separation-individuation process. While the continuing development through the life cycle opens up possibilities of change and growth, the separation-individuation process is nonetheless a seminal experience upon which further development rests.

2

From Mother to the World Outside

The Use of Space during the
Separation-Individuation Process

> We shall not cease from exploration
> And the end of all our exploring
> Will be to arrive where we started
> And know the place for the first time.
> —T. S. Eliot, *Four Quartets*

The moment of birth propels the infant from the warm enclosure of
the mother's body into the open space of the world. For the mother,
the baby, who has been part of her body and a fantasy, now becomes
a reality—a human being totally dependent upon her. The baby is
born into his mother's expectant arms and can become one with her
in a new way—in a symbiotic union. He must then once more emerge
as a separate individual, undergoing a process Mahler, Pine, and
Bergman (1975) have termed the psychological birth of the human
infant—the separation-individuation process. This second, psychological birth, the hatching from the "common symbiotic membrane," the
separation-individuation process, has been described in numerous
publications (Mahler 1963, 1965, 1970, 1971, Mahler and Furer 1963,

Mahler and LaPerriere 1965, Mahler et al. 1975). At the end of this process, the infant has become a toddler with an awareness of himself as a separate being. This awareness involves not only himself, his body now separate from his mother, but includes as well the space surrounding him, space that has become a precious and protected possession. Winnicott (1971) says:

> Whereas inner psychic reality has a kind of location in the mind or in the belly, or in the head or somewhere within the bounds of the individual's personality, and whereas what is called external reality is located outside these bounds, playing and cultural experience can be given a location if one uses the concept of the potential space between the mother and the baby. In the development of various individuals it has to be recognized that the third area of potential space between mother and baby is extremely valuable according to the experience of the child or adult who is being considered. [p. 53]

The space surrounding the self is not part of the self, but it is not part of others. It has the quality of being a possession and yet is not, as are other possessions, either tangible or definable. How far does it extend? With whom and under what circumstances can it be shared? When is it friendly and protective, and when frightening and vast? When does it isolate, when does it connect? When is it inaccessible, like a wall surrounding someone? When is it open to include others? And how does the space outside relate to the space within?

> It is useful then to think of a third area of human living, one neither inside the individual nor outside in the world of shared reality. This intermediate living can be thought of as occupying a potential space, negating the idea of space and separation between the baby and the mother, and all developments derived from this phenomenon. This potential space varies greatly from individual to individual, and its foundation is the baby's trust in the mother experienced over a long enough period at the critical stage of the separation of the not-me from the me, when the establishment of an autonomous self is at the initial stage. [Winnicott 1971, p. 110]

Intrapsychic events are experienced within a space. We may be filled with joy, with expectation, or with fear and sadness. We may be empty, drained, or filled and complete; at times we may be overflowing, unable to contain our emotions. Sadness as well as happiness can make our tears flow over. Extremes of fear or pain can make us lose the contents of our bladder or bowels.

At the completion of the separation-individuation process, the child emerges as a separate small individual surrounded by space that both separates and unites him with his mother, a mother who now exists not only on the outside but also as inner presence that regulates the sense of well-being and safety and enables the child gradually to exchange the omnipotence of the mother–infant unit for a growing sense of his autonomy and competence. If the process fails, the space that both separates and unites is not available, and the individual is threatened by engulfment or unbearable isolation. Asch (1966) holds that claustrophobia is not necessarily symptomatic of a phallic conflict. It is his belief that

> identification with the fetus inside the mother is associated with two fantasies of dread. One, the danger of being squeezed out passively, abandoned and flushed away like a bad, smelly stool; this involves the fantasy of birth as an anal process of separation from the mother; it is pre-genital and does not involve the father. Two, the danger of being passively chewed up, dissolved and digested, to be fused with the mother on the most primitive level, with a terrifying loss of identity. These are two distinct anxieties with mainly anal and oral drive derivatives. One is a fear of separation from mother while the other is its opposite, a fear of complete fusion. One involves abandonment by the object, while the latter consists of loss of the self-representation. [pp. 712–713]

In this chapter I shall consider the space between mother and child as it constitutes itself and grows during the separation-individuation process. This results in space that becomes the possession of each individual, defining him, giving him room to grow, the possibility of coming and going, and the capacity to separate from and reunite with a loved object. I shall consider the use of space during the subphases of the separation-individuation process, space defined by the child's growing ability both to create it and bridge it. I shall give special consideration also to *transitional spaces*. These are spaces of transition between a mother-world and a world outside. I am referring to spaces such as windows, thresholds, and doors, as well as to vehicles that carry us from one space to the other—cars, trains, airplanes— about which we can develop strong feelings. Finally, I shall try to connect certain basic experiences of space with certain periods of early development. Observations to be cited were made during the course of a research study begun in 1959 by Margaret Mahler and her associates at the Masters Children's Center. There normal mothers with normal babies 6 months to 3 years old were observed four times per week in a playgroundlike setting. The observations began at that point in development at which the child's psychological space coincides with actual space, and continued as processes of internalization gradually brought about the creation of inner space. This inner space is a metaphor denoting the location in which psychic events occur and in which object representations and self representations are held side by side but separate from each other.

Closeness and Distance

Many authors have given attention to two opposing but essentially human needs: the need for closeness and the need for distance; the need for clinging and the need for separating; the need for being one with the mother and the need for becoming an individual in one's own right. Imre Hermann (1936) was the first psychoanalytic theorist who postulated a nonsexual primary object relation drive in the infant. He called it the "clinging instinct" (*sich anklammern*) and its dialectic opposite the "instinct to search" (*auf die Suche gehen*). Hermann considers the mother–child relationship the basic dual union, that is, the primary context from which the development of the individual emerges. Individuation for him starts with the trauma of the necessary dissolution of the primary mother–child union. At this point the child goes in search of new objects to cling to. Spitz, in *No and Yes* (1957), says:

> This tendency to separateness counteracts from the beginning the child's more obvious tendency of clinging to the mother. The simultaneous presence of diametrically opposed tendencies in the child, beginning with birth, cannot be sufficiently emphasized. They have their exact counterpart in the existence of similar tendencies in the mother. With the cutting of the umbilical cord a cleavage takes place between mother and child. They become discrete physical entities. At the same time he is driven by a desperate urge to reestablish the previous state, both mother and child strive for as close a contact as

possible with each other, culminating in the nursing act. But at the
end of nursing they are driven apart again, a cycle which is recap-
tured with each nursing act. [p. 123]

Mahler's conception differs from that of Spitz in that she does not
recognize from the beginning a simultaneous tendency to cling and
to separate. She distinguishes an autistic phase lasting about three
weeks, during which sleeplike states account for far more of the
infant's time than do states of arousal. She finds this reminiscent of
that "primal state of libido distribution that prevailed in intrauter-
ine life, which resembles the model of a closed monadic system, self-
sufficient in its hallucinatory wish fulfillment" (Mahler 1968, p. 7).
At about 3 weeks, the autistic shell is replaced by "a quasi-semiper-
meable membrane enveloping both parts of the mother–infant dyad"
(p. 15). From symbiosis the infant slowly disengages himself during
the separation-individuation process, resulting in an intrapsychic
separation of self and object.

Balint, in *Thrills and Regressions* (1959), describes two primitive
disturbances in object relating; these are described in terms of the
use of space, which, as we will see later, closely resembles its use
during the subphases of separation-individuation. One disturbance
is characterized by the need to cling to objects, and experiences the
space between them as a threat. The other denies the need for objects and has an exaggerated need for open spaces. These, Balint says,
are not opposites. Rather, "they are two different attitudes, possibly
developing or, so to speak, branching off from the same stem" (p. 46).
Both are reactions to the recognition that a blissful world without
boundaries between mother and child is disturbed by the need to accept existence of objects with resistant, aggressive, and ambivalent
qualities. Balint says that

> despite many gradations and changes, there are apparently two ba-
> sic ways in which people respond to this traumatic discovery. One is
> to create an ocnophilic world based on the fantasy that firm objects
> are reliable and kind, that they will always be there when one needs
> them, and that they will never mind and never resist being used for
> support. The other is to create the philobatic world which goes back
> to life prior to the experience that objects emerge and destroy the
> harmony of the limitless, contourless expanses. . . . This world is col-

ored by an unjustified optimism—originating in the earlier world of primary love—that enables the philobat to believe that his skills and his equipment will be sufficient to cope with the elements—the substances—as long as he can avoid hazardous objects. [p. 68]

We feel that these disturbances described by Balint originate during separation-individuation, the process of gradual disengagement from our symbiotic beginnings. Inasmuch as they are both disturbances in the use of space, they are of particular interest to us here.

There are two kinds of space: enclosed space and open space. The model of the enclosed space is the womb. Lewin, in his paper on claustrophobia (1935), states that true claustrophobia is regularly connected with fantasies of being in the womb and of one's own birth. Open space is the world outside following separation. Closed spaces are protected, open spaces are exposed, but either one without the other is terrifying. The enclosed space, no matter how beautiful, becomes prison or exiles us when we are denied or deny ourselves the possibility of leaving it. On the other hand, the open road leads nowhere. It becomes the plight of the refugee who is denied the essential human need for protection and belonging. In children's games the zone of security is often called "home," the symbol of the safe mother. However, children's games also contain the other element, that of the open space that must be conquered with skill and daring. Balint (1959) writes:

All thrills entail the leaving and rejoining of security. The pleasure experienced in either of these two phases, that is, either when staying in security or when leaving it in order to return to it—are very primitive, self-evident and apparently in no need of explanation—although it must be stated that not every adult can enjoy them equally. [p. 26]

According to Mahler's theory of symbiotic child psychosis, the cause for this severe disturbance lies in the fact that though the infant is maturationally ready to take the first steps toward separation, he can be emotionally unable to do so, because of "a deficiency or a defect in the child's intrapsychic utilization of the mothering partner during the symbiotic phase, and his subsequent inability to internalize the representation of the mothering object for polarization" (Mahler 1968,

p. 32). This results in panic, the fear of engulfment and abandonment. In classical cases of symbiotic psychosis, the child is not comfortable with mother and often pushes her away vehemently, yet he cannot function away from her. This intolerable state provokes the building of a wall of secondary autistic defense against all object relating.

All spaces are essential for human development: the enclosed mother space, the open, outside world spaces, and spaces of transition between the two. People move with varying degrees of ease between the two spaces. Although the wish to move, to travel, is ubiquitous, there is always some degree of reluctance at the moment of leaving, not to speak of the more severe forms of homesickness and travel phobia.

> In long-range planning for a trip, I think there is a private conviction that it won't happen. As the day approached, my warm bed and comfortable house grew increasingly desirable and my dear wife incalculably precious. To give these up for three months for the terrors of the uncomfortable and unknown seemed crazy. I didn't want to go. Something had to happen to forbid my going, but it didn't. [Steinbeck 1972, p. 19]

The Space between Mother and Child

There is no space between the nursing infant and the mother. The infant at first has no knowledge of space, no knowledge of an outside world, or of the mother as a separate entity. During the symbiotic period, autonomous ego functions develop as the baby begins to find the breast, to gaze into mother's eyes, to listen to her footsteps, to look at bright colors or moving objects. All of these come and go; they come from somewhere and they go somewhere. They provide the first rudimentary experience of space, even though this space is not yet felt to be outside. By the age of 5 months, the beginning of the differentiation subphase, the infant starts to strain away from mother. As he does this, he has already acquired the means with which to bridge the space he is creating. He strains away from mother because the world out there lures him, but as he does this he can take in, feel the mother better from this distance he has created, and he can reach and grasp her body; he can grasp, but he cannot yet let go. The ability to let go of grasped objects develops somewhat later, providing a new lesson in space: objects fall, disappear, can be retrieved. During the differentiation subphase one can at times observe the conflict between the desire for mother and the breast, and the lure of the outside world; between the need for a space between himself and mother, and the desire to undo that space. An infant at that age often acts as though he wants to devour the mother, to literally attack her with an open mouth—the ultimate undoing of the space between them.

Even before the infant has sufficient control of motility to be able to reach out, he can engage his mother actively with his eyes, and elicit a response from her. During the differentiation subphase, seeing itself, looking at people and things not mother, becomes a most pleasurable activity. The nursing baby under 5 months of age seems to gaze steadily into the mother's eyes, but from about 5 months on, the baby, after the first hunger is satiated, will actively look around and follow both visual and auditory stimuli. As soon as the first hunger is satisfied, the world out there competes with the breast. The world out there becomes an enticement and impetus, though the libidinal energy with which the urge to explore is invested is still supplied directly by the mother. The "undernourished" child does not have desire or energy to explore, or the explorations become painful rather than pleasurable, an aspect of early stranger or strangeness anxiety. The ability to distance visually precedes the ability to reach and explore tactilely, at first the body and face of the mother, but, increasingly during the differentiation subphase, the faces of others, as well as interesting objects in the environment, especially objects attached to people, such as jewelry and eyeglasses. The exploration of the "other's" face or body during the differentiation subphase is often followed by a return to close bodily contact with mother.

In our observational study of separation-individuation, certain infants would explore the environment most actively while in mother's lap, if given sufficient freedom to explore in the mother's vicinity. Others, especially those too closely enveloped by the mother, would actively push away from her, seemingly struggling for greater freedom. In an extreme case of this sort, we found one little boy who actually preferred to be held by adults other than his mother during this period. Other children, while exploring from mother's lap, seemed suddenly overcome by distress and simply could not integrate closeness to mother with the exploration of others; they could not give up one for the other. Steven, a child of this sort, rather early in life seemed to resolve the conflict by ignoring his need for closeness and turned his energies to exploration of the outside world. Interestingly, though, he especially liked to explore the inanimate world. It seemed a more neutral ground that would diminish the conflict between closeness and distance. Even early in life he seemed to prefer to explore through his play with toys. He would endlessly push cars and trains about, and would especially enjoy seeing them go in and out of tunnels. In addition to the more obvious meaning of actively playing at separation, the play also enacted the passage from closed to open spaces and vice versa.

Each phase of the separation-individuation process seems to have its own optimal distance between mother and child. While this varies with each mother–child pair, according to their temperament and predilection, one might possibly see these variations as the outcome of the process of mutual adaptation between mother and child. In other words, then, the optimal distance for each child during a given subphase would be a compromise between what might be optimal for a particular phase of development and what would be possible for a particular mother and child. To illustrate: during the differentiation subphase the available instruments for distancing and approaching are the eyes and the reaching-out arms and exploring hands. The optimal distance thus would be one allowing the infant maximal use of these instruments while preserving the maximal amount of closeness compatible with the emerging need for distancing. In order to distance, the baby has to be somewhat apart from his mother and yet close enough to be able to reapproach her. Thus, the optimal distance is no longer attained by the mother's holding the infant closely in her arms as during the symbiotic phase, but by holding the infant loosely enough to leave torso and arms free for exploration; in this position he can pull away from mother far enough to look at her from a greater distance. The infant held too closely will push away and, as a last resort, prefer to be held by others. The infant whose mother's hold is painful or uncomfortable will push away and prematurely try to be on his own. The infant placed at too great a distance by the mother will experience the distancing process as painful, will clamor to be held, and will cling. In all cases the infant begins to have a voice in determining distance or closeness during this first phase of the separation-individuation process. The space explored and created during the differentiation subphase, from about 5 to 8 months, is a space between mother and child. The space surrounding the mother—especially her feet—as well as the space surrounding the child is essentially enclosed. Open spaces are as yet inaccessible.

The Space Out There

The differentiation subphase is at about age 8 months succeeded by the practicing subphase. As his ability to bridge the space increases, the creeping and crawling infant creates a new space between himself and his mother. He can now bridge the space, as well as create a space not only by looking and reaching, hearing or being heard; he can now bridge the space with his body, as he can actively leave his mother and then return. During the practicing subphase there is a great investment in developing ego functions, as well as in the world out there. The baby is relatively oblivious of the mother, as he is not yet fully aware of his separateness. Mother is the home base to which the baby periodically returns to restore his waning energies. However, there are times when he creates a distance greater than he can comfortably bridge. Then suddenly he can be overcome by the feeling that he cannot return to mother. Yet on the whole, if during the differentiation subphase the infant had operated largely within the mother–child space and had eventually learned to know and respond to her as a special person, during the practicing subphase the most important space is out there. The practicing infant seems almost compelled to seek out open space, and he does this in an elated mood. As the mother is still experienced as part of the self, the space is usually not frightening; the practicing infant is actually surprised when he falls and mother is not automatically at hand to rescue him. Balint (1959), in his description of the philobat, brings to mind the practicing infant:

> The philobatic world consists of friendly expanses dotted more or less densely with dangerous and unpredictable objects. . . . The philobat's illusion is that apart from *his* own proper equipment he needs no objects, certainly no one particular object. . . . The philobat feels that using his equipment he can certainly cope with any situation; *the*

world as a whole will "click in" and he will be able to avoid treach-
erous objects. . . . The philobat feels that it is within his power to
"conquer the world. [pp. 34–35]

This description is most reminiscent of the description of the practicing subphase, the love affair with the world, the elated mood, the
feeling of omnipotence emanating from the mother's still being experienced as part of the self.

While the optimal distance during the differentiation subphase was
found on mother's lap or at mother's feet, the optimal distance during practicing is found in the space out there in the outside world.
His mother is within reach of the distance modalities, close enough
to be heard, to hear, to be seen, to be joined for emotional refueling
in case of need or fatigue. The mother is needed as a stable point.
She should not step in too quickly when a child finds himself in difficulty, but neither should she be unavailable in that situation. In
other words, she should be neither intrusive nor aloof.

We may look at some children's attempts to adapt to situations in
which optimal distance is unavailable. Susan, for instance, whose
mother had been able to enjoy close physical contact but did not want
to be bothered once the child started to move away, became more
insistently demanding during the beginning practicing period. She
insisted, for example, that her mother pick up a toy for her. What
seems to have happened later is that Susan, since her mother would
not give freely, was to some extent fixated at this level and continued to make demands upon her mother. This did not leave her free
to relate to the other-than-mother world, and in particular made it
difficult for her to relate to other children.

Doris manifested the opposite problem. Her mother allowed her
ample freedom to explore, was always watchful, always ready to support and help with voice or action. However, she was unable to provide her daughter the gentle push that would convince her that her
mother was confident she could function in the world outside. Doris
showed some evidence of fixation at the level of needing her mother
in case of trouble. She showed strong separation reactions and difficulties with new situations, a character trait that remained characteristic of her.

Jason was a boy who could not outgrow the elated state accompanying the feeling that he could conquer the world. He was a motor-

minded little boy who started to walk freely at the early age of 9 months. His mother was a depressed woman with a rather poor image of herself. It was most important that her son be precocious, a narcissistic completion of herself. She was in great awe of her little boy. She was burdened by his early walking, as prematurely walking toddlers are a burden to any mother. Jason's mother, in awe of her fledgling, was the very opposite of Doris's. The latter could not convey her confidence in her daughter's ability to manage on her own. Jason's mother, on the other hand, seemed to impart to her son the idea that he could manage no matter what. She did not temper his age-appropriate feeling of omnipotence with her own ability to be a rational judge of danger. She allowed him total freedom, and Jason never seemed to learn to be a judge of danger himself. Recklessly he would throw himself into space. He was forever falling, but, interestingly, he hardly ever cried. It was as if the sense of omnipotence and of his own invulnerability dwarfed his physical pain.

Leaving and Returning

At approximately 15 months, the beginning of rapprochement, an important change occurs. In the course of practicing, the toddler becomes aware that his mother is not automatically at hand, that he cannot always get back to her when he wants, that she cannot automatically shield him from all pains and frustrations. In other words, after a period of practicing encounters with the outside world, as well as with his mother, the toddler is repeatedly faced with feelings of helplessness. Thus, he becomes aware of his separateness. An important change occurs in the direction of his movement and experiences in space. While the practicing infant generally moved out in the direction of the big world, protected by the illusion of mother's magical presence, the rapprochement child moves back toward the mother. However, he does not return empty-handed. It is most characteristic of him to bring objects found in the big world back to mother and to deposit them in her lap. During differentiation, the space was confined to the space between mother and child and the space immediately surrounding them; during practicing the space seemed to have no limits; during rapprochement we see clearly for the first time the movement in space that becomes so important from then on, the movement that is truly essential, namely leaving home base (the mother) and returning. But this is by no means easily accomplished. Earlier, during the phase of differentiation, we described a conflict between the wish to incorporate the mother and to distance from her. During the rapprochement subphase, the conflict between wishing to be autonomous and separate, and yet wanting mother ever present and available becomes enlarged by the cognitive developments that require the toddler to relinquish his illusion of mother's presence in their shared omnipotence. During the rapprochement crisis, the toddler, who wants to have it both ways, often cannot bear either situation—to be close to mother forces him to be more passive than he likes, and to be away from her confronts him with feelings of helplessness and intense longing. Thus, during rapprochement, transitional spaces acquire extraordinary importance.

What is the optimal spatial distance during this period? No longer need the mother be within sight or earshot; now a space close by will suffice, where the toddler knows his mother to be, where he can find her and leave her again. Here, for the first time, the toddler discovers the thrill of leaving and refinding his mother. It is this leaving and refinding of the mother that allows her to be created anew each time she is found (Winnicott 1971). Each time the toddler finds her he brings along a new piece of the world outside, and each time he leaves her he takes with him a part of her. Increasingly this part is an image, but often it is concrete. Typically a child of this age will take something from his mother's pocketbook and run off with it. During rapprochement the intervening space becomes once again the space *connecting* mother and child. But this space is now enlarged by the toddler's growing capacity for locomotion, perception, and beginning symbolization and internalization.

In discussing the space between mother and child during differentiation, we mentioned that at times the infant seemed to be in conflict over closeness and distance. During rapprochement, in the enlarged space, the conflict over closeness and distance becomes central. The space between mother and child now turns into a space of conflict between them. At times the toddler insists on shadowing every move of his mother, knowing her whereabouts, controlling her; at times the opposite behavior, driving her away, becomes characteristic. The toddler is forever running away from mother, escaping, yet expecting to be swept up in her arms. Another characteristic pattern is that of veering away, going toward mother, and in the last moment changing direction. The period of rapprochement is one of indecision. On the one side is a fear of reengulfment; on the other side is the fear of abandonment. The optimal distance is thus one that allows for back and forth movement between toddler and mother, with all the pushes and pulls that this entails. It calls also for a place at some greater distance from her—a resting place where the toddler can exercise his newly emerging capacities and interests in the nonmother world, but where the mother is nevertheless available when he needs her.

A child caught up in the rapprochement struggle, unable to resolve his dilemma, in reminiscent of Balint's description of the person who clings to objects and cannot manage the spaces between them.

During the rapprochement subphase, which requires that the toddler reconcile his need for both mother and outside space, transitional spaces take on particular importance. These are spaces that allow the toddler to remain in both places at the same time. For example, before entering a room he might stand on the threshold, hesitant either to come or to leave. Alone in a room, away from his mother, he can console himself by looking out the window, which allows him to stay in a space away from mother and yet be in contact with an outside in which his mother can come and go. Then at certain times a toddler of this age might need to have the door open when he is away from mother; on the other hand, he might not be able to settle down unless it is closed. Playing with doors—closing and opening them, playing with the doorknobs—is another activity that seems important. At Masters Children's Center, where the observational study of the separation-individuation process was conducted, a new space had to be created to meet the needs of toddlers at rapprochement age and beyond. The room where mothers, observers, and babies were together suddenly seemed too small. The toddlers gradually began to leave whenever the door was open. The staff created a toddler room across the hall, where toddlers could be without their mothers. This was a new and nonmother world. The door, the threshold, and windows of that room became transitional spaces, spaces a child could enter when he missed his mother, but did not want to interrupt his nonmother play. Another room that took on special importance to him during this period was the cubby room, where mothers and children hung their coats when they arrived. It had a large window facing the play yard. This became a transitional space par excellence. Apparently prompted by a wish to find their mothers, children would often leave the toddler room. However, they would often change their minds and go to the transitional cubby room instead. There, in a symbolic manner, they could be close to the world of mother and home, since their mothers' coats were there; but they were also symbolically in the world outside, which they could watch through the tall window. Usually, after a short sojourn in the transitional room, they returned to the nonmother toddler room, which provided space for expanding ego functions and a respite from conflict with the mother.

Thus, as the sense of being a separate individual develops, so does the need for a variety of spaces (mother, outside, transitional), and so does a proprietary feeling toward such spaces. Now a child can push another child and fight for the special space of his mother's or a mother substitute's lap. A child can now fight to sit next to a particular person or in a particular chair that he might consider his. Also at this time, certain moving objects, such as tricycles or kiddie cars, become the most treasured possession, and I believe, transitional spaces. These most coveted objects lend additional speed and power to the incessant coming and going, leaving and finding mother, and in addition become small home bases on wheels. Often the child who leaves them still considers them his property, his home base, and becomes upset if another child sits on his tricycle or kiddie car.

The rapprochement subphase coincides with the anal phase of psychosexual development. During the anal phase, awareness of inner spaces as well as transition from inside to outside is strengthened by the toddler's growing awareness that the contents of the bladder and bowel are his property to give or withhold. At the same time an inner representational world begins to have more and more power and reality.

The rapprochement subphase is followed by an initial attainment of object constancy. This implies a growing acceptance of separateness and an increasing internalization of the love object. Mother becomes more an internal presence, and the child between 2 and 3 can imagine and accept her being elsewhere. Thus the need for incessant coming and going is diminished. The child is better able to accept temporary separations, substitute adults, and can become absorbed in activities in the outside world. Symbolic play begins to substitute for the actual doing. A child of that age, instead of going to mother, can begin to play at being mother, father, or baby. A child of this age can begin to play house or castle or cave, and so find symbolic representations of the enclosed mother space.

The Use of Space
as Therapeutic Communication

Furer (1974) maintained that the subphases of the separation-individuation process, while they cannot be directly reconstructed in the verbal content of analytic treatment, nevertheless play an important role in the establishment of the basic transference and therapeutic alliance. One would assume that the patient's use of space is an important communication to the analyst. This has been described by Winnicott (1971), Khan (1973), and Searles (1973).

I would like to give a few examples in the treatment of children where the use of space in the analyst's office was of special importance in working out problems arising from the separation-individuation process. These were not verbalized in therapy, but served as the background music, the atmosphere in which the treatment took place. Peter came to treatment at the age of 4. He suffered extreme separation anxiety and it was many months before he would come to his treatment sessions without his mother, even when she promised to wait for him in the waiting room. Peter also wet and soiled his pants, and was generally willful and uncontrollable. He was a cherished child, good-looking and intelligent. He had been an active baby and his mother had experienced his early motor development as a threat. She had been happy with him when he was an infant, but trouble began when, during the practicing and rapprochement subphases, his intimidated mother interpreted Peter's precocious activity as willfulness. Rather than being quietly available, she fought with him, unsuccessfully tried to control him, and frightened him with unpredictable outbursts of anger. When Peter was 2, his baby brother was born, and Peter could not reconcile himself to having a rival. At the beginning of treatment he repeatedly acted out family scenes that

ended in cataclysms of destruction. In these he was both the perpe-
trator of misfortune and the rescuer, identifying alternately with the
victim and the aggressor. During a later phase of treatment, Peter
became interested in books about space and time, the heavenly bodies, and prehistoric animals. He insisted his therapist read these to
him while he sat on a swing, moving toward and away from the therapist, who had to sit in a fixed position. In this play he seemed to
reenact experiences concerning his mother and outside space, experiences in which he controlled closeness and distance. This was not
interpreted, but was allowed to unfold.

Jimmy was a boy whose sister was born when he was 18 months
old. From early on he had shown a strong, clinging attachment to
his mother, who felt quite helpless in the face of it. She felt inadequate as a mother and feared that she, without wishing to, prevented
Jimmy from becoming an individual. Jimmy was a quiet, withdrawn
little boy who experienced treatment, especially any verbal intervention, as an invasion. It was almost impossible to find a workable distance. One Valentine's Day the therapist gave him a white chocolate
lollipop. He asked the therapist to sit close to him but not to talk while
he sucked the lollipop, which he said reminded him of milk. He remarked how hard it was to suck but not bite the lollipop. He said
how good the session was and again implored the therapist not to
talk. The session apparently recreated a symbiotic union, a good
mother prior to separation. Again this experience was allowed to
develop.

Maria[1] was a little girl with an intense ambivalent relationship
to her mother. Her parents had separated after a long and violent
struggle. While home with a babysitter, Maria had an accident in
which she blinded herself in one eye. For a considerable period in
therapy she regaled her therapist with insatiable demands for objects
that would never satisfy her. Finally she invented a game in which
she created a space under a table for herself, then hung blankets over
it and demanded that the therapist supply various objects for it. This
space had to be re-created for her by the therapist prior to each session. She played in it quietly by herself, while the therapist had to

---

1. I wish to thank Dr. Linda Gunsburg for sharing this material with me.

be watching and available outside. After many months of playing this game, Maria emerged. She no longer needed her special place, and she was now able to relate to her therapist in a new way, on a more mature level. She allowed some give and take, and recognized the therapist as a separate person rather than as an extension of herself.

These examples show how problems of space, of closeness and comfortable distance, of being able to come and go, are worked on by patients in the therapeutic situation as an accompaniment and counterpoint to what is said in words. Feelings of well-being and safety are achieved when feelings about space belonging to preverbal times are re-created by the child in actions or words, allowing for freedom to move with greater ease from enclosed mother space to the space out there. As the conflict is worked through, both spaces become more available. This does not imply that the problem is settled once and for all. Conflicts in this area will recur throughout life, but they are less overwhelming once the essential conflict of the rapprochement crisis is at least partly worked through and resolved.

We have shown how the baby moves in the course of the subphases from being one with mother to beginning awareness and eventual exploration of ever widening areas of the world outside. We have seen the toddler move back and forth from mother to the world outside. Eventually, a space within becomes available which allows for the fantasied creation of both spaces.

Some Thoughts on the Importance
of Home Space

Throughout life *where* one is and not just *with whom* affects one's mood and sense of well-being and safety, and people vary widely as to the varieties of space in which they feel most comfortable. From prehistoric times people have devoted time and energy to creating the home space. A young woman during her therapy described her home as a barometer of what was going on within her. More than the clothes she wore, the neatness or sloppiness of her house represented her feelings about herself. When she was a child, her family had moved from a country house that she remembered as sunny and spacious, in which she had felt close to her mother, to a more expensive but smaller suburban home. She never came to love this new home and in it she began to feel more estranged from her family. In adulthood, she forever attempted to re-create the home of her early childhood.

And finally I would like to present a personal experience that demonstrated to me the importance of home space. On a hiking and camping trip in a faraway country, a group of people, most of them strangers to each other as well as to the country, started out together with the knowledge that they would be trekking for more than two weeks through totally unfamiliar mountain territory. A mood of anxiety prevailed on the first afternoon of the trip. After several hours, the first campsite was reached. As each person approached, he was greeted by a member of the working crew who handed each a small bunch of flowers and led him to his designated tent. This small gesture of hospitality in the wilderness provided much to change the mood of the group to one of confidence and friendliness, which helped everyone through the more difficult and strenuous moments that were bound to arise; no words of reassurance could have worked as well as a ready shelter and a bunch of flowers. Home was carried to the vast spaces of the faraway mountains, giving this group of people the reassurance that both of these essential spaces would still be available.

Summary

During the first few weeks of life the human infant, through the nursing care of his mother, becomes united with her in symbiotic oneness. Slowly as the infant matures he begins to differentiate inside from outside, mother from others, himself from mother. As he does this, space between him and his mother has to be created and bridged. Each period of development during the separation-individuation process has an optimal distance between baby and mother. Exploration of different spaces—mother and world out there—eventually results in cognitive awareness of separation and relative helplessness. Thus, during rapprochement there is a continuous need to traverse the space separating infant from mother. Yet at the same time, the space surrounding the self becomes a precious possession, and space within becomes a reality reinforced by toilet training and the ability to retain or deposit bowel and bladder products. With the advent of beginning object constancy, the inner world of thought and fantasy allows for the symbolic representation of experiences in space—thus widening the world outside as well as securing the home space.

As the realization of the irreconcilability of home and outside space becomes a reality, transitional spaces become a necessity for comfortable functioning. In the outside world these transitional spaces must contain elements of both mother and world outside: the home away from home, the home on wheels, the freedom to come and go, a place to play. It is more difficult to conceptualize the transitional space within the representational world, but it seems that the ability to think and to delay gratification creates a safe space within, mediating between passionate longings for mother and need for distance from her. The concept of transitional space based on observations in a toddler study is an extension of Winnicott's transitional object. The initial and primitive experiences of differentiation of self from mother seem to contain parts of both. Transitional spaces serve a similar function in the widening world of the toddler in his movements from mother to the world outside.

3

Ours, Yours, Mine

Fights over possessions—often fought with a fierceness that in no way seems warranted by the possessions themselves—are all too familiar to those in close contact with young children.

But this attachment to "things" does not end with the end of childhood; it is an important and often plaguing part of adult life as well. There are those who hold onto all the bits and pieces that they have accumulated, whether they are of objective value or not; and there are those who like to live with the bare minimum of possessions. There are those who can give away their possessions but cannot share them; and there are those to whom possessions become most valuable when shared with another person. There are those who know how to take care of their possessions, and who always know where they are, and those who forever lose or misplace them. We could go on and on describing attitudes toward possessions, and it is quite clear that these are deeply ingrained and hard to modify. This chapter will describe uses of inanimate objects as they unfold in the course of the separation-individuation process, with special emphasis on rapprochement, as well as developing feelings of possessiveness toward those objects. It is my thesis that attitudes toward objects reflect the beginning sense of one's own self as separate, emerging from the former state of dual unity with mother.

Psychoanalysis traditionally has connected the attitude toward possessions and such character traits as stinginess or generosity to the anal phase of development (Fenichel 1945). The stool part of the self is eventually relinquished—the first true gift to mother. The anal phase coincides with that subphase of the separation-individuation process designated as rapprochement, that crucial time from 15 to 24 months when the toddler becomes aware of his separateness, a time during which the intrapsychic self and object representations become well established. I will attempt to show how the developing sense of self, unfolding through the separation-individuation process, is worked out not only with mother and others but also with inanimate objects in the outside world, and how in turn it influences attitudes toward such objects, beginning with holding on and letting go of them, and eventually possessing or sharing them. Holding on or letting go does not require the recognition of a separate human object; giving and taking does. I will trace some of the developmental steps that lead to the realization of "mine," "yours," and "ours" by examining how these concepts arise in the course of the separation-individuation process from 5 months, the height of symbiosis, to somewhere in the third year when an intrapsychic differentiation between the self and object has been attained.

A study of the concepts of "mine" and "yours" emphasizes that aspect of the separation-individuation process that propels an individual to take possession of his life and enjoy it, which in turn helps him tolerate the losses that are entailed in becoming a separate individual, and thereby renouncing a symbiotic oneness with mother.

The sense of "mine" and "yours," according to our observations and the symbiosis theory of human development (Mahler et al. 1975), seems to develop out of an earlier sense of "ours" that starts with the symbiotic union between mother and child, widens with the expanding space between them, and finally expands toward interactions with the other-than-mother world—a world that is "other," but onto which some of the mother attributes are displaced as well so that the investment in it becomes libidinal.

In the discussion that follows, I will consider the importance of the space between mother and child, the function of transitional and shared object within that space, and the gradual development of the concepts of "mine" and "yours."

In our observations of psychotic children we noted that certain aspects of development—which in normal children seem fleeting— happen so slowly and laboriously that they can be observed as if with a magnifying glass. Simply for the purposes of contrast and comparison, and to highlight the normal development of a sense of "mine" and "yours," I have included clinical vignettes from our study of infantile psychosis (Mahler 1968).

The Space between Mother and Child

Mahler's theory of human symbiosis postulates that at the beginning of life and for the first five months or so mother and baby constitute a dual unity, and for the baby an omnipotent system. At this time, there is no outside world for the child; the outer world, as it develops, happens in the space between mother and child. This space at first is created by mother's comings and goings. On the baby's side, the space between self and object begins to be created by the baby in the beginning of the differentiation subphase, when he begins to look around and pushes away from mother's enveloping arms. Thus begins a process of distancing from mother and exploration of the world outside. But as the baby creates this distance, he also gets a different view of mother. The differentiation subphase begins at the height of symbiosis at around 5 months of age. We found that those children who had an unusually close symbiotic relationship, in which the mother experienced special pleasure, started to differentiate and seek distance most actively; in one case, where the mother acted out her own symbiotic need, the child sought distance almost vehemently. Sammy,[1] whose mother was symbiotically enveloping, for a while actually preferred to be held by adults other than his mother, adults who would provide him with greater opportunity to visually explore

---

1. Some of the children mentioned here are also described by Mahler, Pine, and Bergman (1975).

the environment while being held. The seeking of distance during the differentiation subphase coincided with greater awareness of mother as a special person, even if this awareness, as in Sammy's case, was a negative one.

Winnicott (1971) says that play and creative activity take place in the space between mother and child. In the study of the separation-individuation process in average mother–child pairs, it was literally that space which was observed, a space very small at first, slowly expanding with the growing capacities of the baby, and traveled over and over again, first with the reaching arms, the searching and finding look, the listening and hearing ear, and finally, with the growing capacity for independent locomotion, the entire body.

During the earliest beginnings of the study on separation-individuation conducted in a playroom-like setting, the mothers and babies were free to create the space that was optimal for each of them as individuals, as well as for each particular age. How this space was used and traversed eventually led to the formulation of the subphase theory of separation-individuation (Mahler et al. 1975). For instance, there was a little girl, 1 year old, preciously and precariously performing daring feats of climbing and balancing at a distance from mother. Her courage seemed to be for the benefit of her mother, who felt that girls had to be tough and could not be taught independence early enough. This mother–child pair seemed separated from each other to an exaggerated degree, and both mother and child gave some signs that they entertained longings for greater closeness. Martha was the first child of this family in the study. Subsequently, we saw the same mother with three more children—all boys—and were impressed with her ability to fulfill their needs as lap babies. When we had first seen her with Martha we did not as yet have any conception of subphases, and we were therefore not aware of two important points. One, what seemed like premature separateness on the child's part was only partly that—it was also to an extent the child's desire and need during that time to explore the environment even at the expense of the former closeness to mother. We were also unaware of the fact that this mother, who seemed to us not to be providing enough mothering to her separating 1-year-old, was more at ease with her children during the symbiotic stage and was able to give them a solid start in life during that period of dual unity. In addition, being

fledgling observers, perhaps, we were not fully aware of the importance of the actual space between the mother and child, that is, of
the fact that the space between mother and child is created by both
in the course of the separation-individuation process. At the beginning there is no space, as there is yet no consciousness of self and
other, but as the space is created it becomes the common orbit. While
the symbiotic unity is an illusory "we" experience that cannot last,
the space between mother and child is a true "we-ours" experience,
as it evolves with the differentiation in the child's psyche of the object and the self-representations as separate entities from the self-
object representation of the symbiosis.

Another mother–child pair observed early in the study was Tommy
and his mother, who showed the opposite of what we saw in Martha
and her mother. Tommy was a quiet little boy, slightly anxious and
restricted in his movements, and with a tendency to stay quite close
to his mother. The mother was very eager to talk about her feelings
toward Tommy when he was first born, and said she had then found
his demands quite intolerable. When he first woke her up at night,
she remembered crying and feeling that she no longer had a life of
her own. During the first weeks and months of Tommy's life, she
would frequently feel compelled to rush out of the house to go shopping, since staying home with him made her feel dreadfully confined.
At around 1 year of age, when Martha had seemed so prematurely
separate, Tommy seemed overly close. And later, during his second
year, he became very anxious about his mother's whereabouts, and
would need to be close to her at all costs. If she would leave him, he
would respond quite often with severe temper tantrums. This mother–
child pair was observed long before characteristics of subphases had
been delineated, and what we did not know at the time was that the
shadowing behavior seen in Tommy was only in part a function of
this particular mother–child relationship; it was also a phenomenon
characteristic of the age later designated as the rapprochement
subphase. Tommy's mother, for whom motherhood had been such an
enormous struggle as long as the baby was totally dependent on her,
functioned much more comfortably with a growing, individuating child
who allowed her more separateness and *Lebensraum*. Tommy, who
had seemed so troubled earlier, developed very well during his third
year.

Once the child is able to move away independently, he seems to rediscover mother as he returns to her. Once he is able to move away, albeit only the tiniest distance at the beginning, he experiences not only a new view of the world but a new view of the mother as well. As the baby's locomotor functioning matures, he is able to move away further, his world begins to widen, there is more to see, more to hear, and more to touch, and each time he returns to mother he brings with him some of the new experience. In other words, each time he returns he is ever so slightly changed. The mother is the center of his universe to whom he returns as the circles of his explorations widen.

How much pleasure there is in the actual finding and refinding of mother perhaps partly depends on how much the mother permits the child the illusion that by finding her he has just created her (Winnicott 1971). If she is too intrusive, it is as if he were being deprived of this process of creating her as he refinds her. If, on the other hand, she is too elusive, the process of creating and finding becomes too much of a strain. One little girl we saw gave up on her efforts to some extent, and instead of finding and creating mother, turned to herself. Her favorite activity was rocking in front of a mirror.

For the psychotic child the adaptive and creative use of space between himself and mother becomes impossible; indeed, this space does not seem to exist. Instead of space, there is only the dread of abandonment or engulfment—in either case, annihilation of the developing self (Mahler 1968). In treatment of psychotic children, this space, the shared reality, may slowly be created by the therapist who acts as a bridge between mother and child, and who slowly and patiently teaches both mother and child that a space can be created that is not too dangerous. The mother must learn that the total rejection she has experienced is only the reverse side of desperate need, and the child must learn that his needs can be fulfilled and that interaction with an "other" can be comforting and pleasurable (Mahler 1968).

Objects and Their Transformation
into Possessions

According to Mahler's theory of human symbiosis, for the first five or six months of life mother and baby constitute a dual unity. The transitional object (Winnicott 1953) of the early months is an object found by the baby that stands between the self and the object world and provides a safe intermediary area of experience that allows both separateness and fusion.

We have observed a related phenomenon in babies during the differentiation subphase, that is, from 5 to 8 months, when they develop a special interest in objects that seem to be a part of the mother and yet are not, namely such objects as the mother's jewelry or her glasses. Why do these detachable objects hold such special fascination, and why are they especially suitable as comforting objects? I believe that these objects represent both mother and the outside world. Thus they may serve both as a confirmation of the early "we"[2] and "ours" experience—one moment part of the mother, the next moment part of the self, a self not yet fully experienced as separate—and at the same time are experienced as not-mother, that is, part of the world outside. Thus, while confirming the symbiotic experience, they also serve as vehicles in the process of differentiation. Winnicott makes the point that the transitional object, though it already exists, is created by the baby. The prototype for this is the way in which the mother gives the breast to the infant, allowing him to create it as he finds it, that is, allowing him the illusion that he has created it. Carrying this concept a bit further, one might apply it to a cherished activity in young children, then they find things in the outside world and act as if they had just created them. We can observe children creating the outside world anew as they find it, and invest it with their own unique way of seeing it. This is intimately bound up with the libidinal investment in mother. The shiny pebble found at the beach by the older child may be like the shiny bit of jewelry found on the mother by the baby.

Thus, during differentiation, the baby's interest in mother's possessions may be seen as a function of his wanting to own and incor-

---

2. "We" as used here is a primitive feeling state that does not require self–object differentiation. The feeling of "we" referred to is psychically experienced as the "me" of primary narcissism that still dominates the symbiosis. Only gradually does this archaic "we" experience develop to include differentiated "me" and "we" experience. However, it is the author's contention that even in adulthood intense "we" experiences retain an element of the archaic "we."

porate her while at the same time be separate from her. The differentiating child makes mother, or parts of her, part of himself. He does this by investigating and manipulating parts of her, especially those he can take off, like jewelry or eyeglasses. These inanimate objects are invested with libido that stems directly from mother, but in contrast to the transitional object they cannot be totally possessed—only borrowed. They may be used but they cannot be used up.

Thus, already during the first few months of life there are two kinds of inanimate objects that take on a special importance and serve the infant in the process of becoming separate. First, the transitional object, described by Winnicott, that is given by the mother and created by the baby; second, the borrowed object that is discovered and thus created by the baby but is ultimately kept by the mother. Thus, it would seem that the transitional object serves the illusion of oneness while the borrowed object serves separateness in a shared place.

During the practicing subphase (10–15 months) the child actually begins to move away from mother as he learns to move on his own. His relative obliviousness of her is determined in part by the pleasures in his own functioning and the widening of his world. But it also seems that, even though separated in space, he still acts as if mother were somehow part of him, with him. In other words, symbolically he takes her along. He greatly enjoys the world of inanimate objects. He picks them up, examines them, and drops them. The world is there to be explored. He usually will easily accept one object or toy as a substitute for another. He might cry briefly when something is taken away, but on the whole the world seems too big and too interesting to be bothered by small frustrations. Objects or activities that seem to be most comforting during the practicing stage are those that seem to confirm the toddler's sense of his omnipotence, which is still shared with mother. For example, we found that an unhappy child of that age could be comforted by being allowed to play with a light switch, turning lights on and off, preferably while being held up by an adult, or else by working a toy such as a jack-in-the-box or top, whose movements he can actively control and which contain some element of surprise and magic.

Mahler's theory states that during the differentiation and practicing subphases of the separation-individuation process, the child gradually comes to a dawning awareness of his separateness. While in the first months of a baby's life the mother comes and goes, toward the end of the first year the baby himself begins to go and come back. During the subphase of rapprochement, beginning at about 15 months, an important change takes place. Mother is now seen as a separate person out there, with whom one might share one's possessions and one's experiences. She can no longer be experienced as part of the self and thus the relationship has to be reestablished and reaffirmed over and over. Moveable objects at this point seem to serve the purpose of affirming over and over the connection between toddler and mother. Toddlers at this age are indefatigable in depositing objects in mother's lap.

During the rapprochement subphase, the toddler has achieved a first real awareness of separateness. The bringing of objects to mother, just as the earlier act of removing objects from her, seems to serve two different functions: one, to bridge the gap by giving *her* what he now begins to experience as *his*; the other, to put into mother's lap for safekeeping what he wants to return to but at the moment does not want to use. Earlier, what isn't used is simply discarded, no longer exists. In many instances, in the same action one can see elements of opposing tendencies—to affirm separateness, and to maintain oneness. At one level the mother is an extension of the self; her lap is part of the infant. At the other, separateness is recognized and dealt with.

When we compare these stages in the normal child's attitude toward possessions to those observed in the psychotic child, we observe marked distortions. Psychotic children have not developed to the point of separateness experienced by average normal children during the rapprochement subphase. This can be seen by the way in which they relate to the inanimate world. The transitional object of the normal baby becomes the psychotic fetish (Furer 1964)—the total absorption with an object or activity that represents the mother, that is clung to with desperate feeling, and that seems to represent the merged identity without which the child would be totally lost or destroyed. A psychotic child whose fetish object is removed from him will break into desperate tantrums. Whereas the transitional object of the normal child is needed mostly at times of fatigue or unhappiness or at bedtime, the psychotic fetish object is held onto almost constantly. It is most characteristic in the observations of such children that while they may hold on frantically to their psychotic fetish (Furer 1964),

objects in general are cathected only during the moment of the immediate usefulness. It is difficult to describe satisfactorily how a psychotic child during the phase of denial of separateness will dispose
of a toy. It is not put away, it is not thrown away, it is not handed to
another person. Rather, it is treated as if suddenly it no longer existed. That part of relating to objects that serves separateness is
strenuously rejected.

Rachel, whose separation-individuation process during her first
two years of treatment has been described elsewhere (Bergman 1971),
at first would not touch objects or toys at all. Later, she discarded
them as if they had never existed, and still later, after she had developed a rudimentary sense of self, demanded that her mother or
the therapist find any object that she could not find. Mother's refusal
or inability to do this would send Rachel into a rage. The child absolutely refused to look for anything herself. Thus, like the toddler
during the rapprochement subphase but typically for the psychotic
child in highly exaggerated form, Rachel, increasingly aware of separateness, attempted to undo it by insisting that mother act as if still
part of her. Like the toddler during rapprochement, she created an
impossible situation between herself and mother, acting this out with
inanimate objects that she could not truly possess. To Rachel, during this period of beginning separateness, her whole world had to be
mother's lap; or rather, mother's lap had to be powerful enough to
extend into all of Rachel's world. For years afterwards Rachel was
unable to take care of any of her possessions. To her mother's great
exasperation, she would lose and forget everything; she never knew
where anything was.

Returning to the normal child in the rapprochement subphase of
separation-individuation and his growing sense that objects in the outside world can be part of him, belong to him, but can also be part of
someone else, that such possessions can be used, manipulated, held
onto or given up, lost or destroyed, we found that at around 15 or 16
months a clustering of several phenomena occurs: (1) resistance to
being dressed or undressed; (2) increasing desire to have or do whatever the child saw others having or doing; (3) nonacceptance of sub-
stitutions for wished-for possession; (4) conflict over holding on or
giving up of a possession that another child wanted; and (5) object-
directed aggression in defense of one's own property or interest.

During the following month (16–17 months) we found an increase in possessiveness, but we also found the most frequent source of anger involved having one's autonomy interfered with, not being allowed to do as one wished, to do things by oneself, and so on. In other words, we found a stronger push toward individuation.

Another month later, 18 to 19 months, constitutes the height of the rapprochement crisis. This is a time when some degree of disturbance in the area of object relations is a universal phenomenon (Mahler 1966, 1971). The bipolar, ambivalent pull—"to be separate" and to be "fused with the object"—creates what we have called this crisis. The rapprochement crisis is complicated by the fact that for the child this is not only a time of painful awareness of separateness and vulnerability, but also of defense against this awareness. The child may thus swing back and forth between an exaggerated independence and an exaggerated dependence, with attempts to coerce the mother to be ever-present and powerful. From these opposite poles, the child seems to say to mother, "I am me. You cannot touch me or tell me what to do." Or "You must be a part of me, fulfill my wishes, and be ever-present." As part and parcel of this crisis, the child experiences on the one hand the fear of being abandoned, alone, unloved, and on the other hand the fear of being reengulfed, overwhelmed, swallowed up. Around the rapprochement crisis we found an interesting cluster of phenomena: (1) increased independent functioning; (2) greater self-assertiveness; (3) increased use of the word "mine"; (4) increased ability and wish to play at some distance from mother; (5) increased awareness of body sensations (for instance, making faces in front of a mirror, water play, riding on the rocking horse, etc.); and (6) competitiveness over possession being the most frequent source of anger.

Thus, what we seem to find is that the rapprochement subphase was ushered in by a great pleasure in sharing possessions, in give-and-take, in using mother as an extended part of the self but also as a separate person with whom to share. But along with greater awareness of separateness seemed to go a greater need to assert the budding self, a greater need to compare it with others, and a greater resistance to intrusion and interference with one's wishes. It seems that in the midst of all this we find a moment of conflict about whether to hold on or give up, and then an increased need to defend one's possessions with one's growing awareness of self, which is frequently expressed by insistence on what is "mine."

The Importance of Clothes

During the second half of the second year, when the toddler begins to insist on his autonomy by saying "no" (Spitz 1957), dressing, undressing, and diapering generally become a battlefield between mother and child. Clothes and wraps during that period seem to have a very special meaning, or rather at this age we seem to see the beginnings of the importance of clothes.

Clothes are not-me possessions that are most closely connected to the "me." They are part of the body, and yet they are taken off and put on. They have color, texture, they can be alluring and soft or hampering and hard or rough. They circumscribe individuality or identity. This function of clothes can be observed later in childhood when boys and girls play dress-up by putting on someone else's clothes and become that person. Hats and shoes often seem to have an especially symbolic meaning, perhaps because they are most easily put on and taken off. The special significance of these articles of clothing is indicated by such common sayings as, "I would not like to be in his shoes," or "I'll put on another hat."

In normal development, clothes seem at first to be experienced as part of the self, and quite early in life it seems that pride in the self can be expressed through pride in one's clothes—again, often shoes and hats. During the rapprochement subphase clothes begin to have special significance.

Peter was a little boy in our study of normal children whose mother had a particularly difficult struggle over dressing and undressing him. When he first started to play in our toddler room, that is, the room where 2- to 3-year-olds could play together at some distance from their mothers, he went through a ritual where he would stop at the threshold, wait to be greeted there by his toddler room teacher, and would then show her his pants. She would admire them, and finally he would enter the activities of the playroom. Charlie, on the other hand, would come in wearing his jacket and hat. He would stand on the sidelines and observe. If urged to take his jacket off, he would leave the room, sulk, or cry. If left to his own devices, he would eventually take it off on his own and then slowly enter into play. Donna, a little girl who had difficulty in separating from her mother, but who could play well and happily once she had made the separation, developed a pattern of pulling at her clothes while she was in the throes of a conflict over leaving mother.

It seems that clothes begin to have symbolic meaning as a result of the rapprochement conflict—and it may be at a particular moment of the conflict. This could be the point when the toddler not only becomes increasingly aware of his own separateness and vulnerability, but in addition becomes aware of sexual differences as well as of the loss of his feces. At this time the taking off and putting on of clothes by the mother becomes a threat to developing body integrity, while on the other hand it also becomes possible to displace some of the conflicts about separateness as well as castration onto the use and possession of clothes.

In later development, of course, clothes take on many other meanings, but it is interesting that they again become so very important during adolescence, the second period of individuation (Blos 1967), and can express both belonging (group fashion) and individuality (separation from parental demands).

Psychotic children often experience clothes as an extreme source of discomfort. For Rachel, for instance, buying new shoes was an ordeal. She would often get blisters from shoes, and her mother would only find this out accidentally, as Rachel would never let her know. Very early in life she was said to have pulled off all her wraps and later she went through a long period of feeling simply miserable in her clothes, taking them all off as soon as she came home and complaining endlessly that a hat wouldn't cover her ears, that a belt was not tight enough, too tight, and so on.

Rosie, a severely autistic girl who had been in treatment for nine years, since the age of 3, displaced her conflicts onto clothes in extreme ways. She was about 8 years old when she began to emerge as a separate little girl with a growing sense of self-awareness. At the age of 9 she went to camp with normal children. She was relatively happy there, but began the painful journey of recognizing that she was different from the others. Though she was speaking by then, her speech remained peculiar and her ability to play in adequate ways was very rudimentary. When she returned from camp she drew pictures of her camp experience, and especially concentrated on remembering and drawing the clothes of the other children. From then on, clothes became an obsession, as she hoped that by wearing the right clothes she could undo the differences between herself and others. She would not allow her mother to choose any of her clothes, and buying trips to Macy's became long-looked-forward-to treats and also ordeals of disappointment. Finally, two years later, at the age of 11, Rosie could come to a more satisfactory solution in which true sublimation could replace the earlier displacement. She now began to design and sew her own clothes, an activity in which she was able to excel and elicit the genuine admiration of others.

Another example of conflict displaced onto clothes was displayed by a severely deprived adolescent boy in therapy. This boy denied any need for help. Although he came to his once- or twice-a-week treatment hours with fair regularity, he consistently belittled the therapist and insisted that nothing was wrong in his life and that, if there were, nobody could help him anyway. Following a joint session with his guardian, during which the therapist was able to act as a bridge between them, interpreting some of the mutual wishes and disappointments, this boy brought to his therapy session a pair of badly worn jeans that he wished the therapist to patch with hand-crocheted patches that he had occasionally seen her make. From then on he periodically returned with the same pair of jeans in need of patching, and along with this his resistance to admitting his own needs gradually diminished. It seemed that he could use his torn jeans as a symbol through which he could begin to admit some need for patching of his own self.

Play with Toys and the Acceptance of Separateness

To accept fully one's separateness is a lifelong task and one way in which this task is continually worked on by children as well as by adults is through the use of objects.

By the second half of the second year, children become capable of enjoying the world of objects in a new way, namely through beginning symbolic play (Ekstein 1966, Galenson 1971), mostly still on a nonverbal level. What are some of the most favored toys of this period? Which ones seem to help the toddler master some of the conflicts and anxieties he experiences, such as mother or parts of the self (feces) disappearing, about being in control, that is, being omnipotent, strong and powerful, and being a helpless baby and cared and provided for? Puzzles, blocks for building towers, balls for throwing, nesting cubes, and other toys that make things appear and disappear, as well as dolls and teddy bears, are toys with universal appeal for the toddler during this period. They are used in ever so slightly different ways by each child, indicating not only the extent of his skill and ego mastery, but also the particular way in which the conflicts over separation-individuation as well as psychosexual conflicts are experienced at the time.

All of these early games are played at first in the space between mother and child, and it is one of the characteristics of the child in acute conflict over separation that he is unable to play. When this acute conflict is settled, either by the child's allowing mother to leave or accepting a substitute, or by mother's remaining close enough to satisfy him, the child is usually able to return to play. In a state of acute longing, most children are not able to turn to play, but will, rather, turn to direct instinctual gratification, such as food, autoerotic activity, or, in other circumstances, sleep. Sometime in the third year, along with the ability for verbal communication, the child can use toys at a higher symbolic level to play out experiences of the past or anticipated in the future. This type of play no longer uses the space between mother and child in as direct a way as before, but already depends on the ability to internalize and identify.

Looking at books and being read to is an activity that is of particular importance and interest to toddlers beginning at the time of rapprochement. Going back to the concept of finding and creating, here we may have an activity that allows the toddler to create the story of his activities and life, his budding self as he relates to the world around him by finding it in stories. Sometimes these stories can be directly concerned with the child's life—"When Susie goes to sleep . . ." or "When Daddy comes home. . . ." Sometimes the stories can be about animals, animal mothers and babies, by which the process of being cared for as a baby can be enjoyed in a doubly removed way: first, by way of a story; second, displaced on animals.

The following examples of children around 2 years old show how play can help the child deal with developmental tasks and conflicts.

Here is a description of Teddy, 2 years old, reported by a play session observer: "Teddy asked for a puzzle. He chose the puzzle with the vegetables. He worked on the puzzle very seriously, taking each piece out, looking at it, and carefully putting it back again. He identified some of the vegetables in an original way. So, for instance, he called a bunch of celery, 'flowers.' He recognized the carrot and the potato, pretended to eat them, and said 'tough.' Then he said, 'my puzzle.' "

Teddy at this time was very concerned with toilet training, and when he had a bowel movement in his pants he would say "me BM." Here individualistic ego activity—fitting together pieces of a puzzle— goes hand in hand with working out anal conflicts.

Peter, at the same age, loved to build high towers and knock them down and build them up again. Also, Peter, a child who very early seemed to have turned away from showing direct concern over his mother's whereabouts, was particularly interested in building tunnels with blocks, making the train go in and out of the tunnels. He seemed delighted to see the train reappear through the tunnel—his way of coping, we thought, with his mother's comings and goings.

Three girls during the rapprochement subphase used ball play in slightly different ways. Wendy, who always needed to relate rather exclusively to one adult, used the ball play as a way of interacting with an adult. Donna, who was very concerned with separation, used the ball play more in an active, coping way, throwing the ball away, then running after it, scooping it up, sometimes saying, "Mommy, Mommy," as she did so. Harriet, who had a very disturbed relationship to her mother, would lose balls and then want the observer to retrieve them for her.

Thus, the rapprochement period is ushered in by a growing wish to share with mother. The space between mother and child now takes on more and more meaning in terms of being a space that bridges a gap between the now more separate self, alone out there in the big world, and mother, whose presence and availability take on renewed importance as the awareness of separateness increases. As the awareness of separateness becomes more threatening, the mother becomes both the restorer of well-being and the person who threatens or interferes with separate functioning. It seems to be at that point that possessions become important and are recognized as "mine" and eventually reluctantly renounced as "yours." It may be that at that point the old comfortable sense of "ours" becomes impossible, and has to be replaced by an eventual ability to share on a higher level. But it may also be that all sharing, shared experiences, shared possessions, when they give a feeling of pleasure and fulfillment, retain some of the flavor of the early "ours" experience.

Summary

I have attempted in this chapter to show how a sense of "mine" and "yours" seems to develop out of an earlier sense of "ours" that starts with the symbiotic union between mother and child and widens with the expanding space between them to include shared possessions as well as shared space. The realization of "mine" and "yours" emerges at the height of the rapprochement subphase of the separation-individuation process, confirmation of and insistence on separate experience and possession. Along with that emerges a possibility to use these possessions to reenact and master the conflicts connected with separateness.

I have tried further to show that perhaps creative experience in Winnicott's sense can be applied not only to the creation of the transitional object but also to the creating of the mother as a separate person. The expanding space between mother and child, which belongs to both, is bridged at first by what happens in that space and later by activities displaced onto objects in the outside world, such as clothes, and eventually toys.

Finally, I have considered the first experiences of "mine" as an important step in individuation that may have repercussions in later attitudes toward possessions which form an important part of each person's life style.

4

Speculations on the Development of Gender Role Characteristics [1]

The paper entitled " 'Consistency' and 'Contradiction' in the Development of Gender Role Characteristics" raises a number of very interesting questions. Why is it that gender role development rarely seems to go beyond the conventional conformist stage, which adheres to gender stereotypes? As the author correctly states, assignment to stereotypic gender roles results in the suppression of important qualities for both sexes. This is not really adaptive. Why then, we might ask further, are the sanctions imposed by society for androgyny so severe that by and large people will sacrifice those aspects of their character that do not correspond to what they have been taught to believe is male or female? I shall discuss briefly some ideas about development of gender identity as I have come to see it based on my

1. This chapter is a commentary on L. Furby (1983), " 'Consistency' and 'Contradiction' in the Development of Gender Role Characteristics," *New Ideas of Psychology*, vol. 1, no. 3.

psychoanalytic work with patients and my research is psychoanalytically oriented observations of mothers and infants. Thus, I will jux-
tapose Furby's discussion of external pressures that result in internal structures with observations on intrapsychic internal problems
that have to be faced by any child in the struggle to achieve identity
and, in particular, gender identity.

The author uses the example of language development to demonstrate that the developing child has a tendency to apply rules rigidly
when these rules are first perceived. This stage of randomly applying rules is later followed by a stage in which rules are more flexibly
applied. When it comes to gender development, an interesting situation occurs that in some ways is almost a reverse of that described
in the development of language. This, I believe, may be one of the
roots of the difficulty in reaching more mature development of gender roles. In language development, rules, when they first are perceived, are overapplied across the board to be followed by a stage of
realization of exceptions: therefore, the need to sharpen one's observations and learn about exceptions. How about the observation of gender differences? At the beginning of the second year of life the child
begins to observe the anatomical difference between the sexes and
eventually arrives at the rule that boys have penises and girls do not.
At a somewhat later age another rule becomes evident, namely, that
girls will become women who can have babies inside their bodies
whereas boys cannot. The problem with these rules is that there are
no exceptions to them. Gender-linked characteristics develop somewhat later and are in part based on observation by the child of the
gender-linked attitudes and actions of adults in his or her environment; for example, that boys should not cry, that only girls should
play with dolls, and so on. Early on, however, the observation of the
rules of anatomical difference to which there is no exception runs
counter to the omnipotent desires of the infant toddler, namely, the
desire to create one's own rules according to one's wishes and needs.
It may be, then, that the rigidity with which gender characteristics
are later assigned has one source in its defensive function, namely
as if to say, "It is not true that I might want to be other than I am."
The defensive position can then result in suppression of those gender-linked characteristics that do not correspond to the more stereotyped expectations.

When we observe the play of little children at the end of the second and during the third year of life, we can often see them act out the desire to be able to reverse what is not reversible, namely gender. There are many symbolic ways in which girls act out their desire to have a penis like the boy and in which boys act out their desire to be able to have a baby like the girl. For example, a little boy 2½ years old during an observation put a ball inside his shirt and said that it was a baby. He gave it a name. It was a boy baby. Then he put another ball, a much smaller one, inside his shirt—a little baby like his younger brother who was born when the older child was 18 months old. He gave the little baby a name very similar to the one he had given the first one. Then he found an empty coffee can. He said it was his Mommy and he put it under his shirt and then another object that was Daddy. (Note the symbolism of the balls as boys and the container as Mommy.) What was the little boy acting out? The wish to be like Mommy—that is, to be able to produce a baby from his body. This was a time when he was very much attached to her and did not want her to leave him. Therefore, to be like her, to be her, was also an expression of this wish to have her with him always. The overcoming of omnipotence is one of the most painful and difficult aspects of separation from the mother. In this case we can see omnipotence transformed into play, which is the constructive outlet for its expression. If the child's omnipotent play were interfered with by the parents and if the boy were harshly told he was a boy and could not have a baby or nurture a baby, this would force him to suppress his androgynous feelings and, thus, a rich part of himself.

Parental attitudes toward gender of the child start from birth. For example, a mother of a week-old infant boy was struggling with conflicting feelings and pieces of advice she had been given. The issue was whether to feed the baby whenever he seemed to want it or to attempt to impose a schedule. The father, in observing the mother's struggle, admonished her not to make a "sissy" out of his son. Here we see a father already, at such an early age, imposing a gender stereotype and intimidating the mother in her attempts to nurture. Robert Emde (1980a) in his work on social referencing has shown the important impact on the young infant of the mother's facial expression. We may assume, therefore, that the way in which parents reflect their feelings about the baby's gender is in some way registered by the baby.

Play and fantasy serve the purpose of gender role transcendence. Gender role transcendence, however, also implies a threat, not only because of the sanctions of society but also because it implies a threat to body integrity and body image. The imagined damage to the body perceived by the girl, when she sees the boy has a penis and she does not, easily turns into a feeling of being damaged that eventually can contribute to a sense of ineffectiveness. The fear of losing a treasured part of the body for the boy by imagining to be a girl may contribute to exaggerated feelings of invulnerability and fear of expressing feelings of communion or intimacy with a woman who is perceived as a threat.

Mature gender identity that does not sacrifice internal correspondence will include for both sexes the fundamentally human tendencies of communion and agency. Reaching of mature gender identity is a developmental process and goes along with the process of reaching mature object relations. Both are an achievement that follows a complex developmental path and depends on many factors. The early mother– and father–child relationship during the stages of separation-individuation and the attainment of beginning libidinal object constancy importantly influence the development of the sense of identity (Mahler et al. 1975). I believe that the groundwork for gender identity is laid during this period as well. The parent's attitude to the child's gender, as well as the relationship they have with each other, we assume to be important building blocks of gender identity.

In this brief discussion I hope I have shown that the child comes to live in a social environment, whatever that might be, with the given of his body self, which includes maleness and femaleness, and with parental attitudes (which in turn are influenced by the society in which they exist) that surround his incipient awareness of himself as a human being.

5

Considerations about the Development of the Girl during the Separation-Individuation Process

Freud repeatedly stated that he knew more about the sexuality of boys than of girls. In his paper entitled "Female Sexuality" he emphasized the importance and intensity of the preoedipal attachment of the little girl to her mother. He said:

> When we survey the whole range of motives for turning away from the mother which analysis brings to light—that she failed to provide the little girl with the only proper genital, that she did not feed her sufficiently, that she compelled her to share her mother's love with others, that she never fulfilled all the girl's expectations of love, and finally, that she first aroused her sexual activity and then forbade it all—those motives seem nevertheless insufficient to justify the girl's final hostility. Some of them follow inevitably from the nature of infantile sexuality; others appear like rationalizations devised later to account for the uncomprehended change in feeling. Perhaps the real fact is that the attachment to the mother is bound to perish, precisely because it was the first and was so intense. The attitude of love probably comes to grief from the disappointments that are unavoidable and from the accumulation of occasions for aggression. [1931, p. 234]

This quotation shows that Freud had some inkling of what we now understand better by way of the study of the separation-individuation process with its regularly occurring rapprochement crisis and its necessary resolution.

I will attempt to show how issues of separation-individuation influence the development of the girl child during that period of development and beyond. A brief overview of the separation-individuation process as conceived and conceptualized by Mahler (1963, 1966, 1968) will serve as a background for the discussion of female identity formation with clinical examples of two girls and their mothers. My discussion will focus on the second year of life, in particular on the subphases of practicing and rapprochement.

The symbiotic phase is seen as the bedrock of the individual's identity, which begins to be formed before separation-individuation begins. Mahler (1968) describes the mutual reflection of mother and child, which, she says, reinforces the delineation of identity. Of special importance in this process is the mother's selective response to the infant's cues.

Lichtenstein (1961) sees in the early mother–child unit, and not in its breaking up, the primary condition for identity in man. He says,

> the very extremeness of the symbiotic relation of the human child to his mother—usually described as the long dependency of the human infant on the mother—becomes the very source of the emergence of *human* identity. . . . Just as an organ within an organism is both "separate" and "symbiotic," the infant is one with the mother but simultaneously bears a primary relatedness of a part to a whole. . . . The organ of an organism has an identity in terms of its functions within the organism, thus the maternal umwelt (which includes the unconscious of the mother) ordains an organ-function to the child, and it is this primary function in which I see the nucleus of the emerging human identity. [p. 202]

Core identity, as defined by Mahler and Lichtenstein, is most likely from the earliest time different for girls and boys.

Kleeman (1976) emphasizes the learning experience about one's gender, which he believes to be more crucial than innate differences for the formation of gender identity. From the beginning, the parents' knowledge that "my baby is a girl" organizes a whole set of cues

to the infant that eventually become part of the baby girl's self experience. Stoller (1976) defines core gender identity as the sense we have
of our sex. It is "the central nexus around which masculinity and femininity gradually accrete. Core gender identity has no implication of
role or object relations; it is, I suppose, a part of what is loosely called
'narcissism' " (p. 61). Thus, core gender identity begins to be formed
at birth; but I will attempt to show here how it develops during separation-individuation into a girl's unique sense of herself as female and
how this sense of herself expresses itself by way of what may be called
her identity theme.

Holland (1978) distinguishes primary identity (something
actually in the individual) from the person's identity theme, which
also remains constant throughout all the changes in a person's life
and lifestyle but is something inferred by someone from outside. He
says, "To the extent that I find it convincing to look at human lives
as identity themes and variations on those themes, to that extent will
I find the hypothesis of a primary identity convincing. To that extent, I can believe that the identity theme I infer from outside for
someone coincides with some intrinsic unity inside the individual" (p.
177).

I intend to investigate the identity theme as it develops in interaction between mother and daughter and pertains in particular to
the girl's sense of herself as female. In examples of two mothers with
their girl children I will infer the girls' identity themes; thus, I will
look from the outside, and I will also discuss how these identity
themes seem to have been imprinted on their daughters by the mothers' perception of them as female. My clinical material is taken from
Mahler's original separation-individuation study (Mahler et al. 1975).
Although the separation-individuation process actually begins at the
height of symbiosis and the beginning of differentiation (around 4 to
6 months of age), I will concentrate on observations of girls as they
go through the practicing and rapprochement subphases that cover
approximately the second year of life. I have chosen this period rather
than the earliest one because, by then, presymbolic action and beginning verbal communication are more understandable to the observer; by then, through her behavior, and later her words, a girl
can give us some indications of her own dawning sense of herself as
female. I will also discuss the outcome of the process during the fourth

subphase "on the way to object constancy," and beyond to a time when the children were seen in a follow-up study.[1]

The observational study of the separation-individuation process was begun by Mahler in 1959 at the Masters Children's Center, and its results have been described in numerous publications by Mahler and co-workers (1963, 1966, 1971, 1972a,b, Mahler and LaPerriere 1965, Mahler et al. 1970) as well as in the book entitled *The Psychological Birth of the Human Infant* (Mahler et al. 1975). Mahler asked herself how normal babies attain a sense of separateness and individuality in the caretaking presence of the primary love object, the mother. She hypothesized the symbiotic origin of human existence according to which the mother and infant form a dual unity from which the infant slowly emerges in a series of steps to become a separate human being with an intrapsychic sense of constancy of the self and the object. Mahler (1971) postulated that the longing for the symbiotic mother, who was part of the self and at one time was able to provide safety and well-being, is an existential aspect of human existence and that this longing for the erstwhile all-good mother "before separation" remains with us throughout the life cycle.

Differentiation from symbiosis begins when the infant has formed a specific attachment to mother and shows a desire to explore the nonmother world. The infant does this visually and tactilely, mostly from the vantage point of mother's arms or lap. With the advent of independent locomotion at around 8 to 9 months, the circles of the infant's explorations widen. As the baby ventures out further, there is more to see, more to hear, more to touch. But mother is still at the center of her world, and the baby needs to take her for granted and to return to her periodically for *emotional refueling*. The elation that is characteristic of the practicing subphase (from about 10 to 15 months) derives on the one hand from the excitement of mastery and the pleasure of exploration, and on the other hand from the feeling of still being one with mother. Emotional refueling is an important phenomenon of that subphase. It describes the way in which a tired

---

1. The follow-up study has been supported by the Masters Children's Center, New York, NY, and by the Rock Foundation, New York, NY, Margaret S. Mahler, Consultant, John B. McDevitt, Principal Investigator, Anni Bergman, Co-Principal Investigator.

baby receives sustenance from brief physical contact with mother and has renewed energy to go forth into the world again with zest and pleasure to begin the unending explorations anew. This is a blissful time for the developing child because for a brief period of a few months the child can literally have it both ways: to venture forth into the world, to explore, to be separate, and yet at the same time to be one with mother and have the sense of safety and protection that this entails. This brings along with it a sense of invulnerability, which is important to remember when we discuss the development of the little girl.

Beginning around the age of 15 months an important change occurs when the infant, who has now become a toddler, becomes increasingly aware of her separateness. Cognitive and motor development have now advanced to a point where the illusion of unity, oneness, can no longer be maintained. The child for us in this chapter, the little girl, now often finds herself alone and painfully aware of her helplessness and vulnerability. Along with this awareness there is also a disillusionment in mother, who no longer can provide solutions as automatically as she could before. The need for emotional refueling is now replaced by a need to share with mother every new accomplishment and pleasure. But concomitantly there is also a need for autonomy and therefore a rejection of mother's help and interference. What we observe is behavior that Mahler has termed *ambitendency*: alternately a wish to be on one's own and to have mother present to provide solutions, only to reject them as soon as they are forthcoming. This behavior culminates in the rapprochement crisis at around 18 months, which is resolved through partial internalization and identification as well as by turning to the father, who rescues the child from the struggles with mother. It is with the resolution of the rapprochement crisis that partial object and self constancy are attained, which make it possible for the child to feel and function more separately. One of the important shifts that happen during the rapprochement subphase is a change in mood toward a more discontented and sometimes even sad mood, which has been described by Mahler (1966). Mahler hypothesized that depressive moods in women may have their origin in the coincidence of realization of sexual difference with the struggles of the rapprochement crisis, that is, with the realization of separateness and vulnerability.

In what follows I will discuss the identity formation in girls during separation-individuation from the point of view of four findings
that importantly interact with each other.

The Discovery of Sexual Difference

It was found in the early years of the separation-individuation study
that girls discover the sexual differences between themselves and boys
at a much earlier age than had hitherto been thought, that is, in the
early months of the second year of life. The impact of this discovery
depends on many factors, some maturational, some dependent on the
mother–child relationship, and some dependent on events in the outside world. Roiphe (1968) took the finding of the early discovery of
sexual difference in girls further and postulated an "early genital
phase" that, he believes, brings with it an important reorganization
of the total personality. By way of observational research, Galenson
and Roiphe (1971, 1974, 1976) have explored further the phenomenon
of the early genital phase. Their findings show the impact of the early
awareness of genital differences on children's subsequent development. They hypothesize a causal connection between an extreme
preoedipal castration reaction and the later development of a basic
depressive mood change in the girl. Galenson and Roiphe (1976), like
ourselves, found that the discovery of genital difference takes place
at an earlier age than Freud had suspected. In addition, they have
described how, in girls, castration responses to the sexual difference
are important organizing influences and determine not only the girl's
subsequent psychosexual development but other aspects of her personality as well, and they emphasize in particular the influence of
early sexual development on symbolic function.

The Rapprochement Crisis and Its Resolution in Girls

It was found in Mahler's study of separation-individuation and confirmed by Roiphe and Galenson that girls have greater difficulty in
resolving the rapprochement crisis than boys. Whereas boys seem to
be more able to turn away from the struggle and invest the world
outside with energy, girls tend to become more enmeshed in the
struggle, which in some cases prevents them from fully turning their

energies to the outside world. For example, Donna, who was described in *The Psychological Birth of the Human Infant* (Mahler et al. 1975) as well as by McDevitt (1979), is an example of a girl who had such difficulty. Seemingly she had had an ideal early relationship with her mother, who was always available yet never seemed to be intrusive. However, during rapprochement she was unable to engage in pleasurable explorations in mother's presence because she was too anxious about mother's possible departure. She would anxiously cling to mother while she longingly watched other children play. On the other hand, when the separation was accomplished, that is, while the mother left the room for a brief period, she was then free to participate in play. It is possible to trace Donna's anxiety over separation from her mother to a series of traumatic events. Following a medical procedure during which the girl was strapped down in a helpless position, she developed a stronger than usual castration reaction. Donna clearly blamed her mother for what she experienced as an insult to her body. The castration conflict, combined with the ambivalence to a mother hitherto all too available and not encouraging of the child's separateness and individuation, seems to have contributed to a general inhibition in Donna. This was confirmed at the time of the follow-up study when Donna was found lacking in assertiveness and spontaneity.

Identification vs. Disidentification

In a paper delivered at the 1979 Margaret S. Mahler Symposium in Philadelphia, Mahler (1979) drew attention to the fact that girls face the difficulty of having to identify with the same mother from whom they also have to disidentify in order to resolve the rapprochement struggle. In all probability this is similar to what Jacobson (1964) has described. She discusses the differences between total identification based on wishes for union with the mother and ego identifications, that is, identification with selective qualities of the love object.

In order to achieve separateness, the infant, who, beginning at the height of symbiosis (around 5 months of age), by then differentiates mother from others, must begin to differentiate herself from mother, that is, must begin to recognize that she and mother are not one. This process, which takes place within the libidinal context of the baby's relationship with both parents, is only partially a perceptual-cognitive one. By the time of the rapprochement subphase, almost a year later, maturation has proceeded to such a point that realization of separateness becomes not only a cognitive-perceptual reality but has to be accepted emotionally as well. The impact of this realization results in a rapprochement crisis characterized by the simultaneous wish for and fear of separateness and autonomy. The little boy is aided in this process of differentiation from mother by identifying with father. The little girl has a more complex task. She, too, has to emerge from symbiosis with mother and attain realization of separateness. For her, too, the father is the important other, but she has to identify with her mother to confirm her own identity as a girl while at the same time she has to disidentify, differentiate from her, to establish herself as a separate individual. Abelin (1980) postulates three steps in the process of early triangulation—the last one different in boys and girls. He finds that at around 18 months gender identity emerges more readily in boys, generational identity in girls. Generational identity establishes the self "between two objects along one linear dimension" and the girl's "generational self-image derives from two identifications within the mother/baby/self triangle" (Abelin 1975, p. 300). In other words, the little girl sees herself as mother's baby or wishes to have a baby like mother.

The Mother's Attitude toward Her Own
and Her Daughter's Femininity

It is my impression that the girl's femininity and the impact on her of the sexual difference are closely connected with the mother's sense of herself as a woman and her feelings about her daughter as a girl. In subtle ways the mother communicates to her daughter what she wishes her to be, what she feels that she can be, and what she feels that she might be. The girl, on becoming an individual in her own right, has to come to terms consciously and unconsciously with her mother's conscious and unconscious expectations. Stoller (1976), in discussing core gender identity of the girl, postulates as one of the factors of importance "the unending impingement of the parents', especially mothers', attitudes about *that* infant's sex and the infant's constructing these perceptions, via its developing capacity to fantasy, into events, i.e., meaningful, motivated experiences" (p. 61). Grossman and Stewart (1976) emphasize the importance of parental attitudes toward the sex of their child:

to the child, the meaning of the discovery of the "anatomical distinction" will depend on a complex variety of preparatory experiences. The timing of this discovery will be important, since the child's cognitive and libidinal levels will naturally play a part in his interpretation of this new information. Narcissistic conflicts and the child's relations to both parents will determine the final result. Parental attitudes toward the sex of the child, toward their own genitals and sexual relationships, will aid or disrupt the child's integration of the awareness of the genital differences. [pp. 206–207]

From the point of view of these four findings and considerations, we will now turn to observational data that will illustrate the complexity of female identity formation. At an early age, probably during the late practicing period, with immature cognitive capacities the girl notices the anatomical differences between the sexes at a time when the sense of separateness is not firmly established, thus at a time when mother is still expected to provide magical solutions. During early rapprochement, the renewed closeness to mother is helpful, but the rapprochement crisis demands that the girl disidentify from mother sufficiently to become a person in her own right, and feel safe enough from fear of reengulfment to identify selectively with qualities of the mother (Jacobson 1964). How the girl will achieve this task is importantly influenced by the mother's attitude to a girl child. This attitude of the mother is colored by her own sense of herself as a woman and by the meaning to her of a girl child. In relating to her daughter, the mother probably relives important aspects of her own separation-individuation process. The process for the girl child, which I hope to be able partly to illustrate, is unique to each mother–child pair. It will never be simple, and it will importantly shape each child's ultimate sense of herself as a woman, which will include her behavior as a mother.

The examples of two girls from an observational study illustrate the interplay between the recognition of sexual difference, the resolution of the rapprochement crisis, the vicissitudes of the mother–daughter relationship, and how this is influenced by the mother's feelings about herself as a woman.

The two girls chosen for illustration of this complex interplay have in common that both of them had older brothers; thus the exposure to the anatomical difference took place naturally from the beginning within the family. Both girls grew up in families in which the father had an important role. Both mothers stayed at home and devoted themselves full time to their families. The manifest, openly expressed attitude toward femininity was very different in these two mothers, and it is this openly expressed attitude that is considered here as having an important impact on the children and in playing an important role in the formation of their identity themes as girls. (If we had access to the unconscious fantasies of the mothers about their own femininity during their daughters' separation-individuation process, we would add the mothers' unconscious fantasies to the complex interplay of forces we are attempting to describe.)

Clinical Examples

Anna and Her Mother

We first saw Anna when she was 10 months old and her brother was 2 years old. From the beginning the mother felt ill at ease with her girl child and openly stated that she would have preferred a boy. The reason for this, she said, was that Anna's presence forced her to experience her own feelings about herself as a woman. She thought that girls and women had a hard lot in life because they always had to worry about their looks and their weight in order to please men.

Mrs. A. was a very beautiful woman. Although she complained about the woman's lot in having to please men, she was on the whole more interested in, and more at ease with, male observers than female ones. She was not very sociable and did not easily talk about herself; especially, she rarely talked about her own childhood. She much preferred talking about her husband and his family.

While Anna's mother worried a great deal about her own looks as well as her daughter's, she did little to make the child look pretty. One always had the impression that mother felt she had to work so hard at being a woman that looking after yet another female person was simply too much trouble. When Anna was 13 months old her mother worried whether her hair would curl, and said that a boy was much easier to care for. As if in response to mother's comments, Anna began to imitate her brother and want what he had. Mother told of a poignant incident in which Anna's brother would not lend her his gun and Anna cried inconsolably. Anna's father, whom Anna loved dearly, insisted that the brother had the right to keep his gun for himself. Mother was sympathetic to Anna's plight, but, typical of her ambivalence toward females and toward herself, she could not find a solution to Anna's problem. Whereas mother said in her presence that it was better to be a boy, she on the other hand did not make any gesture to help her to assert herself vis-à-vis the boy. Thus, Anna was caught. The gun, we may assume, was already a symbol of masculinity. Although she was told it was better to be a boy, she could not get any support, from mother or father, to share in her brother's masculinity.

We have no direct evidence that Anna was aware of the sexual difference, but we would suspect that she was. This awareness may have been a particularly painful one for her because her mother expressed so many feelings about how hard the lot of a girl was. We may infer that sexual awareness may have been present from some of Anna's behaviors. For instance, she became increasingly possessive and wanted whatever her brother had. Another interesting and relevant observation made at this time was that Anna looked anxiously for her leg and seemed to think that she had lost it because she was sitting on it and could not see it.

By now Anna had already begun to show great love for her father and sometimes showed preference for him. Mother took this as an indication that she was not a good mother to her little girl. She could not see what was very obvious to observers, namely that Anna was always immediately responsive to her mother's attention. Though her mood was on the whole low-key, she would immediately become active and cheerful when mother paid attention to her. Most of the time, however, Anna was quiet and subdued. In other words, Anna experienced the omnipotence and elation typical of the practicing subphase in a delayed and muted way.

When the family came back from summer vacation (Anna was about 18 months old), mother began to toilet train her, and their relationship improved. Because her self-esteem as a mother was low, mother had been greatly relieved when Anna began to be more sepa-

rate and autonomous. She did not want Anna to be part of her because she did not feel good as a woman.

As Anna became more separate, an interesting phenomenon occurred within the mother–child relationship on the mother's side; that
is, mother began to hide her own needs behind Anna's. It was striking how often Anna's mother expressed her own feelings and needs
by way of talking about Anna. For example, when she seemed depressed, she complained that Anna never smiled; when she herself
seemed to feel tired and in need of being cared for, she told Anna to
ask an observer to wipe her nose. Mrs. A.'s interviewer was struck
by his observation that Anna's mother found it very difficult to express her own needs in a direct way. It was almost as if Anna was
becoming the mother's alter ego, a very interesting observation in
view of Anna's later development. Unconsciously she was also drawing Anna closer to herself.

At the age of 20 months, Anna became toilet trained and, at the
same time, according to mother, began to develop a ferocious will of
her own. She became more clinging and demanding, more openly
jealous of her older brother, and insisted on being right in the middle
of the family. Anna referred to her brother as "the boy" rather than
by his name. At the same time she began to show more active interest in being a girl. She liked to look in the mirror and paid more
attention to her clothes and hair, an important identification with
mother. Mother reacted immediately by expressing concern that Anna
would become just like all the other little girls who were interested
only in their appearance. Noticing Anna's blossoming femininity,
mother again withdrew from her. She went and had her ears pierced,
which can be seen as her effort to concentrate on *her* femininity rather
than on Anna's.

On the whole, the period of early rapprochement was a positive
one for Anna, as she was able to demand more attention from her
mother who responded by spending somewhat more time with her.
By the age of 21 months, Anna was fully toilet trained, her language
development was excellent, and so was her symbolic capacity as she
began to express herself through fantasy play and show a lively interest in books, pictures, and stories.

At this time Mrs. A. announced that she was four months pregnant. Mother's pregnancy coincided with Anna's growing separation.

It came at a time when Anna was beginning to show the first signs of identifying with mother, and mother in turn seemed to be relinquishing her own needs by expressing them through Anna. We may speculate on some of the emotional significance of the mother's pregnancy at that time. Was it the creation of new union at a time when Anna was becoming more separate? Or was it an anxious flight from an overly close relationship with her daughter that was experienced as painful, and that, from the beginning, had to be defended against?

Whatever the mother's unconscious reasons for her pregnancy might have been, Anna reacted to it by losing her pleasure in being a little girl. She began to talk about herself as either the baby or the boy. Following the birth of her baby sister, Anna went through a renewed period of rapprochement crisis. She withheld her stools, became extremely demanding, and was unhappy both in her mother's presence and absence. Anna's mother became increasingly desperate and was upset with herself for being so worried. She developed a fear that her hair would fall out, a fear that she would lose her own beauty and femininity. She also blamed herself for her feminine vanity because she felt this interest interfered with her ability to be a good mother. She constantly struggled to improve herself, which interfered with her capacity to be attentive to her little girl. This seems to have been the essential dilemma for her—the burden of femininity.

The situation of intense struggle between Anna and her mother continued throughout the third year of Anna's life. There were better times, which were often triggered when Anna was given tangible proof of love by her mother. Mother sometimes gave Anna sweets, which she craved, and at times Anna showed pride in the clothes that her mother had made for her. Eventually, improvement occurred when Anna identified with her older brother and often enjoyed boy's play. She was able to take pleasure in her body. She also enjoyed all kinds of fantasy activity, and on a particularly good day she would imitate Superman. She became elated when she was able to play out her denial in fantasy. The fantasy of being Superman probably contained two wishes: one, to be a boy, the other, to be the all-powerful symbiotic mother—the mother before separation-individuation (Mahler 1979). If this is so, it would confirm the contention of Fast (1979), who sees the formation of gender identity as a process of differentiation that requires the reunciation of the omnipotent state of being that each gender experiences in a different way.

At the end of the separation-individuation period, however, Anna continued to have a very conflicted and ambivalent relationship with her mother. She was far from comfortable with her self-image. The struggle over urine and bowel control continued, as did the struggle over her sexual identity. She alternately saw herself as Mighty Mouse and powerful, or as baby and helpless. Only on rare occasions could she pleasurably be a little girl.

It is interesting to compare impressions of Anna at the end of her separation-individuation process with those of the psychologist who tested Anna at the time of the follow-up study when Anna was 11 years old. The report states: "Anna is a pleasant, wholesome-looking, 11-year-old girl. She does not smile, she is serious, straight-laced and 'grownup.' Anna's speech pattern is clipped and precise with little voice modulation or variation. Her characteristic attitude is 'I'll do anything you ask me to do, don't worry about me, I can manage any hardship.' " When the tester asked if she minded when people smoked, she replied, "Oh, yes, but don't let that bother you. I mind naturally when my father smokes because it's not good for him, not because I mind. I really don't mind and it probably has nothing to do with my allergies. You can really smoke if you want to." Here again we find replayed the words that mother said so often to Anna when she was an infant, namely, that the lot of the girl is a hard one and that girls have to give up a lot in order to please others, especially if they want to please men. Later on in the test, when Anna was asked what kind of animal she would like to be, she said, "A bird, birds can fly, and I'd be the kind that people don't shoot. And I'd be a cardinal and make sure I'm a boy bird because he looks better."

Thus we see in Anna first a compliance with mother's wish that she not be feminine and then, at the time of the temporary resolution of rapprochement, attempts to take more pleasure in her self and concomitantly to become more feminine. Following mother's withdrawal and the birth of her baby sister, Anna showed a renewed surge of ambivalence and envy. She withheld stools, became clinging and demanding, and seemed to renounce her own separate feminine identity.

A school report about Anna described her as a girl who developed a twin-like relationship with a best friend. Her need for a twin-like friend indicated that she probably hadn't resolved the separation-individuation process well enough to feel good about herself without the availability of another person to confirm her own separate individual identity. But the need for the twin-like friend is also reminiscent of the way in which mother had related to Anna when Anna first became more separate, namely, by hiding her own needs behind the needs of her daughter.

Mary and Her Mother

Our second case, a little girl named Mary, was chosen for the sake of comparison and contrast. Like Anna, Mary had an older brother. Like Anna, Mary had a devoted and involved father. Mary's mother also talked a great deal about her husband, on whom she depended for help. Mary's parents were very much a couple, and her father was a source of emotional support for her mother in the task of child rearing. Mary's mother expressed her pleasure in their relationship and her pleasure in being a woman. She had had a profession before marriage: both marriage and motherhood were a choice.

From the beginning, Mary's mother was happy with her. She clearly stated that she was happy to have had a girl (she had had great difficulty in accepting her first baby, a boy), and she said that a girl was a gift to the mother. During the entire first year of her life, Mary was said to have been a very easy baby for her mother to take care of. An interesting change occurred around 13 months of age, shortly after Mary began to walk. At this time the family was taking weekly trips to a nearby weekend house. On that particular weekend, Mrs. M. had forgotten to bring Mary's bottle and decided that this was a good opportunity to wean her. This was the time when Mary was taking her first steps, and her older brother, who seemed to have experienced this as a threat, suddenly became quite aggressive toward her. A week later, Mary's mother reported that Mary had become aware of her brother's penis and had tried to touch it.

The taking away of the bottle, the trip to the weekend house, the beginning of walking, and the awareness of sexual difference all seemed to have coincided and brought about a pronounced change in Mary's mood. Mrs. M., in reporting on the weekend, said, "I don't know what has happened to my sweet little girl. She has always been so good and happy. This weekend she was unhappy all the time. She would lie down and cry and have temper tantrums over the slightest frustration. I took her to the doctor, but the doctor found nothing wrong with her. He thought that maybe Mary was teething." During observation time, Mary found it difficult to stay in the room. She wanted to rush out constantly, and she was very possessive about a doll carriage, which she attempted to push around all morning. Here is the first indication of something that was later to take on great importance, namely, that Mary dealt with disappointment and distress by clinging to the mother-baby relationship (Abelin 1980). This started a period of extreme jealousy on Mary's part toward her brother, Bobby. Whenever mother paid any attention to him, Mary clamored for attention and also began to imitate Bobby.

Mrs. M. felt quite helpless and overwhelmed by this turn of events and found it very difficult to attend to both children equally. Mary also developed a sleep disturbance and regularly woke up in the middle of the night. Mother said that she was beginning to become aware of Mary's bowel movements, and she began to toilet train her. Mary strongly turned to her father and developed what mother called a "love affair" with him. When he came home in the evening, she would cry until he picked her up. Mrs. M. was surprised by Mary's attachment to her father and said that Bobby at that age had never had a similar attachment.

From about 13 to 15 months of age, Mary became more and more aggressive and possessive. She wanted not only what her brother Bobby had but transferred this aggressiveness to our Center, where she struck out at other children. She also became vulnerable, crying hard and lying down on the floor whenever she was hurt or frustrated. At around 14 months, she developed a fungus infection in the urinary area. Thus, Mary seems to have been unable fully to enjoy her practicing period. This seems to have been interfered with by her awareness of the sexual difference, which coincided with beginning to walk, her brother's reaction to her at that time, and the mother's sense of disappointment that Mary was no longer her "sweet little girl."

By the time the family returned to the Center after summer vacation, Mary was 18 months old and had changed considerably. She was beginning to show a pleasurable awareness of her whole body.

She seemed to have coped with the early castration reaction and penis envy by investing her whole body with pleasure. She often went to the mirror and lifted up her shirt. When mother put a new coat on her, she went to the mirror and looked at herself pleasurably. At home she liked to go around without clothes on. At the height of the rapprochement crisis, Mary turned her anger toward her mother and became less aggressive with her brother. She continued to imitate her brother and no longer wanted to wear dresses.

Curiosity about the body and body functions was expressed in Mary's symbolic play (see Galenson 1971). At the Center she teased another little boy by taking the hat off his head, crushing it, asking someone to fix it, and then putting it on her own head and laughing at the little boy. Mary became very interested in going to the bathroom and enjoyed riding on the rocking horse. But she also frequently went to the playpen and pretended that she was a baby. When mother said that she was a big girl, Mary angrily replied that she was a baby and sat in the doll carriage. Mary's desire to be a baby at this time may have been a way to cope with her castration anxiety. She followed her brother to the bathroom, watched him while he urinated upright, and tried to do the same.

By the age of 26 months, Mary's aggressive behavior, which had begun when she had first become aware of the sexual difference, began to alternate with periods of feminine tenderness. She became quite affectionate with little boys and often kissed and hugged them.

It appears that, by the beginning of her third year, Mary had come to terms somewhat with being a little girl and had resolved her rapprochement crisis to some extent. She turned strongly to her father and began to enjoy more cooperative play with other children; however, her concern with the sexual difference remained in her play and in verbal communication.

During various points in the year Mary shifted back and forth between being more masculine and aggressive, and more feminine and coy. She sometimes wore dresses, and it seemed that she began to imitate mother. She was proud of a headband and didn't want to be without it. Finally, toward the very end of the year, Mary's mood seemed to shift, and she became more depressed and low-keyed. She developed a separation reaction, which remained quite strong for several months, and she became more clinging and whiny and wouldn't let her mother leave.

Mary tried to woo her mother, hugging her and bringing her cookies. Once when the mother was absent from the room, Mary asked, "Where's my mommy?" When she didn't get an answer, Mary threw the mother doll on the floor and screamed, "Mommy is thrown on the floor. I threw her on the floor."

We see in Mary, throughout the third year, a continued rapprochement struggle with penis envy and castration anxiety. At the end of the third year there is a suggestion that Mary gave up some of her omnipotent demands for a penis and at the same time became more subdued. It is hard to say at which point in development Mary's rapprochement struggle changed toward a more oedipal struggle with mother. But it seems quite certain that hostility toward mother increased during the third year and that the attachment to father, which had begun at around the age of 12 months, became deeper and more intense.

The follow-up study showed that Mary, at the age of 8, still struggled over the sexual difference and over accepting herself as a girl. During the tests, Mary was resentful about the demands made upon her. This attitude was defensive inasmuch as Mary, afraid to be found lacking, became quite upset when she didn't know an answer to a question. She would give a silly answer before she would allow herself to show that she cared enough to try to think and reflect. The tests found that Mary withdrew from situations that might evoke defeat or criticism.

At 8 years of age Mary was competent and independent. Body narcissism, which had begun a little after she was 1 year old and peaked at 20 months of age, continued to be important. It expressed itself mainly in her interest and excellent performance in gymnastics. At the same time, she retained for herself the privileges of being the baby in the family. This was encouraged by her mother, who, in her own life, had not received enough privileges of a baby. When her mother made demands on her, she often told her mother that she was still a baby, and her bed was filled with all her old stuffed animals.

The escape into babyhood seemed something like a shared fantasy between mother and child, a shared fantasy of symbiotic bliss when Mary was the perfect baby-gift to the mother and the mother the all-good mother "before separation" (Mahler et al. 1975).

She identified with the maternal aspects of mother while keeping femininity and female sexuality in abeyance. Enjoyment of her own body in sports and gymnastics could be seen as identification not only with her brother but also with her mother, who was a very active woman. The relationship between mother and daughter at the time of the follow-up study was a harmonious one.

Discussion

I have elucidated some of the struggles of the little girl during the period of separation-individuation in relation to her establishment of gender identity. We assume that during the first year of the girl's life the mother has already treated the little girl in accordance with her own feelings about the child's gender. Early during her second year of life, the girl begins to recognize the anatomical difference between herself and the little boy. We believe that the recognition of the sexual difference is a developmental process. How the girl experiences and deals with what she sees depends on the state of cognitive development, on the state of self–object differentiation, and on the state of her psychosexual development—all this within the framework of her object relations to mother and father. The girl child also begins to know her own body in relation to her mother's as she begins to develop awareness of her own female identity. During the rapprochement struggle she has to assert herself vis-à-vis the mother— on the one hand to establish her separateness and begin to identify with qualities of the mother, on the other hand to establish her female identity. It is a long and complicated task, unique for each mother–daughter pair, and helped greatly by the relationship to the father, who needs to confirm the femininity of both mother and daughter.

Returning now to a comparison between two mothers and two daughters, I shall go back to the four points discussed at the beginning of this chapter and compare them for the two cases presented.

Discovery of Sexual Difference

Anna: She first noticed and reacted to the anatomical difference between the two sexes early, probably as early as 13 months. This discovery was colored by her mother's constant worries and complaints

about being a girl and by growing up with a brother fourteen months
her senior. It was not directly reported by the mother but could be
inferred from Anna's behaviors.

Mary: She seems to have first discovered the sexual differences
early, at 13 months, during the height of the practicing period proper.
This, combined with mother's decision to suddenly wean her from the
bottle, caused temporary dampening of the elation characteristic of
that subphase, as well as an increase in rivalry and aggression toward her brother.

Resolution of the Rapprochement Struggle

Anna: There was no real resolution of the rapprochement crisis. Following the announcement of her mother's pregnancy and the birth
of her baby sister, she became enmeshed in an intense rapprochement struggle. She became severely constipated and demonstrated
several of Mahler's danger signals, namely excessive clinging and
shadowing, frequent temper tantrums, and splitting of the good-bad
mother image (see Mahler 1966).

Mary: During the rapprochement crisis, aggressivity increased and
was largely directed toward the mother. There was no clear resolution of the rapprochement crisis, which extended into the third year.
Symbolic play revealed concern over body intactness. Mary found
consolation in the relationship to her father, taking pleasure in her
body, and remaining the baby in the family.

Identification vs. Dis-Identification

Anna: As Anna became more separate she also became more like
mother, that is, more feminine. This was poorly tolerated by mother.
Thus, for a while she was happiest when she disidentified from
mother and renounced her femininity to be a boy or, even better,
Superman.

Mary: Mary and her mother had had a pleasurable period of symbiosis and differentiation. As Mary became more separate during
practicing, she discovered her father and brother. But being not-
mother in Mary's case seemed to mean being the baby.

Mother's Attitude

Anna: Mother communicated her conflicts over her own femininity to Anna, who then incorporated these feelings and conflicts into her self in subtle ways. Her desire to be a male cardinal whom no one would shoot is symbolic of her simultaneous wish to be beautiful, a boy, free, and unthreatened by male penetration. Furthermore, the mother showed a longing for her own mother through her tendency to use Anna as a vehicle for the expression of her own impulses and wishes. This need, in turn, was carried further by Anna, who eventually showed a longing for a "bosom friend" who, it seems, would help her establish an identity for herself. Although mother devalued femininity, she guarded her own femininity closely. It seems that Anna withdrew.

Mary: Mary's mother, who professed happiness as a woman, found being a mother difficult. She had experienced her daughter as a gift to mother. But this was difficult to maintain as Mary grew up and experienced conflicts in connection with her discovery of the sexual difference. Mary seems to have internalized the mother's wish that she remain the perfect baby. At the time of the follow-up study, when Mary was 8 and a typical girl with latency interests, the mother reported that Mary insisted on remaining the baby of the family. The tester reported that Mary anxiously defended against any recognition that she might not be perfect.

Both Anna and Mary, perhaps facilitated by the presence of their older brothers, showed early awareness of sexual difference. In Anna's case the awareness has been inferred. In Mary's case it was expressed directly and openly. Interestingly, Mary, whose mother was happy as a woman and happy about the birth of a girl child, struggled more actively and openly over the acceptance of the sexual difference. She found solace in remaining the family's baby and, in partial identification with her mother, in taking care of imaginary babies and her stuffed animals. She also invested her whole body with narcissistic and exhibitionistic pleasure.

Anna, whose mother experienced femininity as a task rather than a pleasure, expressed her feelings about the awareness of sexual difference less directly and struggled less actively over its acceptance. She was happiest when she could deny her femininity altogether and pretend to be Superman. Her rapprochement crisis was more painful than Mary's. The struggle with mother was much more intense and centered around the withholding of her bowel movements and intense separation reactions. Nevertheless, she found a solution that was individual; and, eventually, she may have continued to rework separation-individuation issues by way of closeness to a girl of her own age.

Both girls experienced difficulty at the time of practicing proper and the attainment of upright locomotion. The "love affair with the world" was disturbed, was subdued—a disturbance, it seems, due to the realization of sexual difference that mother could not undo. It would seem possible that this separates the girl from the mother too rapidly and suddenly, and prevents the gradual deflation of omnipotence and illusion of oneness. If this is so, it would help to explain the prolonged rapprochement struggle of the girl. This prolonged rapprochement struggle could then be seen as the girl's wish, and often demand, that her mother remain close and available to make up for too sudden a loss during the practicing subphase. How the mother experiences the girl child and herself as a woman provides the identity theme for the girl.

In the two examples we discussed, Anna's identity theme incorporates both her mother's belief that a woman should be beautiful and that it would be better to be a man. In the case of Mary, her identity theme incorporates her mother's pleasure in herself as a woman and her mother's feeling that the perfect girl baby is the perfect gift to the mother.

Both mothers experienced difficulty with the separation of their daughters as epitomized by upright locomotion. It may be that the mother experiences the daughter's growing separateness as a loss and thus reacts to it in a way that is idiosyncratic and probably connected with her own separation-individuation.

Giving birth to a girl baby may be for the mother a kind of fulfillment of the rapprochement wish for generational identity (Abelin 1975)—which is the double wish to be a baby and have a baby, and through which the loss of the mother during separation-individuation can be temporarily undone. Her own symbiosis with mother may be reexperienced with her daughter, and thus the loss at the girl's growing separation would be a double one—the loss of the baby and the loss of the mother.

6

Thoughts about Stages on the Way to Empathy and the Capacity for Concern

written in collaboration with
Arnold Wilson

The concept of empathy is one that has been receiving an increasing amount of attention in recent psychoanalytic literature. A great deal of attention has been paid to the developmental antecedents of how one adult comes to "know" another's emotional state. The capacity for empathy has been reconstructively traced to various points in human ontogeny. In this way, different understandings of empathy have emerged, shaped by views of the developmental period in which it is thought to originate. Some investigators, for instance, conceive of empathy as a special ability to merge with another and assert that its genesis lies in certain optimal conditions during the symbiotic phase (Greenson 1960, Olden 1958, Schafer 1968). Others view the capacity for empathy as a form of identification and locate its point of origin at a more advanced developmental stage, when self and object are more differentiated (Bachrach 1976, Beres 1968, Beres and Arlow 1974, Fliess 1942). These investigators follow Freud (1921), who noted that "a path leads from identification by way of imitation to empathy, that is, to the comprehension of the mechanism by means of which we are enabled to take up any attitude at all towards another mental life" (p. 110).

The problem of reconciling these two perspectives within a developmental framework has been addressed by several authors. Schafer (1959, 1968) asserts that merging is present in all empathy, but that the most mature form of empathy, which he terms *generative*, is characterized by the simultaneous appearance of merging and an "identification which remains segregated within the ego." Here the empathizer merges while simultaneously maintaining a separate and individual perspective.[1]

Shapiro (1974) examines empathy within a classical developmental framework. At times, he proposes, empathy may serve a defensive function, for "in the case of empathy . . . the denial of the wish or emotion toward the object is absent and a feeling of unity is substituted" (p. 12). In this view, some of the earliest forms of empathy emerge from an infantile matrix of nondifferentiation in which projection and identification are not yet discrete ego functions. Shapiro's formulation is that instead of a shift from "I feel angry" to "I don't feel angry" (denial), the move is to "I feel angry in the same way he (or she) does" (defensive empathy). Later regressions are likely to elicit a mixed deployment of the nondifferentiated identification-projection mechanism, leading to adult distortions in empathy.

Buie (1981) asserts that neither merging nor identification is the necessary forerunner of empathy. He states that merging is not a mechanism of empathy because true object-oriented empathy depends on the development of an inner world of object and self representations as well as introjects, and this commences only at about 18 months of age. Egocentrically oriented forms of empathy may commence during the symbiotic period, but even these do not depend

---

1. Maternal *generative empathy* may well facilitate the developmental unfolding of the capacity for empathy. Sander (1976) describes what he believes is required of the mother, during the first phase of the infant's life (birth to 2½ months), as the capacity to maintain a balance between her intuitive sensing of what the child needs and her objective view of the child. This generative empathy on the part of the mother with her newborn may well set the stage for the reciprocity between mother and child characteristic of the symbiotic phase, during which the infant's capacity for empathy begins to develop.

on merging for their development. Nor, in his view, does the notion of identification as a necessary component of empathy hold up theoretically. Citing Meissner (1970, 1971, 1972), Buie notes that identification is a process that affects the ego by adding new structures. Yet authors who assert that identification is the necessary ingredient for empathy think of it as a process involving already existing psychic structures, without requiring additional structuralization. Buie concludes that "they are either referring to some other phenomenon which is theoretically unspecified . . . or they are simply employing the term identification in a non-technical, descriptive sense" (p. 291).

A question that arises with all these views is: What constitutes appropriate psychoanalytic data for the validation of a developmental hypothesis about empathy? Many of the published reports rely on transference manifestations and reconstructions, so that inferences about the early developmental components of empathy are made from verbal reports of adult patients. The reactivation of phenomena related to empathy in the transference has also been a primary source of data on empathy in the clinical psychoanalytic literature. Data from direct child observation, however, seem to have had little impact in this area. Recently, infancy researchers and developmental psychologists have directed their attention to such related phenomena as early role-taking, social cognition, and similar cognitive and behavioral advances. If analysts are willing to accept direct child observation as a valid psychoanalytic source of data, the results of these studies may prove helpful when interpreted in conjunction with analytic understanding.

None of this denies the role of construction, reconstruction, and transference reactivation as essential sources of psychoanalytic data. Yet our understanding may be enlarged by integrating direct child observation with data from the psychoanalytic situation. Along these lines, we have chosen to use direct observation of children during the preoedipal period to understand the antecedents of the capacity for empathy. Our observations and inferences are informed by psychoanalytic theory and view children through "the psychoanalytic eye" (Mahler et al. 1975).

In examining the development of empathy and the capacity for concern, we use the perspective of separation-individuation. As indicated, many investigators hold that identification, merging, or some state of fusion is the intrapsychic basis for the genesis of empathy. In our view, it is the pathway of separation-individuation itself that shapes the developing capacity for empathy in accordance with the dynamics of each subphase. From this point of reference, we intend to look at how the infant comes to understand, anticipate, and respond to the conscious and unconscious wishes and needs of another person, in particular the mother. Many psychoanalytic theorists hold that the development of empathy should be studied in the context of the unfolding mother-child relationship. So, too, have many infancy researchers concluded that the milieu for the proper development of empathy is the mother–child relationship rather than the peer–peer relationship (Bowlby 1961, Harlow and Harlow 1965, Hoffman 1978, Lewis and Rosenblum 1974).

Developmental Considerations

In Chapter 3 it was shown how a sense of mine and yours, which emerges during the second year of life, is a prerequisite for sharing on a more mature level. This capacity to share on a mature level has earlier sources during the separation-individuation process, in particular during the symbiotic phase and again during the subphase of early rapprochement. It was hypothesized that the mature capacity to share is most pleasurable when the earlier symbiotic pleasure of relatedness with mother is revived. Similarly, it is our contention here that the capacity for mature empathy receives an important increment from the periods of symbiosis and early rapprochement—the periods of greatest intimacy and mutuality between the infant and the mother.

Brazelton and colleagues (1974), Stern (1971), Sander (1977), Emde and colleagues (1976), and others have described in rich detail the fine tuning of early interaction between the infant and the caregiver. A significant contribution of this research has been to revise the notion of the infant as a passive recipient of the mother's care. Instead, the infant, from the beginning, is seen as an active elicitor of care. This discovery has important implications for ideas about early building blocks for empathy, or what will eventually evolve into empathy.

The Symbiotic Phase

The mother's empathic understanding of her infant's needs and states during the symbiotic phase is counterbalanced by the infant's early capacity to evoke responsiveness from the mother. By the time the symbiotic phase is reached (2 months), both infant and mother have become fairly adept in eliciting each other's responsiveness and more and more this is accompanied by mutual pleasure. Affect contagion is reciprocal. Mother's pleasure in her infant is immensely enhanced by the infant's smiling, and the infant's smile blossoms forth into more sustained pleasurable expressions, which gradually include a large repertoire of increasingly differentiated and integrated functions (vision, language, motor responses). As Brazelton (1981b) notes, the mother learns the infant's "capacity for attention-nonattention early in order to maintain his attention to her. Within this rhythmic coherent configuration she *and* he can introduce the mutable elements of communication. Smiles, vocalizations, postures, tactile signals, all are such elements" (p. 18). Mahler (1942) may have had something similar in mind when she said, "Between child and mother there exists from the beginning a close phylogenetic bond which is unique and much more exclusive than communication by words and thoughts; it is an interrelationship through the medium of affective expressions" (p. 4).

From the beginning, then, mother and infant mutually respond to each other. Mutual gazing, gaze aversion, mutual smiling, cooing, infant and mother play—these are all important ingredients in the dialogue during the symbiotic phase. Other writers have emphasized the importance of the early mother–child symbiotic relationship to the later development of empathy (Ferreira 1961, Greenson 1960, Olden 1958, Schafer 1968). Most of them, however, see it as contributing to a merging form of empathy. In contrast, we believe that during this early phase, even though self–object differentiation is not fully established, there is a certain amount of differentiation, allowing for the mutual responsiveness. What is unique to the mother–infant interaction during the symbiotic phase is the intensity of pleasure and mutual attunement. *We believe that for mature empathy to fully develop at a later stage, this early pleasurable interaction must have taken place.*

Winnicott (1953) places great emphasis on the phenomenon of mirroring during this phase—to see oneself reflected in the other. He suggests that this mirroring is an important protection for the infant from seeing the other as separate from the self at too early a time. The mirroring function also brings a sense of how one appears to the other, an incipient sense of being perceived by another, and this may be another building block during symbiosis, which complements learning how to elicit a wished-for response from the other. In agreement with Buie (1981), we contend that the concept of merging has been used to subsume *many* phenomena occurring during this phase, which can now be pinpointed more precisely and vividly. Pine (1981), for instance, describes merging as occurring only during certain moments of heightened drive arousal during the symbiotic phase, rather than as a constant prevailing state.

All these recent findings suggest the need to reformulate the notion of the origins of empathy during the symbiotic phase. Instead of empathy based on merging, we prefer to refer to empathy based on *mutual attunement*, which would include a more clearly defined scope of interactions between infants and their caregivers. Winnicott's (1953) notion of transitional experience seems relevant here, in the sense that it is these early interactions of mutuality, attunement, or communion between mother and infant that are revived throughout the lifespan and become a reservoir of creative experience.

Stern (1983) distinguishes several modes for mother and infant "to be" with each other. In particular, he distinguishes between *state sharing* and *state complementing*. Here, it would seem, lies the root of two paths toward empathy: one based on feeling the same as another person (state sharing), the other based on responding in one's unique way to the stimulus coming from the other person (state complementing). State complementing, the earliest nonmerger road toward empathy, develops into mutual cueing. Selective cueing has been described by Mahler and Furer (1963) as the way in which an infant learns to preferentially send those cues to which the mother has responded. This presumes an early form of empathy on the part of the infant, an anticipatory sense of response of the other to the self, concomitant with an accommodation of the self to the other.

Differentiation

The differentiation subphase begins during the height of symbiosis, at about 5 months of age. Presumably, the mother is now thoroughly and specifically known through all the child's sensory modalities, as is heralded by the specific smiling response, unmistakably directed toward her. A unique attachment has been formed. Although mother and infant are intensely at one with each other, the infant now begins actively to take in more and more of the nonmother environment.

It is no longer necessary or possible for the mother to be so perfectly attuned to her growing infant. Indeed, that she is not promotes both the creation of the transitional object and the sending out of more specific signals for her to provide for the satisfaction of the infant's needs. The infant, in signaling these needs to the mother, is now also more able to take into account the mother's capacity to respond to his demands.

To illustrate this point, we cite the observation of an 8-month-old boy and his mother:

> C.'s vocalizations have become more specific. He now seems to be mouthing sounds that appear more like words. For instance, at one point his mother asked him if he wanted a cracker, and he seemed to be repeating that sound. C.'s mother was a mother who responded exquisitely to her child's signals that indicated those capacities which lead to increasing individuation. She was much less able to respond to signals which indicated her child's needs for physical closeness.[2]

Here we see an 8-month-old's preference for giving those signals to which his mother can best respond. This we would characterize as an example of empathy that has its source in the differentiation subphase.

---

2. This mother–infant pair was observed in the separation-individuation study of normal infants conducted by Margaret Mahler and her associates at the Masters Children's Center (see Mahler et al. 1975). This research is supported by NIMH Grant MH-08238, U.S. Public Health Service, Bethesda, Maryland, and FFRP Grant 069-458, Foundation Fund for Research in Psychiatry, New Haven, Connecticut, with Margaret S. Mahler, Principal Investigator, and John B. McDevitt, Co-Principal Investigator.

At this stage, infants more clearly distinguish mother, father, siblings, strangers. By learning that different people react in unique
ways, through "customs inspections" and other means of recognizing
and assessing people, children widen their repertoire of interactions
and signals that elicit responses from the other. During this period,
in which stranger anxiety appears, children often mysteriously take
to certain people immediately and recoil from others. It seems, then,
that they "read" the stranger in some way that must relate to the
intimacy and familiarity they have established with their mothers.
There exists an awareness of sameness and difference, based on the
cognitive coordinations that develop during the last quarter of the
first year.

Experiences pertaining to empathy become more varied and complex as the child's world widens and the world beyond the family is
cathected. Children learn about other people's different ways of responding, and are often fascinated and sometimes frightened by
strangers. They experiment with their newly acquired ability to signal and may try in this way to gain the attention of strangers. A little
boy, observed at 8 months, used a kind of shout to elicit a response
from strangers. Once he succeeded, he excitedly initiated a smiling
interaction with the stranger. He had learned that he needed to approach strangers differently from his family in order to gain their
attention. He had also, through his family interactions, acquired the
"confident expectation" (Benedek 1938) that he could initiate pleasurable interactions.

Practicing

The practicing subphase, which begins at about 9 months, is ushered
in by the infant's capacity for independent locomotion. During this
period infants turn to the outside world with much greater energy and
enthusiasm through their ability to move away from mother independently, first by paddling and crawling, and finally by independent
upright locomotion. They seem relatively oblivious of mother as long
as she remains peripherally available—in part because mother is still
taken for granted. We hypothesize that the infant's omnipotence has
not yet been disturbed, so that the infant experiences mother as his
extension. An invisible bond connects the infant with the mother, who

is assumed and expected to be empathic to the infant's alternating needs for freedom to explore and to return for emotional refueling. The mother who is empathically available does not intrude, nor does she prematurely remove herself at this time. In this way the infant can put interactions with her temporarily into the background, gaining the freedom to put his energies into exploration and mastery. It is as if the infant had called a temporary halt to interactions with mother to allow for the push in autonomous and conflict-free functioning characteristic of this period. In other words, we hypothesize something akin to a "moratorium" on empathy in the service of individuation. It may be that too much attention to the mother would counteract the omnipotent belief in her presence and availability.

It is important that it is during this period of growing ability to be at a distance from mother that the beginning capacities for imitation and mental imagery appear. Imitation games previously initiated by the mother now begin to be initiated by the child. Imitation is an early attempt at being like the other, an essential intrapsychic process for the later maturation of empathic ability. As Gaddini (1969) notes, "The psychic protomodel of imitation—'imitating in order to be'— . . . installs itself not in the presence of the object but in its absence, and . . . precisely because of this, its aim seems to be that of reestablishing in a magical and omnipotent way the fusion of the self and the object" (p. 477).

Eventually the practicing toddler cannot help but experience limits to his elated exploration of the world. This brings about a deflation of mood and a painfully growing awareness of separateness, in turn making the toddler more aware of his need for the mother. Along with this greater awareness of his own needs, the toddler develops a greater sensitivity to the feelings of others. The following observations of a 16-month-old boy, Peter, illustrate the developing connection between the awareness of self and other (empathy).

Peter was observed at weekly intervals during his practicing subphase. Around the age of 16 months, a change in his mood was noticed. Only a week earlier this little boy had marched about the world as if he owned it, fearless and intrepid. Suddenly he seemed sober and clearly asked for more attention from and contact with his mother. When an observer mentioned this change to the mother, she agreed and connected it with an experience the day before. The beloved family dog had been taken to the vet and had to be left there overnight. Peter appeared to be very upset for many hours and was comforted by his mother. He was distressed by the possibility of absence of anyone in the family. We assume that the dog was an object upon which Peter displaced as well as projected his concerns. Saying this does not exclude the fact that Peter also missed the dog. When the dog returned, Peter was overjoyed and showered the dog with love and attention.

Peter himself had never been separated from his family for more than a few hours. Nevertheless, he seemed to empathize with his beloved dog, his constant playmate. Peter's behavior at the return of the dog suggests a shift from the height of omnipotence to a growing painful awareness of separateness. We hypothesize that he could no longer take his mother completely for granted and assume that she would always be available to him. His reaction to the dog's absence and return shows a double identification—the dog represented both the mother who could leave and a child who could be left. Peter identified with the comforting mother by comforting the dog, but he also identified with the abandoned dog by imagining the dog's pain.

Peter's reaction calls to mind a point made by Furer (1967), who connects the child's earliest ability to show empathy for another with the sense of loss caused by separation from mother. This sense of loss initiates a wish for incorporation in order to reunite with a loved subject. The reunion is accomplished through temporary and partial identification with the other's affective states. Furer names this phenomenon "identification with the consoler or the comforter."

The vignette of Peter suggests a similar process. Peter became very upset when separated from his dog and was comforted by his mother. Then, when the dog returned, he himself became loving and comforting with the dog. Furthermore, on the subsequent day he became especially attuned to his mother. When another person particularly close to Peter came to visit that day, Peter repeatedly came over to her, trying to feed her and showing affectionate concern by stroking and patting her back. We believe he was reenacting the "loss of dog" episode, which contained an empathic moment of comforting. He showed that the experience of being a comforter had become part of his behavioral repertoire—an early form of internalizing an interactive process (Loewald 1978).

A week before the dog incident, Peter was observed watching his mother tend the garden. His mother was particularly pleased with a bed of red tulips. Peter, an active and curious little boy, did not touch the tulips. When the observer commented on this, the mother noted that when the tulips had first begun to bloom, Peter had touched them and tried to pick them, but then she had said, "Please don't do that. I like them so much. They are so beautiful." Peter apparently responded to the way in which his mother made this request, for on other occasions, when he was asked not to do something because it concerned his safety, he did not necessarily comply. That he did comply with the mother's request not to pick the flowers speaks to the possibility that he empathically understood her affect.

Rapprochement

During early rapprochement there is a renewal of the emphasis on state-sharing functions. (During differentiation and practicing there is more emphasis on state-complementing functions, such as signaling.) In the transition between practicing and rapprochement, children begin to be able to modulate their impulses and to relinquish a phase-specific activity (exploration) in the interests of joining in mother's pleasure. This step may be similar to what Furer (1967) refers to as the beginning ability to neutralize aggression.

The period of early rapprochement, from 15 to 18 months, is one that seems of special importance for the further development of empathy. This is the time at which most writers concerned with developmental issues place the beginning of true empathy (Buie 1981, Furer 1967, Hoffman 1978, McDevitt 1981, Schafer 1959).

The early rapprochement subphase brings a major spurt in individuation, which makes possible the developments leading toward more mature empathy. More and more, the child is forced to recognize that he and mother are separate, and at times reacts by wanting to again experience symbiotic bliss. This regressive pull toward a state entailing less awareness of separateness coincides with an upsurge in the development of empathy. In other words, although there is a regressive component to this period, there is also a progressive component in the child's newly enriched ability for empathic communication. Indeed, the unfolding of empathic ability has an ebb-

and-flow quality. Throughout separation-individuation there is a constant alternation between the development of capacities pertaining to object relating (such as empathy) and those that are more narcissistically invested, such as those found during the practicing period. One should also note that activities deriving from what Stern (1983) calls state complementing enter more prominently into empathy as children come to understand a higher level of sharing, in which their actions may complement those of the other, rather than simply imitating or joining with the other's wishes and needs.

Earlier, we referred to Furer's concept of identification with the comforter. The following vignette of a 17-month-old, Paula, illustrates a different aspect of this identification. Rather than identification with the comforter per se, it reveals something we might call identification with the pleasure-giver. Wishing to give and share is characteristic of the child during early rapprochement, and this may also be seen as an identification with the mother who has been giving to the child.

Paula was taken to the playground by her mother on an early spring day. Her mother had not brought along toys, but many children there had toys that Paula desired. In a way typical of a toddler of her age, she wandered around, picking up toys of the other children. The mother suddenly had the feeling that Paula needed a toy of her own. She picked her up and walked with her to a nearby store to buy a toy. Paula had just learned to kiss, an act which delighted her mother. On the way to the toy store, mother asked Paula for a kiss, but Paula refused. Mother found a ball at the store, which she bought for Paula. Together, with Paula holding the ball, they walked back to the playground. On the way back to the playground, Paula spontaneously hugged and kissed her mother.

To understand this vignette in terms of empathy, it is necessary to assume that Paula understood her mother's concern and wish to make her feel happy. She then identified with the mother and in turn did something she knew would make her mother happy. In this vignette we see both state sharing and state complementing. Paula and her mother shared the happy mood, but the happy mood was brought about by each giving to the other what she empathically understood the other to want.

The wish for symbiotic pleasure and the wish to be separate and autonomous constitute a conflict, which becomes more acute and internalized during the second part of the second year, as the child reaches the rapprochement crisis. Along with a relative sense of help-lessness, a depressive mood often occurs as the mother can no longer consistently relieve the child's sense of aloneness. Thus, there is an unavoidable break in the mother's empathy with her child.

Splitting is a characteristic phenomenon during the rapprochement subphase. We observe something akin to a split in the capacity for empathy, for the memory of the good mother is different from the actually experienced mother. The mother can no longer counteract the developmentally necessary waning of omnipotence. At times when she is seen as bad, a phenomenon occurs that we might call *negative empathy* (M. S. Mahler, personal communication). The concept of negative empathy suggests that at particular moments of acute con-flict or frustration, the child can only empathize with the "bad mother" or, as Mahler (1971) has called her, the mother of separation.

Examples of such negative empathy may be found in the toddler's new suspiciousness of mother and her intentions. Toddlers at this time often display sudden, extreme fussiness in relation to the food mother provides. Also particularly characteristic of this period are fights about getting dressed. One child who was observed during the rapproche-ment period had had a particularly good early relationship with his parents, but now often acted as if mother were about to inflict ter-rible pain upon him when it was time to get dressed. He fought and struggled, and sometimes it would take hours before he agreed to get dressed. A particular aspect of this struggle over dressing seemed to be that the child did not want to give up the clothes he was wearing, sometimes clinging to his pajamas while getting dressed for the day, or, the other way around, holding onto his daytime clothes when it was time to go to bed. The seeming fear was probably overdetermined. In part, it may have been due to projection of his own aggressive im-pulses. Yet it may also have been due to fear of reengulfment and intrusion on his burgeoning autonomy, which had to be defended against to the hilt. Further, clinging to the clothes he was supposed to take off may have been connected with wanting to cling to the old all-good mother, who was not contaminated by frustration and badness.

Characteristically, in this time of struggle, the mother is not treated as the person the child has formerly known her to be. Instead, she seems to become the person to be fought with or clung to—the

person who is the frustrator or the giver of pleasure. During practicing the real mother is temporarily ignored or treated as an object of
convenience in order to allow for the spurt in individuation; somewhat differently, during rapprochement the real mother may sometimes not be perceived because of the child's tendency to see the
mother as all-bad if she cannot be all-good.

As long as the mother is perceived as good, state sharing is pleasurable. But when the mother is no longer perceived as all-good, state
sharing becomes contaminated by her badness. By the time of the
rapprochement struggle, then, identifying with the mother is no
longer as pleasurable because of how she is perceived; on the other
hand, if the child can no longer identify with mother, feelings of loneliness and abandonment may occur. At times the child may seek to
reunite with mother by clinging. Clinging, however, does not take
into account the feelings of the other; it does not contribute to the
development of empathy.

During early rapprochement we saw the beginnings of
indentification with the good, providing mother. During the rapprochement crisis we see a similar phenomenon in regard to the bad,
frustrating aspects of mother. In other words, we see two strands of
empathy—empathy with the good, providing mother and empathy
with the bad, frustrating mother. In our opinion, these two strands—
positive and negative empathy—must become integrated for mature
empathy and the capacity for concern to come about. One might relate this to the idealization and devaluation processes regularly seen
in narcissistic and borderline patients, whose ability to empathize with
the other remains in its primitive mode, split between positive and
negative empathy.

It is not unusual for mothers to ask for consultations because their
rapprochement toddlers have inexplicably turned into little tyrants.
One mother came in for such a consultation because her usually
bright, charming 20-month-old daughter had recently developed intense hostility toward her. Observed in a play session, the mother
seemed quite patient and understanding, eager to please her willful
and disgruntled child. The little girl began to feed and put some dolls
to bed. In between taking care of the dolls, attempting to be loving,
she would stamp around the room and mutter, "Look at the mess,
look at all this work I have to do." Mother looked shocked because

she knew that this was how she herself often felt during this difficult period. She had not at all realized that this was how her daughter perceived her. All her goodness, self-sacrifice, and concern seemed to go unperceived by the little girl at this time.

Eventually, toddlers have to resolve the rapprochement conflicts. Partial resolution of the ambivalence characteristic of the rapprochement crisis takes place by way of selective identification, which brings about primarily libidinal cathexis of the maternal representation—one of the essential determinants of object constancy. As McDevitt (1981) describes it, "In [the] fourth subphase the senior toddler's more complex fantasy, more friendly and cooperative behavior, more mature ego-determined object relations, and increased regard for others, all suggest that his identifications have moved from the previous, primitive imitations to more selective ego identification" (p. 140).

To take this step, toddlers may have to develop some recognition of their capacity to inflict pain as well as to experience pain. At the end of the rapprochement subphase, one toddler we observed showed a tendency to identify with the victims of his aggression. It is by way of "identification with the victim" that an incipient stage of compassion may be experienced. One must know how it feels to be hurt before one can realize that one is capable of hurting another person. This is a selective identification, in which the child does not become the other, but imagines the pain of the other by imagining the other's experience. The toddler we observed had a history of attacking other infants when they interfered with him. At a certain point, he became preoccupied with talking about his own pain, real or imagined. We hypothesize that this preoccupation was a precursor to the ability to develop concern for the other.

Similarly, the same little boy often played a game in which he ordered his mother to cry as he was saying goodbye, leaving the room. In play, he inflicted pain on her that he felt when she left him. How would one analyze this play from the point of view of developing empathy? The boy seemed to be telling his mother how he felt by asking her to have the same experience. He clearly derived satisfaction when he could become the comforter and stop her crying on his return. From the point of view of drive-defense interpretations, we would see this play as identification with the aggressor, as well as an attempt at mastery by rendering active what was passively expe-

rienced. Looking at this play from the perspective of empathic development, we would point to the wish to share important feelings—
namely, sadness over separation and joy over reunion.

Beginning Object Constancy

Good and bad self and object representations become integrated into
a whole-object representation when the subphase of beginning object
constancy is reached. There is a dramatic difference between a toddler caught up in rapprochement struggles and a toddler who has
reached a degree of object constancy. With regard to the development
of empathy, an important change occurs in the child's capacity to show
concern for the welfare of others.

In normal development, the good mother manages to survive the
rapprochement storms without becoming unavailable to the child. The
mother who remains available and nonretaliatory promotes the representation of herself as constant and "indestructible."[3] Once on the
way to object constancy, the child can develop the capacity for selective and "trial" identifications (Fliess 1942) necessary for mature empathy. The child must learn to tolerate separateness, without overwhelming fear of abandonment, to obtain positive, internal, libidinally
cathected self and object representations, which allow for the trial
identifications.

Children who develop object constancy can maintain a balance
between narcissistic needs of the self and object-relational needs pertaining to others. They do not need to be overly sacrificial in order
to please another: they do not have to please another at all costs, nor
do they need to fight their wishes to please mother for fear of being
overwhelmed. Thus, the road of state sharing and state complementing leads to relaxed give-and-take abilities and skills.

A child of 2½ years was at the beach with his parents and friends.
While they were taking a walk, they were attacked by a swarm of

---

3. Winnicott (1963) describes these as necessary qualities in analysts treating patients who maintain what we are calling a perspective of negative empathy. In
   his terms, analysts must let themselves be used and destroyed by these patients
   and yet remain indestructible and nonretaliatory.

mosquitoes. They all ran to the car to drive back to the house in which they were staying. When they arrived at the house, the little boy rushed to the house and called to the person who had been most severely attacked, "Come here, come here." He then rushed to the shower to show her where she could shower off the mosquitoes. He had perceived her discomfort and was concerned with showing her where the shower was.

The capacity for concern and mature empathy is possible only when self and other have been sufficiently separated for the self to be concerned with the other. This advance coincides with the capacity for higher forms of symbolization. It is through symbolization that issues relating to self–other interactions can be played out and experimented with. Children's play and role-taking is a constant way in which these issues are practiced. Although regressions occur, there is nevertheless a qualitative change that seems to take place once the fourth subphase of separation-individuation is reached. This qualitative change endures through regressive episodes and upheavals.

Clinical Considerations

In tracing its development, we saw that the capacity for empathy does not unfold in an uninterrupted linear fashion. There is an ebb and flow of empathic ability, which can be explained by the back and forth flow of the child's developmental momentum toward subphase resolution. At times the attainment of certain subphase functions, which must eventually be integrated within the child's psychic economy, may result in the temporary suppression of competing functions or a slowdown in the unfolding of other, as yet undifferentiated functions. Pine (1971) has alluded to this in relation to locomotion and separation anxiety. The same seems to hold with empathy.

As with other developmental lines (A. Freud 1963), there may be developmental impasses and fixations that lead to impaired empathic functioning. Observations of impaired empathic ability in adult and child patients provide additional insights into the nature of early object relations. Two adult patients—Miss A. and Miss B.—illustrate how a severely disturbed mother–child relationship during symbiosis and separation-individuation may have an effect on the capacity for empathy.

Miss A., a woman in her twenties, of exceptional intelligence and artistic ability, concealed her sensitivity behind a belief that she should interact with others in a mechanical, almost robotlike fashion. She was severely frightened by any deviation from her rigid expectations. She did not complain that she found it difficult to interpret the reactions of others to her; she always felt that she knew they hated her because she was bad. She thus felt there was no use in trying to reach out to others; she already knew what the outcome of the relationship would be.

Although Miss A. was capable of being caring and empathic with plants, animals, and people in need, she tended to project onto these objects her own intense and unmet needs for nurturance. If a plant in the analyst's office was not healthy, she interpreted it as a sign that the analyst was cruel and uncaring toward her. If even a book was leaning or out of place, she expressed pity, concern for the uncared-for object, and anger at the uncaring analyst. A sense of frustration and anger was readily invoked by and in others. With the analyst, for instance, it often seemed as if Miss A. were simply refusing the good nurturance of interpretation and insight. Her omnipotent demands, coupled with helpless clinging, made the analyst feel somewhat like the mother of the rapprochement child, who is expected to do the impossible. The collaborative therapeutic alliance was extremely fragile and easily disrupted.

Growing up with a depressed mother and a sadistic father, Miss A. had lacked the opportunity for rich emotional interactions. Her mother had been physically ill, depressed, and depleted, receiving little or no emotional supplies through her marriage. Thus, during those periods in which development is propelled by closeness and psychological proximity, Miss A. was instead reprimanded for her striving for attachment; she was expected to be self-sufficient and nondemanding at all times. Being well endowed, she eventually gained some satisfactions from autonomous endeavors, which brought little shreds of recognition from her parents. We hypothesize that she never experienced empathic understanding and withdrew into a world in which she might experience a measure of predictability—the world of inanimate objects, which she endowed with animate qualities. In her adult life, she lived out her infantile destiny, in that she could never find anyone who responded to her emotional or physical needs.

She constantly found subtle ways to defy and render ineffective the attempts of others to respond empathically to her.

In sum, Miss A.'s difficulties with empathy made it almost impossible for her to build satisfying relationships. She was lonely, longed for closeness, but was unable to find it. In the transference she had a tendency to attune herself to negativity and could not focus on issues involving the analyst's warmth or concern. The developmental line of empathy seemed to be disturbed in all its phases. There was none of the mutuality of the symbiotic phase. She was not able to take anyone, including the analyst, for granted—a practicing subphase element of empathic ability. Negative empathy, originating during rapprochement, was present in full force. Thus, her capacity for object constancy as well as mature empathy was impaired.

Miss B., a woman in her early thirties, had a tendency toward severe depression, which originated in her disturbed relationship with a severely narcissistic mother. Her father, although a kind man, had been withdrawn, unavailable, and unable to fully counterbalance the mother's sadism and her constant tendency to abandon her child. The mother took pleasure in interacting with her daughter only as long as the child was obedient and subservient to her wishes. The sweet little lap baby of symbiosis, the early rapprochement toddler wishing to please the mother—these phases of the child's development were probably enjoyed by the mother. In the practicing subphase, however, Miss B. was most likely deprived of emotional supplies, thus undermining her autonomy and the formation of an integrated self, at a distance from the mother. The cranky, demanding child of the rapprochement crisis was intolerable for this mother. As a result, during her childhood, Miss B. struggled to appease her mother and extract emotional supplies. This tendency to persevere remained a characteristic feature of her object relating, along with a propensity for a false self. Although she strove for authenticity in her relationships, she was paralyzed by fear of disapproval and the potential loss of relationships. Miss B. was well aware of her tendency to try to elicit emotional supplies from others, but despised herself for it. Thus, she was overconcerned with fairness and evenness in all her relationships.

Tortured by her need always to know what others were thinking of her, Miss B. often imagined the analyst to be critical. She would then become suffused with depressive feelings of badness and worth-lessness. Frequently, she became distressed after personal encoun-ters with friends. She always thought she had antagonized the other person by doing something wrong. The childhood situation with her unpredictable mother was replayed over and over, interfering with her ability to find what she most desperately wanted—companion-ship, understanding, and warmth. On those occasions when these were available, she felt truly happy.

Miss B. had a genuine capacity for empathy, but it was interfered with by her tendency to overidentify or be overconcerned with the internal states of others. Unlike Miss A., however, Miss B. was able to distance herself and observe angry and violent feelings as they emerged in the transference. Her lack of empathy was almost a symp-tom from which she suffered, one which she aimed to resolve. She wished not just to be understood, but also to be understanding. This meant that narcissistic hurts and misunderstandings could be cleared up. Although object relating was painful to her, she never doubted its ultimate value. As a small child, Miss B. had known that it was possible for her to please her mother, although eventually her mother's narcissistic character structure rendered the cost too great. Moreover, her father, though emotionally unavailable, had been a benign rather than a cruel force.

Looking at Miss B. from the perspective of developmental stages toward the capacity for concern, we surmise that her difficulties be-gan very early. Yet she must have experienced moments of symbi-otic attunement, because of her wish to elicit responsiveness from others. Her difficulties may have begun during the differentiation subphase, for what seemed most disturbed was the ability to read oth-ers' cues. This hypothesis fits the picture Miss B. painted of her mother's inability to tolerate independence in her child. During the practicing period Miss B. was not allowed to develop her individu-ality while taking mother for granted. Thus, she was constantly afraid of losing the other's love if she pursued her own autonomous inter-ests, which she was quite determined to do. From these difficulties, it follows that all subsequent stages of empathy would be disturbed.

Contrasting these two cases, we hypothesize that the rapproche-ment crisis was less severe and destructive for Miss B. than for Miss A. because, during the symbiotic phase and early rapprochement,

there was an increased potential for positive affective contacts between mother and child. Further, during rapprochement Miss B.'s
father was present as a noncontaminated other, possibly offering some
refuge and consolation. In both cases, however, we see a complex interaction between the mother's character structure, her incapacities
and capacities for empathy with her growing child, and the child's
internalizations, which were eventually amalgamated in a self lacking in certain abilities for understanding the other's internal states
and expressing concern.

Conclusion

In examining empathy from the perspective of separation-individuation, we have noted that the symbiotic phase and the period of early
rapprochement are the periods in which the forerunners of empathy
are most clearly discernible. By contrast, the practicing subphase,
with its emphasis on mastery, autonomy, and narcissistic enhancement of the self, is a time at which there is a moratorium on the unfolding of the capacity for concern. The periods of differentiation and
the rapprochement crisis are times of tension or imbalance between
active and autonomous exploration of the world away from mother
and closeness to the mother. Optimally, when this conflict is resolved
during the period of differentiation, the path to a full blossoming of
the practicing period opens. Similarly, when the rapprochement crisis moves toward resolution, the way is open for the emergence of
self and object constancy and the attainment of a true capacity for
concern.

   With the two adult patients we described, we attempted to apply
our understanding of early empathic development to the clinical
analytic situation. We hope we have avoided the oft-described pitfall
of oversimplification in presenting these cases and drawing comparisons between infantile events and adult personality outcomes. In both
cases, we believe the parents' character structures interacted with
the child's patterns as they emerged during the separation-individuation subphases and influenced developing psychic structures that
determined subsequent object relations. For both Miss A. and Miss
B., it must be noted, the difficulties in the capacity for empathy were
only one aspect of a very complicated clinical picture. Subsequent

experience that overlays a particular infantile psychic resolution will always alter the nature of the psychic structure. Nevertheless, the original resolution is significant. Although the correspondence with adult structure is not exact, we think it is important enough to merit a return to a consideration of the formative stages of psychic structuralization.

7

The Mother's Experience
during the Earliest Phases
of Infant Development

When I nurse her, she and I look at each other and she'll smile and
sometimes stroke my breast that's not being used. At those times,
M. seems so happy and at peace with the world. It is often contagious because I feel the same way. Often it seems like we are the
only people in this world. It is an ego booster to have M. smile and
look at me as though I am the only important person in this world.

These are the words of one mother, beautifully describing her experience with her 3-month-old infant. When we look at the mother–
infant dyad, we deal with two human beings engaged in a relationship of utmost intimacy and intensity. Mother and infant form a psychobiological unit in which only one of the partners has words with
which to describe the experience. Yet, the intrapsychic experience of
the mother during the early months of her child's life is not easy to
capture. Benedek (1970) observes that we generally know much more
about the child than about the parents' intrapsychic reactions to the
child. She feels that this is because the parents happily accept the
omnipotent and idealizing fantasies of the child.

The child's fantasies, unknown by the parent, yet perceived through his play actions, reactivate in the parent the omnipotent fantasies of his own childhood; in addition, the parent identifying with the fantasies of the child accepts the role of omnipotence attributed to him. The normal parent, in spite of his insight into his realistic limitations, embraces the gratifying role of omnipotence. It induces him to identify with his own parent as he had anticipated being able to do in his childhood fantasies. Whatever the real course of events was between himself and his parents, as long as the fantasies of the child do not become hostile against him, the parent derives from the process of preoedipal identifications the reassurance that he is a good parent and, even more, the hope that he is or can be better than his parents were. [p. 128]

In this chapter I will attempt to describe the experience of the mother during the early months of her infant's life. The chapter is divided into two parts. The first part, which includes a selective review of the literature, is based on my own clinical observations of mothers with whom I have had the opportunity to have in-depth discussions. It is my goal to shed further light on the process described by Winnicott (1956a) as primary maternal preoccupation. I will attempt to show the diversity and richness of the experience for the mother, which depends on many variables including the mother's personality, the circumstances of birth, and the infant's personality.

The second part of the chapter is based on my participation in the research study of the separation-individuation process in normal mother–child pairs.[1] Mothers and infants were observed in a playgroundlike setting several times a week over a period of several years. In addition, mothers were seen in a weekly interview. A picture of each mother's personality and her mothering experience emerged through these observations and interviews, reflecting her ongoing relationship with the child and revealing glimpses of the mother's own past. We used our analytic thinking to understand what we saw and

1. The Study of the Separation-Individuation Process in Normal Mother–Child Pairs is based on research supported by NIMH Grant MH-08238, USPHS, Bethesda, MD and FFRP Grant 069-458, Foundation Fund for Research in Psychiatry, New Haven, CT. Margaret S. Mahler, Principal Investigator; John B. McDevitt, Co-Principal Investigator.

heard in our daily observations and conversations (Mahler et al. 1970). I will focus on two mother–child pairs from this study. I will show the difficulties one mother had during the stage of symbiosis with her son. I will discuss the difficulties another mother had allowing for gradual disengagement from the symbiotic phase and the way the symbiotic phase for this mother–child pair was marked by the mother's abruptness and symbiotic need for her child to be part of her and stimulate her.

For both of these mother–child pairs, I will offer some material from a follow-up study conducted ten years later.[2] I believe it is relevant here: it demonstrates that the difficulties the three children had in coping later had already begun during the period of symbiosis and differentiation. It is of course impossible to say that these patterns in the child were caused by the mother's handling during the first few months of life since we cannot discount the remainder of the separation-individuation process or the subsequent developments during the oedipal phase and latency. Nevertheless, I feel that it is of interest to look at the child's preoedipal identifications with the mother that have their beginnings during the early months of life.

The Mother's Experience

The symbiotic phase, which lasts from about the second to the fifth month, is a blissful period for most mothers and infants. Mahler and colleagues (1975) describe this period.

> From the second month on, dim awareness of the need-satisfying object marks the beginning of the phase of normal symbiosis, in which the infant behaves and functions as though he and his mother were an omnipotent system—a dual unity within one common boundary. [p. 44]

The beginning of the symbiotic phase is heralded by the smiling response of the baby, and it wanes when perceptual and locomotor

---

2. The Follow-Up Study has been supported by the Masters Children's Center, New York, NY; the Rock Foundation, New York, NY; and the Margaret S. Mahler Research Foundation, New York, NY. Margaret S. Mahler, Consultant; John B. McDevitt, Principal Investigator; Anni Bergman, Co-Principal Investigator.

capacities mature to a point where the infant can encompass more and more of the outside world, a process that eventually culminates in "hatching" at around 8 months of age. In order to discuss the symbiotic phase from the point of view of the mother, it is necessary to examine both the preceding period and the period that follows.

According to Winnicott (1956), the state of heightened sensitivity that characterizes primary maternal preoccupation is necessary for the mother of the neonate so the infant can achieve the capacity for "going on being" that eventually results in the capacity to "withstand impingement." These capacities characterize the baby during the symbiotic phase if all goes well. The symbiotic phase is distinctly different from the preceding phase in which the infant has to find a niche in the outside world—a phase in which he must become accustomed to the extrauterine environment. The state of maternal preoccupation, which is described by Winnicott as beginning in late pregnancy, is likened by him to an illness from which the mother has to recover. Loewald (1980) explicates Winnicott by saying that the mother, during certain moments in early motherhood, functions on a level of mentation that is similar to that of the infant—a level of mentation in which there exists "only one global structure, one fleeting and very perishable mental entity that was neither ego nor object, neither self nor another" (p. 73). The state of the mother, I feel, can best be described as a regression in the service of the baby, and it relies on a number of complex capacities. The mother needs to be secure enough within her own self to be able to lose herself in the process of achieving empathy and intimacy with her infant.

Mothers, when they become aware of the way in which they may temporarily lose themselves in the baby, describe loss of the usual sense of time while they are watching their infants. They also describe loss of their usual interest in other relationships or events. Although Winnicott refers to this state as a state approximating illness, we might think of it, rather, as potential illness—an illness that occurs if the mother lacks the ability to freely move in and out of the state of loss of self. Winnicott points out that a mother must be healthy in order to achieve this state, that it is not possible for every mother to achieve it, and that a mother may be able to do so with one child and not with another. Brazelton (1983), I believe, describes a process of achieving this state.

In order to produce [infant's] optimal responsiveness, I had to make myself available to them with a sensitivity to their need for control over motor activity and a sensitivity to their "states." I could feel, anticipate, and respond to subtle responses that allowed me to shape my behavior to them so that they could produce their optimal responses. Joint regulation of adult and infant, then, becomes the necessary base for such responsiveness. . . . The feeling of mutuality, of identification with "the other," must be at the base of successful interaction between parent and infant. [p. 42]

Sander (1976) sees this early phase as the one during which mutuality is established. According to him, it requires the mother's capacity to maintain a balance between her empathy with what she feels the child needs and her capacity to view him objectively. Thus, what would be required is not only identification but also the capacity to emerge from the identified state and observe the infant with some distance. Winnicott (1970) states that it is the mother's adaptive behavior that makes it possible for the baby to find that which is needed and expected outside the self. By means of the experience of good-enough mothering, the baby moves into objective perception. He or she is able to do this because he or she has been given perceptual equipment, an inherited tendency, and opportunity. Winnicott fore-shadowed what infant observers in recent years have emphasized—namely that the baby, from the beginning, has the perceptual capacity for differentiating self from other (Stern 1982).

Mothers vary in their ability to achieve the complex state of regression in the service of the baby. Life circumstances, the birth experience itself, and the experience immediately following the birth are of great importance. One mother whose child was delivered by caesarean section at first felt estranged from her infant and felt a sense of emptiness and loss. However, through the process of physical care for the infant and breast-feeding, she quickly achieved a sense of giving herself up to him: "I gave him my body. It didn't belong to me anymore."

By contrast, another mother, after the easy, natural birth of her first child in the presence of the father (who was allowed to stay in the hospital with her overnight so she was not separated from either her baby or him) felt that her connectedness with the infant was immediate. When asked to describe it she said, "I don't know what to say. It was just like being in love." This mother did not seem to feel an early stage of anxiety, insecurity, or loss. She said the infant was immediately familiar to her and that she connected what she saw now with the earlier sensations of his movements in utero: "I saw him move just as I had felt it when he was inside of me. It was an amazing feeling."

In each case, the description the mother gave of her experience was determined in part by the circumstances of the birth, but also fit well with the particular mother's personality. In the first case, what seemed to be an outstanding personality characteristic was a capacity for total devotion and temporary surrender of self-interest. In the case of the second mother, what was characteristic was a kind of calm self-possession that seems to have easily included her newborn infant. The first mother was intensely aware of having given herself over to her son during the early phase. He was an energetic little boy who nursed so vigorously that his mother's nipples often bled. The mother experienced the symbiotic phase and breastfeeding as a blissful period in her life to which she gave all her energies. She weaned her son when he began to walk at the age of about 8 months. The joy in the exclusive symbiotic attachment gave way easily and naturally to the child's needs for distancing and exploration of the world and resulted in the mother's vicarious pleasure and some relief about being able to return to her own life, which she did gradually.

The second mother did not experience a break at birth but felt immediate connection. However, her experience of the early phase was not one of giving herself up to the baby's care; she had an experience of awe and wonder that very quickly became one of exquisite intimacy. She, too, was breastfeeding and especially enjoyed the night feedings when she and her baby were alone together. She felt early on that her baby responded to her in a unique way. She focused more on the earliest signs of interaction and differentiation than on the aspect of oneness with the infant.

For both these mothers, the experience of the early love for and intimacy with their babies and the early experiences of mutuality and reciprocity were satisfying. Both mothers were able to achieve the mixture of identification and objectivity vis-à-vis the infant that, according to Sander (1976), is optimal for the early phase.

In contrast to both these mothers is a third mother. She also had a baby born by caesarean section and described her earliest feelings following birth as feelings of intense excitement and happiness. This feeling lasted while she was in the hospital. However, once she brought the baby home she felt extremely overwhelmed. Her baby was difficult to care for at first. He was colicky, and she felt herself to be in the throes of strong but conflicting feelings. She described her state as one of disequilibrium. On one hand, she had strong feelings for her baby and felt his presence to be a wonderful miracle. On the other hand, she felt distant, isolated, trapped, and very frightened by his dependency on her. She missed the fact that she had no family nearby, and she had a strong sense of loss of self in surrendering all her needs to his. By the time the baby was 6 weeks old and began to sleep for longer periods, she began to integrate him into her life. It was very important to her to begin to resume some of her own activities and go back to work part time. By the time he was 2½ months old and beginning to smile, she began to enjoy him fully. However, she described how it was difficult for her to find herself again. She said, "I had lost myself to an extraordinary extent. I felt I was sacrificing myself, my self-regulation. I had lost my self-feeling. I didn't know when I was hungry or tired. I was up and down with him." When he began to smile and seemed less vulnerable, she began to see him as a person rather than "that alien thing."

This mother vividly manifests the illness aspect of primary maternal preoccupation. She was, however, able to face these feelings well enough to be able to emerge from them and to achieve a pleasurable, intense symbiotic relationship with her son. Her baby, after a difficult beginning, stabilized and achieved Winnicott's capacity for "going on being."

Winnicott (1970) describes play between mother and baby during symbiosis in which the baby interrupts nursing to put a finger into the mother's mouth. This, according to Winnicott, is a primitive identification of the baby with the feeding mother.

> In this way we actually witness mutuality which is the beginning of a communication between two people; this (in the baby) is a developmental achievement, one that is dependent on the baby's inherited processes leading toward emotional growth and likewise dependent on the mother and her attitude and her capacity to make real what

the baby is ready to reach out for, to discover, to create. . . . Consequently, whereas the mother can identify with the baby, even with a
baby unborn or in process of being born, and in a highly sophisticated
way, the baby brings to the situation only a developing capacity to
achieve cross-identifications in the experience of mutuality that is
made a fact. This mutuality belongs to the mother's capacity to adapt
to the baby's needs. [pp. 250–251]

The baby's widening repertoire of care-eliciting behaviors brings
about the more fully developed mutuality that characterizes the symbiotic phase of dual unity. This is based in part on the programmed
maturational achievements of the baby (i.e., smiling, nestling, and
cooing), but also on the mother having provided the possibility of
mutuality for the baby, which depends on her achievement of maternal preoccupation—the development of her motherliness. According
to Benedek (1970):

> As motherliness facilitates the normal symbiotic process between
> mother and child, it supplies the matrix for the healthy development
> of the child; at the same time as it enables the mother to encompass
> the growing child in her own personality, it also prepares her for the
> individuation of her child and for his separation from her. Even the
> normal maturation of the child represents, in every phase, a new
> adaptive task to parents. [p. 165]

I have tried to show how the first phase of mothering requires a
mother's healthy capacity to regress and recover, to be both part of
and outside the baby—to be, as it were, a transitional phenomenon,
a bridge between the subjective and objective world. The mother's role
during the symbiotic phase shifts; she can now feel much more definitely that the baby responds to her. Sander (1976) calls the period
from 2½ to 5 months the period of reciprocal exchange and sees the
task of the mother to be the stimulation of reciprocity. This is the
period of bliss that has been described so richly in recent years by
Stern (1982) in his description of mother–infant games and by
Brazelton (1983) in the development of his ideas on feedback loops
within the envelope of mother–infant interaction.

Mahler (1979) has called the period of dual unity in which mother
and infant are as within a common membrane the symbiotic phase.
This comprises much more than oneness and the sense of lack of

differentiation and separateness. Pine (1981) has emphasized that merging during the symbiotic phase refers to moments of high intensity rather than to a continuous state, and Mahler has repeatedly stressed that during normal symbiosis a complex interaction between baby and mother takes place. In Winnicott's (1956a) terms, the baby has achieved the capacity for "going on being" and for withstanding impingement and the threat of disintegration. During this period, mothers often describe their babies as delightful, enchanting, and sweet. The baby no longer seems so fragile or helpless, and the mother can proudly reap the rewards of her earlier period of primary maternal preoccupation.

Mahler postulated that the beginning of the separation-individuation process occurs at the height of symbiosis at around 4 to 5 months. At this time, interest in the outside, nonmother world gains a great deal of momentum, and the exclusive, intense involvement with mother lessens. Whereas during the symbiotic phase a mother often describes how her infant stops nursing in order to smile, coo, and interact with her, the infant, during the differentiation subphase, often stops nursing and begins to look around at other phenomena in the environment. Sander (1976) calls this period, which we refer to as the differentiation subphase (the first subphase of the separation-individuation process), the period of early directed activity of the infant. He sees this stage as one in which the infant becomes more active in establishing reciprocity with the mother. If the infant can feel successful in initiating smiling play with mother, he or she learns to anticipate her response and can reproduce some of the joyful excitement by activities associated with his anticipation. As Sander (1976) says:

> The period from 6 to 9 months is a time which demands of the mother a certain keenness in reading and appreciating the cues of her child. It further demands that she respond as appropriately as in the initial period of adaptation. [p. 140]

This is the period of selective cueing. Not only is it necessary for the mother to have heightened sensitivity in reading the infant's cues for interacting, she must also be sensitive to the infant's cues for wishing to interact with others, to cathect the nonmother world (Bergman 1978). The need to distance from mother becomes even clearer and more pronounced during the practicing subphase from 9 to 15 months. Sander (1976) sees this as a time when the infant's demands on the mother become more intense and unremitting. He describes what he believes are necessary qualities of the mother during this period: She needs to be secure in her sense of identity as a mother; this enables her to be flexibly available, protecting the infant from dangers engendered during his or her explorations and occasionally from strong fear of strangers.

> The smooth and satisfactory negotiation seems to depend on the mother's availability to yield or to compromise by keeping the baby in her awareness while she pursues her own interests. . . . The mother who is secure enough in herself and has confidence in the ultimate separateness and integrity of her child can enjoy and yield to this possession by him. When she does so, preserving areas of reciprocity with her child, she acts as a stable base of operations for him as his growing motility and inevitable curiosity carry him away from her. [p. 142]

Sander feels that it is particularly important during this period that the baby be allowed to develop certainty about being the focus of mother's attention. Otherwise, he argues, the baby will be faced with a difficult asynchrony during the second year of life caused by the contradictory needs to assert him- or herself in relation to mother while at the same time still seeking assurance in relation to her.

From the point of view of separation-individuation theory, we feel, similarly to Sander, that it is of utmost importance for the baby to be allowed to take mother for granted, even to the extent where he or she seems oblivious of her separateness, which as yet he or she does not fully comprehend. The child during this period often uses the mother's body as if it were an object to climb on or to lean on, seemingly without any wish for interaction. Mother is not only a home base to which to return periodically for refueling, she is also supposed to be a passive facilitator. From the point of view of separation-individuation, however, we are equally sensitive to the mother's ability to be available as we are to her ability to let go and even to provide a gentle push to the outside world. This is a delicate moment indeed. A mother who unnecessarily retaliates by becoming unavailable, aloof, or uninterested or a mother who continues to draw the child back into her own orbit does not provide the optimal environment for the unfolding of the child's separate self.

A mother who seemed equally sensitive to her child's needs for closeness and for distance described his emergence from a very happy symbiotic period. During the period of differentiation, he went through a difficult time. Old ways of comforting him by rocking and singing did not seem to work any longer. The baby woke up crying at night. When mother picked him up, he wanted to be put down. When she put him down, he wanted to be picked up. His mood changed from even-tempered happiness to crankiness. However, as his motility increased and he entered the early practicing subphase, he once again became much more joyful, and he was now able to let his mother know that he had outgrown the old kind of closeness. She noticed that when he was ready to go to sleep and she tried to hold and rock him, he began to pull away from her and to look at his crib. When she put him into the crib he seemed content. He began to sing himself to sleep as she used to do for him before that. She was both wistful and pleased as she told of his growing up.

In this section, I have tried to describe both clinically and theoretically the experience of the mother during the first year of her infant's life. During this time, she needs to go through a process in which at first she is able to relinquish her usual ways of functioning in the interest of helping her infant achieve regulation and establish reciprocity. As the infant's world widens during the second half of the first year, it becomes the mother's task to repossess her own life in such a way that room is made for the gradual achievement of separateness for the infant. As the infant's world widens, so does the world between the mother and infant. Mothers vary in how they are able to make this transition, which in turn has some influence on how the baby experiences his or her needs for autonomy and intimacy. I will illustrate this with some vignettes from the separation-individuation studies.

The Separation-Individuation Process
in Normal Mother–Child Pairs

In the following vignettes, I shall describe mothers whose apparently insufficiently resolved issues of autonomy and separation-individua-

tion in their own lives seemed to be related to difficulties in mothering their infants. The material for these vignettes was gathered in
informal interviews and participant observations of the mothers in
the group of mothers and infants in our study.

Mrs. A.

Mrs. A. was an intelligent young woman who was understated, self-
deprecating, and complained of being disorganized. She attended our
nursery at any possible opportunity, and it seemed quite clear that
it was a longed-for home away from home for her. She was the oldest of three daughters and strongly attached to her father. Her
perfectionistic goals, which she was never able to live up to, were connected with her father. She said that her father had always expected
his daughters to be perfect.

Mrs. A.'s family had traveled quite a bit during her childhood and
adolescence. She had always been a good student and in that way
had lived up to her father's expectations. While she was in college,
her family once again moved, this time a considerable distance away.
Mrs. A. decided to stay in college and not move away with her family. However, she lost interest in her studies, and her grades deteriorated.

Mrs. A. graduated from college but did not pursue any further
studies and quickly married. It seemed that the marriage offered her
some protection and comfort but not very much pleasure or excitement. In her present family, her emphasis was not on her relationship to her husband or their life together but rather on herself and
her relationship to her children. From all this information, we might
hypothesize that Mrs. A. prematurely turned away from her mother
and identified with her father, perhaps in connection with the birth
of her siblings. Longings for closeness with mother were defended
against, and a depressive mood prevailed.

The relationship to her oldest child, a girl, was central in Mrs.
A.'s emotional life. She described the symbiotic phase with his baby
as having been blissful for herself and the child. It seemed that by
way of caring for her girl child she had been able to experience a
pleasure in femininity that she otherwise denied. She took great pride
and pleasure in her daughter's prettiness and dressed her exquisitely.

When they entered our nursery, the daughter was 1 year old and quickly took possession of the nursery by way of her precocity and charm. Her mother took great pleasure and pride in her and was quite tolerant of difficulties the little girl experienced during the rapprochement subphase.

When her second child, a boy, was born, Mrs. A. seemed to experience a great deal of pain and anxiety around separation from her daughter, who was then entering nursery school. Mrs. A.'s primary maternal preoccupation with her son (Nicholas) was a painful one. She never seemed to know what her infant son wanted or needed. She prolonged feedings endlessly, jiggling him to keep him awake while bottle-feeding him. The baby was difficult—unusually fussy and uncomfortable. Using Winnicott's concept, one could describe him as a baby who did not attain a state of "going on being"; he did not learn to withstand impingement during the early phase. Although there was some improvement in his state during the symbiotic phase and a certain amount of reciprocity became established between mother and infant, there remained a sense of fragility in the baby and in the mother–child relationship. His frequent illnesses and several hospitalizations disrupted what sense of safety and well-being could be established. Nevertheless, Nicholas developed quite satisfactorily during the separation-individuation period. His mother was particularly skillful in reading the cues that indicated his increasing competence and ability to cathect the outside world. She was able to support his separation-individuation process and took pride and pleasure in his good intelligence and his achievements.

For Mrs. A. there seems to have been an important difference in mothering a boy and mothering a girl. We might hypothesize that she experienced her girl child as a narcissistic enhancement, an opportunity to take pleasure in femininity that she could not otherwise allow herself. She had experienced the girl child as perfect and herself as the perfect mother for the child. Thus, in caring for her perfect little baby girl, Mrs. A. could meet the father's wish for a perfect daughter. The perfection began to crumble as the little girl had to face the outside world (i.e., nursery school), a world that did not give her the special treatment that both mother and daughter needed. The mother experienced every blow the child suffered as a blow to herself.

Mrs. A. was not able to experience symbiotic bliss with her son. She often complained that she did not feel herself to be a good mother to him when he was an infant, and he was not a "perfect" child. Nicholas was small and fragile and did not easily find his niche in the extrauterine environment. Throughout his separation-individuation process he remained fragile, and he suffered several hospitalizations.

The follow-up study of Nicholas (at 10 years of age) revealed some interesting personality characteristics harking back to his difficult beginnings. Nicholas had turned out to be an intelligent, high-achieving child. He seemed to be confident and considered himself to be the smartest boy in his class. However, his self-confidence seemed to be very dependent on high achievement. When he was tested, he suddenly became confused and panicky after he had solved a difficult problem correctly. He began to doubt his solution of the difficult problem and thought of several incorrect alternatives. This pointed to a problem in Nicholas reminiscent of that of his mother—the need to be perfect. Also, it was a problem reminiscent of his infancy—namely the tendency to fall apart and lose his bearings when he was under pressure.

Another interesting observation noted during the follow-up study related to Nick's love for stray animals. Like his mother, he liked to take them in the house and take care of them. Here we seem to see a double identification: on one hand, he is identifying with a caretaking mother; on the other hand, he is identifying with a child in need of care. The follow-up tests revealed that Nicholas is a child who strongly defends against impulses and, in particular, passive strivings. His defenses take the form of self-sufficiency and achievement orientation. Again, this was reminiscent of his mother who appeared self-sufficient and cool and had great difficulty in acknowledging her dependency needs consciously. Underneath a seemingly strong ego, one sensed fragility in Nicholas, reminiscent of his early life with mother.

Mrs. B.

Mrs. B. was an older mother and, in many ways, the opposite of Mrs. A. If Mrs. A. understated her capacities, Mrs. B. overstated hers. She tried to be supermother not only to her own child but to the other mothers in our group, ever ready with good advice and knowledge of how to do things. However, underneath the bravado and apparent self-assurance of Mrs. B. observers began to notice her depressive tendencies and a strong narcissistic need for admiration. She constantly overstimulated her baby and when not in direct contact with him or when not engaged in active conversation with others, she would lapse into a somewhat withdrawn state. She described her own mother as a dominating and overly efficient person. She said that she regressed when she went home, allowing her mother to do everything.

Mrs. B.'s account of the way in which she had left home seemed revealing of her own difficulties in establishing her separate identity and in separating from her family. She had grown up in a small midwestern town and was still living at home after having finished college. She was then in her 20s and working in an excellent job. On the spur of the moment she decided to go to New York on a visit with a friend. To her own surprise, she found herself looking for an apartment and a job and very quickly found both. To the dismay of her parents, she decided to move to New York and felt happy and content living on her own, relieved to have escaped her mother's domination.

Mrs. B. rarely talked about her father. She described him as kind and unassuming; she loved and admired him. The man Mrs. B. chose to marry in no way resembled the kind, unassuming father. Quite the contrary, he was a demanding, opinionated, and erratic man. He dominated the family and decided on childrearing methods. His most important demand was that little Seth should never be frustrated. Mrs. B. went along with her husband and seemed to agree with him; she thought of herself as the embodiment of motherliness. She was quite dominating, overstimulating, and seemingly needed her child to be constantly engaged with her.

Seth developed well during the symbiotic phase. He was alert, calm, and smiling. Observers noted that early in the beginning of the differentiation subphase (at around 5 months) he began to attempt to push away from his mother's tight grip. At this time, we observed the following.

Mrs. B. sits him up by holding on to his hands and pulling him up. It looked as if he would rather hold onto his mother than have her hold onto him. He continually tried to loosen his hands from her grip and tried to hold onto her himself.

At the same time, Mrs. B. became concerned because Seth, at nursing time, became distractible and no longer exclusively focused on the breast. She decided that she had to nurse him in a quiet place. She could not accept his playfulness and interest in the world that was natural for his age.

Seth, in turn, preferred to be held by others, who seemed to be a kind of refuge for him. His mother's intense overstimulation of him was designed to get a response from him. I quote again from an observation.

> When Mrs. B. returned, she said, "Where is my baby? Hi, you don't want to see me now. He is totally unaware of me today. He is very tired." She lifted him high in the air before putting him back into the baby's section. He quickly started to fret and she picked him up, at the same time she said, "Why don't you go to sleep?" Mrs. B. lifted him high up and lowered him, shook him from side to side and kissed his stomach several times.
>
> She spent several minutes intensely overstimulating Seth with movement, tickling him, holding him high, taking him down, holding him to her face, saying he wanted to eat her up. . . . Actually, she did not notice that Seth was, for some part of the procedure at least, markedly uncomfortable, nonresponding.

Seth was delayed in locomotor development and in entering the practicing subphase. This might have been because he could not take his mother for granted—an important aspect of the mother–child relationship for the flowering of the practicing subphase. He could not take her for granted because he could not be sure whether she would suddenly overwhelm him or be oblivious to him. It was difficult for Mrs. B. to remain in contact with her child when she was not directly engaged with him. She was abrupt in her handling of Seth, unable to modulate her own needs for closeness and distance.

Seth was 10 years old when the follow-up study was conducted. During the first follow-up interview, it was notable that Seth did not show the same reluctance to speak of himself to a stranger, the interviewer, as had most of the other children. He immediately began to talk about himself and proudly told of his accomplishments. The interviewer had the impression that she was not being related to as a person in her own right. Seth seemed to assume that the interviewer would admire him, approve of everything he said, and want to listen to him. In this way, Seth was reminiscent of his mother and the way in which she had entered our group, overly sure of herself and not taking the reactions of others into account. It would seem that in both mother and child, this seeming self-confidence had a defensive quality.

In the test report, Seth's expectation to be admired and approved of was contrasted to his extraordinary anxiety when he was asked to perform a specific task that seemed to make him feel quite helpless. The teacher's report noted that Seth was not a generous boy, that he was not responsive to the needs of others, and that he would not contribute to the group if the contribution was anonymous. Thus, the wish to be noticed and admired was paramount and defended against by taking for granted that others would be interested in him. It was also notable that Seth was rather compliant. The tester noted that he had difficulty in expressing his own wishes vis-à-vis his mother and would instead try to comply with hers. This compliance seemed like a reenactment of his situation during symbiosis and differentiation when he had been overstimulated and his autonomous wishes had not been respected.

Summary

In this chapter I have attempted to describe the experience of the mother as she attains primary maternal preoccupation, a state that requires an ability to lose oneself in the other and emerge again. I have called this transient loss of self *regression in the service of the baby*. It is this ability in the mother that sets the stage for the attainment of reciprocity during the symbiotic phase.

Reciprocity, or symbiosis, denotes a state of mutuality and homeostasis, a state during which the unique bond to the love object becomes established for the baby and a sense of unique caregiving becomes established for the mother. Reciprocity is a stage of balance between two separate beings—the mother and the baby—that creates the sense of oneness and blissfulness characteristic of the symbiotic phase. During the subphases of differentiation and early practicing, a gradual process of letting go is required of the mother. As

she lets go and the infant begins to attain the capacity for distancing, mutual cueing becomes more and more important.

Mothers vary in their ability to attain primary maternal preoccupation and to emerge from it. The stage of symbiotic unity is unique
in the pleasure it provides for the mother and is a kind of reward for
the dedication and loss of self required during the earliest period of
motherhood. During the stage of symbiosis, the groundwork for further differentiation and autonomy already is laid. However, it is
during the period of differentiation par excellence, beginning at 5 to
6 months, that the mother has to begin to allow the baby's interest
in and relation to the outside world to begin to flourish; it is with the
advent of independent locomotion and early practicing at about 9
months that the baby begins his endless explorations of the surroundings. Most mothers can facilitate or at least allow this process to
happen, but difficulties in the mother may, to a greater or lesser
extent, interfere with the child's unfolding of the separation-individuation process.

In examples taken from the observational study of normal mother–
child pairs during the separation-individuation process, I have shown
how the patterns established during symbiosis, differentiation, and
early practicing become internalized by the child. I have speculated
that disturbances in early mothering are connected to the mother's
own difficulties, which may extend back to her own separation-individuation period. From material gathered during the follow-up study,
it was possible to see how the child attempted to adapt to the difficulties in the mother and to what degree earlier patterns persisted.
In the case of the first mother, Mrs. A., the difficulties were present
at the very beginning in establishing a strong symbiotic relationship
to her second child, and he did not develop a good capacity for "going on being." This was partly offset by the mother's excellent adaptation to the child during the separation-individuation process
(Mahler et al. 1970). In the case of the second mother, Mrs. B., the
difficulty was twofold: first, in the mother's need for stimulation from
her infant and, second, in her difficulty in allowing him to separate
and individuate and thus become a self in his own right. These difficulties seemed to be connected to a difficult relationship with her own
dominating mother. By moving away abruptly and getting married
she had attempted to free herself, but the unresolved aspects of her

relationship to her own mother were relived in her marriage to a dominating husband and the relationship to her child.

Acknowledgment

The author wishes to thank David Pollens for his assistance in the preparation of this chapter.

8

On the Development of Female Identity

Issues of Mother–Daughter Interaction during the Separation-Individuation Process

Psychoanalytic views of feminine development have undergone significant changes in the course of the last thirty years. These have come about in part as a result of our growing knowledge of development in the first two years of life. Knowledge has been gained from both psychoanalytic observational research of mother–infant and, increasingly, father–infant interactions, as well as from the analysis of patients with disturbances in early object relations. This chapter is based on clinical work in these two areas and attempts to focus on early processes of internalization and identification that shape the emerging identity themes. With clinical examples of mother–daughter pairs from observational research as illustration, I present some thoughts about the effects of the mother–daughter relationship on problems of individuation in adult women.

A great volume of literature now exists that attempts to provide descriptive and theoretical models for preoedipal development of female gender identity. Roiphe and Galenson (1981) have focused on the early genital phase, the beginning of genital awareness, and have found important differences between girls and boys. My emphasis will be on the mother–daughter relationship, in particular during the separation-individuation process. My observations are based on the observational research of mother–infant pairs who were seen three to four mornings a week between the ages of 5 months and 3 years.

The development of female gender identify during the first five years of life can be seen as occurring in three progressive steps. First, the development of core gender identity, or primary femininity (Stoller 1976), from birth through the period of hatching at about 9 months of age. Second, the development of female identity as it becomes connected with the child's growing awareness and beginning consolidation of her separateness from about 9 to 10 months until well into the third year. And third, the development of a more complex organization of female identity during the oedipal phase. This chapter will focus on the development of the mother–child relationship between the ages of about 10 months and 3 years, that part of the separation-individuation process that includes the practicing, rapprochement, and on-the-way-to-self-and-object-constancy subphases. It will also focus on the recurrence of unresolved issues from that period of life, as they seem to occur in psychoanalytic treatment of adult women.

The issue of distinguishing oedipal from preoedipal issues in the analyses of adults has caused a great deal of controversy. Pine (1979) makes the important point that manifest material can sound as if it is derived from separation-individuation themes in patients who are in fact well differentiated. The achievement of differentiation is a definitive cognitive achievement and, in that sense, does not affect the analysis of adults. However, the feelings and fantasies connected with one's separateness and the losses as well as the gratifications that are entailed in it, the identifications that begin to be formed during the period of separation-individuation, the pleasure in or conflict about autonomous functioning, even if they have been reworked by the reorganization of the oedipal period, continue to color, to a greater or lesser degree, analytic work with adult patients. The early turning away from mother may result in apparent autonomy but also in an inability to be free from the early ambivalent relationship to mother.

Observational studies have opened our eyes to the power of nonverbal communication that, from the beginning, is two-directional.

Not only do infants communicate their needs and elicit their mothers' caretaking, but they also read their mothers' facial expressions (see Brazelton et al. 1975 in the experiment with the still-faced mother, and Emde 1983 in his work on social referencing). The infant faced with the still-faced mother attempts to engage her, and if she cannot literally falls apart. The infant faced with the "danger" of the visual cliff will look to the mother and in her face will either find the confidence to cross over or will be deterred by anxiety. Beginning at around 9 months—that is, after hatching—infants increasingly understand not only gestures and affect conveyed by the mother's caregiving behaviors, but also words, and concomitantly the infant becomes increasingly able to communicate intentionality.

What may be the significance of all this for the girl's earliest sense of herself as female? The most important revision of Freudian theory probably is that femininity or femaleness—a sense of one's own gender—begins at the beginning of life. The mother and father, in taking care of their infant girl's body convey in their facial expressions, words, and physical handling how they feel about their baby's gender. Stoller's work (1976) on primary femininity is of particular importance here. Kleeman (1976), Grossman and Stewart (1976), Blum (1976), and Tyson (1982) have all spoken to the importance of the early mother–child relationship for the formation of female gender identity. Schafer (1974), in his critique of Freud's psychology of women, writes, "to be consistent with psychoanalytic propositions and findings, one must see the girl and, later, the woman as being in a profoundly influential, continuously intense and active relationship, not only with her real mother, but with the idea and imagined presence of her mother, and with her identification with this mother . . ." (p. 476).

Freud (1931) himself expressed uneasiness with his theory of female sexuality. He seems to have understood the importance of the preoedipal bond between the little girl and her mother. When he tried to explain the girl's hostilities toward her mother, he said, "Perhaps the real fact is that the attachment to the mother is bound to perish, precisely because it was the first and was so intense. . . . the attitude of love probably comes to grief from the disappointments that are unavoidable, and from the accumulation of occasions for aggression" (p. 234).

We might add here that we may be dealing with a phenomenon that involves both mother and girl baby. Perhaps the intense attachment of the girl to the mother has its counterpart in the intense attachment of the mother to the daughter. Freud has spoken of the birth of the boy as fulfillment of the mother's wish for a penis. This would then be experienced as a sense of power, of strength, or completion. But how about the girl? Giving birth to a girl can give rise to the fantasy of creating a new and better self. It can also provide a very special sense of closeness and narcissistic fulfillment. Freud speaks to the eventual disappointment of the girl in her mother. There may well be a parallel process in the mother who has to come to terms with the separateness of the daughter. A young mother whose second child was a girl said, "When I nurse her, she and I look at each other, and she'll smile and sometimes stroke my breast that is not being used. At those times she seems so happy and at peace with the world; it is often contagious because I feel the same way. Often it seems that we are the only people in the world."

A year later, the same mother described how much closer she had felt to her daughter during her infancy than to her son. She said that she now, during the second year of her daughter's life, continued to spend as much time with her as possible. Her rationale was that a little girl needs her mother's love and devotion. Thus it seems that often for the mother, the separating of the daughter, which follows a period of the earliest closeness (symbiosis) is a more difficult and conflictual experience than the separating of her son. We will look at this in more detail below.

Reflections on Subphase Development in Girls

I shall briefly describe some aspects of the separation-individuation process in girls, based on the clinical descriptions of the girls in the Mahler study (Mahler et al. 1975). It is extremely difficult to generalize from in-depth case studies, but the data from the separation-individuation study are both cross-sectional and longitudinal, thus allowing for such an attempt. The individual differences in each mother–child pair probably outweigh the common features. If we keep in mind the limitations of generalizations, however, they might even-

tually lead us to further comparative studies that could help us for-
mulate clinically useful developmental models. Several interesting
observations about gender identity crystallize around the subphase
theory.

We have found that at the height of the practicing subphase, when
the child begins upright locomotion, mothers will at times subtly
interfere with both their daughter's or son's elated mood; however,
they more often show signs of abandonment or loss vis-à-vis the girls
than the boys (Bergman 1982). Since this is observational and not
analytic data, we do not know if they actually feel less abandonment
with boys or if they simply show it more with girls. For example, at
9 to 10 months, Chloe was described as exuberant to ecstatic in her
explorations. Her interest and curiosity in her surroundings were said
to override unhappiness or pain. She showed pleasure in vocalizing
and exhilaration in standing while holding on. There was a shift from
smiling specifically at mother to frequent smiling at others. She was
so preoccupied with her new locomotor explorations that she barely
noticed mother's comings and goings. Mother was pleased with Chloe's
expanding skills and often picked her up abruptly, kissing her im-
pulsively. She seemed competitive with Chloe's attention to others.
Then she suddenly announced that she intended to go back to work
and had already found a job and a babysitter. When Peter, Chloe's
older brother, had been the same age, he too enjoyed his explorations,
and was friendly, sociable, and happy. The mother had tended to
minimize his need for her. She denied or minimized his attempts to
seek her out and had a tendency to pick up and cuddle other babies,
thus demonstrating her longing for the closeness she was losing with
her separating child, which, however, she was not acting on with him.
She tended to hug baby girls.

It seems that early rapprochement, from about 14 to 18 months,
is a time of special pleasure and elation for girls. It seemed at first
as if some girls were experiencing a belated practicing subphase. But
on closer examination, social interactiveness seemed to be responsible.
This starts with mother, but quickly spreads to others, as long as
mother is pleased and approving. During this period, as the girl becomes more separate, her mood and personality take on an individual
character, but she also becomes more sensitive to mother's praise or
disapproval. If mother has indeed resented the girl's moving away

during practicing, she may now be very happy as the girl shows renewed interest in her.

Chloe began to approach mother frequently with an object, toy, or experience to share, and no longer went to other mothers as she had done before. Chloe also went to mother for cuddling or just to sit next to her. When she was unhappy she could be comforted by looking at mother from a distance. As time went on, she sought out mother more frequently for close, affectionate contact. When she explored away from mother, the mother sometimes followed her with resulting pleasurable interchange. She seemed to miss her mother even while she enjoyed active play. She seemed as alert to mother's comings and goings as mother was to hers. Frequently she shared her great pleasure in what she was doing with mother. This pleasure in mother began to spread to other people, especially to her father. When he came home at night, she would sit with a book beside him for a long time while he read the paper. Mother was able to maintain a closer relationship with her than she had had with her son when he was that age.

Another aspect of the mutual pleasure in the rapprochement phase in girls is the pleasure in the beginning identification with mother.

A male observer noted a more feminine way Chloe had of relating to him that included much smiling and offering him a cookie, which she tried to feed him. Her mother was always delighted when Chloe tried to imitate her gestures and sounds. In contrast, Peter, at 15 to 16 months, was said to turn away from mother and adults in general—in a way quite different from his earlier obliviousness of mother during practicing. Mother reported that he was clinging and demanding when tired, which irritated her. At other times he was always into things, requiring her attention. She said, "He's too much to handle!" Typically, Peter did not respond to mother when she returned from a brief absence. He seemed to turn away from her in a hostile or aggressive manner and did not find great pleasure in interacting with her.

As has been discussed elsewhere (Mahler et al. 1975), it seems that the rapprochement crisis is more easily resolved by boys than by girls. One factor that seems to be responsible is the discovery of the anatomical differences. This discovery is often a blow to the sense of omnipotence in the girl, for which she blames her mother.

Mahler (1966) noticed a greater tendency toward depression in girls than in boys. She ascribed it to the anger toward and disappointment in mother for not having given them the penis. We would add to this, on the basis of further scrutiny of the material, that this realization simply adds to the vulnerability that the girl feels as she becomes increasingly aware of her separateness that follows the joyful reunion with mother during early rapprochement. This loss of union seems to be reacted to strongly not only by the girl child, but also by the mother, and comes as a special disappointment to both.

It seems that the stage of on-the-way-to-object-constancy, along with the capacity for concern, is reached in a more definitive way by boys than girls. In girls, the transition between the rapprochement and early oedipal rivalry seemed sometimes harder to discern. If the mother is experienced as an oedipal rival, giving in to her could mean losing the love of the father. To be empathic with mother's needs or wishes could then be experienced as having to give up everything in order to maintain the mother's or father's love. It is this bind that we often see as a fixation point in the treatment of adult women.

Both girls and boys turn to father during the period of practicing and rapprochement. In boys, the disidentification from mother and identification with father is more necessary and probably more encouraged by both parents. If the boy does not manage to move away from mother, serious pathology develops, which is familiar to clinicians (McDevitt 1985). It is more socially acceptable and possible for girls to remain overly attached to their mothers. The boy is helped to identify with father not only through parental encouragement, but also through perceiving himself as male like father (Abelin 1980). Male symbols such as cars and trucks and baseball bats become early favorite toys.

The girl has to identify with the same mother from whom she has to separate, and thus her task is a more complex one. It is my impression that the preoedipal father can help the girl in the resolution of the rapprochement crisis by being available to the girl toddler as the important other and by providing an anchor of strength and security without being overly seductive. It is important to do further research on the attitudes of both mother and father toward the emotional response of the girl toward both parents. In addition, research is needed on the differences between the preoedipal relationship to father in girls and boys, as well as the attitudes of the father toward the girl who seeks closeness in the struggle to disidentify with mother.

The girl's ability to reach a resolution of the rapprochement crisis, and in particular her acceptance of the observation of anatomical differences, is strongly influenced by her mother's and father's reaction to her as a girl. The mother's sense of herself as a woman and her feelings about her daughter as a girl are communicated to the girl in many subtle ways.

The girl, in becoming a separate individual in her own right, has to come to terms, consciously and unconsciously, with her mother's conscious and unconscious expectations. There is an interweaving in the girl's identity formation of her own actual and increasingly intrapsychic experiences with the expectations and wishes of the mother that are communicated in myriad subtle ways. As we now know so well from infant research, the infant is never just a passive recipient of the mother's care. From the beginning, she has a powerful effect on the mother, and shapes, as well as receives, parental attitudes. Thus, what we need to look at are interactions and their eventual internalizations.

A little girl can be seen by the mother as an incipient rival, but she can also be seen as an extension fulfilling some of the mother's unfilfilled wishes as a woman or the reification of some of the mother's own pleasure in being a woman.

In our study, one mother who tended to be depressed seemed not to care about the way in which she dressed or looked, while at the same time she always dressed her daughter meticulously in freshly washed and ironed dresses. This girl, at the age of 13 months, was particularly hard-hit by the observation of anatomical differences and showed a quite severe castration reaction. It was as if her observation threatened her with imperfection since her mother was so invested in making her into what must have been her image of the perfect girl, an image toward which she herself did not even seem to aspire. Another mother always looked beautiful and meticulous herself, whereas her little girl looked quite shabby and disheveled. The mother seemed to have turned her daughter into a devalued part of herself. The mother had rather low self-esteem, and it was as if she demonstrated that fact by the way she dressed her daughter. Yet another mother dressed her little girl in such a way that the two of them looked remarkably alike. The look was fairly colorless. Her child was not her better self, nor was she the devalued self. Instead, she seemed to have been seen as a continuation of her own body.

Reflections on Separation-Individuation Themes in Adult Women

I now turn to problems around separation-individuation issues as they emerge in work with some adult women. Several of my women patients show great difficulty in resolving issues around their rapprochement crises with their mothers; these difficulties show up, in particular, in finding or staying with a partner in a love relationship. These women, attractive and intelligent, are able to perform at least adequately in various professions of their choosing. They are able to attract men and have love affairs, but these affairs sooner or later sour. The real difficulty seems to be in establishing their own homes and families.

What seems to happen is that the required step in individuation has to be sacrificed in order to protect the mother who, whether dead or alive, in the fantasy of the daughter, would perish if she established her own individual love life and family. In fantasy, these daughters believe that their mothers would be destroyed by their separateness and fear retaliation from the envied mother who is the only one who can have the phallus—the man—and the baby.

These women seem to have failed in the task of partial and selective ego identifications. Instead, a kind of global identification process occurs. The mother who is the dreaded and burdensome introject cannot become rival or friend. Instead, she is experienced as a demon who takes possession and the woman experiences herself as helpless and enraged. There exists a strong fear of either being or becoming crazy that seems to come from a feeling of being overwhelmed time and time again by feelings over which she has no control. Identifications are either with the helpless baby or with the powerful and sometimes benign, sometimes demonic mother.

Although these women appear to be interested in finding relationships with men, the man seems often to be put into the role of either the good or bad mother. He is often desired especially when he is unavailable. This of course makes him safer, as an object but also turns him into the early unavailable mother.

The women I have in mind all have in common a history of early abandonment by mother, either because mother was very depressed or because during the second year, the period of practicing and rapprochement, she turned her attention to a new baby. Many of these women seem to have had fairly ineffectual or sadistic fathers who could not act as buffers, or as models for partial identifications. In most cases where the father was more available, he was of immeasurable help to the girl in the attainment of pleasurable, autonomous functioning. But he could not liberate her from the bondage to a depressed and/or unavailable mother who seemed to need the daughter to fulfill her life. More than that, she used the daughter for a kind of reenactment of her own life problems, with the hope for a better outcome. The daughter becomes the slave of the mother's wish.

In the following clinical vignette I attempt to describe how the joint fantasy of a mother and daughter, though it has many oedipal overtones, served as a symbiotic bond between them. The daughter, though seemingly autonomous and independent, experienced a major crisis in her life when she finally reached a point at which she had found a man she wanted to marry and with whom she wanted to have a family. That the man was not approved of by her parents added to but did not cause the difficulty, since unconsciously she felt that no man she chose could possibly please her mother. The mother had constantly expressed the fear that through marriage her daughter would be doomed to a life of unhappiness as her own had been. She always told her daughter that only when she was married would she understand her mother. Throughout the daughter's childhood the mother threatened to run away and leave the family, to find another husband. She told stories of love affairs she had had before her marriage and how she had missed the opportunity to marry a rich man. She often criticized the daughter for having insufficient feminine attributes and virtues.

Though the daughter seemed to make light of these criticisms, she was nevertheless deeply affected by them. On one occasion her mother told her she was beginning to look old. This caused something that looked like an instant aging process in the daughter, who began to feel old and burdened rather than young, attractive, and competent.

As in any adult patient, oedipal and preoedipal issues are inter-mingled. The oedipal defense against the insoluble bond with the preoedipal mother was predominant at the beginning of her treatment. Only later did her feelings of a blissful union with me become avail-able, to be seen as a defense against problems of envy and rivalry.

This daughter, Sarah, was the older of two girls. Her younger sister was born when she was 14 months old. Sarah was a bright and attractive little girl who found many people to take care of her. She had no conscious memories of being jealous of her younger sister or feeling in any way displaced by her. As a matter of fact, she always considered herself lucky because while her younger sister had had to stay at home with mother, she was able to go out into the world. She is intelligent, attractive, professionally successful, and with progress in her analysis, better and better able to sustain close rela-tionships and have a circle of friends.

In the course of her analysis, she began and ended several love relationships because the man she was with was never the right one. In the transference this feeling of not being able to find the right person did not come up. She seemed to be more than satisfied with me and found my interpretations clever and helpful. She seemed, on the surface, fully engaged in her analysis, to which she came regu-larly and punctually. She often expressed wishes to take care of me, as she took care of her friends and her family. Yet in spite of her apparent involvement in the analysis, there was something amiss. She brought dreams like little presents wrapped in paper, but she preferred not to unwrap them. She had the fantasy that she was out in the world, gathering data for me, her analyst.

Thus she was repeating something from her early life—namely to be out in the world, making friends, while her mother was home with the baby, tied down and unhappy. In other words, she seemed to use me as a young toddler uses mother during practicing for refueling, for leaning on, for walking over without much regard for the sepa-rateness of the mother, for that separateness was not yet fully per-ceived. The way in which she picked up men and left them had a somewhat exhibitionistic quality, as if these men, too, were interest-ing objects to be collected.

Sarah finally met a man to whom she was very much attracted. At first, she treated him like a god who had descended from heaven

just for her. Her relationship to him had some of the quality of bondage described by Reich (1940a,b). After the honeymoon was over, she
went into a very different phase of the relationship. She began to be
dissatisfied with him and felt that he did not understand her problems. At first she felt somewhat justified in her attacks of rage against
him, but slowly she began to feel herself a victim of these rages. Yet
she hardly remembered them the next day. It was as if in the relationship she experienced a kind of total identification with her mother
who was prone to sudden and violent rages and despair.

During the course of her analysis, Sarah had slowly become more
aware of early narcissistic hurts by mother and of her longings for a
mother who would in turn be loving toward her. She became more
and more unhappy. In fact, she hardly knew herself as she became
tired, frequently feeling ill, disgruntled, dissatisfied, and unenthusi-
astic about her life. She was ready to give up everything, even her
hard-won professional status. I interpreted how much she seemed to
be ready to sacrifice everything for the fantasy of her harmonious,
blissful reunion with mother, as it was enacted with me. She searched
my words for approval of her relationship because only then, she felt,
could she decide to marry the man she loved. She now quite frequently became enraged with me as she felt I could not help her to
resolve her terrible conflict.

The crisis was reached when she finally experienced herself as if
possessed by an evil force condemning her to eternal doom of unhappiness and even madness—of isolation, burden, and a need to rid
herself of the man she really wanted. Following a dramatic session
in which she talked about this feeling of being possessed, of having
lost her freedom, and in which she recognized this possession as being connected not only with her mother but with her mother's own
fate and with her mother's unhappiness as well as the mother's
rageful revenge of abandonment, she began to once again have more
control over her life and was able to experience more pleasure.

At the same time, a shift in her capacity for object relations seemed
to occur. In her analysis, it took the form of showing what seemed
like genuine concern for me, rather than just using me as she had at
the beginning or blaming me as she did later. She now wondered how
I had felt as she ranted and raved, as she changed her mind daily
about whether or not she would marry her lover.

The story of Rapunzel comes to mind. Rapunzel is given up by her real mother and is taken care of by a stepmother, a sorceress. The sorceress locks Rapunzel in a tower but visits her regularly, climbing up the tower on Rapunzel's long hair. A prince discovers her and also visits her regularly, climbing up the tower on her long, beautiful hair. All is well until inadvertently Rapunzel gives up her secret and tells the mother-sorceress about the prince. She innocently asks the sorceress why the prince climbs the tower so much faster than she. The angry sorceress sends Rapunzel into the forest, and the desperate prince jumps out of the tower window and is blinded by thorns. His blindness is healed by Rapunzel's tears. Bettelheim (1976), in his analysis of the story, points out that the stepmother is not punished. She has acted out of selfish love (the symbiotic bond), not out of wickedness (selfish rivalry). We might take a leap of imagination and translate Rapunzel's tears into her realization of separateness and loss of omnipotence; she realizes she cannot have both the mother-magician and prince for her own.

Sarah eventually married and had children. I would like to close by telling a dream that she had during the pregnancy with her first child. In the dream, she was with a woman friend, a friend she had not seen for a long time and thought she had lost. She was very happy that this friend had returned to her. In the middle of talking with her friend, the doorbell rang; it was a delivery. Someone delivered several large statues that she seemed to have ordered. They were very beautiful and valuable. However, she was shocked when they arrived, and she said to the delivery man that she was not ready for them. He said that he had been asked to deliver them and could not take them back. She did not know what to do since she did not have room for them. She was much relieved when the thought occurred to her, "I will send them to my mother until I am ready." This dream points to the conflict Sarah was experiencing in relation to her first pregnancy. While she wanted a baby, having one also meant making a final and full commitment to her own life and her own husband. The dream, in its manifest content, expresses uncertainty about her readiness. It also expresses the wish that her mother, and of course in the transference that I, should remain available to her as she takes this final step toward separation-individuation. How big a step it is is expressed by the fact that several large statues are delivered. There is also the fear that she will lose her close woman friend when she has a baby. Will the achievement of motherhood and marriage make me, the analyst, unnecessary?

Just as Rapunzel has to give up the mother who climbs up the tower to comb her hair, Sarah has to finally renounce her wish and fear of the all-powerful mother in order to be in possession of her own life.

Conclusion

In giving an example of an adult patient with early problems, one inevitably runs the risk of oversimplification and overapplication of the genetic point of view. My allotted space allowed for a tiny fragment of a long analysis. I believe that Sarah's development and the change in her transference show that freeing herself from the preoedipal mother can be accomplished in the analysis of an adult. Sarah did not achieve a full identity as a woman in which she could allow a man to be different from her and not turn into the both wished-for and dreaded mother without making the basic changes in her object relationships. She could not be fulfilled as a woman with a child of her own until she could separate and renounce the symbiotic tie to her mother, from which she had apparently turned away earlier but which in reality she had not been able to give up at all. The identification with the father was of immeasurable help.

The examples from the normal separation-individuation study serve to show the strength of the tie between the mother and the little girl. It is a tie that can become noxious when the pathology of the mother or early traumas are such that the object representation of the bad mother of separation has to be carried along forever after.

9

Self–Other Action Play

A Window into the Representational World of the Infant

written in collaboration with
Ilene Sackler Lefcourt

From early on, babies, by virtue of their babyness, elicit playfulness in others. Smiles special for baby, unique tempos of speech and body movement, and games passed down through the generations comprise the first mother–infant play. The mother of a 2-month-old baby recently asked us, "Would you like to see our first game?" She and her infant, gazing into each other's eyes and smiling, became engaged in a dialogue. She lifted the baby from her lap, raised him slightly above her head, and said, "bouncy, bouncy!" She then returned him to her lap. The baby moved his body upward and looked at her expectantly. This provided the signal for her to lift him again. After several repetitions he stopped signaling; she was immediately sensitive to the change in his behavior, and the game ended.

The first play experiences, between mother and baby, promote the baby's most rudimentary sense of self and other within the context of an intimate, affectively attuned relationship. The games of early infancy create a mutually regulated action dialogue between mother and infant. The earliest mutually related dialogues provide the foundation for what we will describe as *self–other action play*. Self–other action play is play in which themes of self, other, and self with other predominate and in which the formation, transformation, and interrelatedness of self and object representations take place. We refer to these interactions as self–other action play because the baby playfully enacts many of the salient experiences of self, other, and self with other. We believe that such play contributes to the formation and integration of self and object representations in a unique way. Self–other action play eventually leads to the capacity for role play, which requires at least a rudimentary ability to take the perspective of another. When it emerges, role play becomes a new interactional language. Like spoken language, ideas and feelings are expressed. However, while in internalized language, or thought, ideas and feelings are internally processed, during role play they are enacted. The capacity to role play indicates that interactions with others have been internalized; that is, they have become part of the child's representational world.

Our understanding of the representational world of the infant before symbolic capacity is established has been enriched by researchers who have studied in detail how infants organize their experience internally (Stern 1985). A young infant's representational world is organized by interactions, memories, and expectations (Stern 1985). Recent mother–infant interaction research indicates that interaction structures are represented in a presymbolic form and lay the foundation for symbolic forms of self and object representations (Beebe and Lachmann 1988). In addition to the formation of progressively organized images of self and other, several theoretical constructs of the infant's intrapsychic organization of lived experience with an emphasis on interaction have been proposed: *scripts* by Nelson and Gruendel (1981), *generalized episodes* by Bretherton (1984), *internal working models* by Main and colleagues (1989), and *representations of interactions that have been generalized* (RIGs) and *prenarrative envelopes* by Stern (1985, 1992). All of these formulations refer to the infant's intrapsychic organization and memories of lived experience, and provide babies with a way of preserving the structure and quality of interactions, specific memorable events, and the likely course of events based on average experiences.

Here we will focus on a particular aspect of the infant and toddler's representational experience: the way in which playful interchanges, occurring in the context of the mother–child relationship, provide the scaffolding for evolving representations of both self and other and self with other. Our work draws on that of a number of authors who have argued that significant relationships are the foundation for successful symbolic growth. For example, research growing out of attachment theory (Sroufe 1979) has demonstrated the relationship between the presence of the mother in the child's life and the amount and quality of the child's play. It further demonstrates a connection between the quality of the relationship to the mother and the quality of play. Slade has done extensive research on the influence of maternal involvement on the quality of symbolic play in toddlers. She has shown that "interaction with another appears to bring out higher performance and to provide a critical context for the elaboration and expression of symbolic processes" (Slade 1987a, p. 374). Her data demonstrate the importance of mothers and caregivers' playing with their children. In particular, Slade found that children whose move to the phase of object constancy was compromised were limited in their capacity to maintain the organizational structure or conceptual underpinnings of a play scene. She says, "The failures of internalization which inhibited the resolution of rapprochement were reflected in the structure, coherence, and integrity of play" (Slade 1986, p. 548).

Essentially, Slade's work draws attention to the social construction of the play process, particularly the connection between maternal participation and availability and the success of eventual symbolic representation. Our work is complementary; we are interested in showing how prototypic games played by mothers and infants during each subphase of the separation-individuation process contribute to the formation of internal representations of self, other, and self with other (Drucker 1979, Mahler et al. 1975). While this process of forming representations proceeds outside of the play situation as well, we believe that special qualities and characteristics of play make a unique contribution to the representational world of the infant. Garvey (1977) notes the following characteristics of play:

> (1) Play is pleasurable, enjoyable. . . . (2) Play has no extrinsic goals
> . . . it is more an enjoyment of means than an effort devoted to some
> particular end. . . . (3) Play is spontaneous and voluntary. . . . (4) Play
> involves some active engagement on the part of the player. . . . (5) Play
> has certain systematic relations to what is not play . . . play has been
> linked with creativity, problem solving, language learning, the devel-

opment of social roles, and a number of other cognitive and social phenomena. [pp. 4–5]

These characteristics color playful interactions with delight. These highlighted moments of pleasurable play, often part of basic caretaking activities, are an essential part of mother–infant interaction. In what follows we will look at these kinds of play exchanges (self–other action play) that occur during the successive phases of the separation-individuation process as described by Mahler and colleagues (1975).

Separation-individuation theory, which is based on detailed observational study of the developing mother–infant relationship, enriches our understanding of how play may contribute to the formation of self and other representations during the preverbal and earliest verbal periods of development. Consequently we will examine shifts in play behaviors that occur during the subphases of the separation-individuation process as it unfolds across the first 3 years of life (Mahler et al. 1975). In so doing, we will show that self–other action play serves different representational functions at different ages and promotes the linking and integrating of existing simple representations to form new, more complex representations. Using the subphases of the separation-individuation process as an organizing prospective for the description of self–other action play does not imply that one kind of play or representation is replaced by another. The subphase theory takes into account the overlapping and complex layering of the development of the representational world.

Play with Objects Connected to Mother: Linking Representations (5 to 9 Months)

A baby at 5 months is clearly attentive to the outside world. This marks the beginning of the differentiation subphase, the first subphase of separation-individuation, which takes place from about 5 to 9 months. We will describe two kinds of play during the differentiation subphase that we relate to the formation and integration of self and object representations and thus describe as self–other action play.

The first of these types of play is with objects that belong to mother, such as her jewelry, keys, and eyeglasses. Originally initiated by baby, this play is quickly responded to and elaborated by mother. These objects are of interest to infants at this age because of certain physical attributes that appeal to babies: For example, they are shiny or make special sounds. However, we assume that they are also of special value to the baby because of their connection to mother's body. They belong to mother; they are part of mother; yet they can be taken by baby and thus become baby's. Playing with these objects in mother's presence promotes the mental processes that create a relationship between an inanimate object and the specific person with whom it is associated. It is the relationship, created by the infant between mother and the objects that belong to her, combined with the intrinsic pleasure derived from the manipulation of these objects, that gives the object special meaning. Mental processes imbue the objects that belong to mother with "momminess." This begins when infants cherish and love to play with objects that belong to mother and continues in a variety of ways throughout life. This is play in Winnicott's *intermediate area*:

> The intermediate area to which I am referring is the area that is allowed to the infant between primary creativity and objective perception based on reality-testing. The transitional phenomena represent the early stages of the use of illusion, without which there is no meaning for the human being in the idea of a relationship with an object that is perceived by others as external to that being. [Winnicott 1953, p. 90]

Play with inanimate objects that belong to mother reveals the emergence of the mental capacity to invest an object with feelings one has toward another and transfer attributes of one object to another. This capacity to link and integrate representations is the first step in the developmental pathway to symbolic functioning.

Separation and Reunion Play: Linking Representations of Interactions

The second kind of self–other action play that begins during the differentiation subphase is more clearly interactional. We refer here to games of peekaboo and what we call "I give it to you—you give it to me" and "I drop it—you pick it up." "I give it to you—you give it to me" is the game in which baby hands an inanimate object to mother and mother hands it back to baby. The self–other interaction is repeated several times and is usually accompanied by a singsong phrase. This mother–infant play activity seems to provide the baby with an experience of separateness and connectedness. "I drop it—you pick it up" is the familiar, endlessly repeated activity, initiated by babies, in which the baby drops, and eventually throws, an object and mother retrieves it. We believe that repetition of this sequence—holding on to an inanimate object, letting go of the object, and having the object returned—promotes the formation of representations of expected sequences.

Games of "I give it to you—you give it to me" and "I drop it—you pick it up" deal with issues of letting go and repossessing of inanimate objects that we think are related to issues of separation and reunion with loved ones. When the baby's actions are responded to with playfulness, these activities become pleasurable games of mastery.

The classic game of peekaboo is typically introduced by mother into the mother-baby play repertoire at this time (Bruner and Sherwood 1976). Mother, while pulling a sweater over baby's head, may elaborate the activity of dressing into a game of peekaboo. In another form of peekaboo, mother covers baby's face with a diaper and baby learns to pull it off, or mother covers her own face. The external, self–other action often changes in games of peekaboo as mother and baby interchange roles of hiding and finding. The specific games of peekaboo played by each mother and baby, including the roles played by each, will have their own personal signature and reveal aspects of their relationship.

One special characteristic of these games that deal directly with appearance and disappearance is that they typically are accompanied by crescendos and decrescendos of excitement. The increase and decrease of arousal are mutually regulated and result in an experience of fluctuating, moment-to-moment state sharing (Stern 1985). The reappearance after a brief disappearance evokes the joy of refinding, that is, rediscovering mother. Furthermore, the experience of "making" mother retrieve the lost object enhances the feeling of the self as agent. At a time when babies are increasingly confronted with feelings of loss and separateness, and just on the brink of becoming capable of more independent activities, in particular locomotion, we believe that the emergent experience of self as agent and highlighted experiences of state sharing, that is, attunement (Stern 1985), may be particularly exciting. We are reminded here of Pine's concept of *moments*, which he believes to be structure-building (Pine 1985).

At about 8 months there is a marked change in baby's reaction to mother's absence for even brief periods. Momentary losses of mother elicit a variety of distress reactions (Mahler et al. 1975). In his presentation entitled "The Origin of Conflict During the Separation-Individuation Process," McDevitt (1988) traces the development of anxiety and conflict throughout the separation-individuation period and notes that play becomes an important part of active coping behavior in response to separation toward the end of the first year. Games of peekaboo and "I drop it—you pick it up" after the onset of separation anxiety can provide the baby with experiences of control and mastery over loss and retrieval and over separation and reunion. In the presence of mother, these games promote the formation of representations related to separation and help transform painful experiences into pleasurable play.

A representation of mother as permanent (i.e., a sense that mother exists even though out of perceptual awareness) is promoted by experiences of separation followed by reunion and enables baby to tolerate separations from mother. The expectation during separation that separation will be followed by reunion is a result of the integration of the representation of mother, the representation of separation from mother, and the representation of reunion with mother. These newly integrated representations form the expectation that separations from mother will be followed by reunions with mother and the sense that mother exists even though out of perceptual awareness. These early representations and the ways they are linked together, with both their cognitive and emotional components, contribute to the eventual ability of the baby to tolerate separations.

Transitional Phenomena: Evoking a Representation of Mother in Her Absence

Gradually baby's mental representation of mother may be evoked in her absence. For example, upon awakening a baby may coo or babble, possibly evoking mother's presence. Or baby begins to be able to soothe himself as he has been soothed by mother. Sucking his fingers or making tongue and lip motions and sounds might evoke the feeling of sucking the breast; the blanket or cuddly toy has aspects of the mother's soft body. This process of being able to derive comfort from something that reminds one of mother begins as early as 5 to 9 months and continues in various forms appropriate to the child's developmental stage.

A dramatic and poignant example of the capacity for self-soothing and the way in which transitional phenomena promote self-soothing occurred when Jessica McClure, an 18-month-old girl, was trapped at the bottom of a well for 58 hours (Shapiro 1987). After moments of crying for her mother, she began to sing to herself the songs that her mother sang to her, thus evoking a representation of mother that may have helped her to endure the traumatic separation. The process of attaching aspects of the mental representation formed from knowledge of the actual mother to the representation of an inanimate object (or, in the case of Jessica, a song) contributes to the capacity to evoke the representation of mother during her absence. We are describing a presymbolic process by which not only lived experience determines the formation of representations but also the linking of already existing simple representations, which then form new, more complex representations. The process of linking representations of inanimate objects to representations of mother is an internal activity in which the baby becomes invested. This process contributes to the developing sense of self. Stern (1985) states, "Each process of relating diverse events may constitute a different and characteristic emergent experience. . . . I am suggesting that the infant can experience the process of emerging organization, as well as the result, and it is this experience of emerging organization that I call the emergent sense of self" (p. 45).

We are suggesting that emergent experiences result in the emotional investment of the internal world. Self–other action play constitutes a kind of emergent experience and may in this way contribute to the uniquely human capacity to form symbols. It is not simply that the representation symbolizes the actual object, but also that the emotional investment in the inner sense or feel of mother eventually enables that inner experience or representation to substitute for the actual mother. This is similar to the way in which an emotional investment in representations is necessary for the creation of a transitional object: "It is true that the piece of blanket (or whatever it is) is symbolical of some part-object, such as the breast. Nevertheless, the point of it is not its symbolic value so much as its actuality. Its not being the breast (or the mother) is as important as the fact that it stands for breast (or mother)" (Winnicott 1953, pp. 91–92). The attachment to the transitional object results not only from the fact that it symbolizes the love object, but also that it is an external manifestation of the emotional investment in the developing representational world.

Play Away from Mother and the Internal Sense of Being with Mother (10 to 15 Months)

The next subphase of separation-individuation is practicing (10 to 15 months). During the practicing subphase, there are dramatic increases in physical ability and a great upsurge of pleasure in locomotion and functional play. Infants of this age practice, with great interest and compelling motivation, their quickly emerging capacities to crawl, climb, and walk and their rapidly increasing manipulative skills. Enthralled with their play activities, infants vigorously begin to explore the other-than-mother world and at times appear oblivious to mother.

During this subphase, physical distance between mother and infant can be initiated by baby. The infant no longer has to endure passively being left, but can actively begin to leave and in this way practice separations and reunions. Mahler and colleagues (1975) observed that as long as the mother is not too far away, the infant's practicing subphase behavior continues with exuberance. If the distance is too great or mother is away for too long, the joy in practicing wanes and the infant becomes subdued.

Babies this age crawl and then walk away from mother, returning often, not with the intent to play with her but rather to facilitate their own play. At these times, babies may use mother's body as if it were an inanimate object to climb on, step on, push, and pull—a stepping stone to the world to further baby's activities and to extend baby's reach. The infant's external obliviousness to the actual mother is accompanied by an intrapsychic way of being with mother, and it is this internal sense of being with mother that enables the infant to separate from her.

This internal way of being with mother is related directly to actual experiences with mother. The memories of actual experiences of being with mother are retrievable, when separated from her, when an attribute of the memory is present (Stern 1985). Perhaps the bodily pleasures and elation that accompany play activities during this subphase are the attributes that evoke the internal sense of being with mother. But the reverse is also true: The inner sense of being with mother increases the pleasure in play activities and the mood of elation characteristic of this subphase. Optimal amounts of the actual mother's presence and emotional availability are required in order for the baby to pursue these play activities and to derive pleasure from them. Although exceedingly interested in the other-than-mother world, the infant needs to reestablish frequent eye or physical contact with mother. Furer called this touching base with mother *emotional re-fueling* (Mahler et al. 1975). There is an ongoing interplay between actual experiences of being with mother, the internal sense of being with mother, play in the other-than-mother world, and the pleasure and mood of elation. The interrelatedness of these experiences suggests the integration of inner and outer reality and of self and object representations.

It is central to our thinking that the spontaneous, inner sense of being with mother that enables the baby to separate physically from her is itself an important intrapsychic phenomenon that promotes development. This inner sense of being with mother during the practicing subphase lays the foundation for the later mental capacity to create or evoke the inner sense of being with mother, as desired or needed, when there is a greater displeasure in separateness. (This was seen in the previously noted case of Jessica McClure.) The ability to evoke and sustain representations increases with development and facilitates the formation of psychic structure.

During the practicing subphase, intense pleasure in independent locomotion and newly acquired motor capacities propels the toddler to embrace a new separation and reunion game. Chase and reunion games are a new form of the earlier peekaboo game and serve a similar function. They are initiated by both mother and baby, and often involve a rapid alternation of roles of chasing and being chased. Peekaboo, a self–other action game of separation and reunion, becomes infused with the functional pleasure derived from motor capacities.

Play Re-creating Essential Ways of Being with Mother: Fluidity of Representations

A commonly observed game during the practicing subphase that further suggests the integration of self and object representations is baby feeding mother playfully. This self–other action play suggests an experience of self–other ambiguity, as well as the emergence of self and object representations during play. How does one interpret this play—"I, baby, do to you, mommy, as you have done to me" or "I am now mommy and you are baby; therefore, I feed you as you have fed me"? This game and similar ones provide an actual experience of being with mother while evoking representations of mother, of self, and of self with mother. The ambiguity inherent in this play of who represents whom suggests the fluidity that is inherent in the process of integrating representations.

The use of the pull toy, another favorite play activity during the practicing subphase, raises similar questions about the meaning of play at this age (Shopper 1978). Baby walks proudly, with his pull-toy behind, and looks back at the toy frequently. How do we understand the meaning of this play—"I am mommy, with a pull-toy baby who goes everywhere with me" or "I am baby and have a mommy pull-toy who will go wherever I go"? One might ask similar questions about riding on kiddie cars, which begins to be a favorite activity. Riding on his own car, does the child feel strong and powerful, like his mother? Or does the child now have a pretend parent always available on whom to ride? We believe it is the ambiguity about self–other symbolic meaning that gives these games special power and makes certain possessions coveted in special ways. Once again the very uncertainty of who represents whom reveals an essential fluidity and simultaneity of representations, and the process of linking and integrating representations, forming new representations.

Games of Sharing: Integrating Representations
of Self and Mother (15 to 24 Months)

During the rapprochement subphase (around 15 to 24 months), another important change occurs: the child wishes to share objects and activities directly with mother and to engage mother in play. As the toddler becomes increasingly aware of his vulnerability, helplessness, and smallness, his relative obliviousness to mother demonstrated during the practicing subphase begins to wane. In an attempt to bridge the separation between self and other, children of this age bring many things to be touched and held by mother. During the early rapprochement subphase, a child literally fills his mother's lap with the other-than-mother world. A common playground activity is to wander from mother and return with "treasures" that the child demands to be held and kept by mother. These things range enormously in size and can include everything from favorite toys to objects such as pieces of wood, scraps of paper, metal, and bottle tops. "Each time the toddler finds her he brings along a new piece of the world outside, and each time he leaves her he takes with him a part of her. Increasingly this part is an image. . . ." (Bergman 1978, p. 158). In this way the child creates a physical bridge between mother, self, and the other-than-mother world and facilitates the formation of a psychological bridge. The psychological bridge we refer to is constructed of representations of mother, self, and self in relationship to mother, as well as of representations of inanimate objects. This self–other action play adds to the stability and integration of developing representations of self, other, and self with other.

During the rapprochement subphase, the toddler's newly acquired and valued skills are repeatedly demonstrated for mother in order to receive her admiration and approval. The coming together of mother and toddler in this mutually pleasurable and gratifying way helps the child to tolerate his feelings of vulnerability, helplessness, and ineptness by having his competence mirrored and admired. These shared moments also help bridge the gap of separateness. While observing a toddler jump up and down with mastery and delight, his mother looking on with admiration, one gets the feeling that the child becomes "filled" with mother's admiration and love. This is reminiscent of the way in which inanimate objects touched by mother seem to be transformed by momminess. It is not uncommon during the rapprochement subphase for a child to refuse a cookie unless first touched by mother or to have a hurt healed by mother's magical kiss.

The child's conflicting wishes for autonomy, on the one hand, and for mother to be ever-present, on the other hand, culminate in the rapprochement crises. Attempts at omnipotent control of both self and other are the way in which the toddler tries to solve this inherently insoluble problem. A great need for mother's emotional availability (Emde 1980, Mahler 1963) combined with frequent outbursts of anger often make even brief separations stressful. We will attempt to show how self–other action play helps the child to deal with the conflicts that arise during the rapprochement crisis.

Beginning Role Play between Mother and Baby: Representations of Empathic Exchanges (22 to 26 Months)

During the rapprochement subphase, a maturational leap in symbolic functioning and important developments in play occur. Although we believe that precursors to symbolic functioning or more rudimentary forms of symbolic functioning are evidenced in earlier play, the symbolic meaning of a child's play gradually becomes clearer. The unfolding of this process is revealed during the rapprochement subphase when self–other action play actually takes the form of role play.

In beginning role play, mother often takes a fairly passive role as the child tells her what to do. She allows herself to be used to meet the needs of the toddler's inner life. A common script enacted by children of this age requires mother to cry when baby leaves or to cry when she has been hurt. For example, toddler leaves the room and says, "Mommy cry." Toddler then returns and says, "Here I am. Mommy, stop crying." They hug. This role play is less ambiguous in terms of role designation than the play described during the practicing subphase. Baby plays mommy, and mommy is supposed to play baby. Typically this kind of game is repeated over and over and represents active, pleasurable mastery in play of the painful situation of being left. In a slightly more complex scenario, the mother of a 20-month-old boy reports that he bites her playfully but sometimes quite hard. She pretends to cry. He runs and brings her his blanket, the beloved transitional object, to comfort her. He shifts from being the playful biting baby, or the aggressive hurtful baby, to the comforting caretaker. This game is repeated over and over. Such early forms of role play typically involve the exchange of roles between mother and child addressing issues of vulnerability, separation and aggression, and experiences of empathy, reparation, and love. The ability to play these games, that is, to put oneself in the role of another, requires the beginning ability to objectify the self (Piaget 1962, Stern 1985) and the capacity to link and integrate representations. The representations integrated include representations of mother, self with and without mother, actions of mother, and self performing the actions of mother. This kind of role play reveals early identifications with mother and the working through of issues and conflicts related to separation and reunion and to aggression and reparation. Role play further promotes the integration and elaboration of self and object representations. The integration of self and object representations will eventually result in a self that can be both similar to and different from mother, both complying with and opposing mother, and both loving and hating mother. Role play, with its expansion and elaboration of representations, promotes identification that will be instrumental in the resolution of the rapprochement crisis.

Further Development of Role Play:
The Consolidation and Expansion
of Representations (24 to 30 Months)

As rapprochement conflicts begin to be resolved (around 24 to 30 months), the *on the way to object constancy* subphase begins. With self and object representations now more firmly established, the child is further able to enact a wide range of needs, impulses, and conflicts through role play. Therefore, during this phase, our ability to learn about the representational world of children through their play is dramatically increased. Now role play begins to include characters from the outside world. It is no longer limited to role exchange between mother and child; it begins to include the child's everyday experiences with people such as the mail carrier, bus driver, repairman, police officer, and doctor.

We wish to emphasize that role play that includes characters from the other-than-mother world begins when the self is firmly enough established to be able to put itself in the place of the other; this is the hallmark of the *on the way to self and object constancy* subphase. This expanded role play enables the child to elaborate and consolidate aspects of development that were first established during earlier developmental phases when issues and conflicts were negotiated within the parent–child context. Now the child is able to extend characteristics of self and other, and the relationship between himself and significant others, to the widening world. The roles that are enacted express the child's knowledge of the people who surround him, help the child expand that knowledge, and represent important aspects of the now more consolidated and ever-expanding inner representational world. Such role play reinforces both connections with and separations from emotionally significant others because each role enactment embodies a crucial aspect of the self and the other. We suggest that this kind of role play is directly related to self–other action play that occurred earlier and continues to deal with the basic themes of self–other interaction.

We believe that the internal experience during role play can be best understood in terms of Winnicott's intermediate area of experience (Winnicott 1953). Both a certain fluidity and constancy of self and object representations remain characteristic of role play, and a particular kind of integration of self and object representations and of inner and outer reality occurs. Role play serves the child's simultaneous needs to both express and disguise his impulses, anxieties, and conflicts (Bornstein 1945).

"Mail carrier" is a favorite game of children on the way to object constancy. This role play allows children to continue the pleasure of bringing treasures to mother, a pleasure that began during the early rapprochement subphase. Mail carrier role play, a game that has anal phase components, puts giving and receiving of valued things into a context that assures the child that his gifts will be received with approval and delight. Children of this age have observed that adults are often excited about getting mail and that it connects them with people who are somewhere else. Thus the child not only reinforces the bridge between self and mother, but also acknowledges the relationship between mother and others.

"Doctor," a popular game throughout childhood, begins at this age. Doctor play usually originates as a reenactment of the child's visits to the doctor and gradually is elaborated. Many children alternate between the roles of doctor and patient, while others consistently choose one role or the other. Doctor play provides the opportunity to explore the body, a self–other action play activity that began during the differentiation subphase, and to address concerns about the integrity of the body and the genital difference that become important during the second year. Both passive wishes and sexual and aggressive impulses are expressed. Doctor play is self–other action play that often involves direct and intimate body contact between self and other.

Playing doctor also enables many children to reconstruct and work through traumatic experiences of illness and injury. A 22-month-old girl who suffered a severe injury to a finger that resulted in losing a great deal of blood, an emergency visit to the hospital, injections in her finger and buttock, and a huge bandage that covered her hand completely frequently played doctor in the following weeks. She alternated between playing the role of the frightened, crying patient; the angry, defiant patient; the detached, hurtful doctor; the concerned, healing doctor; the frightened, guilty mother; and the comforting, loving mother. The enactment of self and other roles related to the accident facilitated the integration of representations and the resolution of the impact of the traumatic experience.

Sometimes role play can serve the integration of both masculine and feminine identifications within an appropriate gender role. For example, a 2½-year-old boy whose father was in the construction business chose the role of repairman. He loved tools and was not satisfied with toy imitations. The boy was clearly identifying with his father as he walked around the house with his little tool box, talking to his mother about all the things he was fixing. His collection of favorite tools included the vacuum cleaner, which was regularly used by his mother. Thus the role of repairman included both male and female identifications within a male role. The incorporation of a female identification into a male gender role supported this little boy's growing masculine identity without relinquishing the identification with his mother. In addition, role-playing a repairman probably helped him cope with the discovery of anatomical difference, an important developmental issue of children his age.

"Bus driver" and "elevator operator" are favorite games of separation and reunion. Issues and conflicts from earlier subphases of separation-individuation, as well as oral and anal phase development, are addressed. The child controls the make-believe mechanical door that enables passengers to leave and enter the bus; passengers are dropped off and must wait (and often pay) to be picked up. In this way, the child may be dealing with issues of what goes into and out of the body, as well as issues of separation and reunion with love objects. Perhaps this game of separation and reunion is a new edition of the earlier games of peekaboo. The small toddler feels powerful as he pretends to drive the huge bus and in this way continues to work on rapprochement subphase issues of feeling relatively small and helpless.

"Police," "cops and robbers," "superhero and villain," and variations thereof include the enactment of aggressive impulses or references to them and reveal beginning superego structure formation. Many children alternate between the police and criminal roles, while others exclusively play one role or the other. The good–bad split in roles is a significant aspect of this play and promotes the integration of good and bad, self and object representations. In addition, the police in pursuit of the criminal may be an elaborated version of the earlier game of chase and reunion. Within the child's life experience, the authority of the police is understood to be more powerful than that of his mother and is to be respected by him as well as his mother. This aspect of police play enables aggression mobilized toward mother in response to her limit setting to be modulated, thereby facilitating object constancy.

Role play that includes characters from the outside world captures essential aspects of love objects and simultaneously promotes separation from them. This type of role play integrates and expands representations of self and mother, and reveals the consolidation of representations created by linking representations of mother with representations of self. Because of more advanced symbolic functioning and greater integration of representations, developmental issues and conflicts are addressed in more derivative form, thus facilitating development.

Many of the issues and conflicts addressed in role play during the *on the way to self and object constancy* subphase originate in earlier developmental phases and continue to be issues for life. Many role-play games appear to be elaborated versions of earlier self–other action play. The roles enacted have been observed by the child in his ever-widening world and in some way capture not only internal conflicts seeking resolution or developmental issues to be negotiated, but also significant aspects of the adult that the child is aspiring to be and is already becoming, as well as elements of the external world within which he lives. Role play moves this process beyond the parent–child relationship while simultaneously incorporating it. Resolution of issues and conflicts that first emerged in infancy need no longer be exclusively bound to the parent–child relationship. In this way, role play serves a unique function in development.

Summary

During the separation-individuation process, self–other action play promotes the child's formation and integration of self and object representations and his adaptation to those conflicts and losses that are part of normal development. The capacity to role play, that is, the capacity to reenact one's own lived experience or one's own experience of another, is the culmination of a process that is rooted in earlier forms of self–other action play and, further, promotes the integration of self and object representations. In addition, role-play games seem to share action themes in common with earlier play.

The ability to create relationship between objects, between representations and objects, and between representations is a mental capacity that is required in order to role play. We believe that this occurs for the first time in play during the differentiation subphase when a relationship is being created between mother and those objects that belong to her—her jewelry, clothes, and so on. This developing mental capacity, the capacity to link and integrate representations, is next revealed during the rapprochement subphase during play that creates a bridge between mother and self and between mother and the rest of the world. The second mental capacity essential to role play is the ability to evoke a representation when desired. This capacity is first revealed during the practicing subphase and was described as an inner sense of being with mother that enables the infant to separate from mother. Furthermore, this inner sense of being with mother promotes the integration of self and object representations. We have suggested that the linking and integrating of representations occurs in self–other action play throughout separation-individuation. During the differentiation subphase, play with mother's possessions facilitates the linking of representations of mother with things that belong to her. During the practicing subphase, the fluidity of representations of self and other inherent in certain play activities, and the ongoing mutual regulation of and reciprocity between actual experiences of being with mother, the internal sense of being with mother, participation in play activities in the other-than-mother world, and the pleasure and elation that is derived from those activities, suggest the integration of self and object representations. During the rapprochement subphase, play activities in which child fills mother's lap with inanimate objects, thereby filling mommy with the world and the world with momminess, and play in which the child performs skills for mother, thereby filling the self with mother's loving admiration, promote the integration of representations of mother and inanimate objects and of mother and self. These play activities create a psychological bridge through representations that can connect the separate mother and self.

During the fourth subphase, *on the way to self and object constancy*, play that includes roles from the outside world begins. This occurs when the self is firmly and flexibly enough established that the child not only can put himself in the place of emotionally significant others, but can also extend this capacity to include persons beyond parents and other family members. This kind of role play is related to self–other action play that occurred during earlier phases and continues to deal with the basic themes of self–other interaction. It enables the child to elaborate and consolidate aspects of development that were first established during earlier phases when developmental issues and conflicts were negotiated almost exclusively within the parent–child relationship. During this phase of development, because of more advanced representational and symbolic capacities, those same issues and conflicts can be addressed in more derivative form allowing for the further elaboration and consolidation of development. Resolution of issues and conflicts that first emerged in infancy need no longer be exclusively bound to the parent–child relationship.

Acknowledgments

We wish to thank those colleagues who have made valuable comments on earlier versions of this chapter, and in particular to acknowledge the contributions of Drs. John McDevitt, Robert Michels, and Ethel Person.

Throughout this chapter, *mother* is used to refer to the caretaking other, regardless of gender, and masculine pronouns are used to refer to the child. This has been done to distinguish clearly references to the mother and references to the baby. The unique aspects of the father's role in the processes discussed will not be addressed here.

10

Two Women and Their Mothers

On the Internalization and Development
of Mother–Daughter Relationships

written in collaboration with
Maria Fahey

Introduction

This chapter is based on the data collected from a longitudinal research study that has spanned thirty-five years. The first segment
of the research was the observational study of mother–child pairs that
led to the formulation of separation-individuation theory (Mahler et
al. 1975).[1] This study, begun in 1959 by Margaret Mahler and her
associates, was based on Mahler's hypothesis of the symbiotic origin
of the human infant, who she thought developed a sense of separate
identity during the period of separation-individuation. Mothers and
children met in a playground-like setting that allowed for the comparison of the development of children the same age while each
mother–child pair was studied intensively. The data were collected
by a team of participant and nonparticipant observers, as well as by

1. This research was supported by NIMH Grant MH-08238, USPHS: Margaret
Mahler, Principal Investigator; John McDevitt, Co-Principal Investigator.

senior clinicians who conducted regular interviews with the mothers
and observed the mother–child interaction. Hypotheses about
intrapsychic conflict were formulated from these observational data.
While fathers were observed during occasional visits to the center,
interviews, and home visits, the data on the father–child relationship are in no way comparable to data on the mother–child relationship.[2]

A brief follow-up study was conducted in 1973 during the children's
latency period, and in 1988 the adult follow-up study was begun.[3] The
follow-up study has included series of unstructured, clinical interviews
with the original subjects and psychological testing of the subjects
and their mothers. It needs to be emphasized that the follow-up data
are quite different in quantity and quality from the early data, which
were based on daily observations collected by multiple observers and
examined carefully in weekly research conferences. In contrast, the
follow-up data have been collected by single observers, and the
amount of contact with the subjects have been varied and limited according to the circumstances of each individual's life.

There is a vast time span that has not been covered by our research. Even though children and parents were seen in a brief follow-up study during latency, we do not have ongoing observations of
the lived experience of our subjects and their parents during their
later childhood, adolescence, and eventually separation from home.
While there is a danger of relating early material directly to adult
life without observing the important developmental reorganization
during latency and adolescence, it is nevertheless of interest to see if
meaningful connections can be made between observed early experience and identity themes in adult life. We are looking to see if in the
adult personality organization patterns remain that were observed
early on in the mother–child interactions and if formative early experiences can be identified.

We want to emphasize the importance of the observational data
collected during the preverbal period. Since this period is usually

---

2. Fortunately a great deal of work has been done on the father–child relationship
   subsequently (see, for example, Cath et al. 1982, 1989).
3. Follow-up studies supported by the Rock Foundation: John McDevitt, Principal
   Investigator; Anni Bergman, Co-Principal Investigator.

inaccessible through memory or even psychoanalytic reconstruction, subjects in the adult follow-up would not be expected to remember what was observed. It is therefore of special interest to see if themes that emerge from the observation of the earliest relationship play out in adult life. The fact that we have extensive, detailed observations, both participant and nonparticipant, of mother–child interactions during the preverbal period gives us a rare avenue for studying the influence of these earliest interactions on adult life.

Modern developmental research has shown that the infant is not a passive recipient of caretaking: from the beginning each infant brings into the world her own unique way of responding to and interacting with the caretaking other. These early interactions are like a *cantus firmus* upon which each person composes her life with endless elaboration and variation. A *cantus firmus* is "a 'fixed' song or melody . . . commonly adopted by a composer for contrapuntal treatment. A tune used as a *cantus firmus* remained unaltered in one voice while the other parts proceeded independently. It was as a rule sung in long notes against quicker motion in the counterpoint, with the result that it usually moved so slowly as to become unrecognizable in performance" (*Grove's Dictionary of Music and Musicians* 1954). It is because the *cantus firmus* can become unrecognizable as the counterpoint is built around it that we choose this metaphor. While we do not expect the early interactions between mother and baby to be obviously recognizable in the life of an adult, we shall look for how the earliest mother–child relationship is internalized and wonder how the composition of each person's life is built upon the melody of the earliest relationship.

Clinicians who have worked with mother–infant pairs have shown the significance of mothers' representations of their infants (see Brazelton and Cramer 1990, Fraiberg et al. 1975, Stern 1995). We shall look at how the mother's early representations of her baby translates into behaviors that influence the development of her child's sense of self. The original separation-individuation research was focused more on observing the developmental sequences in the infant and toddler than on the experience of the mother. Since this time, the contributions of attachment theorists have shown the importance of the mother's own attachment to her mother for the development of the mother–child relationship (Ainsworth et al. 1978, Main et al.

1989). Our data on the nature of the mother's attachment to her own mother are not universally available, since this information is based on what mothers revealed in unstructured interviews. The mother's representation of her child is understood better in some cases than in others, depending on how freely the individual mother shared her fantasies and how pressing these were for her. In our experience, it seemed that some mothers interpreted almost all of their child's behaviors in terms of their internal representation, whereas other mothers seemed freer to respond to even the young baby as a separate individual. However, even when mothers respond to the baby as a separate individual, often characteristics are emphasized that confirm the representation, that is, the internal needs of the mother.

One of the unique aspects of the observational separation-individuation research was the emphasis on both longitudinal and cross-sectional methods: individual mother–child pairs were observed over time, and observations of mother–child pairs were continuously compared with each other. These comparisons were a natural outgrowth of the very design of the research in its playground-like setting, where several mother–child pairs were always present. The comparative aspects of the original research, from which patterns in the mother–child dyad emerged, allowed for the formulation of the theory of subphases of the separation-individuation process. We have found in working with the data of the follow-up study that comparing mother–child pairs has proven to be a fruitful method for generating ideas about the continuities between early relationship patterns and conflicts and later compromise formations.

It is important to remember that while the original study focused on the interaction between mother and child, the emphasis was always on the separation-individuation process in the child. In the adult follow-up, the emphasis is even more strongly on the child, now a young adult. We are studying the ways in which early patterns have been internalized and absorbed into the adult personality structure, and we are studying the continuing relationship between the child–now-young-adult and her mother. Our knowledge of the mother herself and the motivating forces that moved her to relate to her child in a particular way is not available with the same clinical richness. However, it should be remembered that observations of mothers and children and interviews of the mothers were conducted by psychoanalysts who were concerned always with understanding the meanings of what they saw and heard.

In examining the data collected on two mother–daughter pairs during the separation-individuation process and during the follow-up studies, we shall be guided by the following questions: (1) How is each mother's representation of her daughter internalized into each woman's own sense of self? (2) How has the mother's representation of her daughter either facilitated or interfered with the process of separation-individuation? (3) In what way is each woman's current relationship to her family, especially to her mother, continuous or discontinuous with the relationship she had had with her mother during the first three years of life? (4) How is the way in which each woman thinks of her mother related to the relationship noted in our early observations of the separation-individuation process? (5) What part do internalization and identification play in the resolution of the rapprochement crisis and the attainment of emotional object and self constancy?

Helen and Her Mother:
From Separation-Individuation to Adulthood

The First Three Years

Helen and her mother started to attend the center when Helen was just over a year old. Helen was an attractive, sturdy, little girl who was unusually competent for her age. She walked and climbed very well and was active but cautious. Her language development was precocious: she already said many words quite clearly. At the center Helen was very social, which her mother attributed to having taken her everywhere without Helen showing any stranger anxiety. One observer described Helen's effect on him:

> I had first seen Helen when she just turned 13 months. Her effect on me was almost immediate and very profound. I realized after some time I had surrendered a certain observational distance. Instead I felt myself captivated and in a state of great pleasure, sympathy, and almost complete admiration for this phenomenal little creature. The energy and vigor of the pretty little child's activity was indeed a joy

to watch. There was a contrast between this child and her mother, who sat very quietly and seemed rather shy.

Helen was able to let her mother know what she wanted, and her mother was responsive. Mrs. H. described Helen as an easy baby who had never slept much during the day. She had not been breast-fed, which Mrs. H. explained in a characteristically matter-of-fact way by saying that she had not been encouraged to do so in the hospital. Mrs. H. emphasized that Helen was a very independent child and had never liked to be held closely as a baby. Observers noted that Mrs. H. responded well to verbal cues. Thus, we might speculate that this mother–child pair created a holding environment in keeping with the mother's predilection that the child be competent and independent and not need much physical closeness. Mrs. H.'s wish that her daughter be self-sufficient may have been connected to her own struggles and some unconscious realization that she, in fact, could not fully fulfill herself because she was still longing for closeness to her own mother, which was not available. Mrs. H. was the oldest of three daughters and talked far more about her father than about her mother. The wish for a caretaking mother was enacted by the way in which Mrs. H. attended the center: she came regularly four times a week and always arrived early. Arriving before the other mothers and children assured her and her daughter special attention. Her own need for attention was channeled through the needs of Helen, who, she said, had difficulty occupying herself at home.

This mother's representation of her first child, a girl for whom she had wished, seemed to be an idealized version of her own self. While Mrs. H. dressed herself in a manner that played down her looks, Helen always came to our group in very pretty little girl clothes Mrs. H. made for her. Mrs. H. may have put her own wishes to be admired into Helen. She emphasized that Helen had no favorite toy or blanket and said that she could remove any toy at home without Helen missing it. However, at the center Helen quickly attached herself to a teddy bear almost as large as herself, which she liked to carry around. Was this teddy bear a representation of mother? Or was the teddy bear a representation of herself to whom she played mother? It seems that the center, where others related to both mother and child, provided enough separation between them to allow for the creation of a transitional object (Gaddini and Gaddini 1970).

Mrs. H. rarely talked about her husband. Later on, she told an interviewer that she had married when she first started college, which was when her own parents had moved abroad. Perhaps after the abrupt separation from her own family, it was important to Mrs. H. to replace her family with a baby of her own. Mrs. H. was so gratified by her little girl, with whom she so strongly identified, that she may not have left room for another person—or even a transitional object—to become really important to Helen. An observer noted the pride this mother took in her child. It seemed to him that the child filled the mother's life and that the mother–child pair gave the impression of amazing self-sufficiency. This appearance of self-sufficiency, however, existed at the center, where they did not have to be self-sufficient. In fact, Mrs. H. had said that she liked to arrive to the center early because she found it difficult to be home alone with Helen. Through Helen, Mrs. H. was able to receive some of the mothering she had missed.

By the time Helen was 15 months old, Helen's father's work took him abroad. At this time, Helen developed a sleep disturbance: she woke up several times each night, her mother unable to comfort her. At the center, a marked change in the child was noticed. Helen started to play bye-bye games and became very alert to people's comings and goings. During the same period she became listless and fatigued, a strong contrast to her former boundless energy. She began to fall more frequently and was generally irritable; she cried a lot and ran to her mother for comforting. Helen demanded food, such as cookies and pretzels and juice. The male observer who had been so captivated by her noted that her former ability to command a response from others seemed to be replaced by an almost desperate appeal for attention and that the feeling of pleasure and joy in her performance was no longer there. Helen became more aware of being wet or soiled, which made her uncomfortable. While Mrs. H. did not talk about her own feelings about her husband's absence, she often stated that Helen didn't really miss her father. A contradiction emerges here between Mrs. H.'s feeling that she and Helen filled each other's worlds completely and Helen's strong reaction to her father's absence.

During this period Mrs. H. talked about her own childhood, especially about her father, a brilliant and successful man who had become severely ill early in his life, after which time he had been cared for by many people. Resentment of her father's need for caretaking by her mother and, as Mrs. H. often emphasized, by other women may have been a source of this mother's ambivalent feelings about caretaking. When Mrs. H. spoke of her college years, she said that she did not do as well as she might have because she felt that nobody was there to care whether she did well or not.

When talking about her husband's absence, Mrs. H. said it was better that he should be overseas rather than in a place where they could visit easily, which would only make it more difficult to adjust to the separation. Mrs. H. seemed to defend herself from the impact of her husband's absence on herself and her child, an absence compounded by the previous times in her life when she had felt abandoned—first by her father's critical illness and then by her family leaving while she was in college. In fact, Mrs. H. also may have been particularly sensitive to separations because she was the oldest of three sisters. Perhaps the feelings about separations that she would not allow herself to feel were expressed by Helen, who began to find separation from or sharing of mother unbearable. An observer wrote at this time:

> Helen has for the first time begun to show jealousy of Mother's attention to other children. She pushed another child off Mother's lap. When the mother was taken out of the room for an interview, Helen cried a lot; it was hard to quiet her. When Mother returned she did not go to her at once, but acted as though oblivious of Mother's presence.

How do we interpret Helen's behavior? The avoidance of her mother may have been an expression of her anger and a way of protecting herself from the pain of renewed separation. This reaction on Helen's part was comparable to her mother's decision not to visit her husband, a decision connected to not wanting to feel repeated pain over separation.

When Helen was around 16 months, observers noted that for the first time Helen's mother came to the center dressed up and wearing make-up. During the following months Mrs. H. continued to give more attention to her appearance than she had when she first came to the center, when all her efforts had been spent on dressing up Helen. It is significant that her attention to her own appearance coincides with a time when she could no longer derive as much gratification from admiring attention to Helen.

When Helen was 19 months, she was left for an afternoon with one of the other mothers, who had a little boy of the same age. Helen and this little boy were bathed together and the mother reported that upon seeing Jay's penis Helen had said that he had two belly buttons. Later she called the penis "Jay's birthmark," perhaps attempting to undo the anatomical difference because Helen, herself, had a birthmark in the genital area. At this same time Helen suffered extreme separation distress and cried a lot when she was left by her mother. On the other hand, she became almost phobic of her mother's efforts to pick her up or comfort her, efforts that resulted in outbursts of rage. We saw in Helen a fairly extreme early reaction to the anatomical difference, resulting in simultaneous need for her mother and rage-fear reactions toward her mother.[4]

Helen was frustrated easily, often breaking into tears. She consumed great quantities of juice, asking for it from all the adults who came into the room. Helen was happiest when she was at the center alone with her mother and the observers. Mrs. H. reported that Helen, who had begun to enjoy using the potty, now began to shun it. Helen's mother seemed very depressed and distraught and was not very attentive to Helen. She complained that Helen was impossible at home, with crying, temper tantrums, and what seemed like incomprehensible behavior. But what bothered her most was, as she put it, "Helen won't let me touch her." Although she accepted help from other adults, Helen would not allow her mother to dress her or put her on the toilet; however, Helen would scream for hours if mother left her with a friend. At the center Helen asked to be taken to the toilet and then refused to sit down. She seemed miserable under urinary pressure but would not wet herself or sit down on the toilet. At the center Helen became very aggressive toward the other children, especially by pulling their hair. She was unable to share her mother or any other adult. Even on better days Helen remained extremely sensitive to any deprivation, such as her mother talking on the telephone or a toy

---

4. This event inspired Roiphe's conceptualizations of the early genital phase, which he further researched with Galenson (Roiphe and Galenson 1981). Mahler (1972b) discusses the relation between castration anxiety and rapprochement.

being taken from her. She broke a crayon in half, then tried to put it together. When she could not, she broke into uncontrollable sobbing for forty-five minutes, from which her mother could not comfort her. While this kind of behavior is typical for children during the rapprochement crisis, it was particularly difficult for Helen and her mother. Helen's mother looked harassed and worn. Perhaps the rapprochement crisis, difficult for all mothers, was especially difficult for this mother because it ended the blissful period in which Helen's precocity matched her mother's representation of her as an idealized part of her own self.

As Helen came to some resolution of her rapprochement crisis she began to internalize her mother's prohibitions by saying, for example, that she should not pull hair. She also began to play with dolls: identification with the mother emerged as both playing mother who prohibits aggression and also playing mother who takes care of the child.[5]

As the rapprochement crisis waned, Helen's mother became sensitive to Helen's asking observers to do things for her. Mrs. H. said, "Now will come the time when she will prefer her teacher to her mother. That's all right, maybe Mrs. K. [an observer] will even take her home." Was Mrs. H. hurt by Helen's turning toward other adults as she recovered from the intense conflicts of the rapprochement crisis? Did she feel rejected because she could no longer be Helen's exclusive love object? Was it an expression of her resentment that Helen could now turn to others, whereas she had clung to mother when in the throes of the rapprochement crisis? Helen reacted sensitively to her mother's expression of feeling rejected by asking her to come over and join in a pretend meal. It may be that the rapprochement crisis was particularly hard for Mrs. H., not only because she had to weather it alone without the help of the father, but also because the demandingness of Helen may have evoked an unconscious memory of the abrupt ending of her own happy relationship with her father, who, when he became sick, became demanding of the mother and other women.

---

5. McDevitt (1997) has shown identification in another subject from this follow-up study as a way to resolve rapprochement conflicts. Furer (1967) and Arlow (1982) have written on the development of the early superego.

When Helen was 2 years old, her father returned, and Helen greeted him by saying, "Hi, Daddy." Mrs. H. said she was surprised that Helen seemed to have remembered her father during the whole year he was gone. Mrs. H. said that she expected Helen to have difficulty in accepting him, which may have been in part a projection onto Helen of what she herself was feeling about the reunion. In fact, Helen did not want to stay with him alone. Perhaps Helen's rejection of her father was in part an accommodation of her mother's wish for an exclusive attachment.

After her father returned, Helen became particularly interested in male observers and used imaginative ways of getting attention from them. An observer noted:

> When Dr. G. [a male observer] came into the room, Helen looked at him for a moment. She was holding the big baby doll, and immediately dropped it on the floor and gave it no further attention. She then started to play with various toys, always with one eye on Dr. G. Also, while she had been fairly quiet until then, she now started talking in a steady stream, accompanying whatever she did with various explanations. When she did not get Dr. G.'s attention, she did not directly clamor for it. She would go and find a new activity to impress him with. In this way she went from playing with the train to playing with the push toys. She then climbed on the window sill, and made up a story about being on the roof of the house and fixing the roof. She then was painting the roof; this reminded her of the sky and she told a story about being in an airplane and going way up into the sky, as she had done during the summer. From this she went to the active toys, such as the see-saw and the rocking boat. Being on the rocking boat set off further associations of swimming in the ocean and sailing a boat on waves.

What we seem to see here is that the return of the father gave Helen the opportunity to identify with him, both by playing out the male roles of fixing roofs and also by making up stories about going overseas. It is significant that Helen needed the attention of a male observer as she played, as if this part of herself could be inspired only by the presence of her father or a surrogate, namely the male observer.

At the same time Helen's identification with her mother continued, and she became absorbed in doll play, feeding the dolls and putting them to bed. Helen played with her teddy bear, put it to bed, and wondered if its head could come off. She then tried to get into bed with the teddy bear and said that it was Mommy's bed. Mother said that when she listened to Helen talking to her teddy bear, she could hear herself talk. Here we see Helen play mother to her teddy bear while she simultaneously wanted to be the baby in her mother's bed.

The return of Helen's father enriched her inner world, as demonstrated in her fantasy play where she could take both male and female roles. His return also necessitated a shift in Helen's sense of herself from being her mother's little girl to being a small child with a mother and a father (Abelin 1975). In her play, Helen experimented with taking different roles and at the same time attempted to come to terms with the reality of the new family constellation. Not surprisingly, this transition was difficult for her, and she became increasingly sensitive to being left by mother. She refused to stay with either a babysitter or her father, yet she wanted to walk in the street without holding her mother's hand.

Around this time, Helen's mother reported a dream in which she had to take an exam, but Helen had taken the exam instead of her and had made a few mistakes. Mrs. H. explained to her professor that it was natural for Helen to make mistakes because she did not yet know the letters. This dream reflects Mrs. H.'s identification with Helen and her fear that Helen might not be able to do well enough in school. At the time when Mrs. H. herself had expected to move out into the world to go to college, her parents moved away, and she stayed behind. Mrs. H. often connected her indifference to doing well academically with having felt abandoned by her parents at that point in her life. Mrs. H.'s fears about Helen's moving out into the world were confirmed by Helen's difficult transition to nursery school. Perhaps the combination of Mrs. H.'s feeling that she was abandoning her daughter to school and also abandoning her exclusive relationship to Helen by having a new baby made it difficult for her to support her daughter's transition to school.

At the time Mrs. H. reported this dream, Helen expressed her own concerns about growing up. For example, observers heard Helen say that when she "will be a mommy, her mommy will be her baby." She also talked about being "a little mommy and growing up to be a big mommy." Helen said that when she "will be big," her mother "will be little," and that she would "grow to be a baby again." Helen expressed some resentment of her father's presence, telling him to "go away again." Thus, at the time of ever-increasing awareness of the inevitable separateness, both Helen and her mother expressed some regressive desire for exclusive attachment. Helen resisted the inevitable separateness in her omnipotent fantasies in which she could undo who she was: she would be a baby or a mommy, but not a little girl who had to face the world. In her play, she alternately identified with mother or with baby. For example, when mother left the room, she filled a bottle with water and said that she would give it to the baby. Then she started to drink from it herself, gurgling and cooing, lying down in the crib and drinking the water from the bottle.

When Helen was 29½ months old, her mother announced that she was four months pregnant. She was very worried about Helen and said, "Helen will be three; it will be just around her birthday. Helen won't like a new baby for a birthday present." Mother talked about the wonderful, special baby that Helen had been, already very interesting when she was only 5 months old. Being the first of three children herself, Mrs. H. knew how the birth of a second child forever undoes the special position of being the only one.[6]

At the center Helen demanded the exclusive attention of observers. She was furious when other children were included in a game of ring-around-the-rosy. At story time Helen pushed away the other children and insisted on sitting on the observer's lap. Later that day, she played on the couch with a little boy, pretending it was a ferry boat. They had a big doll between them and both said that it was their baby. They argued about whether the baby was a boy or a girl. Finally, when her playmate took the doll, Helen had a tantrum and cried, "He's taking my baby away." She was inconsolable for the rest of the morning. One wonders if Helen was expressing feelings about

---

6. The powerful and lasting effect of a new sibling on the oldest child can be seen in the response of a young adolescent to the death of his dog. This boy, who was one-and-a-half years older than his younger brother, blamed the accidental death of his dog, who had been in his family for most of his life, on a visit by a new puppy of his grandparents, which had occurred several days before the accident. He said that his beloved dog had run away and gotten run over because he was upset by the new puppy being brought into his house.

the return of her father or if she was expressing a fear that the arrival of the new baby would take her mother away from her. Perhaps she connected the return of the father with the birth of a new baby.

A few days later, Helen sang the song "The Farmer in the Dell," but changed the words to "the hunter shot the mommy." (Helen used to cry at the story of baby Babar being left when the hunter shoots the mommy.) The song "The Farmer in the Dell" is a song about procreation and coupling, at the end of which "the cheese stands alone." What was Helen expressing by singing the tune to "The Farmer in the Dell" with words about baby Babar being left when the hunter shoots the mommy? Was she blaming her daddy for hunting her mommy, which would leave her alone when the new baby arrives? This echoes Helen's distress when her little boy playmate took the baby doll. Helen began to show marked jealousy and aggression toward all babies. The exclusivity of Helen's union with her mother during her father's absence heightened her feelings about the mother–father union, soon to produce a new baby.

Helen began to reject her father despite his special efforts to give her attention. She said, "I don't want to have a daddy. I want to sleep in Mommy's bed and I don't want Daddy to sleep with Mommy." At the same time she said to her mother, "I will prick you with my scissors and then I won't have a mommy any more. Will it hurt? Will you cry?" (Here she becomes the hunter.) She also told her mother to go home from the center without her: "I will stay here and then you won't have a little girl any more." We can see that Helen was struggling with oedipal conflicts, both negative and positive, and that these oedipal conflicts were strongly tinged by the particular relationship with her mother. At the same time, Helen developed an intense conflict about giving up her bottle. Though she cried out in her sleep wanting the bottle, when her mother offered it she refused it. Helen wanted both to remain her mother's baby and to take her mother's place.

Helen's relationship to her father began to change. Whereas earlier she had tried to send him away, one day she said, "My daddy is a boy. He's not a man. He's a big boy." Then she said she was glad to have a daddy and she liked him. Mother heard her say to a family friend on the telephone, "Someday my mommy will go away, and then I will sleep with my daddy." Helen began to develop some uncomfortable guilty feelings, demonstrated by her blaming others when she did something she was not supposed to do. Along with these advances into oedipal development, both Helen and her mother expressed longings for the earlier baby time. Helen pretended to be a baby needing her diapers changed, and her mother remarked that since toilet training Helen missed being diapered. At home Helen was moody, which Mother thought had to do with trying to give up the bottle. Helen had some bad dreams from which she woke up crying. Once she asked her mother, "Why did you break the roll?" referring to an incident the day before when mother had broken a roll that Helen had wanted to be whole. At this time of oedipal conflict and the expectation of a new baby, the nightmare about the roll broken by the mother can be seen as a regressive recall of the rapprochement crisis, which had been exacerbated by the absence of the father and the observation of the anatomical difference. Around the time of Helen's dream, mother remembered how possessive she had felt about Helen after she was born, not wanting anyone else to touch her, and she expressed worries about who would take care of Helen when she had to go to the hospital for the birth of her new child.

At the age of 31 months Helen had given up the bottle at night, but still asked for it during the day. Her mother reported that she was very nice to her dolls, but "mean and rotten" to real babies. Helen said, "What would happen if somebody ate up all the candy in the candy store and there was none left and the candy store people would cry?" Is Helen worried about the new baby eating up everything? Or is it she who will eat up all the candy so there won't be any left for the baby or her mother? Helen became sick with a very high fever again, and her mother was worried that she might have a convulsion. She sat up with her all night. Helen had several bottles and cried out of her sleep, "I don't want the bottle. I don't want the cup. I don't want the glass." When she woke up she was very upset and rejected her mother. Finally, she got into bed with her mother and had a bottle. Helen, who still had not been told by her mother about the pregnancy, asked many questions. "Where was I when you were a little girl? Was I big when you were little?" After talking to Helen about the new baby, Mrs. H. said that Helen was looking forward to it and played the devoted mother to her teddy bears. Mother still did not talk to Helen about the baby being inside her body because she thought it would be disturbing to her. This demonstrates once again

Mrs. H.'s own regret that she would be disturbing the union between herself and her little girl through the advent of a new child.

Further Development and Adulthood

Helen's transition from the research center to nursery school was difficult for both her and her mother. Mrs. H. had just given birth to Helen's baby brother, who required a lot of attention. Helen transferred the possessive, clinging relationship she had with her mother to the nursery school teachers, from whom she demanded exclusive attention, reacting to the other children as rivals. Mother was concerned that Helen was not treated well enough by her teachers, and thus this first contact with the outside world of school turned out to be difficult for both mother and child. This outcome is interesting in light of Mrs. H.'s comment early on that the time would come when Helen would prefer her teachers to her mother. Did Mrs. H.'s need for Helen's exclusive attachment to her inhibit Helen's ability to become a member of her new nursery school "family"? Helen's difficult transition to school was a disillusionment for her mother because it contradicted her early image of Helen. Mrs. H. began to feel a sense of doom and failure. Helen's difficulties continued to some extent throughout her school years and became especially exacerbated during her early adolescence, when she and her family moved; Helen was extremely shy and had difficulty making friends. Many of her teachers reported that she did not live up to her academic potential.

During her adult interviews, Helen did not speak about her difficult adolescence. In describing her college experience, she said that she had done well, but did not describe her experience as exciting or remarkable. After college, when Helen could not find a job she wanted, she decided to go to graduate school and entered a masters program in rehabilitation. She described her field as one she had fallen into more than one she had actively sought. In this way Helen was similar to her mother, who always stressed her own lack of academic ambition, even though she had attended an excellent college. During the follow-up interviews, Helen underplayed the importance of her professional choice, but in fact she had become quite successful in her field. Helen's style of appearing casual about important decisions is congruent with her mother's style and contrasts sharply to

Helen as a child, who did not easily accept disappointment and was especially sensitive to needing exclusive attention from adults. One wonders when this shift occurred and whether it was connected to leaving home.

After Helen received her master's degree, she began to work in a program that trained people with serious disabilities to make the transition from institutional to mainstream living. This training in basic living skills was intensive, on the job, on a one-to-one basis, echoing perhaps her early desire to be in exclusive relationships with others. Helen rose quickly to become a creator and administrator of these programs, but even in this position she did not seem to appreciate fully the importance of the contribution she was making to the field. Helen was not entirely happy in her professional activities and hoped to continue her studies. Her career in helping severely disabled adults learn to function in the outside world may have allowed her to play the mothering role her mother had had such difficulty playing for her, namely helping her to function in the outside world.

Helen married a man she met at work. He had lost both his parents early in life and had very little family of his own. By marrying a man with little family, Helen may have fulfilled her childhood longing for an exclusive relationship with her mother. She described her husband as someone with whom she got along very well. She also described him as a moody person, and she described how she was able to tolerate and handle his moods: "His moods are unpredictable. When he gets moody, I just sort of let him." Thus, Helen unconsciously played the role of mother to the moody child she herself had been. Helen made the impression of being quite stable in her own moods and not being easily upset; one might wonder if she allowed him to express the moody side of her.

Helen talked quite a bit about the house in which she and her husband lived, an old house they had fixed up together. She described how hard they had had to work and described in detail stripping layers and layers of paint and wallpaper from the walls. The renovating of their old house is of particular interest in connection to her description of how the house in which her husband had grown up had been completely neglected and eventually torn down. She sounded quite burdened by all she had to do, but she liked her house and she liked gardening, an interest she shared with her mother. The theme

of rehabilitation in Helen's adult life is significant because, in helping people function in the outside world, Helen is doing for others
what her mother could not do for her. It is of further significance
that Helen shares this profession with her husband and that she
shares the burden and pleasure of renovating an old house with him,
as if to say it takes two to accomplish such a task.

Helen described her pleasure in her garden and how she and her
mother enjoyed looking at gardening catalogs together. Helen's
mother sometimes visited and helped Helen with gardening. She
enjoyed her mother's visits and described how well her mother got
along with her husband. She felt it was good for her mother to take
a break from taking care of the family—Helen's father and brothers.
Helen's pleasure in her garden and her sharing of this pleasure with
her mother seemed to be an area of unconflicted gratification for
Helen. By working on her garden together with her mother, Helen
seemed to be able to refind her early mother, for whom she was the
admirable little girl.

We shall now present somewhat more briefly another mother–
daughter pair for comparison and contrast.

Karen and Her Mother:
From Separation-Individuation to Adulthood

The First Three Years

Karen and her mother first came to the center when Karen was almost 1 year old. Karen, an attractive, well-endowed little girl, was
described by observers as listless, often sitting quietly in one place,
crawling only to mother and then pulling herself up on mother's chair
to be near her. Mrs. K. had difficulty taking pleasure in Karen. Nonetheless, Karen responded well as soon as her mother paid attention
to her: her face would light up and she would become much more
active. When Karen was 1 year old she actively missed her mother:
she cried and crawled to the door when her mother left the room.
Karen was clearly very attached to her mother but was inhibited in
her capacity for exploration and autonomous functioning.

Karen was the second child; the first was a boy. Her mother had
stated openly that she had not wanted a girl because she felt that

girls were fated to be unhappy, preoccupied with their looks and with the need to be thin to please men. From the beginning, Karen's mother worried about her daughter's appearance and projected her own feelings about the burdens of womanhood onto her little girl. Karen's mother was conflicted about mothering a daughter, yet at the same time she longed for unconditional love from her, a love she felt she had never received from her own mother. Thus, Mrs. K. was observed to be extremely sensitive to what she experienced as rejection by her little girl. For example, when Karen became attached to her father, Mrs. K. said, "Karen wants no part of me. On the weekends she just wants to see her father. I can't be expected to start taking care of her on Monday mornings." Here we see how sensitive Mrs. K. was to any sign that her daughter did not love her enough; perhaps Mrs. K. needed Karen's love to repair the pain of not having been loved enough by her own mother.

When Karen was 13 months old she began to walk, to point, and to say some words. She showed interest in her clothes and knew where her dresses and shoes were kept. Mrs. K. was a very well-dressed woman. Karen's early interest in clothes not only demonstrates her identification with her mother, but also her wish to please her mother. In fact, during this time Mrs. K. was able to be more responsive to Karen. Unfortunately, soon thereafter Karen had an accident in the park: she was standing right next to her mother when she slipped and fell and cut her forehead badly. Mrs. K. took her to the hospital, where she had to have stitches. She described how she was very close to fainting herself and could hardly stop herself from crying. She feared that if she had started to cry, she would never have stopped. Mrs. K.'s reaction to her daughter's accident demonstrates her need for Karen to repair her own feelings of vulnerability. It was almost as if Mrs. K. was so afraid of this vulnerability that she projected it onto her daughter and then maintained a strict distance from her. The traumatic event of this accident precipitated a crisis of separation for Karen. When her mother was out of the room, Karen was inconsolable: she could not take comfort from anything or anybody and even refused ice cream, which she usually loved. It is interesting that Karen became so inconsolable when her mother had felt such a dread of being inconsolable herself. In this way Karen demonstrated an extraordinary degree of empathy for her mother's pain. Mrs. K. reacted by becoming further withdrawn from her daughter, thereby distancing herself from her overly strong identification with her little girl.

Following summer vacation, Karen was 18 months old and in the midst of rapprochement conflicts. Her crisis took the form of clinging to her mother, seemingly an attempt to coerce her mother to fill her emotional needs. Karen was constantly aware of her mother's presence, and any attention from the observers was experienced as a threat to the wished-for closeness with mother; even being looked at by an observer would result in Karen's running to her mother. We see here a kind of splitting, in which contact with the mother is perceived as good and wished for, whereas contact with the outside world is perceived as bad and to be warded off. At this point Karen's exclusive need for her mother made her unable to take advantage of the other available resources.

One day Mrs. K. came to the center elegantly dressed, wearing jewelry and make-up, and complained that Karen had no clothes and that she would have to go shopping for her. In fact, observers often noted a discrepancy in Mrs. K.'s careful attention to her own appearance and relative lack of attention to Karen's. Mrs. K. related the story of a hysterical crying attack Karen had had one night during the summer. She had been so upset that she was shaking, and mother had been afraid that Karen was having a nervous breakdown from which she would never recover. Just as during Karen's accident she was afraid she would have cried forever if she had let herself begin to cry, we again see Mrs. K.'s projection of her own vulnerability onto Karen. It is significant that Mrs. K. told this story on a day when she presented herself as a woman of the world, quite a contrast to a woman who needed a little girl to make her feel whole.

Despite her mother's inattentiveness, Karen continued to seek closeness to her mother. She would stand close to her mother, look into her face, pat her from time to time, and ask to be rocked on her foot. Whenever she got closer to mother, she could then tolerate attention from observers. Karen could be available for attention from others when she felt more secure with her mother.

Around the age of 19 months, Mrs. K. began to toilet train Karen and was able to take more interest in her daughter. Characteristically, Karen's positive reaction to her mother's attention was almost immediate. Mrs. K. began to dress her daughter in more attractive clothes, and Karen started to look in the mirror. By the age of 20 months, Karen began fantasy play, placing dolls around a table with cups and saucers. She became more friendly to observers and was able to let her mother leave the room without clinging or crying. Thus, there seems to have been a resolution of the intense earlier crisis, which was helped by her beginning symbolic play in which she could enact a happy family. Toilet training proceeded well. Karen began to identify with her mother and played flirtatiously with a male observer. She liked to dress up and enjoyed putting on observers' jewelry, which she showed off to her mother. Karen also played a game that she had learned from her brother. Thus, identification with her mother and also her older brother seems to have helped in the resolution of this rapprochement crisis.

The relatively blissful period of positive rapprochement and sharing between Karen and her mother ended when Karen was 22 months old and Mrs. K. announced she was four months pregnant. Karen became demanding, asking her mother for specific things rather than just for her presence. Battles of will began that eventually focused on the issue of toilet training, which earlier on had been a positive shared experience. Karen became frequently constipated and at times would not go to the bathroom for three to four days.

Karen began to seek her mother's attention in negative ways and to oppose actively her mother's suggestions. Of particular importance was a behavior that seems to have been the origin of a pattern that continued in Karen's adolescence and into adulthood. Karen began to be more adventurous, climbing up to dangerous places in spite of her mother's admonitions. This behavior, in which Karen would endanger herself and Mrs. K. would have to come to her rescue, assured her of her mother's attention. It also, however, can be seen as a literal enactment of Karen's intrapsychic conflict, namely that Karen's separateness from mother was inhibited by the simultaneous need to cling to her.

During Karen's third year, the struggles continued. When Karen was 30 months old, her mother said, "Karen is driving me crazy." She described a visit to the paternal grandparents during which Karen had cried, clung to her, and not allowed her to "do anything, even speak to the relatives." At the center Karen had difficulty staying in

the toddler room without her mother, but when with her mother continued to fight and struggle with her. This was different from the
time at which Karen had clung to her mother but was always accepting of any attention her mother offered her.

At the climax of Karen's struggles with her mother, which took
the form of severe constipation, Karen revealed a fantasy during a
play session at the center: she said, "I have a horsie in my stomach."
Karen became very attached to a little toy horse that she took home
from the center, kept under her bed, and did not allow anyone to
touch. Earlier on, observers had noted Karen's attachment to the
rocking horse in the playroom, which she often sat on for long periods and refused to let other children use. It may be that this rocking
horse represented the mother from whom she did not want to separate. Perhaps sitting on the rocking horse provided her with feelings
of comfort that she did not get enough of from her mother, who held
her only rarely. In addition, rocking on the play horse must have
provided her with genital stimulation, as did the withholding of stool
and urine. In taking possession of the little toy horse and not letting
go of it, the horse became a kind of transitional object. It may have
represented the attachment to mother—the big rocking horse—as well
as a primitive identification with mother, who she said had a baby
in her stomach like Karen had a horsie in her stomach. The difficulty in separating from mother became an unconscious fantasy in
which having mother and being mother are merged. This kind of
identification with mother could not help Karen to resolve her rapprochement struggles: if Karen's identification with her pregnant
mother took the form of not wanting to relinquish her bowel movement—the horsie in her stomach—this identification was tainted by
the conflict. Eventually Karen would have to relinquish her bowel
movement and with that the fantasy that she, like mother, could have
a baby. Karen's mother's negative feelings about being a woman made
it difficult for her to soften her daughter's disappointment. However,
once the baby was born, Karen actively participated with mother in
caring for the new baby, a pleasurable activity for both of them.
Karen's new identification with mother's care for the new baby and
with the cared-for baby ameliorated their conflicts.

Because the representation of her girl child was both negative and
narrow, Karen's mother could not be steadily emotionally available

during her daughter's separation-individuation process. Fluctuations in her availability had an effect on all aspects of the separation-individuation process and made it difficult for Karen to achieve an identity separate enough from her mother to gratify her own needs. Karen, who was an intelligent and attractive girl, eventually could find satisfactions in her life apart from mother, but carried the burdensome aspects of the bond with her mother into her adult object relations.

Further Development and Adulthood

Although the problems of her conflicted relationship with mother continued in her preschool years, Karen was able to make a good adjustment to nursery school. Her play was rich and imaginative; her concentration was outstanding; her language was very articulate; and her ability to get along with other children and teachers was quite satisfactory. In follow-up school visits, observers remarked on the liveliness of Karen's expression and manner, which they contrasted to her subdued and sad mood at the center. Karen seemed to have found in nursery school a safe and enjoyable haven from turbulent family relationships. Her problem with constipation persisted in spite of medication, and it continued to be a battleground between her and her mother. In fact, Karen told an observer who inquired about why she didn't go to the bathroom that not having a bowel movement made her mother angry. The constipation was also painful to Karen and contained layers of fantasy connected with birth and death: upon seeing a dead bird, she wondered if the bird might have died while having a bowel movement. At times Karen expressed a negative self-image, saying that nobody liked her and that she did not like herself. She identified strongly with her older brother and at times wanted to wear only boys' clothes. Karen's ability to make good use of her school experience and her identification with others enabled her to grow despite the difficulties in the relationship with her mother.

When talking about her mother in the adult interviews, Karen said how carefully and well her mother had chosen all her schools and how important her school experiences had been. While Mrs. K. could not be sufficiently attentive to Karen's needs herself, she had enough

awareness of her own difficulties with Karen to know that life outside would be important and that she could provide nurturing school
settings. Not surprisingly, Karen chose to become a teacher and found
great satisfaction from this profession. School reports during Karen's
latency and adolescent years always emphasized her intelligence and
creativity. However, by the time she got to high school, Karen's personal difficulties began to interfere, exacerbated by the trauma of her
parents' divorce during this period. In the adult interview, Karen
described unsatisfactory relationships with boyfriends, who were demanding and not appreciative and respectful of her. Karen described
how the painful turbulence of her adolescence quieted when she
started a college well suited to her, at which time she also began
therapy. Being in therapy brought her closer to her father, who also
entered therapy at the time, partly because of his concern for Karen.
Karen left her boyfriend, who she felt was unwilling to make the
relationship work. Here we see how, while Mrs. K.'s representation
of her daughter seems to have influenced her difficulties in relationships to others and to herself, Karen's experience of her mother as
someone who could help her find support outside the family—as she
did by choosing good schools—became an important theme in her life
as she continued to find support for herself outside the nuclear family, both in relationships to extended family and in her wish to be
helped by and to be helpful to others.

The year after she finished college, Karen moved away from home,
supported herself doing office work, and eventually started graduate
school in education. She shared a home with her younger sister, who
attended the same graduate program. Karen described her close relationship with her sister, and said that she liked the fact that she
and her sister could talk about everything and share their experiences. Then she said, "We rely on each other too much. We're always
together, we always do things together, and we both feel that we need
to break away because we're not helping each other get boyfriends,
because we just sit around and talk all the time. Maybe we have
physical needs, but we don't have mental needs as much as somebody else might because we can fulfill that for each other." While
Karen derived comfort and stability from sharing her life with her
sister at that time, she longed for a satisfying relationship with an
intimate other.

Karen had difficulty thinking of herself as an attractive young woman, and she was especially troubled both by her tendency to be overweight and with her mother's continuing preoccupation with her weight and weight in general.

While Karen was very well aware of the burdensome aspects of her relationship with her mother, she nevertheless spent time with her and was compassionate toward her. Eventually Karen moved away from her sister, which she experienced as a very positive step. While Karen had wanted to move away from her sister, the internal experience of the separation may still have been one of being abandoned by a maternal object. She once again became involved in a relationship with a man that turned out to be destructive to her. However, Karen felt a strong pull to stay with this boyfriend and work on the relationship. This pull reflected an omnipotent fantasy that if she tried hard enough, she could make any relationship work. It also reflected a sense of being the one at fault, a continuity of Karen's old dilemma with her mother, where the origins of and responsibilities for the difficulties and conflicts in their relationship could not have been clear to her as a child.

While Mrs. K.'s early representation of Karen as a little girl contained her sense of the burdens of being female, it also contained a sense of herself as being inadequate in fulfilling Karen's needs. The compensation Mrs. K. found for this by providing good other sources for furthering Karen's development has continued to be an important asset to Karen's life. During the follow-up interviews Karen was, of all the subjects, the most open and the most willing to share her internal world. In fact she appreciated the interviews and thought that they had been quite helpful to her. Karen's use of the follow-up interviews is another example of how she learned to turn to the outside world for support, and it eventually became possible to help her get good therapeutic help, which she seems to have been able to use well. It is interesting to note that Karen's mother eventually did start a new career that was fulfilling to her.

Discussion

We have discussed the development of Helen and Karen during separation-individuation and early adulthood. We will now briefly review and compare their development, keeping in mind the questions raised at the beginning of the paper.

Helen's mother saw in Helen an ideal little girl who she could present for the world's admiration with pride. Helen and her mother were an uneven couple in which Helen was attractive, vital, and admirable, whereas her mother appeared very quiet and withdrawn. They functioned well as a couple as long as the child could shine, possibly enacting the idealized and wished-for part of the mother's self representation. In contrast, Karen's mother saw in Karen a little girl who would have to suffer her whole life the burdens of being female, which meant having to please men and to deny her own pleasures and satisfactions. Karen's mother could not present her daughter for the admiration of the observers. Karen and her mother were also an uneven couple, almost the mirror image of Helen and her mother. Whereas Helen's mother seemed to receive gratification from the observers' admiration of her daughter, Karen's mother's seemed in need of admiration herself and was unable to obtain narcissistic supplies from admiration of her daughter. Karen's mother's outlook on the life of a woman seemed to make her feel doomed as the mother of a girl.

While Helen's mother was able to experience fulfillment for narcissistic wishes through the birth of her baby girl, Karen's mother could not experience such satisfaction from her daughter. When Helen had difficulties, her mother tended to deny them or be overwhelmed by them. Karen's mother, on the other hand, defended against the effect of Karen's troubles on her by distancing herself. During Karen's rapprochement crisis, however, when she was confronted with Karen's intense need for her, she rallied to be more available. In contrast, the appearance of Helen's rapprochement struggles interrupted the mother's representation of the ideal mother–daughter couple, which made it difficult for Helen's mother to be emotionally available to her.

In considering how this early mother–child interaction affected Helen's self representation, we see a little girl who started out life exuberant and confident become demanding, clinging, and aggressive, and who later on had difficulty getting along with people outside the family, such as teachers and peers. Her father's absence further narrowed the range of people to whom Helen could relate and with whom she could identify. The birth of two brothers further strained the representation of her as her mother's special child. During her second year the discovery of the anatomical difference was particularly difficult for her. Helen remained vulnerable to disappointments and perceived failures.

In contrast, Karen started out lacking in motivation and confidence. She did, however, turn to her father and to her brother for stimulation and identification, and later on she was able to turn to people outside the family, such as teachers and friends at school. In addition she benefited from identifying with her mother caring for her baby sister, and also with her baby sister as she received her mother's love and care during early babyhood. At school Karen was able to develop her interests and creativity and find appreciation for them.

When Helen and Karen began to be interviewed, they were close to the age of 30. They had both graduated from college and were living on their own at varying distances from their parents. Helen was married, and while both Helen and Karen had professions, neither was yet completely settled in her professional life. Both Helen and Karen kept in fairly regular contact with their families.

As an adult Helen had made a good adjustment and was able to create a life for herself that included marriage and a profession. Her relationship to her family of origin showed appropriate concern, neither overinvolved nor uncaring. Difficulties of her early life, particularly in the mother–child relationship, were not recalled by her. Helen retained a special relationship with her mother that was reminiscent of her wish for an exclusive relationship with mother early on: she liked her mother to come and visit her and her husband, and enjoyed being with her. Gardening was the activity she most liked to share with her mother. Helen felt these visits were beneficial for her mother as well as for herself.

As an adult Karen still struggled with unsatisfying relationships and was not satisfied with herself. She was, however, able to enjoy her work and activities with friends. What was striking about Karen as an adult was her energetic search and hopefulness about being able to create a healthy life for herself. Karen retained a close relationship with her younger sister, harking back to the time when Karen had been able to benefit from her mother's love and care for her new baby sister.

Helen seemed to have renounced the liveliness apparent at the beginning and seemed to suppress her disappointments and experience her resentments in an impersonal way—against fate rather than anyone in particular. She did not express her affects very strongly, probably an identification with her mother, who was always understated and undemanding. While Helen had made a more stable adjustment than Karen, finding a home and relationship, she seemed to be less open to new experiences and to reflection about herself. Karen, on the other hand, continued to go through a great deal of turbulence, but was actively searching for her place in the world, for meaningful work, and for close relationships. Helen seems to have identified with a somewhat depressed mother who never quite got from life what she deserved.

As an adult Karen continued to be burdened by the difficulties in her early relationship with her mother and by the difficulties that she still experienced in getting needed narcissistic supplies from others. She suffered from the negative aspects of her mother's representation of a female child and of women in general, and had difficulty taking pleasure being attractive or desirable. While Karen indeed seems to have internalized her mother's burdensome representation of her, Karen also identified with her mother's search for self-realization and enrichment. Mrs. K.'s continuous search for self-realization, present already during Karen's infancy, was on the one hand an obstacle to her ability to be a reliable source for Karen's needs for nurturing, but on the other hand seems to have given Karen the hope that by continued searching she would find her own happiness. Karen identified with the part of her mother that was determined to have a better life. (It is interesting to note that Karen's mother eventually did embark on a new career that she found very fulfilling.) In addition, she had been able to receive strength from her identifications with her brother and her father,[7] her father's extended family, as well as her teachers. Mrs. K. had been able to encourage Karen's relationships with the outside world and to provide environments that were enriching for her. Karen remains open to the possibility of change.

---

7. Benjamin (1991) has described the importance of identification with the father for the girl's development.

During the early observational research, what was observed most closely was the interaction between mother and child as it evolved during the course of the separation-individuation period and the interplay between the early mother–child relationship and the child's capacity to develop her own resources, possibly in concordance with the mother's predilections as well as her unconscious needs and desires. The goal of the early research was to study the separation-individuation process, that process by which each child develops a self representation separate from the representation of the mother. The original study did not focus on understanding the separate development of the mother through which she had arrived at her particular mothering style. During the early study, it was observed that identification with the mother was an important avenue for the development of the separate self. In examining the data from the follow-up study, we find that identification with the mother goes beyond identifying with her mothering and includes identifying with other aspects of the mother's own being that might be less directly connected to the mother's interaction with the child. By the time we look at the adult subjects, important other identifications have also played a role in determining the character and lifestyle of each daughter. Helen's mother turned to the outside world in a more limited way than Karen's mother. Helen, like her mother, turned to the outside world in a reserved way. Karen, on the other hand, continued to look to the outside world, partly an identification with her mother, but also to fill a need that was present in her development from the beginning. Again this was evident in the way in which Karen was very open to the adult interviews as a new experience in her life that might offer new understandings and directions. Thus, while Helen's development was influenced by her mother's representation of her as a wished-for baby girl, Helen also identified with a mother who had limited expectations for her own life. Karen's development was influenced by her mother's representation of her as a girl child in a world where it is burdensome to be a woman, yet Karen also identified with a mother who struggled for self-realization.

As analysts we try to reconstruct beginnings; as researchers we attempt to understand outcomes. In both cases we draw inferences from observed behaviors to internal conflicts. Psychoanalytic work, whether in the psychoanalytic situation or in psychoanalytic observations, deals with unconscious processes at which we arrive from observations of the psychic surface. In analysis the multifaceted interactions of life are funneled into and made sense of in the exclusive relationship between analyst and analysand. In observational research the original exclusive relationship is made sense of by observing how it spirals out into the multifaceted and complex interactions of later life situations.

Observational research of the kind described adds to our knowledge of intrapsychic development as it interacts with lived life, which begins with mother and infant and branches out in ever-widening circles. In the longitudinal, psychoanalytically oriented observational research presented here, we can glimpse how internal representations develop. Helen and Karen's representations of self and other had their foundations in the way in which they were originally conceived in the minds of their mothers. In turn, each mother's conception of her daughter influenced the ways in which she interacted with her daughter. These early interactions provided the ground upon which each daughter built her sense of herself in relation to others, as new experiences, based on expanded capacities to perceive the world outside, broadened the world built on the first relationship. We can now return to our metaphor of the *cantus firmus*. We hope to have shown both how the earliest mother–child interactions continue to have a powerful influence on the composition of one's life, and we also hope to have shown the possibilities for unpredictable and creative use each child makes of the earliest interactions as her world widens, other voices enter in, and variations and transformations occur.

11

Autonomy and the Need for the Caretaking Other

written in collaboration with
Maria Fahey

Introduction

The title of the symposium at which this chapter was first presented,
"Through the Seasons of Life: Separation-Individuation Perspectives,"
raises two questions. How does the separation-individuation process
continue throughout life once a degree of self and object constancy is
reached? How does the unique way in which each person passes
through the separation-individuation process influence the way he
or she experiences later phases of development and later life conflicts
and crises? It is this second question that we will attempt to address
by describing the interactions of a mother–child pair during the child's
voyage through the separation-individuation process. In particular,
we will focus on the way in which this particular child was able to
use his autonomous functioning to compensate for the fluctuations
in the emotional availability of his mother. This reliance on autonomous functioning played itself out in different ways at different phases
of his development and remained characteristic of him into young
adulthood.

The excitement of the practicing subphase, with its narcissistic investment of both the self and the world outside, reaches its height with the achievement of independent locomotion, especially upright walking. During this time of development, toddlers use their mothers to facilitate their explorations of the world, and they return to their mothers at regular intervals for close contact called *emotional refueling*. The development of autonomy during the practicing subphase can fill the toddler with joy and the mother with pride as she watches her baby's locomotor and verbal capacities unfold. The development of her baby's autonomy can also fill a mother with anxiety for her baby's safety, or with feelings of loss as she must gradually accept her baby's growing separateness. During the rapprochement crisis, the toddler becomes aware, sometimes painfully, of the pitfalls of autonomous functioning and separateness. Margaret Mahler emphasized the importance of the mother's emotional availability during the difficult period of rapprochement conflicts. At the achievement of emotional object and self constancy, a further level of autonomy is reached: with the resolution of the rapprochement crisis the inner presence of the caretaking other enables toddlers to tolerate separateness and helps them to overcome feelings of vulnerability and inadequacy.

The analysis of adults has revealed how, for some patients, the issue of the mother's emotional unavailability during the earliest phases of development casts a shadow over all intimate relationships in later life. For such patients it seems that no later love object could compensate for their feelings of unhappiness and dissatisfaction experienced during this early period in life, and thus these patients could never be satisfied and could never accept the shortcomings of chosen others. They did, however, often show more than adequate capacities in their autonomous functioning. The question emerges: How does such overdevelopment of autonomy in the face of inconsistent availability of the other affect the development of object relations in early and later life? The analytic issues, namely to what extent and by what means it may be possible to help patients rework these early issues and reach a better and more satisfying capacity for object relationships, will not be addressed here. Instead, we shall describe the development of autonomy during the separation-individuation process in one of the subjects of the original study, a boy who turned out to be an extremely bright and capable adult.

David was observed with his mother from the age of 3 months to 3 years in a nursery-like setting,[1] during which period his mother's emotional availability was inconsistent. David went through the separation-individuation process with no more than average difficulties, and when he began nursery school at the age of 3 he had no trouble separating. Though his teachers were impressed by his talents and exuberance, they found him difficult to integrate into the group.

David was seen in a brief follow-up study during his latency years, and he was not seen again until he took part in the adult follow-up study, which began twenty-five years after the original observations had been completed.[2] This leaves a very large gap in the observational data, especially during the important transformational period of adolescence, which we know of only from his own descriptions as an adult. During this time, an important event took place in David's life: his parents separated, and his mother moved out of the home into a place of her own, coincident with the time David's older brother left for college. Thus, David lived alone with his father during adolescence. In his first adult interview, he spoke a great deal about his development as a self-reliant person and eventually described himself, with reference to the research, as being "overindividuated." In this context, David spoke about how he had not really experienced his mother's leaving as a great loss. In fact, at the time he found it was easy to live with his father, who gave him a lot of freedom, and found it difficult to comply with his mother's requests for weekly visits.

As an adult, David showed a high degree of autonomy in his functioning in the world. He described himself as a juggler of the many areas of his overly busy life, always trying to balance personal obligations and pleasures, relationships to many friends, a demanding professional life, and his creative life as a artist. At first it seemed that the joy and pride in his juggling ability was ample compensation for the extraordinary efforts he had to make to keep everything

---

1. For a fuller description of this study, see the introduction to "Two Women and Their Mothers" (Chapter 10 in this collection).
2. The original research was supported by NIMH Grant MH-08238, USPHS: Margaret Mahler, Principal Investigator; John McDevitt, Co-Principal Investigator. Follow-up studies supported by The Rock Foundation: John B. McDevitt, Principal Investigator; Anni Bergman, Co-Principal Investigator.

in the air. Later, during the adult follow-up interviews, which were
followed by weekly therapy sessions, David became more aware of the
conflicts he was trying to master by his juggling, and eventually
became more aware of his needs for caretaking others.

David and His Mother: The First Three Years

Three to Six Months

David was a healthy, well-endowed infant, the second child in his
family, three years younger than his older brother. Our observations
of David and his mother began when David was 3 months old, at
which time Mrs. D. was observed breast-feeding with pleasure. In one
of her first interviews, she talked about David's week-long hospitalization for a severe digestive problem, which had taken place when
he was 1 month old. Mrs. D., who had spent the days with him at the
hospital, had been very upset and annoyed with the surgeon for suggesting that she wean David while he was in the hospital. Observers
were therefore surprised when Mrs. D. completely weaned her 3½-
month-old son in just two days. After the weaning, observers noted
that she looked tired and sad and complained about David's bad ap-
petite. Mrs. D. was observed to be less engaged in feeding David. She
said that she weaned him because she would soon be starting classes
and also because she had to help David's older brother, Jay, get adjusted to nursery school. Later on, she also gave as a reason for
weaning the fact that her nipples had been sore. For the two weeks
following the weaning, David ate little and cried a lot. However, two
weeks later, when David was 4 months old, mother and baby were
much happier. Observers noted that David was responsive to people's
voices and especially to the voice of his mother, which was often soothing to him. He smiled and vocalized when he was put into the playpen with one of the other babies. At around this time, Mrs. D. went
away for the weekend with her husband and older child, leaving
David at home with her mother. She reported that when she returned,
David did not greet her in any special way; she felt that David indiscriminately smiled at everyone and did not yet recognize her as special. Mrs. D. also reported that David did not react negatively to
having been left during the weekend. At the center, observers no-

ticed that she did not interact much with David or speak about him during her interview. Already ambiguities in their relationship emerged. Did David indeed not greet his mother happily because he was angry at being left for the weekend? If so, did Mrs. D. then feel rejected by her son and conclude that he really did not need her? Or did she deny David's reaction to her as special because being needed was too painful? Whatever the dynamic underpinnings, Mrs. D. reacted by neglecting both herself and her son. In the next weeks, unsatisfactory interactions between David and his mother were reported. Observers noted that Mrs. D. was dressed more carelessly than usual, as was David. When David became sick with the croup and a high fever, mother did not become significantly more attentive.

How might we make sense of the emerging pattern of Mrs. D.'s interactions with her son? It seems that Mrs. D. had begun to see her son as a survivor: he had bounced back after the hospitalization and after the weaning, and he had seemed not to react negatively to being left for the weekend. Perhaps it was David's apparent resiliency that allowed Mrs. D. not to worry about him even when he became sick. David seemed to show his mother his capacity to go on being would not be disrupted by potentially traumatic experiences. Mrs. D. in turn felt that he did not really need her special protection and nurturing, a feeling that was for her both depriving and reassuring and might explain the pattern of her interrupting periods of joyful relatedness. It is of further significance that David's mother denied her own need for his show of love for her: she insisted that David did not miss her.

Six to Eight Months

When David was about 6 months old and began to turn toward the outside world, it was reported that mother and child seemed to have regained some of the pleasure they had had before the weaning occurred. This development coincided with David's ability to propel himself, to engage adults actively and to reach for objects. He was an active baby and began independent locomotion at the age of 7 months. When David had a minor fall, Mrs. D. became upset, and said that this was the first bad experience in his life and that he would never be the same. In fact, Mrs. D. was right that David would never

be the same: he had entered a new developmental phase—early practicing—which meant that he would need her in new ways. Mrs. D.
had difficulty adjusting to this next developmental phase, which demanded that she simultaneously let go of and protect her son, and
observers noted misattunement.

By the time David was almost 8 months old, the first separation
reactions were observed. Mrs. D. reported that at reunions David not
only smiled at her, but also brought his whole body forward toward
her. She was elated as she told an interviewer that David had tried
to feed her what he was eating, commenting that this was very precocious. David touched and mouthed his mother. She also reported
that he had begun to imitate her by patting her and making sounds.
The next day Mrs. D. was quiet and withdrawn, and complained
during an interview that David was demanding and only enjoyed playing with toys in her presence. Here we see that while David's mother
was able to enjoy her son's ability to connect to her, she was once
again puzzled by his need for her. At the center, David cooed, chanted,
and touched his mirror image, possibly reacting to mother's withdrawal by turning toward himself. On a particular day when David
was described as being in a good mood, happily exploring while in
his mother's presence, Mrs. D. was able to hold him securely and
comfort him well. After she left the room, he cried over a small hurt,
spat up several times, and then collapsed suddenly with fatigue. He
accepted a bottle from an observer and seemed to be falling asleep.
However, when his mother returned he started to cry vigorously, as
if her return had reminded him how much he had missed her. One
day David was brought to the center by another mother. He was
markedly quiet and less active than usual, yet when his mother arrived he did not seek her out actively. At the time he was interested
in an observer's glasses and jewelry. When Mrs. D. asked to borrow
the observer's gold pendant with which he was playing, David's interest in it markedly decreased. Later that day David's mother was
very worried when he had a minor fall and followed him around to
make sure he wouldn't fall again. Was Mrs. D. worried that she was
losing his love because he turned to an observer in her absence? Was
she angry at him for being happy with an observer in her absence
and rejecting her? If so, did this anger, of which she may not have
been fully aware, make her frightened that some harm would befall

her son? The next day, an observer noticed a black spot on the roof of David's mouth, which turned out only to be a piece of cookie. When mother realized this she almost cried with relief: she had been frightened that it was a hole in the roof of his mouth. This incident further illustrates her fear about David's intactness and needs to be considered in the context of the early damage to David's digestive system for which he was hospitalized at the age of 1 month. This event must have been very frightening for Mrs. D., who never expressed any feelings about it. We speculated earlier about Mrs. D.'s fantasy of her son as a survivor and relatively invulnerable. Perhaps this fantasy could not hold up at moments when she felt rejected by him.

During early practicing, we saw David's development proceeding well: good locomotor development, good autonomous functioning, and expectable separation reactions. Mrs. D.'s reactions to David, on the other hand, remained inconsistent. She intermittently was able to enjoy him and his attachment to her. On the one hand, mother wanted David to be independent; on the other hand, she was fearful of his autonomous functioning and attachment to others. Her ambivalence manifested in being alternately overly protective and worried about his survival and imperceptive about his basic needs.

Nine to Eleven Months

At 9 months, well into the practicing subphase, David enjoyed exploring the environment and smiled broadly at people he recognized. While exploring he often paused and oriented himself in relation to his mother and other adults in the room. Mrs. D. reported enthusiastically that David now rejected baby food and ate whole foods. During an interview she heard a child crying in the nursery. She went to see if it was David, and indeed it was: he had burst into tears during a game of peekaboo, which clearly had made him miss his mother. During his tenth month David continued to develop well and Mrs. D. was particularly well attuned and able to appreciate and enjoy him.

At 11 months an observer described David and his mother as "a study in contrasts": David was lively, energetic, and exploratory, and his mother was quiet and depressed. It seems noteworthy that once again a brief period of pleasure in her son was followed by a depressive period in her. At 11 months, 3 weeks, Mrs. D. reported that David was developing a sense of humor and playing elaborate peekaboo games. She also described that he was very friendly and exploratory with strangers. Observers began to notice a growing need for David to be at the center of his mother's and other adults' attention. During an interview, one observer noticed that David, who was in the room, seemed to notice when the conversation was not about him and would then initiate some approach behavior. While David was developing so well and enjoying exploration, play, and interactions with others, he simultaneously developed an intense attachment to his bottle, so much so that he would hold his bottle with one hand while busily playing with the other. Mrs. D. reported that the bottle went everywhere with him at home, as it did at the center.

While David's growth was certainly in keeping with expected developmental capabilities, we can also see how he was able to use his new capabilities to cope with his mother's tendency to depressive withdrawal and her inconsistencies in attention. He developed ever more inventive ways to engage her and others; he developed what was possibly a more than average need to be at the center of attention; and he developed the ability to satisfy two needs at the same time, namely the need for mother-qua-bottle and the need for autonomous functioning.

One Year

At 1 year, David took his first steps. The enormous impact of independent walking on the mother-child relationship has been described:

> [W]alking seems to have great symbolic meaning for both mother and toddler: it is as if the walking toddler has proved by his attainment of independent upright locomotion that he has already graduated into the world of independent human beings. The expectation and confidence that mother exudes when she feels that the child is not able to "make it" out there seems to be an important trigger for the child's own feeling of safety and perhaps also the initial encouragement for his exchanging some of his magic omnipotence for pleasure in his own autonomy and his developing self-esteem. [Mahler et al. 1975, p. 74]

At this time, when the mother's confidence is so important for the child's own feeling of safety, an observer noted that David seemed to want more physical contact than his mother offered. As we have seen,

David expressed his need for being allowed to hold on to mother through his strong attachment to the bottle.

Fourteen to Sixteen Months

At 14½ months David seemed eager to be growing up. He ate regular food and refused to sit in the high chair. He also said his first words. Observers noted his skills at manipulating toys and making up little games for himself. David showed further signs of his individuation through his awareness of his bowel movements. At the center, he became very interested in a baby, patted her head, and said "nice, nice." At just over 16 months, David showed behaviors typical of early rapprochement, bringing toys to mother and observers. When mother was out of the room, David moved around less, smiled less, and did not play with any toy for a long time. When she returned, he rushed to her smiling. During this happy period for David, observers noted that Mrs. D. again seemed anxious and depressed. It is noteworthy that despite his mother's intermittent availability, David seemed to have developed a secure attachment to her.

Seventeen to Nineteen Months

At 17 months, Mrs. D. said that David was getting more wonderful every day and that she never knew she could enjoy a baby so much. She had asked her husband to spend more time at home with David. Mrs. D. reported that David was ecstatic when with his father alone, and that he would walk around saying "Daddy, Daddy, Daddy." At the center, it was noted that some of David's activities seemed to be imitations of father—loading up a wheelbarrow or building a house. Observers noted that Mrs. D. was very quiet and looked sad and depressed. Once again, this mood seemed connected to having spoken about her special pleasure in David. She took him to an interview, hugged him, and said, "I really can't bear to part with him." At this time, when Mrs. D. expressed reluctance about letting go of her son, he became more aware of her leaving him, clinging to her upon her return. She reported that he would call for her at night and eventually go to sleep with a bottle. What is interesting here is that strong feelings about separation are expressed by both mother and child. At this time David, still holding on to his bowel movements, became very interested in toileting activities of others and would rush to bring them toilet paper. He also became aware of pairs of tools and adopted the role of providing the needed other half. For example, Mrs. D. described how David always brought her the dustpan when she swept, and one time, when she already had the dustpan and the broom, David took it from her and then brought it back to her. It is typical of toddlers during rapprochement to demand of mother to make whole something that has come apart. Here we see David taking on that role himself: instead of demanding that mother make things whole, he demands that he be allowed to play this role. Mother also described how David waited for his father at the door at the time he would come home. He gathered objects connected with an activity as soon as she mentioned it. Once when he woke sick during the night, she changed him and did not bother to put rubber pants over his diaper as she usually did. He picked up the rubber pants and said, "Put on." An observer at the center noted that David could be described as "happily compulsive. . . . He is not driven to do things out of frustration or desperation, but rather seems to enjoy bringing things to their logical conclusion." David liked to help his mother and said "helping" when imitating her. At home, he would run and get out the vacuum when the cleaning woman came. He called for his stroller when they were about to leave the house. It is interesting that during this period David developed a fascination with running faucets. We might wonder if David mastered his anxieties about separation and castration with this object that assures continuity.

Twenty-One to Twenty-Three Months

At 21 months David rushed to his mother when she returned from an interview, arms raised to be picked up. She held him and then put him down. Very shortly thereafter he went over to a baby on the mat and hugged her several times gently, smiling very sweetly. While his mother was out of the room, he had gone over to the baby several times, but did not hug her as he did with mother present. Mrs. D. smiled with great pleasure while watching him.

While David was able to master some of his anxieties through playful activities, he continued to be averse to toilet training. He sat on the toilet for long periods of time, but didn't do anything except say, "No, no," and looked frightened. An observer noted that David wanted to be in control of situations. He liked to control his parents' comings and goings by being the one to open the door, and he became distressed if they left too quickly. He insisted that a fork be next to his plate even when he ate with his fingers. During this time, some aggressive behaviors began to be noted.

At 22 months, David began to show further signs of rapprochement conflicts. He became possessive, did not want to share crayons with another little boy, and took the little boy's place at the table when he got up. Later he took toys away from the same little boy and said, "Mine." An observer noted that he did not want to play with them, but seemed merely to want to possess them. In the playroom, David wanted all the toys for himself. When mother came back from an interview, he did not want to leave her lap. He slapped away an observer's hand as she turned the page of a book she was showing him. Mrs. D. said, "He wants to be very independent and do things all by himself as long as he sits on my lap." In this way, Mrs. D. expressed her perception of his simultaneous need to be with her and to be independent.

At around 23 months it was noted that David's play was purposeful and that he went to his mother and asked for her help when he could not accomplish something. Mrs. D. was well attuned and helped him in age-appropriate ways. David began to use the word "I." An observer noted that David seemed to understand that he could entertain his mother and that she was very absorbed in him, found him very funny, and was very invested in his antics. David's mother was more talkative and connected than usual and paid more attention to her appearance, with a new haircut and new clothes. During this time of attuned attention from his mother, David became more agreeable and less determined to have his way. An observer described how David began to push away a younger child who tried to take his toy, but stopped himself and gave him a hug and patted him. Mrs. D. said that David had become very easy to handle. He was able to accept his mother's comings and goings and substitute caregivers. He also had become more amenable to toilet training.

A month later, David began to speak in full sentences and use the word "you" correctly. He imitated Jay and said, "I win," when he finished a game. When he played with puppets, he used a squeaky voice. Mrs. D. reported that at home he wanted to be with his father a lot. He imitated him working around the house and took immense pleasure in working alongside of him. He also imitated mother doing housework, but preferred father. David now ran to the toilet after he urinated and was very uncomfortable when his diaper was wet. Though David pushed away his mother when she approached him with a diaper, he also would not use the toilet.

Around the time of his second birthday, David seemed to have reached some resolution of rapprochement conflicts. He was accepting of brief separations from his mother and was able to show his loving feelings toward her while at the same time he strongly identified with his father and his brother. At times Mrs. D. appeared happier and calmer than usual, but at times she looked withdrawn. Another important family event occurred at this time: father took a new job and had much less time to be with his family. Mrs. D. reported that David no longer talked about his father, didn't call him, and didn't seem very much aware of him. It seemed from these reports that David reacted to father's sudden unavailability not with open protest, but by withdrawing. At his second birthday party, observers noted that his mother was also withdrawn. David played by himself and refused to participate in any party rituals, such as sitting down at the table with the other children. He ate his ice cream before everyone else. Thus, David seems to have reacted to his parents' unavailability by withdrawing and becoming less related.

The Third Year

Back at the center after summer vacation (2 years, 3 months) David seemed very happy. Observers noted that his language development was remarkable and that he remembered everything about the center in great detail, including a specific book about fire engines, which he insisted an observer find for him. David used the toilet to urinate standing up, though he refused to have a BM when his mother thought he needed to. At 2 years, 4 months, when David was left at the center by his mother, he refused the bottle she had left for him and drank his milk from a glass. He was whiney and did not engage in fantasy play. David played with another boy, sometimes amicably, sometimes with struggles over toys, and would not accept substitute toys for the one he wanted to take from this boy. When Mrs. D. arrived back at the center and then left the room for an interview, David noticed her coming and going but did not react much. When mother was finished with the interview, he gave her a broad smile and showed her what he had been doing. Mrs. D. also reported that recently when father took his older brother out alone, David did not cry (as he typically did) but stayed close to her. Here we see David developing the ability to accept being left by turning to the available caregiver. Interestingly, during this same period, an observer noticed David withholding urine and connected this withholding to his mother's absence. While David was able to make good use of substitute caregivers, there was some sense that David felt compelled to hold onto himself. He also may have been trying to gain control over his urinary function at a time when he seemed to have to come to terms with the fact that he could not control his parents' comings and goings. David did not want the toilet flushed and was particularly scared of the loud flushing noise.

David continued to struggle with aggressive impulses, especially in connection to his father and brother. On the one hand, David became very protective of his older brother: When a 6-year-old girl made threatening gestures at Jay at the playground he said to her, "You leave my brother alone." On the other hand, when his father took him along with Jay to the Museum of Natural History, he became so frightened of a tiger that he insisted on leaving. Following this, he developed sleeping difficulties and insisted that his mother stay with him until he fell asleep. Further evidence of these struggles was observed at the center. One day, David was withholding his stools and was more aggressive than usual, attacking other boys for no apparent reason, and on the same day he cradled animals in his arms tenderly, putting bandaids on them because they were sick. David's concern about bodily injury grew: one day when his mother had a bandaid on her finger, he became so distressed that he demanded she take it off. He became scared of the camera, and would not allow his picture to be taken. At the point of David being so fearful, he said with great excitement that he wanted to fly a helicopter when he grew up. Mrs. D. explained that he had said this ever since watching the cars on the street, which, he said, "moved too slowly." Perhaps this

wish is an early sign of a tendency to use manic defenses and omnipotence in the face of helplessness and anxiety.

During the second half of the third year, David's play became
wilder and more competitive. His mother, who was interviewing for a
job, seemed preoccupied and would drop him off quickly at the center. David looked sad when she left him; he was aggressive; he was
unable to follow through activities as he usually did; he withheld
urine, and cried, "I want my Mommy." Observers noted that his
strong reactions to her leaving him were difficult for and puzzling to
Mrs. D. At around this time, Mrs. D. took a job and had her mother
bring David to the center. David became toilet trained; however, as
Mrs. D.'s time at work increased, David became increasingly hyperactive, difficult to control, and at the same time, shy. Mrs. D. reported
that David had become more "of a rascal"; however, she did not connect his behavior to her absence, and, in fact, said that he did not
miss her. David clung to the bottle. On David's third birthday, Mrs.
D. switched her day of work to be at his party, and observers noted
that he was his old self with mother present.

Further Development and Latency

David's nursery school teacher reported that he was brought to his
first day of nursery school by a babysitter to whom he paid little
attention. The teacher described that David appeared "happy, excited,
and self-directed," and reported that he was particularly self-directed
in the block area, where primarily he built roads. In his rich fantasy
play, he mostly took on the roles of transportation workers. In her
report, David's teacher noted that he was anxious about finishing
what he began, and she felt that this anxiety kept him from realizing his full potential. He also refused to comply with cleaning up:
his tendency was to make creative excuses and sneak away. David
was intellectually precocious and related to adults as "intellectual
equals." In relating to other children, David tended to play alongside
them rather than with them. He was not aggressive toward other
children, and hit out only in self-defense or when acting as self-as-
signed judge in a dispute between other children. All David's nursery school teachers commented on his love of school and learning,
his superior intellectual abilities, and his enthusiasm and energy.

David's transition to nursery school was easy and positive, though one can see how earlier issues around separation and separateness between him and his mother affected his ability to complete tasks, to take the point of view of the other, and to play interactively.

At age 10½, David was seen in a brief follow-up study that included psychological testing, interviews, and school visits. He came to the testing session with his mother, and when she offered to wait for him, he said, "I don't care if you do. I don't care if you don't." She decided to leave, and was somewhat late arriving back to pick him up. During that time, David became noticeably anxious, alert to every sound. However, when she did return, he was uncommunicative and surly. Here we see an old pattern: David asserts his autonomy, and his mother has trouble seeing and responding to his simultaneous needs to be both independent and cared for. She seemed to have responded to her feeling of rejection by keeping him waiting, and he was unable to express directly that he was in fact made anxious by having to wait for her. The tester remarked on David's excessive doubting during the test. Perhaps this doubting was connected to his reluctance to reveal himself, and also to his experience of having his cues misread by his mother and by not being able to read hers predictably.

It is not surprising that what emerges from David's reports from nursery and elementary school is that David was really quite puzzling to his teachers, who found him hard to guide and control. They could not really read him, which is particularly interesting in light of the ways in which his mother sometimes misread his cues. An observer who made several visits to the classroom felt that his teachers often misread him and had negative expectations of him. He was not fully accepted into the classroom community by his teachers, to whom he was an enigma and to whom he gave the feeling that they were not needed and could not have an effect on him. In both his family and his school, David eventually was perceived as egocentric.

When interviewed during the latency follow-up, David went by himself, and was very friendly and forthcoming, eagerly sharing his interests and accomplishments. He came across as unusually independent for a boy his age and proudly talked about the fact that he would travel alone a great distance for art lessons. During his first interview, he appeared eager and cooperative and cheerfully agreed

to return for another session. Nonetheless, he never did return for
another interview, further illustrating how David existed on a thin
line between autonomy and the inability to respond to the needs of
others. Early on, David seemed to have internalized that he might not
be responded to, and that his needs might not be met. Left to
draw on his own resources, he became prematurely independent,
denied his need for supportive caretakers, and denied the need of others to be responded to fully by him. The question emerges whether
this difficulty in David's object relating was defensive in nature or
whether it was due to an incomplete resolution of separation-individuation issues.

Adult Follow-up

During the adult follow-up interviews, David described his years at
a top high school as a time during which he was more or less
unsupervised. He had been an excellent student and an accomplished
artist. After his mother had left the family and his brother had left
for college, David had lived alone with his father in the home in which
he had grown up. He described how his family did not stay in close
contact and how he had learned that his mother had left the family
when he had returned from camp at the age of 14. At the time, he
thought that he did not mind because it was easier to live with his
father, who did not put any restrictions on him. David described
how he created "families" for himself. For example, he became very
attached to the owner of a record store where he spent many hours.
He also built up a large family of friends, many of whom remain very
important to him.

David was accepted to several excellent colleges and had chosen
to attend a prestigious university a great distance from home. With
a mixture of pride and amusement, he spoke of his arrival to college
as a freshman, on his own with his backpack and his bicycle, in contrast to the other first-year students, who had been accompanied by
their parents. His college career was academically very successful,
and in addition he became a Resident Advisor in his dormitory during the second year of college—a position generally held by seniors
and graduate students. After graduating from college, David settled
in the city of his college, where he lived with a friend and supported

himself. Eventually he decided to return to New York, where he took on the difficult task of becoming his aging father's caretaker. He lived on his own but managed all of his father's financial and health affairs, which he found in great disarray. While he felt burdened by these caretaking tasks, he also experienced gratification in doing this difficult job and in his father's pleasure in being with him. David was very happy to have returned home; he described that while away he had resisted strong attachments because he had always felt that he would return.

During the period in which the follow-up interviews were conducted, David was actively striving for a closer relationship with his mother both directly and through connections to her extended family and heritage. David was attached not only to his mother, but also to her family of origin, and he regretted that none of them lived nearby. He realized that at times he had appeared aloof and that he needed to show his mother how much he valued her. However, her availability to him was not constant; her loyalties were divided between her present husband and her children. There seemed to be a clear connection between David's longing for the available mother and his search for a suitable partner with whom to share his life. The search for continuity is an outstanding characteristic of David's life at present and one wonders whether there is a connection between this search for continuity and the absence of consistent availability in his earliest relationship. David's contacts through his interviews continued, and he eventually asked to be in therapy. The main reason for this was the realization of his difficulties in maintaining an intimate relationship. He felt very burdened in his life by the responsibilities of a demanding job and the needs of his father. He began to experience longings for being taken care of and realized that, in spite of his many close friendships, he at times felt very lonely because he always had to provide for himself and for others and found it very difficult to ask for anything for himself.

A conflict exists between David's search for continuity and his tendency to disrupt continuity. At the beginning of his therapy, David frequently missed sessions or came late. These absences and latenesses were always easy to account for because of his many responsibilities and busy and changing schedule; however, it seems that slowly he became much more cognizant of the regularity and reliability of the presence of the therapist, who did not respond to his fluctuating availability by withdrawing hers. In the therapeutic work, David has come to realize how much effort he has always put into making himself lovable and how much what he considers an excessive need for approval and acceptance has limited the experience and expression of his authentic self. He can now tolerate being on his own while he is looking for a partner with whom he can have a truly mutual relationship. Along with these changes, David has developed a greater awareness of the needs of the other; recently when he met a woman he liked very much, he didn't try to overwhelm her with attention. He was very respectful of her needs separate from his.

Discussion

We saw in David an infant and toddler who seemed to have developed very well through the process of separation-individuation even though David's mother seemed to keep herself from fully realizing the special connection and mutual pleasure in their relationship. As we study the observations on David's separation-individuation process, what emerges is the mother's sense that she did not have a strong effect on her son. Her sense of David as a survivor may well have developed already when he was 1 month old and lived through the trauma of a serious illness and hospitalization. She was able to be relatively unconcerned when she was not available to him, yet at the same time she was overly sensitive when David did not pay attention to her. Eventually, she began to see David as unavailable, and he in turn developed precocious autonomous functioning, beginning even in nursery school. We have shown how the pattern of David's mother's fluctuating emotional availability affected David in his journey through the separation-individuation process and eventually on his journey through childhood and adolescence. We have also seen how it affected his personality structure and his view of himself in relation to significant others.

It seems that David and his mother together constructed a myth that David was self-sufficient and indifferent to his mother's efforts in caring for him. The myth of David's invulnerability and self-sufficiency created by them was so powerful that eventually when Mrs. D. left David and his father, after his older brother had left for college, it allowed David not to miss his mother at that point, but to experience her absence as something of a relief because it would allow his autonomy and independence free range.

We have described how, during rapprochement conflicts, David dealt with a sense of helplessness and rage (often observed during this period) by identifying with the caretaking other and taking on that role himself. Here we see autonomy developing as a defense against helplessness, an affect that must have been unbearable to this child who could not fully rely on the supportive presence of his parents. David's defensive identification as the helper seemed to lead to a premature and insufficient resolution of rapprochement conflicts and may have spared him the full experience of anger at his parents for the ways in which they were not there for him. While David did experience aggressive impulses, it seems he rarely acted them out against his parents. Thus we see how identification, which is one of the avenues to healthy resolution of rapprochement conflicts, can also be used to avoid facing conflicts and can lead to a defensive autonomy, comparable to the development of a false self, in Winnicott's sense (Winnicott 1960). Indeed David seems to have become overinvested in his autonomous functioning: when he was seen in his first adult interview, he spoke at great length about his self-reliance and how early it had developed.

While David described how his parents had not been there for him at important periods of transition, he did not express resentment, but rather felt pride in how well he had managed on his own and how rich a life he had been able to create for himself, beginning in his latency and adolescent years. This uncompromising investment in his self-reliance was often experienced by others, especially his mother, as his being emotionally unavailable and narcissistically invulnerable. He himself saw his development as precocious, and described himself as a teenager who was "very, very self-reliant, very brash, very rude, very determined, with a lot of my own ideas." This uncompromising self-reliance was also a way of dealing with his anger at not being taken care of by showing his caretakers that they were not needed.

While great differences exist in the extent to which mothers are able to be emotionally available to their children, maternal emotional availability is necessarily limited for all children, and thus all children must cope with the fact their mothers are not as available as they might wish. In studying the detailed observational data of mother–child couples, we have noticed that how a child responds to mother's unavailability seems to be influenced by gender, and have observed that the danger for boys is to turn to the outside world, giving up mother too soon and then feeling a lack in ability to communicate and relate to an intimate other. The danger observed for girls, on the other hand, is to stay overly involved with mother and to transfer the sense of unfulfilled longing and wishes to excessive longing and pursuit of an intimate other in adult life.

While at times David's needs were not met by his parents, at other times they were loving, admiring, and attuned to him, surely an important factor in his good development. In addition, while in some ways his mother's representation of him as invulnerable, precocious, and competent was limiting, in other ways it was empowering. David certainly has been able to use his intelligence and competence to create an enjoyable and productive life for himself. Yet, as emerged in his adult therapy, David's self-reliance, juggling, and exaggerated, defensive autonomy has prevented him from realizing his longing for a relationship with mutual caretaking and availability. Recently, David has become aware that being taken care of and having an intimate other is what has been missing in his life. He has also begun to face the depressive feelings about not really having a close family. In Kleinian theory, reaching the depressive position implies a process of mourning, which Mahler also describes as characteristic of the rapprochement subphase, when the toddler has to come to terms with aloneness, separateness, and relative helplessness (Mahler 1966). We saw how, during the rapprochement subphase, David defended against coming to terms with helplessness by taking on the role of the helper who provided the missing other half. David had not fully experienced the aloneness of the rapprochement subphase, and later on had not mourned his mother's leaving the family. Steiner (1992) describes the stages in reaching the depressive position:

> A critical point in the depressive position arises when the task of relinquishing control over the object has to be faced. The earlier trend, which aims at possessing the object and denying reality, has to be reversed if the depressive position is to be worked through, and the object is to be allowed its independence. [p. 53]

We have described how in his most recent relationship David is providing space for his love object to be separate.

It is significant that David was able to ask for therapeutic help in the context of being a subject of a longitudinal study; David was able to ask for help in a situation where he could also see himself as a helper. In this way he is repeating the known conditions under which he can be loved. The danger is, of course, that the defense is built into the setting that he has chosen and that he is spared the risk of giving himself over to an unknown other.

An important question that we have not yet addressed in this chapter has to do with the application of earliest development to the adult personality with relatively little direct observation of the intervening transformational periods of latency and especially adolescence. From what we do know, it seems that David continued the trends of adaptive and defensive autonomy that had begun during his separation-individuation process without major transformation. The question emerges whether there are some character traits that develop during the separation-individuation period that remain relatively fixed throughout the life cycle. In his recent book, Allan Schore (1994) describes the separation-individuation process, and in particular the practicing period, as a time that is "marked by the emergence . . . of a structure that contributes to autonomous emotional functioning, that is, to the self-regulation of affect" (p. 92). Schore says, "These dramatic affective transformations are critical to the establishment of permanent characteristics of the emerging personality. Perhaps more than any other time in the life span, the individual's internal state is externally observable and susceptible to socioenvironmental influences" (p. 93).

Schore's formulations, which are borne out by our own observations, correspond to research findings of contemporary attachment theorists who have shown the lasting nature of early attachment patterns. The possibility that certain character traits that first emerge in the separation-individuation process last throughout the life cycle needs further investigation. The present follow-up study in which we are engaged will give us the opportunity to look at this question in greater detail in a number of cases.

In David's case, we have gained insight into the origin as well as the lasting nature of the way in which he was able to compensate

for difficulties in his early relationships through the development of
his autonomous functioning, which provided pleasures and satisfaction for him and his mother. We can also see the way in which autonomous functioning allowed him to be unaware of the way in which
caretaking others were not meeting his emotional needs. It seems that
the continuity that our study has provided for David and the therapeutic help for which he has asked has brought about a shift that
will make it possible for him to begin to find a new way to regulate
affective interchanges.

12

Love, Admiration, and Identification

On the Intricacies of Mother–Daughter Relationships

written in collaboration with
Maria Fahey

Introduction

This chapter is based on the data collected from three research studies. The first of these was the observational study of mother–child
pairs during the separation-individuation process, from 6 months to
3 years of age.[1] This work was begun in 1959 by Margaret Mahler
and her associates, and was based on her hypothesis of the symbiotic origins of the human infant, who she thought developed a sense
of separate identity during the period of separation-individuation. The
study focused on the mother–child pair. Mothers and children met
in a playground-like setting, and the development of children of the
same age was always compared while each mother–child pair was
studied intensively. The data were collected by a team of participant
and nonparticipant observers as well as by a senior clinician who con-

1. This research was supported by NIMH Grant MH-08238, USPHS: Margaret
   Mahler, Principal Investigator; John McDevitt, Co-Principal Investigator.

ducted regular interviews with the mother and observed the mother–child interaction. A brief follow-up study during latency consisted of interviews with both children and mothers, psychological testing, and school visits. Thirty years after the original research, an adult follow-up study was undertaken by two members of the original team of observers. This study has included series of interviews with the original subjects, psychological testing of the subjects, and thorough reworking of the original data.[2] It needs to be emphasized that the adult follow-up is quite different in scope than the original research, in which data were based on daily observations by multiple observers. The data of the follow-up study have been collected by single observers, and contact with the subjects has been much more limited, especially because most of the subjects now live in various parts of the country.

The data gathered on the adult subjects is studied in the context of the data collected on the mother–child pairs during a period that was largely preverbal. The availability of the extensive mother–child observations of the preverbal period provides an unusual window through which the influence of the earliest mother–child relationship on adult life can be viewed. However, we are faced with the difficult question as to whether direct connections can be made between early childhood and adulthood without taking into account the intervening formative experiences of later childhood and adolescence, of which we have only a glimpse gained from the intermediate follow-up study. This intervening period is accessible to us mostly through the accounts of the subjects, based on the memories they wish to share. This clearly is a limitation; however, the preverbal period is usually only available through reenactments in the transference in the analytic situation. The fact that we have actual observations of mother–child interactions during the preverbal period gives us another avenue of studying the influence of these earliest interactions on adult life.

In this chapter, two mother–daughter pairs who have been participants in all aspects of the longitudinal study will be described: the course of the daughters' development during separation-individuation,

<hr>

2. Follow-up studies supported by the Rock Foundation: John McDevitt, Principal Investigator; Anni Bergman, Co-Principal Investigator.

a glimpse of their development during latency, and the life of the daughters as it has evolved in early adulthood. One of the unique aspects of the observational separation-individuation research was the emphasis on both longitudinal and cross-sectional methods: individual mother–child pairs were observed over time, and observations of mother–child pairs were compared continuously with each other. These comparisons were a natural outgrowth of the very design of the research in its playground-like setting, where several mother–child pairs were always present. The comparative aspects of the original research, from which patterns in the mother–child dyad emerged, allowed for the formulation of the theory of subphases of the separation-individuation process. In working with the data of the follow-up study, comparing mother–child pairs has proven to be a fruitful method for discerning patterns of ways in which the experience of the mother–child relationship can influence adult life.

It is important to remember that while the original study focused on the interaction between mother and child, the emphasis was always on the separation-individuation process in the child. In the adult follow-up, the emphasis is even more strongly on the child-now young adult. We are studying the ways in which early patterns have been internalized and absorbed into the adult personality structure, and we are studying the continuing relationship between the child-now young adult and her mother. Our knowledge of the mother herself and the motivating forces that moved her to relate to her child in a particular way is not available with the same clinical richness. However, it should be remembered that observations of mothers and children and interviews of the mothers were conducted by psychoanalysts who were concerned always with understanding the meanings of what they saw and heard.

Mary and Laurie

As adults Mary and Laurie have been able to create satisfactory lives for themselves and have maintained good relationships with their mothers. We know that both Mary and Laurie were desired daughters: both of their mothers had expressed preference for a girl child in their initial interviews at the center. While both mothers experienced great satisfaction from their girl children, the emphasis here will be on the differences in how each mother derived pleasure and gratification from her daughter.

On Laurie's first birthday her mother held her close and talked about her loving feelings and how she had never experienced such feelings before. Laurie's mother was very sensitive to Laurie's attachment to her. Mrs. L. talked a lot about her pleasure in Laurie and how from early on she was able to quiet her daughter just by talking to her when she was upset. At 8 months Laurie had cried for the first time when her mother left her, and mother was proud and pleased by this clear sign of Laurie's unique attachment to her. Mrs. L. also described with pleasure Laurie's attachment to her father. At the center, Laurie was described as lively, vigorous, and curious. She was content and peaceful, yet active and interested in the world around her.

Mrs. M. described how she was completely absorbed by her baby, Mary, during her first year. She described how she and her daughter spent all their time together, how she had always taken her daughter everywhere, and that Mary had never shown any stranger anxiety. Mary was described by her mother as a very independent baby who had never liked to be held closely. Mrs. M. felt that Mary had always been able to let her know what she needed. At the center, Mary was admired by the observers for her unusual competence. She walked and climbed very well and her language development was precocious. She said many words quite clearly, and her mother said she had a very good ear and had been able to imitate sounds from early on. Mary was able to let her mother know what she wanted, and her mother was responsive.

Here, the contrast between Mrs. L. and Mrs. M. emerges. Mrs. L. was most pleased by her little girl's attachment to her and by their mutual pleasure in closeness and the uniqueness of their relationship. Mrs. M. was also pleased by her relationship with her baby, but emphasized Mary's independence and ability to relate to others. In what follows, we will look at each girl's separation-individuation process to the achievement of object constancy and consider how each mother's greatest pleasure in her daughter influences storms that arise during the separation-individuation process. In particular, we will look at each mother–child pair's navigation through the rapprochement subphase and the process of its resolution.

Laurie and Her Mother: The First Three Years

Two weeks after her daughter's first birthday, Mrs. L. said that for the first time she had been angry with Laurie when she had insisted on playing in the toilet bowl. After removing her several times, she had finally yelled, whereupon Laurie went into a corner and cried quietly. Her mother was quite shocked by this and worried that she could break her wonderful spirits. She recalled the strictness of her own upbringing and talked about her determination to be different. Around this time her husband encouraged her to take off one afternoon a week from child care to go shopping.

At the age of 13½ months Laurie began to walk, but preferred to crawl and usually walked only when asked to by her mother. Perhaps Laurie experienced walking alone as too much of a separation from her mother and therefore would only walk when encouraged by her mother. Mrs. L. also seemed to express some ambivalence about Laurie's growing up and out of the blissful union of babyhood, and by the time Laurie was 14 months old, observers noticed some misattunement. One observer described their interaction:

> Laurie has been put down by her mother and apparently wishes to be held some more. She cries when she is put down. Mother says, "Laurie, Laurie, what's the trouble?" She does not pick her up, and Laurie continues to stand near her. Later Laurie seems to have recovered and plays by herself crawling about. She walks to mother and looks at her. Mother does not see her and turns away from her. She then walks a bit away from mother, and there seems to be a kind of almost playing at falling, which happens for a while. Then Laurie walks to mother and just as she arrives at mother's chair, mother gets up to get some coffee.

At the age of 14 months, Laurie continued to feel vulnerable and to be easily upset, crying at small frustrations and hurts. Laurie also became more aggressive and demanding. She began to run away and had to be watched closely. She often wanted exactly what her brother had and began to imitate him. Mrs. L. reported that for the first time Laurie was not happy when she woke up in the morning and was not eager to get out of bed. Mrs. L. said, "My sweet little Laurie, who has always been so good and happy, was unhappy all weekend. She would lie down and cry and throw tantrums over the slightest provocation." Laurie was extremely jealous of her older brother and wanted everything he had. When Mrs. L. left the room, Laurie was inconsolable, yet when taken to her mother her mood did not really improve.

Thus at just 14 months, Laurie was displaying behaviors typical of the rapprochement crisis, and Mrs. L. was baffled and upset by the loss of Laurie's blissful babyhood. It is interesting to note that the rapprochement crisis occurred so early for this child, where there had been some inhibition of the full enjoyment of the practicing subphase, perhaps because the pre-practicing union was so important. When at 16 months Laurie started to sleep through the night, her mother said, "Laurie's growing up so quickly." Laurie loved food and made humming sounds while eating. Her mother wondered if her zest for life had something to do with her love for food. Mrs. L. loved to cook and thought that food was such an important part of life. On a deeper level, she must also have connected Laurie's love for food with Laurie's love for her.

Around the age of 17 months, Laurie made a great spurt in cognitive development, which took the form of remembering and evoking events from the past. She made great strides in language. Mrs. L. reported that for the first time Laurie had come over to her and given her a spontaneous hug and kiss, which touched her very deeply. Mrs. L. talked about wanting another baby, but not wanting Laurie to become a middle child. At 18 months there seems to have been a resolution of the rapprochement crisis. Laurie began to imitate her mother and liked to do things with her, like putting things in their place, such as dirty laundry into the hamper. She also imitated her brother and did not want to wear dresses or play with dolls. As she became reconnected to her mother following the rapprochement crisis, Laurie also guarded her budding autonomy, and became sensitive to the interference of other children and aggressive toward them.

When Laurie was 2 years old her family moved to a new apartment. Laurie cried from the time her crib was put into the moving van until it was in its new place. Once the crib was there Laurie was all right again. It seems that the crib took on a special symbolism for her, which is interesting in light of Mrs. L.'s special feeling about Laurie as a baby. At this time Laurie herself began to be aggressive toward other babies. When her mother stopped her by telling her she was a big girl, she got very angry and said, "No, I'm a baby." Laurie spent a lot of time sitting in the big doll carriage at the center. She was possessive and unwilling to share anything. At the center Laurie screeched at one of the babies, who had followed her around and pulled himself up on a chair. Mrs. L. said, "This is the most venom she has right now. She really hates babies. My sweet little Laurie. I couldn't imagine that she would ever be like this." Here we see that both Laurie and her mother had feelings about the loss of the special union they had felt when Laurie was a baby. Even though her crib could be moved to her new house, and she could be consoled about the loss of her old house, she could not be a baby again, and maybe therefore hated other babies, who could have what she could no longer have.

At around the age of 2 years, there was a further resolution of the rapprochement crisis as Laurie's language development progressed. Once again Laurie became more purposeful in her play, and she liked to listen to and tell stories. At times she could tolerate sharing the attention of an observer with another child, and her periods of aggression toward babies began to alternate with periods of tenderness. Here we see how Laurie began to identify with her mother, who loved her and treated her with tenderness.

A big step in individuation was noticed first by Laurie's mother, who reported a shift in Laurie's relationship to her older brother. Until now she had imitated everything he did and wanted. For example, she had always taken ketchup on her hamburger because he did, but now she decided that she wanted her hamburger without ketchup. Along with this new step in individuation, Laurie seemed to have begun identifying with her mother in a new way, namely by internalizing her prohibitions. On the playground, when Laurie saw another child putting sand in his mouth, she said, "Mommy say, 'No, don't eat that.'" Thus the asserting of her own individuality went hand in hand with internalization of her mother's prohibitions. At the same time, she became more possessive of her father, calling him "My Daddy," and asking him to do things for her instead of asking her mother. Thus, a new level of triangulation occurred, indicating a loosening of the exclusive mother–baby bond.

At the age of 26 months, Laurie seemed well on the way toward emotional object constancy. Observers noted how she now showed her understanding of the feelings of others. Laurie also referred to the future and the past. When she didn't like to be left by her mother she would say, "Mommy will come" or "Mommy will take me home." Laurie was very able to express her feelings to her mother. She managed well in her mother's absence, and when her mother returned she immediately said to her, "I did not want you to go away." Then she went on playing. Once when she was at the center without her mother and an observer asked, "Where's Mommy?" Laurie answered, "Shopping." When asked when Mommy would return, she looked down at her new shoes and said, "Mommy always buys me new shoes." In this way Laurie showed that she could keep the connection to the good mother in her mind and was not easily thrown by questions from a strange observer. After her mother had returned, she again went out to pick up Laurie's brother from school and asked Laurie if she wanted to go with her. Laurie said, "I want to stay here while you pick up Bobby. Then you come back and pick me up." She hugged her mother and said goodbye.

When Laurie was 31 months old, Mrs. L. talked about how confident she felt about Laurie, who seemed so self-sufficient. What is notable here is that Laurie's mother, who had had some difficulties as Laurie began to show signs of growing up, especially during the practicing subphase, seems to have been able to accept Laurie's self-sufficiency at the point it was more free from conflict. However, Mrs. L.'s ambivalence about how much she should baby her daughter remained discernible when Mrs. L. reported how Laurie had suddenly given up her pacifier. One night, Laurie had announced that she didn't want the pacifier any more but woke during the night, became very upset, cuddled up with her father, and asked for the pacifier. Mrs. L. gave it to her and worried whether she had done the right thing. Laurie did not ask for it again. Around the same time she became very proud of a band that she was wearing in her hair that she did not like to be without. We might ask what the meaning could be of this new strong attachment to a hair band. Was this a new way of being close to her mother, the band being a symbolic tie between them and a sign of identification with her mother, wearing her hair in a grown-up way? Laurie's mother had worried whether she had discouraged her from growing up by giving in to her demand for the pacifier. In fact, the opposite may well have taken place: as long as the pacifier symbolizing mother was available, she could in fact enjoy closeness to mother in a new way, wanting to be like her.

Mrs. L. reported that Laurie was developing a very strong prefer-ence for her father and a renewed strong identification with her brother. During one observation at the center, Laurie played that she was Bobby and wanted her mother to play the role of Laurie. She said, "I am Bobby. Feel my muscles." Later, playing with play dough, she rolled it into a long piece and said, "Look at the big snake." She started to eat it and spit it out and said "Bobby spits, and I am Bobby." When mother scolded her, Laurie insisted that she should telephone Daddy so she could tell him what had happened. She did not play with her dolls, and only liked the stuffed animal her father had given her. Thus, at the age of 2 years and 9 months, Laurie showed signs of an oedipal attachment to her father. At the same time she began to have much greater difficulty separating from her mother. She did not like to be left at home with the babysitter she knew very well, but demanded to go everywhere with her mother. During an inter-view with Mrs. L., Laurie insisted on remaining with her mother and then could not become involved in play, remaining continuously aware of her mother. She called her father on the play telephone. Mrs. L. reported that Laurie was jealous of a new kitten in the family, and she also reported that Laurie had asked her father to sleep with her and this new kitten in her bed.

One day, when she was 35 months old, Laurie was extremely up-set, and upon arrival at the center she screamed and did not want to stay. Mrs. L. explained that before leaving she had been wearing dressy shoes and red boots and had then refused to wear these and had demanded her white ski boots instead. Mrs. L. had complied with her wishes, but when they were out on the street Laurie wanted to go back home and change her boots again, and her mother refused. Upon arrival at the center, Laurie refused to take her coat off and sat on her mother's lap fully dressed. Mrs. L. seemed very distressed and looked pleadingly at the observer. At the time oedipal conflicts emerge, posing a new threat to losing the exclusive early bond with mother, we see the return of typical rapprochement behaviors. Mrs. L. seemed very distressed and puzzled. An observer encouraged Laurie to play with a new doll, and Laurie took her mittens off. Mrs. L. was then able to interest Laurie in dramatic play with dolls sit-ting around the table and said to Laurie, "Oh, here is a family having breakfast." The other children joined Laurie and they continued to play. In this way Mrs. L. showed her sensitivity to Laurie, even though she said she was feeling so helpless. In play she took Laurie back to the breakfast table that preceded the tantrum and reassured Laurie that the family would remain intact and withstand her attachment to her father and hostility to her mother. Eventually Mrs. L. left the room for an interview. At first Laurie said nothing and continued to play as if she had not seen her mother leave. After a few minutes she asked where her mother was and then threw the Mommy doll on the floor and screamed, "Mommy is on the floor. I threw her on the floor." Laurie became increasingly reluctant to go to the center, which she associated with being left by her mother. Mrs. L. was able to convince Laurie to go to the center by reassuring her that she would not leave her.

Summarizing Laurie's third year, we saw at first a calm period during which she was able to tolerate separations from her mother and in many other ways showed she had indeed overcome the rapprochement crisis and reached a degree of object constancy. With the advent of the oedipal conflict, as indicated by her strong turning toward her father, we saw an increase of hostility toward the mother and a resurgence of separation reactions—temper tantrums and refusal to be left by her mother. The wish to be mother's baby remained present throughout but may also have been replaced in part by being father's baby or having a baby with father, as illustrated by accepting only the stuffed animals that her father had given her and expressing a wish to sleep in bed with father and the new kitten. During the time of beginning oedipal conflict, expectable regression to typical rapprochement behaviors occurred. Mrs. L. was able to respond reassuringly.

Laurie: Further Development

Laurie made the transition to nursery school fairly easily. At the time her competition with her brother was still very much in the foreground. She fought with her mother about clothes: she liked to wear very feminine clothes but was very particular about them and would not wear clothes if she perceived the slightest thing to be wrong with them, possibly a displacement of a fear that something could be wrong with her own body. An observer described her as being very tomboy-ish and at the same time very feminine.

It was characteristic of Laurie throughout her latency years and beyond that she kept both the male identification with her brother and father and the female identification with her mother very much alive. During a home visit, Laurie proudly showed the observer her large collection of stuffed animals, which were on her bed. She liked all kinds of physical activities from dancing and gymnastics to ball playing and skiing and at one point became very involved in going to circus school. At the same time Laurie recalled that during her latency years she liked to be with her mother a lot.

Laurie as an Adult

In looking at Laurie as an adult, our focus here will be on the way the mother has continued to take pleasure and satisfaction in Laurie's development, even if how she developed was very different from any-thing she might have envisioned. It seems that Laurie's mother is able to respect and enjoy Laurie's separateness and difference, and that this has not alienated mother and daughter from each other but has instead provided the opportunity for new bonds to be formed because of the mother's efforts to share in Laurie's present lifestyle.

At one point during the follow-up interviews, Laurie was given the opportunity to look at a videotape from the original study of her-self as a baby with her mother. Laurie was very moved and spoke about how she had always known that her mother loved her, but actually seeing how tender and loving she was with her as a baby almost brought tears to her eyes.

Laurie recalled her close relationship with her brother during childhood and her desire to be always included in everything he did. Laurie has maintained a very close relationship with her brother and his family, has become a close friend of her sister-in-law, and also continues to enjoy skiing and hiking alone with her brother. Laurie expressed appreciation for her father, who had always included her in the games he played with Bobby, and as an adult Laurie conti-nues to share interest in team sports with her father.

The themes that had been so important at the time of Laurie's rapprochement resolution, namely closeness and identification with her brother and identification with her mother, especially by way of cooking and eating, were still very strongly present. In one of her adult interviews she recalled her favorite toy—a little toy oven in which she had baked little cakes. Food and cooking was a very important part of Laurie's adult life, and she involved not only her brother and his family but also her parents in her health-oriented eating. In an interview, when Laurie and her mother talked about early memories, Laurie remembered a game in which she would come from her bedroom downstairs into the living room to visit mother with her baby doll, and Mrs. L. would make tea for them.

In a joint interview, Mrs. L. and Laurie remembered that when Laurie was around 8 years old, going shopping together was always a disappointment. Laurie would want certain shoes her friends had that her mother found too expensive or unsuitable. Eventually the shopping trip would end in disappointment, and they would go home sitting at opposite ends of the bus. Laurie said, "I can remember we always liked different things. I'd say, 'I like this' and you'd say, 'No, that's not right.' And then you'd say, 'Why not get this?' and I can remember sometimes saying, 'Well, okay, it's not that bad.' But I would never wear it because I didn't like it. And I can definitely remember that I would get very sulky and sullen and angry that I couldn't have what I wanted. I hated that." Laurie and her mother's recollections about shopping are interesting in light of the observation thirty years before in which Mrs. L. had left Laurie at the center and when asked, "Where's Mommy?" Laurie had said, "She's shopping. She always buys me new shoes." Shopping had been Mrs. L.'s way of taking time off from Laurie, yet she maintained a connection to her daughter by shopping for her. It is interesting that both Laurie and her mother recall joint shopping trips in later life as disappointing.

Later in the interview, Laurie's mother remembered her wishes to see her little girl in dresses. Laurie in turn remembers not wanting to wear frilly dresses and wanting the same clothes as her brother. Laurie said, "I felt a little bit trapped in this image, like I couldn't wear a skirt or a dress even if I wanted to." Then Laurie remembered her mother crocheting a little miniskirt for her that she liked. Laurie had chosen the colors, and Mrs. L. remembers buying leotards to match. Laurie said that she loves shopping now and that even though she and her mother have different taste they like the *idea* of going shopping together, and they like to look at each other's clothes. Laurie said, "We have fun together." And her mother agreed, "We are good pals, I would say, really I think so. I would say to this day I couldn't ask for a better daughter." Laurie said, "I feel the same way. I love my mother."

Having presented Laurie and her mother in some detail, we will now briefly outline another mother–daughter pair's journey through the separation-individuation process.

Mary and Her Mother: The First Three Years

When Mary and her mother began to attend the research center, observers found Mary to be captivating, in contrast to her mother, who faded into the background. Mary and her mother attended very regularly and usually came early. Because they arrived before the other mothers and children, they were assured special attention. Mrs. M. may have found in our center a place comfortable for her where she and her daughter were supplied with mirroring attention, perhaps attention for which the mother unconsciously longed. This is different from Mrs. L., who basked in the attention given to her by her little girl. For Mrs. L., it was the loving attention from her daughter that made her feel good as a mother, whereas Mrs. M. felt good as a mother when her child was admired for her precocity and attractiveness.

Though Mrs. M. had remarked that Mary was an easy baby, she reported that they arrived early because she found it hard to be home alone with Mary who, she said, had difficulty occupying herself. This contradiction illustrates the gratification Mrs. M. derived from being watched as the mother of her little girl, whom she seemed to see as an idealized version of her own self. Mary always came to our group in very pretty little girl clothes that Mrs. M. made for her. This was in contrast to the way Mrs. M. dressed herself, always playing down her looks. Thus she may have put all her own wishes to be admired into Mary. One observer noted the pride this mother took in her child. It seemed to him that the child filled the mother's life and that the mother–child pair gave the impression of amazing self-sufficiency. One observer described watching her:

I had first seen Mary when she had just turned 13 months. Her effect on me was almost immediate and very profound. I realized after
some time I had surrendered a certain observational distance. Instead, I felt myself captivated and in a state of great pleasure, sympathy and almost complete admiration for this phenomenal little
creature. The energy and vigor of the pretty little child's activity was
indeed a joy to watch. There was a contrast between this child and
her mother, who sat very quietly and was rather shy.

Mary was at the height of her practicing subphase, enjoying her explorations and precocious locomotor capacities. This period ended
abruptly when Mary was 15 months old, probably catalyzed by the
sudden absence of her father, whose work took him abroad. Mary
developed a sleep disturbance: she woke up several times each night,
her mother unable to comfort her for quite a long time. At the center, a marked change in the child was noticed. Mary started to play
bye-bye games and became very alert to the comings and goings of
everyone. During the same period she became listless and fatigued,
which contrasted strongly to her former boundless energy. She began to fall more frequently and was generally irritable; she cried a
lot, demanded food, and ran to her mother for comforting. An observer
noted that the former confident expectation and the awareness of her
ability to command a response from others seemed to be replaced by
an almost desperate appeal for attention. The feeling of pleasure and
joy in her performance was no longer there. Mrs. M. did not connect
these marked changes in Mary to the absence of her father. It would
appear that Mrs. M.'s life was so filled by her daughter that she could
not see how her daughter's life was affected by anyone other than
her, even the father. Mary began to fight for unique possession of
her mother and eventually of other adults at the center. The period
of Mary's upset became more acute when she was 17 months old,
around the age of the expectable rapprochement crisis. During this
time Mary became almost phobic of her mother's efforts to pick her
up or comfort her. These efforts simply resulted in more anger toward mother. Mary was frustrated easily and broke into tears. She
consumed great quantities of juice, asking for it from all the adults
who came into the room. Mary was happiest when she was at the
center alone with her mother and the observers. Mrs. M. became depressed and distraught and had difficulty being attentive to Mary.

She complained that Mary was impossible at home with crying, temper tantrums, and what seemed like incomprehensible behavior. At the center Mary became aggressive toward the other children. Even on better days Mary remained extremely sensitive to any deprivation, such as her mother talking on the telephone or a toy being taken from her. Mary's mother looked harassed and worn and worried about her daughter. Perhaps Mrs. M. was especially hard hit by her child's rapprochement crisis because it was such an abrupt ending to the period during which Mary could be the ideal baby and she could be the ideal mother.

As Mary came to some resolution of her rapprochement crisis she began to internalize her mother's prohibitions by saying, for example, that she should not pull other children's hair. She also began to play with dolls, acting toward the dolls the way her mother acted toward her. Identification with the mother emerged as both playing mother who prohibits aggression and also playing mother who takes care of the child. At this time Mary's mother became sensitive to Mary turning to observers. She felt easily rejected and jokingly remarked that Mary would some day prefer her teacher to her.

Throughout Mary's further development, Mrs. M. continued to express her concerns about the loss of the exclusive relationship between her and her daughter. For example, when Mary was 2 years old her father returned from abroad. When Mary greeted him as if she had always remembered him, Mrs. M. was surprised and seemed to experience Mary's remembering and welcoming her father as a sign of the loss of their exclusive relationship.

Another event which further threatened the exclusive relationship was Mrs. M.'s pregnancy, which she first spoke about when Mary was 29½ months old and she was in her fifth month. Mrs. M. was very worried about Mary and said, "This will be the end of Mary. She will be 3; it will be just around her birthday. Mary won't like a new baby for a birthday present." She talked about the wonderful, special baby that Mary had been, already very interesting when she was only 5 months old. Mrs. M.'s worry that Mary would not be able to tolerate a sibling was heightened by her own worry that her cherished relationship with her daughter would be forever changed. In fact, Mary became increasingly demanding of exclusive attention. At the center, for example, she wanted to play ring-around-the-rosy with an observer and was furious when other children were included. At story time she pushed the other children away and insisted on sitting on the observer's lap. She showed marked jealousy and aggression toward all babies. It was almost as if Mary began to enact her mother's fear about the dissolution of the perfect and exclusive mother–baby union, where Mary was the center of her mother's and the observers' attention.

When Mary was 31 months old, her mother reported that she noticed for the first time Mary accepting a disappointment without crying, which made her mother sad because it further signified her daughter's growing up. Mrs. M. was reluctant to tell her daughter about her pregnancy or the new baby coming and was surprised when it turned out that Mary already knew because she had been told by another mother who was also expecting a new baby. When Mary's mother spoke to Mary about the baby herself, she said that Mary was looking forward to it. Observers noted that in her play Mary was the devoted mother to her teddy bears. Thus, despite her mother's concerns, at this point Mary was able to use the idea of a new baby in the family to identify further with her mother.

Mary: Further Development

Early on when Mary came to the center, all eyes had been focused on her, a precocious, beautiful, verbal little girl. When Mary left the center to go to nursery school, it was a difficult transition for her and her mother. Her mother had just given birth to Mary's baby brother, who required a lot of attention. Mary demanded exclusive attention from her nursery school teachers and reacted to the other children as rivals. Mother was concerned that Mary was not treated well enough by her teachers. Thus, this first contact with the outside world of school turned out to be difficult for both mother and child. These difficulties continued to some extent throughout her school years and became especially exacerbated during her early adolescence when the family moved and Mary had to adjust to a new school and community. Mary was extremely shy and had difficulty making friends. Her teachers reported that she did not live up to her academic potential. Once again, mother was very disappointed and anxious and took Mary's difficulties as a sign of her failure.

Mary as an Adult

In looking at Mary as an adult, we will focus on how the nature of her early relationship with her mother was ongoing in her adult life. During separation-individuation—and maybe beyond—the ending of the exclusive relationship had been painful to both. It seems that in adult development, the relationship was preserved by way of Mary's identification with her mother. Mary worried about her mother, perhaps comparable to how her mother had been worried about her. She felt that her mother was not realizing her own potentials and was instead continuing to serve the needs of others, especially her brothers and father. It was important to Mary to have her mother come and stay with her where she and her mother could enjoy things together and her mother could be freed of some of her typical family responsibilities.

Mary did well in college and in her profession, which she described as having fallen into rather than having actively sought. In this way she was similar to her mother, who always stressed her lack of academic ambition even though she had gone to an excellent college. In her interviews Mary underplayed the importance of her professional choice, but in fact she had become very successful in her field. Mary's style of appearing casual about important decisions is congruent with her mother's style and contrasts sharply to Mary as a child who did not easily accept that she was not the only child and the star. On the other hand, she rose to the top of her field, though she did not regard this as a big success. Mary was not entirely settled in her current professional activities and planned to continue her studies.

Mary married a man she met at work who had lost both his parents early in life and had very little family of his own. In this way, she may have fulfilled her childhood longing for an exclusive relationship with her mother. She described her husband as someone with whom she got along very well, but who was moody. She was able to tolerate and handle his moods, and said, "His moods are unpredictable. When he gets moody, I just sort of let him." Thus, Mary may unconsciously have played the role of mother to the moody child she herself had been. Mary made the impression of being stable in her own moods and not being easily upset. One might wonder if she allowed her husband to express the moody side of her.

Mary described her pleasure in her garden and how her mother
sometimes visited and helped her with gardening. She enjoyed her
mother's visits and described how well her mother got along with her
husband. By working on her garden together with her mother, Mary
seemed to be able to find again her early mother.

Discussion

It is interesting to compare two mother–daughter pairs who are similar and yet very different. Both mothers had wished for a daughter
and both were very happy with their girl babies. While both mothers
derived great pleasure from their girl babies, there is a crucial difference.

In the case of Laurie, the greatest pleasure seemed to come from
the mother's realization of her baby's love for her, which triggered
the mother's loving and tender response. The inevitable difficulties
in the relationship, beginning during the second year of life, were
reacted to with ambivalence and insecurity about how much to allow
Laurie to remain a baby as she grew up so fast. This ambivalence
may have been mirrored by Laurie's ambivalence about growing up,
especially during the practicing subphase where she was able to walk
but would at first do so only with her mother's encouragement. Notwithstanding these ambivalences and conflicts, Laurie's mother
seemed to remain quite secure in her love for her little girl and her
little girl's love for her. The continuity of her child's primary attachment to her was not threatened by her awareness of Laurie's attachments to others—especially her love for her father and her identification with her brother. It is important to note that the father was
present as the important other for both mother and daughter.

Mary's mother, on the other hand, seemed to derive the greatest
joy in Mary by being able to admire her and by Mary's ability to elicit
the admiration of those around her. Mary's mother's pleasure and
need for attention from her daughter were expressed more indirectly,
as if the mother had to defend against her need for more direct expressions of love from her daughter. This may enlighten the observation that the mother took greater pleasure in her daughter's practicing subphase, which distances mother and baby in space while
preserving the power of the mother's watchful presence, than in close

physical contact. While Mrs. M. took pleasure in the admiration of the observers of Mary's practicing, she could not easily acknowledge the importance of others in Mary's life, including her father.

When Laurie was difficult, her mother frankly showed her disappointment, but was able to recuperate from the disappointment fairly easily, perhaps in part because of her close relationship to her husband, with whose help she could be more attentive to her own needs. Mary's mother tended to interpret Mary's difficulties as a more personal reflection on herself, and it was harder for her to recuperate from the disappointments. She tended to deny her own needs and did not have the presence of a supportive husband, nor did she seem to seek other close, supportive relationships. Laurie's father provided support for both mother and daughter as well as offering himself for closeness and identification. Mary's father, on the other hand, was absent during an important period in the life of both the mother and the child, but the child seemed to fill the mother's life so much that she did not need him and therefore could not identify with her daughter's need for him.

In adulthood, Laurie's interests and lifestyle were different from her mother's, and these differences inspired Laurie's mother to learn from and share in Laurie's new life. Mrs. L. accepted that Laurie was different from her and wanted to bridge that difference by becoming involved with Laurie's interests. Laurie's choosing a lifestyle different from that of her family may reflect her identification with her mother, who had voluntarily left her country of origin at a young age and met her husband while traveling. It also may reflect her identification with a mother who had expressed a desire for a mothering style different from the one she had been raised with. Laurie also seems to have identified with her mother's joy in homemaking: her love for food, cooking, and homemaking remain important elements in her life, though she has given them a coloring very much her own. Laurie's father and brother, who had been important objects of identification in her early life, remain present as important others in her adult life as well. It would seem that Laurie's ability to enjoy life has its source in an identification with her mother's joy in her as a baby.

As an adult, Mary has moved away from home and has a profession, but her basic lifestyle is not very different from that of her mother. Like Mrs. L., Mrs. M. likes to share in her daughter's life and does so by visiting Mary and helping her with gardening, an activity they both enjoy. These visits are pleasurable for Mary not only because of what they provide for her but also for what she feels they provide for her mother. Mary seems to have identified with her mother's need for exclusivity by forming a relationship with a man in whose life she could be the exclusive love object. As a baby, Mary did not have the opportunity to identify with her father or older siblings—her relationship with her mother was, in fact, exclusive. In adulthood, Mary seems to pursue her own individual desires less than Laurie, perhaps because Mary had identified with her mother who had not pursued her own intellectual interests. Although she had the tendency to underplay her achievements, Mary had created an independent and constructive life for herself.

By comparing Laurie and Mary during separation-individuation and then again in young adulthood, we hope to show the subtlety and complexity in which the earliest, preverbal period of development—and in particular the earliest relationship with mother—may be recognizable in the character structure and emotional life of the adult. In the light of present knowledge about the mother–infant relationship, it is interesting that Freud thought about identification as a form of attachment. In his lecture on "The Dissection of the Psychical Personality" (1933), he says that identification "is a very important form of attachment to someone else, probably the very first" (p. 63). Through the cases of Mary and Laurie, we see how the outcome of the process of identification reflects the nature of the mother's attachment to the baby. The child's first identification with mother is influenced by the ways in which the mother experiences her child's attachment to her.

Laurie's mother reacted with joy to the love she felt from her baby daughter. This basic joy with which the mother reacted to Laurie may have given Laurie the freedom to pursue her life without being inhibited by how well she performed. The things she shared with mother as a little girl she later incorporated into her own lifestyle.

Mary's mother reacted with joy and pride to Mary's abilities and to the admiration Mary inspired in others. As Mary grew up, she could not always continue to evoke admiration from others, which upset her mother, who wondered who was at fault—herself, nonadmiring others (such as her teachers), or Mary. Mary may have

have experienced Mimi as the ideal child—the good child that she herself could not be. Through Mimi, Rosie seems to have recovered aspects of the childhood she wished she could have had.

Rosie spoke lovingly of her husband and felt he was patient and kind. However, she was also aware that he sometimes tended to confide more in his mother than in her. Although she could not yet speak the language fluently, she understood everything and realized her husband often discussed serious matters with his mother rather than with her. Rosie reacted by becoming more acutely aware of her own internal struggle—a struggle she described as being between the child and the woman in her. The child was demanding, had a quick temper, and tended to be resentful; the woman was appreciative, patient, giving, and kind. Rosie set high standards for herself and blamed herself when she could not live up to them.

As an adolescent, Rosie had come to understand her childhood illness as an angry turning away and escape from the realization that she could not be the ideal child of her fantasies. As a young mother, Rosie struggled once again with the desire to be perfect, and she suffered from her perceived imperfections, vulnerabilities, and weaknesses. However, she was able to face these conflicts and feelings rather than turning away from them through denial, projection, and avoidance. Rosie was capable of genuine love and concern for her children. As a mother, she was able to revisit and further repair the wounds of her own childhood, the pain of which remains vivid in her mind. Through the birth of her daughter, Rosie seems to have been able to experience a kind of rebirth: in nursing and caring for her baby girl, she experienced complete happiness and bliss, perhaps for the first time in her life. As Rosie mothers her daughter through the phases of development, she herself emerges as stronger and eager to become more fully adult. At this time Rosie began to talk about wishing to take over more of the household chores, to become more of a companion to her husband, and to be more fully responsible for her own life.

Discussion of Development and Treatment

While it is difficult to compare the development of a severely disturbed child to the process of normal development, it is of interest to look at

the major changes in Rosie's development in terms of resolution of
conflict and crises that all children face, and to see in what ways an
intensive treatment could help a disturbed child experience an expectable developmental process, though in a different time frame.

The first question is: How can one help an autistic child who is
not relating to others accept the presence of a caretaking other? How
can that caretaking other then help set in motion basic processes of
affect feedback and regulation, eventually leading to basic trust?
Through a long-term, intensive treatment process like the one I have
described, which includes both the child and the mother, the autistic
child can come to recognize the mother as a caretaking other, and
the mother can come to feel that her child, no matter how strange or
disturbed, needs understanding and responsiveness even as the child's
behavior seems to show indifference and rejection. The hope is that
eventually the child will give up the autistic defenses, recognize her
emotional needs, and become able to express them in a comprehen-
sible way.

How did Rosie manage to change? How did she make the transition from one phase to the next? It is striking that each change was
preceded by a crisis. The change from autism and symbiosis to hatching, the first words, and the beginning of symbolization, which happened between the ages of 6 and 8, was preceded by her separation
from her family in a summer camp. The change from a violent rapprochement crisis to beginning object constancy and the emergence
of communicative language, which happened at the age of 8, was preceded by first her mother's and then her own accident. And finally,
the change toward a therapeutic alliance, the capacity to reflect, and
the initial working through of her obsessions happened at the age of
11 when she began to come to therapy sessions on her own at my
office.

Each of these important steps, then, was preceded by a challenge
and crisis that her treatment could help her use to grow rather than
cause her to regress. The mutative point in the first transition seemed
to be the recognition of her feelings of despair when she was left at
camp, saw it get dark, and had the feeling that her parents would
never come back. When she returned from camp, though she had
become toilet trained and appeared calmer on the surface, she had
in fact retreated to autistic defenses. She dramatically enacted her

feelings of loss by giving up her psychotic fetish and love object, the piano. Eventually through my interpretation of her play and anxiety on a particular day when her mother had left and it became dark, I could begin to help her recognize and express her feelings of despair and eventually to experience and express her real affect of sadness. This experience brought her closer to both me and her mother and, at this time, she began to use words, most importantly "Mommy." Notwithstanding the retreat into a more autistic state, one wonders whether the traumatic experience of absence was in the end instrumental in helping her come to a realization of the importance of her love objects.

When Rosie was around 8 years old and in the midst of violent rapprochement struggles with her mother and me, her mother had a painful accident for which Rosie felt guilty because of rageful feelings toward her mother. This guilt made it possible for her to attempt to repair the damage that she felt she had inflicted and to empathize with her mother's pain. The wish to make reparation is an important aspect of reaching *depressive position*, in the Kleinian sense. The capacity to empathize and identify with her mother brought about a resolution of rapprochement struggles that allowed for further development. Through her fantasies and obsessive preoccupations Rosie could now express her wishes for omnipotence in more sublimated forms. In her fantasies, which she expressed mostly by way of her drawings, she saw herself, for example, as a famous cello player commanding a large audience. The choice of fantasy instrument in connection to having given up the piano is of some interest. While playing the instrument was lived only in her fantasies, a cello is an instrument—unlike a piano—shaped like a maternal body, around which the player wraps herself. One might in fantasy experience the cello as a huge phallus and a maternal body, representing perhaps the love for the father without the loss of the mother.

By the time Rosie was able to come to her treatment sessions alone, she to some extent had weathered the early developmental conflicts, both preoedipal and oedipal. She now no longer blamed her suffering on her parents or on me, and she became increasingly aware of her internal struggles, which took the form of severe and consuming obsessions. Rosie portrayed her struggles in voluminous, detailed drawings and stories. As the meaning of one obsession would emerge through treatment, the obsession would subside only to be replaced by another. We came to understand how the struggle with the various obsessions was an attempt to come to terms with typical preadolescent and adolescent struggles of establishing a separate female self in the context of her atypical development and her mental illness. Once she had become a separate self, she began to go through a long period of mourning for what she now recognized as the loss of a normal childhood, as well as jealousy and envy of those whose development seemed characterized by loving closeness to parents. However plaguing her obsessions, and however hopeless the struggles against them often seemed, Rosie struggled valiantly to become a more independent person and create a life of her own.

One could describe the many years of this treatment process of terms of Winnicott's conceptualization (1971) of the necessity for the analyst of severely disturbed patients to survive being destroyed. According to Winnicott it is the destruction and survival of the object that eventually makes it possible for the object to be used. This struggle to survive was ongoing for both Rosie and me. I feel it is important to conceptualize what made it possible to endure the struggle. Perhaps the most important was Rosie's intelligence, vitality, and talents that enabled her to use music, art, and eventually writing to express her inner life. Furthermore, it was the willingness of Rosie's parents to live with an extremely difficult and demanding child and adolescent and to endure the pains of her struggles for so many years. Finally, and not least of all, the existence of a setting that allowed for such intensive therapy provided support and supervision[4] and the conviction that intensive, long-term psychoanalytic treatment can offer the possibility to disturbed children to develop and lead fulfilling lives in the regular world in spite of the pain and difficulty of coming to terms with both internal and external conflicts and difficulties.

---

4. I am grateful to Rosie and her parents. I am also grateful to Margaret Mahler and the staff of the Masters Children's Center. In particular I would like to thank Manuel Furer, who supervised the case for all the years of treatment and helped me to remain hopeful and to develop creative ways of understanding and helping Rosie. I am also grateful to Rosie's art therapist, Edith Kramer, and to all those who were therapeutic companions for Rosie, particularly Judith Lobel, Elissa DeWitt, Chip Crosby, and Jill Rosenblum.

Appendix A
Rosie's Development as Seen by Her Art Therapist
Edith Kramer

I began to work with Rosie when she was 9 years old. Since Rosie's art work clearly showed talent and meant a great deal to her, it was felt that she might profit from coming to my studio every Sunday. This proved to be also an important respite to her mother, who often fell asleep on the couch, exhausted, while Rosie and I worked. It was my task to be nonintrusive and yet available, to turn toward Rosie, but also to endure that she did not seem to take notice of me and did her work all on her own. I found a solution to the problem of staying connected to Rosie for hours without interfering with her work by doing something I've never otherwise done as an art therapist: I started painting portraits of her. Because I could interrupt my own painting at any time, I was able to stay available during the hours that she spent working. At the time Rosie seemed oblivious to what I was doing. However, when she visited me as a young adult, her interest in my observations of her became very clear. She was enormously interested in the portraits I had painted of her and was very happy when I gave her one of them. It was also interesting that during this visit, at which time she was already the mother of two children, Rosie fell in love with a painting I had done of an early snowfall up in the mountains, where small purple flowers were sticking out of the snow. She wanted and bought the painting. I thought it very beautiful that she would pick a painting with this image, as the small flowers blooming through the snow symbolized quite poignantly her own development.

When I first met Rosie, she was obsessed with facades. She drew big houses with beautifully detailed doors and windows. At the time, Anni Bergman connected this obsession to a traumatic event. Rosie, angry at her mother, had run out of her apartment, down the stairs, and stood out in front of her own building. Her mother found her outside looking at the building. This actual event was probably also an enactment of her feeling herself outside her family and maybe outside herself, all of which entered into her fascination and endless drawing of facades (see Figure 13–7).

After Rosie worked through her obsession with facades, she became obsessed with crowds. She had to travel by car on the West Side Highway when going to her therapy and talked endlessly about the crowded West Side Highway, about which she also made many drawings. Rosie felt the highway was much too crowded and that the world was too crowded as well. Some of these drawings were very primitive, not at all in accordance with her ability and her previous works. The primitiveness of these works seemed to have something to do with Rosie's having broken through the facade behind which she could be isolated from the world. Her development exposed her to feeling threatened, which took the form of the obsession with crowds and particularly crowded highways (Figure 13–8). This pressure seemed to leave her no time for detailed drawing; the people of the crowds appeared to her as stick men lacking individual features.

Figure 13–8.

As Rosie came out of her isolation, she also became more aware of her body, which seems to have been related to an obsession that followed, namely with the cello. She wanted to play it, she talked about it, and she drew a series of pictures about it. There was a strong exhibitionistic and competitive component to this obsession and, while she could not learn to play the cello, she was able to produce beautiful paintings of playing the cello, and she also asked me to paint a picture of her playing the cello. One painting in the series (Figure 13–9) seemed to be in preparation for going to camp and wanting to have something to show to the other children. Her fascination with the cello was an illusion: it could not materialize and remained a

Figure 13–9.

fantasy. Yet the art work Rosie did around the cello was some of the most normal work she had done.

By the time Rosie was 10 years old, she had entered a belated oedipal phase. Her feelings of competitiveness with her parents and her death wishes became very frightening to her. She began to chant the word "tomb," which became unbearable to her parents, who forbade her to say the word. In her art therapy sessions, Rosie painted crosses with dates on them that she then scribbled out, showing how unbearable these thoughts were to herself (Figure 13–10). Whenever Rosie drew people during this tomb period, they always had cartoon faces, which was a very subtle way of representing the death wishes (Figure 13–11). We see in Figure 13–11 Rosie's picture of herself dreaming a dream. The dream is scribbled out, but one can see that it deals with death, which she attempts to undo by scribbling over it. She gave herself a smiling cartoon face.

Rosie's next major obsession was with the Attica prison uprising, when she was around 12 years old. She became terrified that she might become a victim and be imprisoned in Attica. This was another obsession so unbearable to her parents that she was forbidden to talk about Attica at home. Rosie worked out her fear during art therapy sessions by spending several sessions making a picture of a "Mrs. Attica," who grows prisoners in a flower pot. I greatly praised this work and encouraged it because I felt her black humor to be a way for Rosie to master her fear (see Figure 13–4). The following summer Rosie went on vacation instead of going to camp. She had a very good summer and returned quite changed. She drew herself as a real person (see Figure 13–5); however, in her drawing she wears a striped bathing suit that is reminiscent of the striped prisoner clothes. The little island in the distance had the word "Attica" on it, which was then scribbled over. By turning Attica into a distant island, Rosie very concretely distanced herself from the Attica obsession. At this point, she began to become jealous of all the cute little girls in the world who had easy, normal childhoods. She talked about a cute little girl who had been drinking out of a fountain in a big supermarket (Figure 13–12). Rosie said with wry comprehension of her situation, "Yes, you're very cute, but you don't know what it is to be a victim."

A period of profound mourning and suicidal fantasies followed, during which Rosie produced her most exquisite art yet (Figure 13–

Figure 13–10.

Figure 13–11.

13). Her pieces from this period were very small drawings, perhaps an attempt to concretely minimize these suicidal fantasies. After this series of drawings, Rosie did not come to work with me for a few years. During her last year in high school, she decided she wanted to come and do some art with me again. We had a difficult time at the beginning because Rosie wanted to do very conventional, cute, teenage art work and wanted help from me in a way she could not be helped. We were at an impasse. Then one day she came to a session and found in my studio a poinsettia past its bloom and a bunch of daffodils. Rosie took the daffodils, beheaded them, and stuck the flowers onto the poinsettia, thus creating an new, artificial, nonviable plant. I praised it and told her she had made a great invention. I then suggested that she make a painting of it, which she did. Rosie painted a beautiful watercolor of her invention (Figure 13–14). During her next session she painted a watercolor again, this time of a bouquet at my studio. She worked in a very straightforward manner, talking all the time about the act of painting, for example, about how she was mixing colors. This painting was to be a birthday present for her mother (Figure 13–15). It seems that Rosie had to do something absurd— something I could have never foreseen—before she could paint a beau-

Figure 13–12.

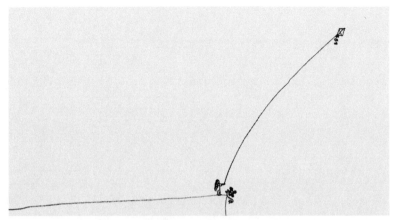

Figure 13–13.

Figure 13–14.

Figure 13–15.

tiful watercolor that was suitable as a birthday present for her mother. Rosie decided that she needed a good set of watercolors of her own, which her parents bought for her. She then decided that she did not need to come to work with me any longer.

The next time I met Rosie she was a young adult, and she showed me some of her new work. Painting has remained her most important avenue of self-expression and of mastering problems during stressful periods in her life. In fact, Rosie's art work seems to become more alive and poignant when she goes through difficult times. When she visited me as an adult she told me that the most important thing I had done for her was never to criticize her. In her art therapy, Rosie was allowed to do what she needed to do without questioning or interpretation. Thus, her art therapy could contribute to her finding her true self in a unique way and in fact gave her a respite from the much needed work of her analysis.

Appendix B

Rosie's Development
as Seen by Her Therapeutic Companion

Jill Rosenblum

When I first met Rosie, she was 9 years old. She had a limited, highly accented vocabulary and a remarkably expressive face with deep blue penetrating eyes. She was a beautiful little girl with an incredible creative energy. She was fearless, agile, and unpredictable. The first day I arrived at her house I entered and was almost run over by Rosie, who was impersonating a wildly careening car on the highway. She accompanied her movements with loud, inspired sounds. Rosie was self-conscious about her limited and often unintelligible speech. She lived in a largely Hispanic neighborhood, and she created an elaborate ersatz Spanish dialect, wonderfully inflected and rhythmic. She was often hesitant around other children. The intensity of her play, its individualistic quality, and her speech difficulties all helped to estrange her.

Rosie was very observant. We often discussed differences in people's appearances, with differing skin colors coming in for close scrutiny. Rosie thought she would look good with blue skin. I bought some blue theatrical make-up, and we went ice skating with sky-blue faces. We were noticeably different and attracted a good bit of attention at the rink. Somehow the very tangible difference had a freeing effect on Rosie, and she responded to the other children without her usual defensiveness. This event sealed a bond between us: I had not only not rejected her imagination, I had joined in with it.

Sometimes with children whose emotional balance is precarious, seemingly insignificant events can assume great importance. Around Easter we were walking past a candy store in which delicate, elaborately decorated Easter eggs were being displayed. We stopped to admire them. Rosie wanted one and we went in to purchase it. It was very expensive, and I had very little money. I decided that I couldn't afford it. As we left the store I looked at Rosie and saw that her lips were trembling and that she was beginning to cry. I asked her if that egg was really so important to her. She looked up and said, "You didn't know, Jill? You didn't know?" We went back into the store and purchased the egg. She must have felt I had known how valuable that egg was to her and was willfully depriving her of something very meaningful. Rosie, who so often seemed to exist in another world, had found something in this world that she prized and she was heartbroken at the thought of losing it.

I was very privileged to work with Rosie and will never forget the sensitivity and intelligence she displayed and the effort she made to emerge from her private realm.

14

"I and You"

The Separation-Individuation Process in the Treatment of a Symbiotic-Psychotic Child with Adult Follow-up

Introduction

Rachel was 4 years old when she was brought to the Masters Children's Center by her mother. She presented a typical picture of a symbiotic-psychotic child. She clung desperately to her mother, seemingly in an attempt to coerce her to function only for the purpose of fulfilling *her* needs. There was no pleasure in closeness for either Rachel or her mother. Rachel was rigid and panic-stricken. At the slightest frustration she would break into piercing screams. She would not permit her mother any independent existence. For example, she could not tolerate her mother to converse with anyone, either in person or on the telephone.

Rachel showed a mixture of symbiotic and autistic defenses. While she used language, it was never for direct communication, and she did not put words together in a spontaneous way, but instead quoted from books, records, songs, and television commercials. She would also parrot words and phrases said to her by people in her environment. Since everything she said was merely an echo of what she had heard, the reversal of personal pronouns was a natural consequence. When speaking of herself, she would say, "You get dressed," "You eat your dinner," "You go to the park," and so on. Although she spoke fairly clearly, her voice was lifeless and unmodulated, as were her facial expressions and body movements. Even her frequent shrieks seemed to lack emotional participation. She did, however, use quotations with astonishing accuracy as a way of conveying her feelings. When she was angry with her mother, for example, she might say, "the poisoned apple," or "she's dead, of course," quoting from fairy tales and folk songs.

Rachel was a pretty child, with lovely blue eyes and long, tightly braided hair. She was always clean and neatly dressed; her face was set in a tight, smilelike grimace. Her motility was severely restricted: she had a broad, toddlerlike gait, and walked cautiously, with small steps, climbing one step at a time, like a 2-year-old. She would never run and was unable to climb, swing, throw a ball, or use her hands in any kind of manipulative activity. Instead, she was always either bouncing from foot to foot or jumping and waving her arms.

Rachel showed no interest in toys, except as objects to chew on; she liked small objects she could hold in her mouth. When given a doll, she would undress it and then discard it. She spent many hours during the day listening to records or looking at a particular book that caught her fancy. She worked strenuously at shutting out the outside world; when she was unsuccessful, she reacted with anger and fear. If anyone tried to interest her in a new toy, she would ignore it. If she was not permitted to do so, she would knock it down, drop it, or break into loud shrieks. She would not look at a new book or listen to a new record, nor would she wear new clothes. A trip to the shoe store was an ordeal for her mother, who could not quiet her screams. Her mother had found only one activity that would interest Rachel: the spelling of words usually had a soothing effect.

Rachel had innumerable fears: of strangeness and strangers, especially of children; of going in cars; and of all kinds of household machines including the mixer, the blender, the vacuum cleaner, and especially the washing machine.

There was a complete breakdown in communication between mother and child (Mahler and Furer 1960): Rachel would climb onto her mother, tear at her body, clamoring, it would seem, for the very closeness and warmth her mother felt she had tried to provide but which was not accepted by Rachel as a baby. The mother was stiff and proper, intellectual, perplexed, trying desperately to make her child behave in a more normal, age-appropriate manner—yet clearly afraid of her own and her child's feelings and trying to keep the child at a distance, since she was not able to interpret her distorted behaviors as a need for closeness.

Rachel and her mother lived in an isolated world. The parents had separated when Rachel was 2½ years old. With her child's difficulties and her own tendency to be overly critical of herself and others, the mother had since found it impossible to keep up normal social relations.

History

Adopted at birth, Rachel was the only child of a middle-aged couple who had been married for ten years. Rachel's mother, the youngest of a large immigrant family, remembered her own childhood as devoid of love and pleasure; her own mother, worn out by work and poverty, had been an excellent housewife but had had little time to share in the emotional life of her children.

As we have seen with other mothers of severely disturbed children, Rachel's mother had had the fantasy that being a mother would help her undo the deprivations of her own childhood. Her hope was cruelly disappointed by this child, who seemed unable to accept her, who did not develop "confident expectation" (Benedek 1938), and who kept alive in the mother the distrust that stemmed from her own childhood.

Rachel's father was a kind man, though he lacked spark and enthusiasm. The mother complained that her husband had withdrawn emotionally from her when the baby came, and had, for the first time in their married life, become very demanding. When Rachel began treatment at the age of 4, her parents had been separated for about two years.

Rachel's mother reported Rachel had been an easy baby to care for, requiring little attention. She did not like to be held and cuddled, a disappointment to her mother. Rachel sat up by 8 months, crawled by 10 and walked at 15 months. Mother reported that she toilet-trained herself at the age of 2½ years.

From birth on, Rachel had manifested extreme skin sensitivity. She had not liked diapers or clothes, or being covered, and she would manage to wriggle out of any wrappings at an early age. Rachel's hypersensitivity also manifested itself in violent reactions to minor hurts, such as vaccinations or small mishaps like soap in her eyes.

Rachel's mother had first become concerned about her child when she was 1 year old, after they returned from spending the summer in the country. She had found herself perplexed by Rachel's lack of interest in toys, her tendency to crawl away from her, and her unresponsiveness. At this same time, the difficulties in the marriage became acute, eventually resulting in the parents' first separation, which was preceded by a physical fight at which Rachel was present.

Rachel's real difficulties started in her second year, at which time she became intensely negativistic and fearful. When she was 2, the mother had to spend a few days in the hospital; when she returned, Rachel was even more unresponsive than she had been earlier. When she was 2½, the parents, who had reunited briefly, decided to separate for good.

Rachel's condition now worsened rapidly. She spent a good deal of time simply rolling on the floor, rocking, and screaming in panic when anything was asked of her. She was not able to show either pleasure or sadness, which sustained the mother in her belief that Rachel had not reacted at all to her father's leaving. At the time Rachel began treatment, her father had completely withdrawn from any contact with her or her mother. While Rachel's mother complained bitterly about his lack of interest, she denied any effect of his absence on Rachel.

When, at the beginning of therapy, Rachel's need for him was discussed with the father, he responded very positively. He began to see Rachel regularly twice weekly, and to attend her therapy sessions once weekly. While he tended to be passive and withdrawn, he was consistently loving when Rachel approached him. In the early therapeutic sessions, recognition of Rachel's feelings of loss in connection with the father's absence seemed to bring almost instant relief to the child. The screaming, which at first had been almost continuous, subsided.

Treatment

First Year (Age 4–5): Symbiosis and Differentiation

Prior to coming to the Masters Children's Center, Rachel had been referred to several day treatment centers, none of which was satisfactory because the mother was unwilling to comply with their request that she leave Rachel. Thus, the treatment design we offered was ideally suited to the mother's needs. We proposed not to break the symbiotic bond between Rachel and her mother, but rather to take advantage of the child's and mother's wishes and, with the therapist acting as a catalyst, to reverse the destructive process and create a more satisfying relationship between them.

Rachel's mother responded well to the demands of the intensive treatment program (four times weekly for one-and-a-half to two hours). She was willing to give her all. Rachel too responded very rapidly to the initial phase of therapy, the creation of the symbiotic milieu. Her angry shrieking stopped within the first two weeks, quickly replaced by pleasure in physical closeness and in simple games of the sort one might play with an infant. She loved to be held, fondled, rocked, carried about, and covered up, which she would call "making cozy." She also liked to play in the water with all her clothes off and then to be wrapped in a towel or sheet.

All this surprised Rachel's mother, partly because she expected much more grown-up behavior from her 4-year-old, and partly because she said that, as a baby, Rachel had disliked being held. One could surmise that a harmonious, mutually pleasurable symbiotic relationship had never existed between Rachel and her mother. Nevertheless, Rachel seemed to have made some progress along the way of separation-individuation, but then regressed under the impact of trauma—a temporary separation from her mother when she was in the hospital, the fight between her parents, and the separation from her father. While Rachel had regressed as a consequence of these traumatic separations, closeness to her mother seemed to create a state of panic as well. The wished-for closeness with her mother seemed to elicit the simultaneous fear of being overwhelmed. Thus, Rachel was caught in the impossible dilemma where both being close to and not being close to her mother were unbearable and caused her to retreat into an autistic world of her own.

In the tripartite treatment setting, the wished-for closeness became less threatening, diluted by the introduction of a third person, the therapist. In Rachel's case, much of the early treatment consisted of introducing slowly and abundantly the kinds of experiences that, in normal development, happen naturally and almost imperceptibly, paving the way for the gradual discovery of self and other (Spitz 1957, Winnicott 1965).

Before the separation-individuation process could begin, a pleasurable, libidinally gratifying, symbiotic relationship had first to be established. Rachel demonstrated her denial of herself as a separate person in a number of ways. In her speech patterns, she not only avoided the use of personal pronouns, but also left gaps in her communications that would have to be filled in by her mother. She never communicated a wish directly, and what she did say was always a quotation—either from a story or record, or from a storehouse of phrases that she had heard. Another characteristic aspect of her speech was the tendency to repeat words and phrases over and over, until they turned into nonsense syllables. One could thus observe how she constructed her own code, her own autistic secret language.

Rachel expected her mother and her therapist to be partners with her in her symbiotic world. For instance, early in treatment we played the xylophone together. First we played the same song over and over without variation. Then, one day I sang, to a slightly altered tune, "You can play another song." Rachel, anxious at first, adapted this variation and made it part of her unalterable pattern. Every activity, at that time, was accompanied by a particular pattern of songs or conversations. If I did not play my prescribed parts, Rachel would shriek; if shrieking did not instantly produce the desired response, she would help herself by saying or singing my part. Thus, rather than accept the fact that I was not part of her, not subject entirely to her will, and not totally predictable like a phonograph record, she would regress to the autistic pattern of supplying the desired response herself (Elkisch and Mahler 1959).

As Rachel obtained gratification of her symbiotic needs and began to experience pleasure in the primitive games and interactions between the two of us, as well as with her mother, her relationship to her mother began to change. The earlier clinging disappeared, and instead a certain degree of obliviousness to her presence developed, at least in therapy sessions. However, Rachel still expected her mother to be there when she needed her, for example, to find a lost object. Rachel's earlier clinging had been a futile attempt to force her mother to satisfy her infantile needs for responsiveness and interaction. However, her desperate clinging was incomprehensible to her mother because she simultaneously rejected her mother's attempts at closeness. As therapist, it was my task to act as a bridge between mother and daughter, who were so desperately alone and so desperately longing to be together. Once the therapeutic situation began to provide Rachel and her mother with the satisfactions they had missed, Rachel's desperate need for her mother's continuous presence subsided.

Rachel continued to have many ways of denying her separate existence, some of which were curiously symbolic. For example, one day on finding a set of plastic letters in the playroom, she looked for the letter "I" and started to chew on it. Her mother said that at home they had a similar set of letters and that Rachel consistently ate all the "I's." Rachel's relationship to her own body was consistent with this self-denial. She treated it as though it were not part of her. Even though she was toilet-trained and went to the bathroom automatically, she would never look at either her stool or herself, and neither would she touch herself. She managed to perform her bodily functions in an almost dissociated, completely mechanical way.

As Rachel began to show signs of growing trust and beginning self–object differentiation, she started to move more freely. She bounced and jumped, and showed interest in climbing. She learned to climb a ladder, and was very proud of this accomplishment. She loved music and dancing. Her mother, who was also very musical, knew many songs, and both she and I sang a lot to Rachel during the first year of her therapy. Many hours were spent playing the piano for her while she rocked on a rocking horse. Later, I used piano playing and singing to talk to Rachel about difficult subjects, which she would otherwise refuse to hear about. Later in her treatment, when Rachel started to play the piano herself, she also chose songs with words that bore some relationship to problems with which she was dealing at the time.

Within an atmosphere of greater comfort and confidence, it became possible, with the help of Rachel's mother, to understand some of the child's codelike communications. Eventually it became possible to understand some of the fears underlying her autistic and symbiotic defenses. For example, Rachel's mother brought Rachel's favorite book to a therapy session and showed me Rachel's favorite page, which depicted a big animal pinned down to the ground, accompanied by a text of a rather violent content. When I asked Rachel whether this reminded her of anything, she lay down across two chairs in a most uncomfortable position and said, "Nice baby." Whatever Rachel said at this time was a repetition of something that had once been said to her. Thus, in this case, Rachel took words her mother must have said to her many times and connected them with a frightening picture— a picture that conveyed violence on the part of both the attacker and the victim. This in turn reminded her mother of how, when Rachel was a baby, she had always screamed in terror upon being wrapped in a towel after her bath and had always managed to wiggle out of her blankets. The child's behavior and the mother's memory together allowed me to begin the task of deciphering and reconstructing early traumatic experiences.

Another type of signal communication was more clearly related to the therapeutic situation. One day I sensed Rachel felt particularly close to me; she enjoyed hugging me and climbing on me. While looking out the window, I told Rachel that I saw a little girl going to the store across the street. This was the first time during her therapy when she seemed to show interest in and react to something in the outside world that was pointed out to her. For a long time thereafter, whenever Rachel craved closeness, she would go to the window and say, "The little girl goes to the store." I used this signal communication to show Rachel how much she actually did want closeness and tenderness, and how she was afraid to ask for it directly.

As a consequence of such interpretations, Rachel began to show her need for affection and approval, first of all from her mother. For instance, after tripping or falling, she would go to her mother and say, "Kiss it." Parallel with this development, however, she became increasingly demanding and coercive toward her mother—a defense commonly used by symbiotic psychotic children to reestablish their omnipotent world of symbiosis with mother just when the walls of that world begin to crack. Mother complained that Rachel was not satisfied to do things *with* her, but quickly took the role of being the mother in control.

At this stage Rachel's development in her treatment paralleled the first subphase of separation-individuation. She began to show some interest in other children and no longer avoided contact with them. Her wish to play with other children showed her dawning awareness of herself as a separate being, but her approach to them showed equally how dawning her sense of self was. One day Rachel's mother reported with great excitement that Rachel had made a friend in the park, a little girl who had been kind and outgoing toward her. Rachel responded, and the two little girls played together for a long time. Rachel played by following the other child about and imitating her without seeming to be quite aware that this other child was her own age and size. For example, when Rachel wanted to reach for something, she went up to the little girl and held up her arms, seemingly in the expectation that the little girl would lift her up—that is, that the child would respond as her mother might.

It was interesting to note that at the same time as Rachel showed growing interest in the outside world, she also actively sought distance from both her symbiotic objects, especially her mother. Not only did she pull me out of the room every so often, leaving her mother behind; her mother also reported that when Rachel had awakened one night with a stuffy nose and the mother tried to sit with her, Rachel pushed her away and ordered her back to bed. In her therapy sessions Rachel became interested in playing with doors, different from earlier hide-and-seek games she had played. Her new games entailed more active approach–distance behavior and showed her interest in active distancing.

As Rachel continued to turn toward the outside world, she acquired new skills on the playground, such as climbing on the jungle gym and swinging. Even though these activities caused her great anxiety, she showed an unusual determination to conquer her fears. The first time she tried a new activity, she would scream with anguish; thereafter, she would rapidly master the situation and return to the same activity with relative ease and mounting pleasure. Once Rachel was ready to struggle with an anxiety-provoking situation, she no longer needed reassurance. The quiet presence of her love objects and their participation in the pleasure she took in her expanding world provided her with enough support.

During this period Rachel started to have a very different look about her. The empty, staring expression and the fixed grin began to disappear as modulation of affect began to be reflected in her face. She cried real tears and could be comforted after a hurt. Mother commented that crying with pain or tears had been extremely rare and that until now Rachel had cried only in rage or fear (Mahler 1961).

Words spoken both *to* Rachel and *by* her began to have more meaning; they were used less and less as parts of a codelike signal language. Rachel began to describe activities that were actually going on. Games involving physical contact, such as running and catching, still remained very important to her, and at contact one felt Rachel's body become alive and relaxed.

Rachel's interest in her body took the form of oral exploration. She took a small baby doll and dropped it into a glass of milk, then took it out of the milk and licked it. Rachel's mother explained that at home Rachel tried to lick her own body and tried to reach inaccessible parts of it (Norman 1954). At home she started to explore her genitals and began to wipe herself after going to the toilet. She also began to look at herself. One day she pulled her tights down and said, "Two knees."

As Rachel started to show more interest in and awareness of her body, I put increased emphasis in therapy on the games that mothers play with their much smaller babies: we started to look in the mirror at her eyes, nose, and mouth, touching these parts and naming them. This exploration happened in an atmosphere of great intimacy and physical closeness between us. It was climaxed by Rachel's saying for the first time, with great emotional involvement, while looking in the mirror: *"I and you!"* We then invented games that combined words with pleasurable body feelings, in order to strengthen the emerging sense of I-ness and you-ness. One such game, which Rachel especially liked, was blowing at each other and saying, "I blow on you."

Rachel carried her growing ability to be separate one step further. She asked me to play the song "The Farmer in the Dell." I had played this song for her many times, but previously she had never been able to sing the last verse, "The cheese stands alone." Instead Rachel would sing, "The cheese stands alight." I had interpreted Rachel's inability to sing this last verse by telling her that she did not want anyone— not even the cheese—to be alone. On this day, following soon after the day Rachel and I played the "I and you" games, she sang the song first in her usual way and then sang, "The cheese stands alone," looking at me proudly as she sang.

Later in the same session, she had difficulty with a toy that kept breaking. I talked about how difficult it was for her to have me help her, because if I did help her, instead of magically making things turn out right, we became "I" and "you," which made her feel afraid of being alone. Thereupon she accepted my help and said softly, as if to herself, "I love you." She found the baby doll and started to chant, "Ah baby, sweet little Rachel." The monumental change of Rachel's ability to accept that she could be alone grew out of her trust that I could be in her world with her, after which point tolerating separateness no longer threatened her with total annihilation. With the awareness that people are separate, which earlier had been equal to annihilation of the self, she could now experience the need for love and caring. She played with a family of dolls for the first time, causing the mother and the baby doll to sit in the rocking chair together and play at cooking and feeding (Norman 1948).

Now that Rachel could acknowledge loving and being loved, she became more aware of her desires and wishes. However, she had to face the challenge of being disappointed when her wishes were not met by the outside world. A while back, Rachel and her mother had been accustomed to pass by a bakery every day where mother bought Rachel her favorite pastry. One day the bakery did not have this pastry, whereupon Rachel ran out of the store screaming. Thereafter, she refused even to walk by the store. Now, however, further along in her treatment, she started to talk about the bakery and about wanting to go there. When she got to the bakery, however, she closed her eyes and refused to go in. By closing her eyes, Rachel attempted to protect herself from the potential disappointment: it was better for the bakery not to exist than for it not to have what she wanted. As Rachel became more related, she faced the loss of protection of her symbiotic omnipotence.

The fact that Rachel was beginning to have a greater awareness of an outside world (which could be either gratifying or disappointing) was confirmed by a story her mother told. One day Rachel had been playing at home and had lost a toy she wanted. Her mother could not find it but had to go shopping nevertheless, leaving Rachel with a babysitter. When the mother returned from her shopping, Rachel ran to meet her and said, "Mary found it. Nice Mary." The mother thought Rachel's reaction was remarkable because Rachel had finally been able to appreciate and enjoy consciously something that had been done for her by someone else.

With increasing satisfaction in her relationships to others, Rachel became able to delay gratification. Earlier, only immediate gratification seemed to make any sense to her. If intermediary steps were necessary for the fulfillment of a wish, the wish itself would be forgotten in the process. For example, once when Rachel wanted to go outdoors, I told her we needed to get her coat first. She cried as if she hadn't understood what I had said. After agreeing to get her coat, however, she then lost sight of the original wish and made no further move to go outdoors. However, as her ability to recognize and appreciate when satisfaction of her needs came from a source outside herself, she developed a sense of time, and especially a reliable concept of the future. She also developed a greater sense of reality, an understanding of cause and effect, and with that a greater ability to master anxiety. For instance, she became willing to accompany her mother to the hitherto much-feared laundry room, and to accept mother's promise that they would do something nice afterward.

At about this time I stopped acting as the symbiotic, need-fulfilling partner and started to make greater demands upon Rachel, since she now had greater resources and a greater ability to endure anxiety and frustration. Instead of limiting herself to gestural and indirect demands, Rachel slowly became able to use words to ask for things. On one occasion she struggled to make me understand by gestures and by moving my arms as if they were her own that she wanted me to make a see-saw for her. When I did not comply, she was then able to ask for what she wanted by using words. Interestingly, she said "Oh, the see-saw," thus saying what she imagined I would say to her once I understood.

As Rachel became more of an individual, Rachel's mother started to investigate her own narcissistic investment in her child (Olden 1958). She found that up until then she had seen Rachel too much as a reflection of herself and considered how during the child's early life, she had expected too much of Rachel and had reacted too strongly when Rachel failed to meet these expectations. She thought her own anger had been needlessly intense and unpredictable. She wept frequently during her private sessions with me, saying she had noticed she was weeping a great deal when not with Rachel. Mother talked a great deal about her own childhood, particularly the suffering she had experienced because of a lack of mothering. She realized being a mother was one of the ways in which she had been trying to make up to herself for what she had not had as a child. It seemed she was mourning both the mother she didn't have and the mother she couldn't be.

Second Year of Treatment (Age 5–6): Practicing and Rapprochement

Rachel brought to her first session following summer vacation some postcards I had sent her. She put them on the table, looked at them and said, "Hugs and kisses." She would not talk about anything she had done during the summer, but went around the room looking at and briefly touching all the familiar toys and objects. She had some favorite words at that time, which she now asked her mother to repeat over and over. They were words that had to do with the passage of time such as "still" and "until." Later in that same session, Rachel showed, in primary process fashion, her awareness of feelings brought on by the separation and reunion.

Rachel talked about parcels, which her mother explained by referring to the story about Ant and Bee in which Bee was sad and Ant gave her presents (parcels) to make her feel better. I connected this story to the postcards and presents I had sent to Rachel during our separation. Then, referring to the song "Parlez-moi d'Amour," Rachel said to her mother, "Sing 'parcels'" (to Rachel the song title sounded like parcels). In this way Rachel showed she was able to appreciate my sending her parcels as a sign of my love for her. Typically, the way in which she showed this was disguised by a story and a French love song—through the use of primary process associations.

During this same session Rachel picked up a baby doll and said, "The baby is screaming." Her mother remarked that Rachel would never say a baby was crying. In the very next session, however, Rachel picked up a baby doll and said, "The baby is crying." Her mother also reported that Rachel herself had cried with tears on saying goodbye to her friends on the playground. From then on, Rachel was able to cry from sadness (as earlier she had started to cry from pain). This ability to experience genuine sadness at separation rather than anger emerged together with her growing ability to experience loving feelings, even in the face of separation and disappointment (A. Freud 1965, Jacobson 1957).

I believe Rachel's behavior during the session after vacation showed she had been able to retain an inner positive image of me during our separation: I had become a good outside object, internalized and relatively stable. Rachel had developed a degree of "confident expectation" and was on the way toward developing object constancy. She now understood that after a separation I could and would again become available to help and comfort her and that it was safe to enjoy loving and being loved. At this point Rachel had entered the practicing period, the second subphase of the separation-individuation process, characterized by an increased investment in the environment— a "love affair with the world"—as well as by greater narcissistic investment in her own functions and body.

Rachel still did not communicate directly but rather spoke for the other person: for example, she would say, "I will push you on the swing" or "Mommy push you," when she wanted to be pushed. I began to question Rachel about her inability to ask directly for something she wanted. One day I said to her, "I wish I could understand why you cannot ask for things for yourself, and then I could help you better," to which Rachel replied, "Ring-around-the-rosy." Her mother explained that during the summer she had been afraid of the ocean and had overcome her fear by playing ring-around-the-rosy. Characteristically, Rachel's response was rich in associations and meanings, which her mother could help us to understand. Rachel's fear of asking directly for my help was as big as her fear of being engulfed by the ocean. To ask for help is to acknowledge dependence on, as well as separateness from, the other, and with that the possibility of annihilation, should the help not be forthcoming. Poignantly, Rachel conjured up an instance in which her mother had effectively helped her face her fear by playing a game in which they hold hands and "all fall down." Thus the disastrous play outcome is shared with the other and can be overcome. Through repeating the game one can control and master the fear.

One day Rachel asked me to play on the piano a song I did not know. When I indicated that I could not, she became furious and refused to sing the song to me. Rachel's mother said sadly, "This is so often what happens at home: Rachel won't help me and she won't let me help her." Thereupon, Rachel began to sing to a familiar tune, "I help you and you help me, and so we will sing together." I spoke to her about her conflicting wishes: on the one hand she wished to have us as part of herself and for us to know all her thoughts and feelings without her having to express them; on the other hand, she wanted us to love her and to do nice things for her that she hadn't asked for or even, in a sense, "wanted," like sending parcels. Rachel listened with rapt attention, and something seemed to click in her. At the very next session she asked me directly for the first time, "Push me on the swing," and "Please sing once more."

At around this time Rachel started to play with a small baby doll while talking about "baby cream." Her mother explained by recalling the big jars of Desitin she had used when Rachel had eczema starting in the second half of her first year. Mother said that both she and Rachel had hated the cream, but it was the only thing that helped relieve the eczema. Thus the reconstruction of the past continued with the addition of more detail and a more intense reliving of old affects.

As Rachel became able to replay some of these old memories in her sessions, there were periods of much angry screaming. When she screamed she would often look in the mirror, as if she needed to assure herself she was still there and unharmed. One day she reminded her mother of a story her mother had read to her about an old goat who wanted to get her way, and of another about a troll who was so angry he stamped his foot and then disappeared under the ground. Through play and storytelling, Rachel, together with her mother, made it possible to recall and work through frightening memories, especially those connected with terrifying rage and destruction of the self or other.

At home Rachel seemed to try to master her fear of the disappearing garbage by helping her mother dispose of it. Her fear of her own and the object's rage—as a result of which objects disappeared or were destroyed (Winnicott 1953)—was beginning to loosen. In her play she went back to the older sources of such overwhelming rage to a time

when her mother's attempts to care for her were indeed experienced
as catastrophic. This period was difficult and explosive for both Rachel
and her mother. Only after it became possible to make Rachel aware
of her annihilation panic and to reassure her that she was loved regardless of her destructive impulses, did she quiet down and earnestly
go about remembering in play and words some of her early traumatic
experiences. First came the rash and the baby cream. A baby doll
was amply creamed and powdered session after session, even though
Rachel had been afraid to touch the sticky baby cream at first. This
play went on until it could be linked to castration fear. One day Rachel
called the feared Desitin "vagina cream," and touched her genitals,
saying sadly that she had a cut. During this time Rachel was very
concerned about her body and keenly aware of any small wound, for
which she required an ample supply of band-aids. Her eczema recurred at a particular spot on her arm, at the bend of her elbow.
Rachel would scratch until it was bloody. The eczema on her elbow
could now be connected to the eczema she had had in her diaper area
when she was an infant. Rachel could now be shown how she had
perceived her mother's treating her eczema as "hurting" her, when
in fact her mother had been trying to alleviate her pain.

Another incident that had been traumatic for this hypersensitive
child came into consciousness. Rachel said, "The medicine chest," and
then "Vaporub." Her mother recalled that when Rachel was about 2,
shortly following the first separation between the parents, she had a
severe cold and was unable to sleep at night. Mother put Vaporub
on her chest to relieve the congestion, but Rachel was terrified and
screamed for hours. This incident too was played out and worked
through in great detail.

The playing out of traumatic incidents of this sort was always
accompanied by an intense struggle on Rachel's part. Sometimes it
seemed she could barely distinguish between the doll and herself. She
would say, "No, no, she's not sick. She doesn't have a rash. It's all
gone. It's all better." At the same time there was a strong, quite admirable determination in Rachel to keep bringing up painful and
frightening situations and work them through.

Rachel now began to play a new kind of game with her dolls. Instead of playing with only the baby doll, she started to arrange all of
them in family situations. Then she would say, "They all lived in a

little apartment—a father, a mother, a brother, a sister, and a baby." At the time Rachel started treatment, the first toy she became attached to was a frog which reminded her of a small toy frog her father had given to her when she was 2 years old, which she had subsequently lost in the toilet bowl. Rachel's feelings about the loss when her father left home now came up as she played out her wish for a united family.

For several months, while working hard in her therapy sessions and facing much conflict and anxiety therein, Rachel also went through a period of happy involvement, both at home and at nursery school. In the fall she had started to attend a neighborhood cooperative nursery school two afternoons a week. She was already familiar with the teachers and children whom she had regularly met at the playground used by both the school and the clinic.

In the beginning, even though she loved to go to school, she experienced great difficulty and anxiety in certain situations, for instance, at story time when the teacher gave her attention to the entire group, a situation over which Rachel had no control. Another difficulty was over some small animals in a cage: Rachel became compulsively drawn to them and was at the same time terrified of them. (Her teachers thought she was terrified by her impulse to hurt them.) Rachel would shriek with hysterical laughter at the small furry creatures. At first she was unable to play with the children to whom she reacted with similar excitement and hysterical laughter. Following the therapeutic work about being "made to disappear" like the troll and the garbage, her anxiety lessened in the nursery school and she began to take part in group activities, to use materials, and to play with the other children.

It was a description by her very devoted and patient teachers of this kind of play that first brought to my mind that what they were describing was reminiscent of the "love affair with the world" during the practicing period. Rachel now seemed to be in love with her life, especially with her nursery school. When it was closed at vacation time or even on the weekends, she could not imagine the building was empty: in her fantasy her beloved teachers and classmates were always there.

After several months of this relatively happy time of Rachel's practicing period, her behavior once again became very disturbed, culminating in a rapprochement crisis. Characteristic of Rachel's therapy, the change was ushered in by the introduction of a new story. While caring for her baby doll, Rachel would give her a bath and wash her hair. But one day she dropped the baby doll in the water and said, "She fell into the water until she reached a *lot*." Mother explained the reference to a story about a kitten who looked into the water, mistook its reflection for another cat, and jumped in. The kitten fell down until it reached a *rock*[1] but was eventually saved. This story seemed to represent Rachel's struggle to find her self image, to see herself as a separate person—to reach a *lot*. Rachel's feelings about the dangerous nature of this undertaking was symbolized as falling into the water.

Up until this time, Rachel had been most interested in a baby doll to whom she gave the name Snow White, a name that seemed to express Rachel's ambivalence about being her mother's baby. At this point, Rachel became interested in a new little girl doll—no longer a baby doll—to whom she gave the name Cricket. As she came to identify with the new doll, she insisted on having two girl dolls: Cricket and the "other Cricket." It seemed that when she dared to become a separate individual, symbolized in her identification with a girl doll, she had to reassure herself by having two.

By now Rachel had fully reached the rapprochement period of her separation-individuation process. In normal development this period represents the peak of the separation-individuation struggle during which the toddler, who has been practicing separateness from mother without being fully aware that mother is not ever-present, slowly and sometimes suddenly has to face that neither mother nor the world is at his omnipotent command and disposal. Even in normal development this realization can lead to strenuous attempts to force mother to be ever-present, ever-sharing, ever-fulfilling of every wish and whim. Suddenly the child's frustration tolerance, which expands so significantly during the preceding practicing period, disintegrates. Thus, rapprochement is characteristically a period of temper tan-

---

1. Changing a word to one with a similar sound was a characteristic way in which Rachel tried to defend against her anxious thoughts and feelings. Thus, "rock" to "lot."

trums, sleep disturbances, and moodiness (Mahler 1966). It is also
the period of rapid language development. Both possessiveness and
pleasure in sharing are indicators of the growing sense of separateness and identity.

Rachel's rapprochement crisis became apparent first in nursery
school, where it revolved around Rachel's relationship with a gentle
little girl, Nancy. The two girls had a special game together: Rachel
would come very close to Nancy, look into her eyes tenderly, and say,
"Hippity hoppity." Nancy would then repeat the words. And so the
game would go back and forth without variation until Nancy could
no longer take it. Rachel would become enraged by Nancy's refusal
to continue the game and would become aggressive with Nancy, who
would never hit back. Soon Rachel's aggressive behavior spread to
her relations with the other children. Rachel became uncontrollable:
she would pull chairs out from under children, push them down, pour
water on them, and pull their hair. When she was separated from
them she would shed bitter tears and promise to be good, only to start
the same cycle all over again upon being allowed to rejoin the group.
She was also intensely provocative with her teachers, attempting to
do everything that was forbidden.

At home she became most demanding of her mother, who complained that life with Rachel had not been as hard as this since they
first started treatment. Rachel now insisted on her mother's participation in her play and tried to control every move. She insisted that
both she and her mother take off their clothes at home: she would
wear only pajamas and her mother was required to wear a house-
dress. This demand seemed to be an attempt to regress to symbiotic
closeness with mother.

Rachel insisted on sameness between herself and her mother in
many ways, even at some sacrifice to herself. For example, if mother
did not want to eat the same dessert, Rachel would forgo eating it
herself. Once more the relationship took on the quality of Rachel's
wanting to force her mother to be part of herself.

Rachel had developed another problem with regard to her clothes.
She had endless difficulties in putting on her hat, complaining that
her ears were not covered, and she developed a strong attachment
to an old coat, which she treated like a transitional object. She refused to wear a new coat to which she gave the name, "the meet coat."

With considerable effort we established that several months earlier Rachel had met another child in the park wearing an identical coat, which shocked her. Since that time Rachel had refused to wear her new coat and became attached to her old one. It seemed that meeting another child in the identical coat threatened her newly emerging, unstable sense of self, and that her old coat thus took on the qualities of a transitional object that helped her to hold on to her tenuous ability to maintain her own individual entity and identity (Mahler 1958, Winnicott 1953).

At the time Rachel may very well not have fully cathected her body boundaries yet; thus, clothes were particularly bothersome to her because she could not decide whether they were part of her. She expressed fear of losing part of herself, an anxiety that was at its peak as she became more separate and felt more acutely vulnerable and helpless. These feelings must have been particularly acute when she was at home alone with mother, for it was during these times that the old patterns recurred of trying to force her mother to be the symbiotic partner. For example, she demanded that her mother finish her sentences or guess her thoughts. She also became intensely preoccupied with wanting to know where situations or experiences had gone after they were over, even if they had been unpleasant (Elkisch 1956). For example, she would ask, "Where did the rash go?" Once she added, "I ate it up." After a vacation she asked, "Where did the vacation go?" At the same time she developed a great fear and dislike for men, probably related to her awareness of her father's absence from the family, as well as of sexual differences.

The changed behavior in Rachel was first manifested in school, later at home, and last in her therapeutic sessions. There too she eventually became more aggressive and negativistic. She no longer accepted necessary limitations but would instead run away and attempt to do what was forbidden. When she became angry with me, she would take my chair and carry it into another room. At the same time she became interested in the physicality of loving, and arranged the dolls hugging and kissing in various positions. Primal scene fantasies entered into her doll play. Often she had the mother and father doll hugging each other, or she would make the father doll throw the mother doll. She also became much more aware of people's moods, of their being happy or unhappy, and she anxiously insisted that her mother and I smile and be happy. She made up a story about a baby pig that was thrown away because it shouted and screamed.

The fact that her love objects did not always fulfill her wishes threatened Rachel's feelings of omnipotence and made her acutely aware of her separateness and vulnerability (Geleerd 1958). The rage at her little friend could be understood in therapy as a displacement of her rage toward her mother and me, a rage she was afraid to express directly for fear of retaliation by us. I offered this interpretation to Rachel and encouraged her to express her angry feelings toward both her mother and me, in words and gestures. At the same time it was decided with the nursery school teachers that Rachel would be sent home if her aggressive behavior continued, in order to make her experience the fact that both she and the other children needed to be protected. When she was sent home, Rachel was indeed terribly upset. But the next day, when she was allowed to return, she began the day in the same wildly aggressive way, and her teachers decided once again to send her home. This time Rachel cried so hard they felt compelled to give her another chance. Rachel sat down and asked her teachers to draw a picture of a little girl. Following that, she wrote (she had recently taught herself to write, just as she had taught herself to read), "If I bother Alice, I will have to go home, but if I don't bother her, you can play with her." Another child, moved by Rachel's anguish and by her attempts to control herself, said, "Yes, if you are good, we will play with you." The teacher then suggested ways in which Rachel might play with the children, ways that were different from the way she played with her mother.

Suddenly the teacher felt herself in touch with Rachel. At last, she thought, she could feel empathy with Rachel's wish for love and sharing. With the help of her teacher, Rachel did learn to approach the other children in a more acceptable way and her behavior did improve. For the first time she began to be able to understand and accept "pretend" games, a further sign that her own sense of identity was becoming more secure.

It was dramatic to observe how Rachel's recently acquired ability to write helped her to master her impulses. At the beginning of treatment, she had brought up new material by quoting from stories and poems. Later she had added play with dolls and had uttered single words that were the code to some past event. As she became interested in writing, she added another way, namely, asking me to write certain words or phrases that, with the help of her mother, would lead to the reconstruction of early traumatic events. Finally she started to write by herself. Rachel's mother said often she had been able to tell what problems Rachel was struggling with simply by seeing the situations she had left her dolls in. Now she began to find sheets of paper covered with writing. At first, the writing was difficult to decipher, but it improved steadily.

Rachel worked out the resolution of her rapprochement crisis—the crisis of separateness—in her doll play. For a while, Rachel had been playing with a doll family consisting of a father, mother, and one little girl. She had named these dolls respectively Laurie, Lauren, and Laura, and then added another girl doll, who was always passive in the play, who never did anything but just be there. This doll she called Urgie. In playing with the dolls called Lauren, Laurie, and Laura, Rachel seemed to alternate between thinking of herself as Laura, the little girl, and as Lauren, the mother doll. I said to her that it seemed to me as if Laura and Lauren were the same person, to which Rachel answered, "And Laurie too." Then she played that Laurie was the king, Lauren the queen, and Laura the princess.

For the first time, she then played with a small girl doll to which she had given her own name, Rachel. On that same day, when her mother left the room, she did not respond with her usual jumping, which served both as a discharge of tension and as a way to hide the underlying affect. Instead, she went to the piano and looked forlorn. The mood of sadness over separation from her mother was finally able to emerge; her state of separateness no longer had to be denied. She sat in my lap and said, "Love me." Then she picked up the doll she had always called Urgie, looked at her thoughtfully, and said, "Urgie, mergie, urgie, mergie."

Before this, Rachel had given no clues about the Urgie doll's role in the play, nor about her strange name. Now it seemed as if Urgie might represent Rachel's *urge to merge*. The concept itself was not strange to her; we had often talked about her wish to be one with her symbiotic objects. The use of such abstract language, however, seemed quite incredible, although Rachel's ability to comprehend, use, and at the same time concretize abstract concepts had always been an outstanding characteristic of hers (Despert 1940, Norman 1954).

It seemed quite clear, at any rate, that something of great importance was going on. I said, "So it is Urgie-Mergie who makes Laurie-Laura-Lauren all have the same name and be like one person?" Rachel said, "I want to throw it away." She asked to have the window opened and threw Urgie-Mergie out. It was interesting that Rachel was apparently able to feel the urge to merge as another person within her compelling her, not allowing her to be herself.

Many important changes followed in the wake of this session, in which Rachel had been able to do to the doll what she herself had been so terrified might happen to her. Earlier, Rachel had thrown blocks and sand; she had also attempted to throw children in school off their chairs or into water. In this session, however, she was able to express in play both the urge to throw away and the fear of being thrown away; and she could furthermore express the idea that there was something within her—Urgie-Mergie—of which she wanted to rid herself.

Bringing this issue into the treatment situation made the danger less real, since in play the doll could be and was retrieved, and the action repeated, slowly interpreted, and put into the context of her feelings, both past and present. Rachel herself had developed a fear of falling out the window, as well as a fear of the toilet. It became possible to make her aware of her need for love and to help her to keep in mind that feeling loved and cared for could alleviate her feeling of aloneness and rage when her partner was unable to fulfill her demands. Rachel then gained sufficient courage to express feelings of rage toward me in word and action.

Rachel had now entered the period of verbal communication, symbolic representation, and object constancy. This stage of the process is characterized by a capacity for internalization and by the establishment of self and object representations, with increased self-esteem and self-love. The most important gain of this period was the consistent use of communicative secondary-process functional language. She began to use "I" and "you" consistently, and she could now express much more directly how she felt in everyday life situations and in play (Furer 1964).

With the establishment of her separate identity, Rachel became able to take part in and enjoy many new activities. Most important was the development of the ability to use "pretend" play and the ability to draw and paint representationally, even though her drawings were primitive and monotonous (at first faces and then figures). She gave names to these drawings and put them into many different contexts.

It was as if windows to the outside world had now been thrown open, allowing for the exchange of more genuine feelings and enabling Rachel to dare to reach out and to begin to gain pleasure from the real world and from her love objects. Once established, this quality remained with Rachel. She seemed to know and accept the fact that she was separate. She no longer had to deny unpleasant experiences; she gave up the anxious pretense of being always happy. Above all, she seemed to know from then on that the "I" needed to love the "you" and to be loved by the "you."

Follow-up and Discussion

In the above description of the treatment and development of a psychotic girl between the ages of 4 and 6, I hope to have shown how the world of a psychotic child, which appears to be incomprehensible, can be made sense of through the treatment process. I also hope to have shown how recognizing the phases of the separation-individuation process and identifying these phases as they unfold in a delayed and distorted manner can bring order and meaning to what otherwise seems chaotic. The foundation of such treatment is the therapist's willingness to enter into the psychotic child's world and to recognize the ingenuity of its own peculiar logic. I believe that the aim of treatment of psychotic children is not that they become "normal," but rather that they develop a sense of their unique self and learn to form meaningful and caring object relationships. Treatment should enable them to learn to function adequately in the world as it helps them to accept the ways in which they are unique and different from others.

In her years of treatment, Rachel gradually was able to accept and function in the world while being fully aware of the difficulties she would always face of fully fitting into it. During her further growing up, Rachel had to weather finding her sense of identity which, for psychotic children, eventually requires a process of mourning for a lost, "normal" childhood. It also requires the ability to accept the particular difficulties in growing up with which they will always have to struggle as long as they continue to live in the real world.

In the case of Rachel, we can see the strength and creativity needed by such a child to overcome nameless dreads. We also see the strength, creativity, and perseverance needed by the mother to use an alliance with the therapist to tolerate living with her child and, together with the therapist, to help her child develop into a separate person with a viable sense of self.

Looking back after a recent visit with Rachel, it is clear that indeed she emerged from her treatment with the strength needed to continue to develop in the world. Now in her late thirties, Rachel is living in a stable relationship with another woman and works on and off as a librarian, which is also the profession of her partner. She is very much aware of her past difficulties as well as remnants of those in her present way of functioning. Rachel has not given up her strong connection to the world of the unconscious. Not only are her memories of her childhood and her treatment very much alive in her, but she continues to find a place in her life for her creative inner world through the writing of poetry, composing of music, singing in several choirs, and adherence to religious rituals which were not part of her upbringing but which she discovered as an adult.

In a recent interview, Rachel talked about retaining strong positive feelings about her early treatment, though she said I might have helped her more with some of her cognitive difficulties, which have been diagnosed as Attention Deficit Disorder. She also talked about having been quite seriously depressed for many years and how she eventually sought psychiatric help, at which point she was put on a mild dose of imipramine, which she has found helpful. Asked how she experienced Attention Deficit Disorder, she said that she thought she had difficulty processing and understanding interpersonal situations: she wasn't quick enough to pick up people's messages and communications.

Rachel talked about having searched for and found her birth family and that this was very important to her because she felt that she now had relatives. Her birth sister has recently had a baby, and Rachel is very excited about this and showed me pictures. Rachel continues to be on good terms with her mother. Their relationship can weather disagreements: for example, Rachel described how her mother is not happy about her being religiously observant.

In discussing her early treatment and my writing about her, it seemed that Rachel is quite clear about the essence of our therapeutic work. It is very important to her to be out in the open—both as a lesbian and as a person with certain disabilities. She very much wants her story to be told, would like her real name to be used, and even suggested the title: "Searching for Rachel: Psychoanalytic Work with Seriously Disturbed Children." I think one could say that Rachel not only feels that I searched for her but that I found her—or helped her to become herself. It was very impressive to me how well she understood both where she had come from and where she is now.[2]

2. I am very grateful to Rachel and to her parents, who steadfastly supported her treatment and managed to live through very difficult years with her. I am also grateful to Margaret Mahler and the staff of Masters Children's Center, and especially to the School for Nursery Years, which supported Rachel as she learned to tolerate and enjoy the company of other children.

Appendix

The Inclusion of a Symbiotic Child
in a Normal Nursery Group

Judith Lobel

At the time of her diagnostic evaluation, prior to coming to Masters Children's Center, Rachel was described as avoiding other children, preferring to engage in solitary activity. However, after she had been in treatment a few months she began to show interest in the children in the group of 4-year-olds I was teaching at the cooperative nursery school for normal neighborhood children, which was housed in the same building.

Her first contacts with the children took place when she would come out to the play yard. At first she paid little attention to the other children; in the midst of their activity she seemed to build a wall around herself and her therapist. Although she did not interact, she nonetheless appeared to enjoy herself in the children's company, and frequently expressed a desire to go to the yard where she knew they might be. Gradually, she began to watch them, and by November she would join briefly in their play, for example, taking turns on the slide.

She soon discovered the nursery room. As in the yard, she began by paying little attention to the children, which was particularly noticeable when the room was filled with busy activity. At these times she focused on peripheral and inanimate objects, such as the phonograph, and would soon want to leave. However, when there were just a few children in the room, she would take the opportunity to investigate toys and materials and watch them. Even when she had not appeared to be watching the other children, it sometimes became clear that she had because she would go over to toys they had been using as soon as they left them. At around this time she began to beg her therapist to take her to "see the children." By January these visits had become a regular part of her therapy sessions. She was usually reluctant to leave the nursery and often, before doing so, she would look into each child's eyes, squatting down if they happened to be on the floor.

Rachel now frequently joined in activities such as dancing, using Play-Doh, and painting. She observed the other children attentively and frequently imitated them. At times it appeared that she did not understood the meaning of the actions she imitated. For example, after another child pretended to talk on the telephone, Rachel picked up the phone and parroted some words. Gradually, the number of interactions of which Rachel clearly grasped the meaning increased and she responded with appropriate affect and sustained excitement.

The following September, the staff and parents of the cooperative nursery school agreed to Rachel's participation in the fours' group on a twice weekly basis. The parents knew of Rachel as a child who screamed and acted strangely but who was very eager to be with other children.

During her first few days of nursery school, Rachel seemed to be bursting with happiness and excitement over the presence of so many children. She quickly learned all of their names and had to know at all times where each child was. She took attendance the moment she came into the room: "Where's Joshua? Where's Amy?" She continued to ask for those who were absent and would answer her own question with the explanation she had been given earlier, "Where's Bobby? He's sick. He'll be better soon."

Rachel's first approaches to the other children were physical. She would poke, pick up, or embrace them, particularly the girls, and they would have a hard time releasing themselves from her strong grip. She appeared to be overstimulated by them and unable to control her impulses. She became more excited and anxious when they screamed and ran from her.

Rachel spent a good deal of time watching the children and briefly trying one sensory material after another, with the exception of paint, which she used in an intense and compulsive way. She was unable to join in group activities and was allowed to paint while the group met for story and to have juice served to her at the easel. Although she was not pressured to join group activities, she appeared tense during them. She would suddenly stop painting and approach the group. Then she would stiffen, arch backwards, and laugh in a strident, hysterical way. Sometimes, when a teacher was reading she would put her face in front of the teacher's and laugh hysterically.

Gradually, through observing the other children and approaching them in her clumsy physical way, Rachel began to develop ways of interacting with them. These early interactions were extremely limited, ritualized, and essentially dyadic. She tended to restrict each pattern of play to the child with whom it had originated. These patterns often involved being chased. With Bobby, Rachel would say, "Bobby chases me, Bobby kills me," and then run away from him. Soon she began to push Bobby to induce him to chase her. John would try to keep her from getting out of the jungle gym, and she would say, "John puts me in jail." When she would escape, he would chase her.

Because of her disruptive behavior it became clear that she would need to have someone who would stay by her side and act as a buffer between her and the other children. The individual attention of a student teacher who was assigned to her helped calm her during group times and transitions, and greatly facilitated her integration into the group.

The winter months were marked by impressive social and intellectual accomplishments, including Rachel's teaching herself to read. At first she wrote the word *wood* over and over again. This word, to which she would sometimes add an s, did not seem to have a communicative purpose. By Christmas time she could write all three of her names, and shortly after this she astounded the children by writing their names.

Though she continued to approach children physically, she also began to find other ways of relating. Gradually more elaborate interactions evolved. Furthermore, her physical approaches were not always rejected. For example, Amy declared that she didn't mind if Rachel picked her up. Such a gesture usually meant that a child had developed some understanding or empathy for Rachel. With Amy this acceptance was followed by other marks of friendship; for example, Amy and Rachel would work side by side at the easel, even exchanging compliments on each others' paintings.

The children had varying degrees of tolerance for Rachel. One little girl, Francie, was consistently accepting of her and characteristically responded to her with patience rather than annoyance. On the other hand, Amy's friendly and understanding disposition toward Rachel easily broke down in the face of Rachel's infantile qualities. Amy would sometimes band together with Judy, who seemed personally disturbed by Rachel and was generally antagonistic toward her.

Like Rachel, Judy was an only child who lived with her mother because of her parents' separation. At the beginning of the year, Judy had difficulty joining other children's play. She was quite rigid and if the children did not play just as she wanted, she would be upset and would not play with them. Judy's mother expected a lot of her, including that Judy "understand" about her parents' separation. This demand may have contributed to a certain hurt and angry quality about Judy. It was characteristic, for example, that when another child bumped her she was sure that it had been done on purpose. If one pointed out to Judy that the other child was distressed to see her so upset, Judy would reveal a capacity to melt and would appear relieved and appeased. Having taken over her mother's exacting standards of behavior, Judy was naturally annoyed by Rachel, who was in many ways so infantile and who, in particular, had such poor impulse control. Perhaps Judy was also jealous because Rachel was given love just as she was. In any case, Judy, who was herself so sensitive to exclusion, reacted by making Rachel the unacceptable one and by trying to exclude her.

My role as teacher was to explain to Judy (and others who were disturbed by Rachel) that in some ways Rachel was not as grown up as she, that all children could not do the same things, that Rachel was trying very hard, and most of all that Rachel really wanted very much to be friends. I believe that one of the great values of including Rachel in the group was that the emphasis on tolerance made it possible for Judy to make significant changes. In the course of the year, Judy became a great deal more flexible and accepting of herself. In the end she was also able to show a limited empathy for Rachel.

Amy and Judy would show their dislike of Rachel by making comments and faces at her. Rachel would retaliate by calling them "stupid." Sometimes Rachel would initiate this name calling without provocation from the girls; she seemed compelled to stir them up. This unprovoked aggression greatly angered them and they would in turn lash out at her. Rachel would become frightened by their physical assaults, and cower and back away from them; nevertheless, she would continue the name calling.

Interestingly, during the winter months these incidents did not dominate Rachel's adjustment in the group; she was too busy practicing her newly acquired social and cognitive skills. In fact, during this period she was the pride and joy of the mothers and teachers, who were so pleased with her progress that they decided to increase her attendance to three days a week.

During the winter months, Rachel developed a pleasurable relationship with Francie. This relationship was less exclusively dyadic, and their play often included other children. It also involved more varied themes, which were apparently very meaningful to Rachel. Francie was an imaginative child who could play nicely with several other girls without competing for their attention. She was able to be lively, but was generally rather gentle with a kind of adult-like neutrality. Francie would initiate play by moving near Rachel and taking part in whatever she was doing. However, at a certain point— which we later came to think of as the end of Rachel's *practicing period*—Rachel lost interest in the quiet, warm play she had had with Francie, and became intensely attracted to Nancy.

The relationship between Rachel and Nancy was at first marked by tenderness. Nancy was easily moved to sympathy for others. She was largely involved in friendships with other girls with whom she played out family themes, and she usually took the role of mother. Nancy's role with Rachel was also motherly: she was consistently tolerant and generous toward Rachel even when she made unreasonable demands. On several occasions Rachel became attracted to toys that Nancy was using, and Nancy repeatedly gave them to Rachel. Nancy also gratified Rachel's wish for physical contact, letting Rachel put her head in her lap, stroke her hair, and dance with her.

However, the friendship between Nancy and Rachel began to take on a darker tone as Rachel became desperately intent on perpetuating their interactions and preventing Nancy from moving away. For example, one game that developed between the girls went as follows: Rachel would look into Nancy's face in a tender way and say, "Hippity-hoppity." Then Nancy would repeat this to Rachel; Rachel would repeat it again, and so on. Nancy would eventually tire of this game and want to stop, but Rachel was insatiable and could not bear to stop, nor could she bear any variation. After a while Nancy became afraid to play this game, which enraged Rachel, who would follow Nancy around, grabbing hold of her arm and preventing her from doing anything else.

Rachel's aggressive behavior toward Nancy escalated, until during the first two weeks of May, it took up most of her day, while mine was dominated by the need to restrain her. None of her earlier constructive activities interested her. She was dissatisfied with everything, yet, at the same time, she seemed very much aware of the other children. It appeared that this awareness led her to notice differences between them and herself that left her dissatisfied, angry, and jealous.

While Nancy remained the special focus of her aggression, Rachel now attacked the other children as well. She tipped over chairs on which they were sitting. She pushed them into the sandbox when it was filled with water. She came close to dumping a pail of water over one of the biggest boys. She knocked down block buildings. Whenever a prohibition was stated, Rachel seemed compelled to violate it. If I announced the fire escape was out of bounds Rachel would immediately climb it. Similarly, she would flick the overhead lights on and off and turn the water faucets on and off.

It seemed that in choosing Nancy as the primary object of her love and aggression, Rachel made a realistic assessment of Nancy's personality: she chose a child who could be nice to her in a motherly way. To help Rachel control her attacks on the other children, it was necessary to teach her that the consequences of her aggression would be separation from Nancy and from the group. On the day following the punishment of being sent home from school, Rachel was again very aggressive. I was about to send her home again when Rachel, sitting at a table, began to write: "If I bother Nancy then you have to go home. If you are nice to Nancy then she will play with you." She covered several sheets of paper with such phrases, and the directness of her wish and her great effort to control her anger made it possible for me to sympathize with and help her by reflecting this back to her.

It was touching that Judy and several other girls who were also sitting at the table where Rachel and I were writing and talking overheard us and became more sympathetic as well. Judy echoed Nancy and said: "Yes, if you're good we'll play with you." At story time several girls put their heads in Rachel's lap and announced that they liked her. Rachel loved this contact but was able to stay with the story rather than demanding that the contact continue.

During the two remaining weeks of school, Rachel was generally more quiet and less provocative. Though she mostly seemed to revert to parallel play, she played very near the other children and watched them more intently than ever. It seemed to me that she was on the verge of approaching them in a new way. Her mother reported that outside of nursery she was now able to approach children directly and ask them, "Do you want to play?"

Rachel seemed to recognize her wish to play with Nancy and also to accept that she could not force Nancy to play with her. She seemed more and more clearly to be asking me to reinforce her self-control. About two or three times a day she would make it necessary for me to repeat briefly the punishment of removing her from the group. She would bring this about with a resurgence of aggression, now usually indirect, yet still disruptive. She seemed to need these "time outs," after which she could once again play contentedly.

I was impressed by the social gains Rachel was able to make in the course of the year and also by the tremendous effort that they had entailed. She had needed to observe the children and laboriously learn how to interact with them. She had needed to curb her longing for exclusive interaction with Nancy as the price of remaining in the group. She seemed to emerge from the experience with increased resilience and a capacity for more complex and modulated interactions.

15

Using Insights from Observational Research of Mothers and Babies in the Therapy of Preschool Children [1]

The City University Child Center

Introduction

This chapter describes the City University Child Center, a therapeutic treatment center begun in 1976 and ongoing until 1995. The center was an integral part of the Clinical Psychology Ph.D. program at The City University of New York, primarily to teach clinical psychology students how to work with seriously disturbed preschool children and their families from economically disadvantaged backgrounds. It was a model program within the community and encouraged visitors interested in learning more about a developmentally and psychoanalytically oriented approach to young children with a variety of language and attachment disorders. Professionals, including teachers, day-care workers, music and art therapists, child psychologists, and

---

1. It is impossible to list all the colleagues who over the years have collaborated on this project. I would like to thank Steven Ellman and Lawrence Gould for their unflagging support during all the years of the center's existence. It would have been impossible to keep it going without them.

psychoanalysts, visited from many countries including Spain, Italy, Sweden, Finland, Germany, Brazil, and Australia. I have presented our work at conferences and seminars both in the United States and abroad, including the Infant Psychiatry Conferences in Lugano (1990) and Stockholm (1987). In addition to serving as a teaching and model institution, the center also provided clinical psychology students with the opportunity for case studies and research. Papers co-authored by students have been published in psychoanalytic journals and several students have written their doctoral dissertations on particular clinical and theoretical issues drawn from their research and clinical experience at the center (Bergman et al. 1983, Bergman and Chernack 1982, Voyat 1978, 1980).

Historical Background

The center began in 1976 under the direction of Linda Gunsberg, Gilbert Voyat, and me. Sadly, Gilbert Voyat died a few years after this work was begun. Each of us had become interested in starting this treatment center based on earlier work in child development research and clinical practice, and each of us brought our unique background to this project. Voyat was a Piagetian scholar with a particular interest in psychoanalysis and cognitive developmental psychology. He had previously used Piagetian testing in assessing the cognitive development of psychotic children. I had done intensive psychoanalytically oriented long-term therapy using the tripartite treatment design with several autistic and symbiotic psychotic children at the Masters Children's Center with Margaret S. Mahler and Manuel Furer (Bergman 1971, 1985, Mahler 1968), and I had worked as co-investigator of normal mother–child pairs studying the normal separation-individuation process (Mahler et al. 1975). Working simultaneously in the normative study and as a therapist with psychotic children provided a unique opportunity to study the distortions of normal development in severely disturbed children. Linda Gunsberg was a practicing child psychotherapist with a particular interest in education. She was interested in setting up a treatment center and in gaining a more profound understanding of psychotic children.

We set out to devise as ideal an environment as possible for the treatment of severely regressed psychotic children from economically

deprived backgrounds.[2] This setting consisted of a therapeutic classroom, individual psychotherapy for each child, and therapeutic companionship. I had developed the role of the therapeutic companion
in my previous work with psychotic children (see Chapter 13). We
knew that the kinds of children our center would serve could not
function in a traditional classroom setting because the severity of their
disturbances required almost constant individual attention. The classroom design would combine the availability of one-on-one relationships with adults with the opportunity for the children to develop a
beginning sense of being with each other.

The Developmental and Object Relational
Approach[3]

Based on our knowledge of early development within the caretaker–
child dyad and our knowledge of the beginnings of intrapsychic conflicts, our approach was developmental as well as psychodynamic. We
aimed to create for each child a facilitating environment. It was
Winnicott (1964) who said there is "no such thing as a baby . . . if you
show me a baby, you certainly show me also someone caring for the
baby, or at least a pram with someone's eyes and ears glued to it" (p.
99). Winnicott (1956b) described the early mother–baby relationship
in terms of the mother's primary maternal preoccupation, during
which the mother relinquishes some of her own adult functioning to
identify with her infant. This is what provides for the infant a sense
of "going on being." Bion (1962) writes about the mother's reverie,
which signifies her ability to receive her baby's projections, to contain them, and eventually give them back in a new form. He believes
that the therapist similarly acts as a container and that this is instrumental in transforming somatic discharge into beginning

2. This work was supported by HEW Grant #02907: A Model for the Development
   of a Professional Training Program to Educate Severely Emotionally Handicapped
   Children from a Psychoeducational Approach. Principal Investigator: Gilbert
   Voyat; Co-investigators: Anni Bergman and Linda Gunsberg.
3. I would like to thank Arnold Wilson, who began his work as a therapeutic companion when the center began, for helping me to conceptualize the therapeutic
   approach.

mentation (Bion 1967). We attempted to create an environment that allows for the creation of a mind that can develop along expectable pathways. Our most important therapeutic task with children suffering from severe pathology was to create meaning. We became particularly aware of the need for the creation of meaning when most of the children in our center were psychotic and we needed to make sense of their bizarre communications.

For the psychotic child there seems to be more pleasure in private and autistic referential symbolization than in object directed communication. To the psychotic child progress toward shared meaningfulness and communication seems impossible. Instead, the child clings to psychotic, private ideation.

In order to better grasp the withdrawal of the psychotic child, let us compare his struggle with the struggle of a normal 3-year-old child to reconcile his private world of desire for omnipotence with the public rules of a game. This 3-year-old was playing a game in which he could follow the rules but found the possibility of not winning the game intolerable. He changed the rules of the game enough so that with the tacit consent of the therapist with whom he was playing, he was able to win. In fact, he played the game by himself while the therapist was relegated to the role of onlooker. In the end he jubilantly exclaimed that he had won the game, inviting the therapist to applaud his success. He had gratified private desires, rejected for the moment the competitive challenges of the external world, and yet he was fully aware of altering the rules. He followed them enough so that he could derive pleasure and satisfaction from his triumph and could ask the therapist to participate in it. He had not given up nor had he destroyed the game. He could fulfill two purposes simultaneously, having both accepted and rejected the demands of reality. A psychotic child, by contrast, would destroy the game and obliterate the rules in the service of an omnipotent yet unenjoyable and unshareable triumph over the external world.

In the treatment of a psychotic child it is the therapist's task to *construct* meaning. In the treatment of a normal child we attempt to *discover* meanings that exist yet are obscured by the defensive processes. In a psychotic child such meanings seem at first almost nonexistent and therefore have to be created. Green states: "[W]hen we are dealing with a psychotic, it is we who infer the existence of underlying fantasies. These are not, in my opinion, situated 'behind' the empty space, as in neurotics, but 'after' it, i.e., they are forms of recathexis" (Green 1975, p. 8).

Thus it is through the thinking and acting of the therapist that shareable thinking becomes possible. Our thoughts must fill the empty space, which is empty of meaning but filled with bizarre communications, products of the chaotic inner world of the psychotic child. Our meanings must resonate with the clutter yet at the same time represent a way of first organizing and then overcoming the chaos. Again we turn to Green to describe this difficult bind:

> The search for a balanced exchange is difficult. If one fills the emptiness prematurely through interpretation, one is repeating the intrusion of the bad object. If, on the other hand, one leaves the emptiness as it is, one is repeating the inaccessibility of the good object. If the analyst feels confused or amazed, he is no longer in a position to contain the overflow which then expands without limit. And finally, if one responds to the overflow with verbal overactivity, then even with the best of intentions, one is doing no more than responding with an interpretive talon. [Green 1975, p. 8]

The construction of meaning is greatly helped when the tripartite treatment approach can be used, because often the mother who lives with the child is able to fill in events from daily life that are alluded to in a distorted way by the child, which makes it possible to anchor the meanings we construct in the life of the child and the relationship with the mother. However, it is important to realize that the correctness of an interpretation at that stage is less important than the process, which demonstrates to child and mother over and over again that what appears bizarre and incomprehensible can be understood.

The situation with less disturbed language-delayed children is different because their communications are less bizarre and less stereotyped. However, we found that what we had learned from working with psychotic children is of great importance in these less disturbed children, because especially at the beginning of treatment, we often have to work with nonverbal communications.

The interpretation of the nonverbal communications is an important aspect of the individual therapy. It is through the understanding of the child's body language, to which the therapist must be attuned and able to translate into words, that it becomes possible for therapist and child together to develop a narrative that provides a sense of existing beyond the moment, creating a common past, and being able to anticipate a common future. We compare this to what the mother intuitively does with a preverbal child. The approach here is very different from one that demands or requests the child to say things with words, because it accepts and participates in the child's developmental level of the moment while providing the child with the opportunity for developmental growth. This is by no means an easy task, and can at times be very frustrating and upsetting for the therapist, especially when the child expresses very strong feelings without being able to provide very quickly the opportunity for understanding what these feelings are about. For example, we had one little girl who began to cry inconsolably during her therapy sessions. It was very difficult for the therapist to accept that she was not doing something bad that was causing the child's terrible sadness, but that in fact she was providing a place for the child in which she could be allowed to be herself, even if this meant sadness and tears. Eventually some understanding could develop about the cause for the sadness, which in this case was connected to the departure of a beloved grandmother. The child in this case was expressing not only her own sadness, but also the sadness of her mother about the loss of the grandmother. The child and therapist together could eventually create a narrative that captured the meaning of her inconsolability.

Here it is important to remember that what we do as therapists parallels what the mother of the prelinguistic child does intuitively. With children who are disturbed in language and object relations, it is possible that the mother's intuitive understanding of her nonverbal child was absent and that a nonverbal dialogue had never developed between them. By the time they come to our treatment situation mothers have often given up trying to communicate, but they nonetheless expect and hope that with the repair of the language disorder the child will magically function like a normal child. While a child's growing ability to use expressive language certainly has a beneficial effect, the mother must face that speaking—one step toward more mature object relating and cognition—does not make the child magically normal.

We found that many of the children who came to our center with almost no language at the age of 3 developed language fairly rapidly in our therapeutic environment. We were fully aware that language delays can have many different origins and we provided speech therapy through the speech pathology department of the university. In the therapeutic part of our program we were particularly concerned with the effect of speech delays on the ongoing object relationships with the parents and with the developmental difficulties that ensue when language is not available at the point in development at which it would facilitate the developmental process of separation-individuation, of the attainment of object and self constancy, and of the ability to develop shared meanings that can be expressed in words. We believe that every child with a delay in language development—even when such a delay is entirely neurologically based—suffers from special difficulties during the rapprochement subphase of the separation-individuation process. During this phase of increased ambivalence language becomes a mediating tool with which to span the newly perceived gap between child and mother (Mahler et al. 1975). During rapprochement "verbal communication becomes more and more necessary: gestural cohesion on the part of the toddler or mutual preverbal empathy between mother and child will no longer suffice to attain the goal of satisfaction" (Mahler et al. 1975, p. 79). During the rapprochement subphase language can provide the toddler with a new sense of mastery. The child can now ask to have wishes fulfilled, demand mother's attention even from a distance, and express the delights of reunion (Mahler et al. 1975). Slade and Bergman (1988) point out that both expressive and receptive language increase the ways in which the child can interact with others. "The development of language and conceptual skills allows the child to express his wishes and the widening range of his affective experience and permit him to understand better parental explanations and limits" (p. 182).

All these areas of increasing pleasure, control, and interaction are jeopardized when the child is unable to use language at the appropriate time. The words that can ease the difficulties of the rapprochement subphase are lacking. The toddler has more difficulty both in structuring his internal world and getting his needs met from the external world. Parents' inevitable disappointment and anxiety about

OURS, YOURS, MINE

the child's deficiencies interfere with their ability to provide the pride and recognition so necessary for the development of self-esteem. Both mother and child are prone to increased feelings of frustration and failure. The rapprochement crisis becomes intensified and can become a point of fixation.

Daniel Stern (1985) emphasizes the importance of the acquisition of language in the service of union and togetherness. He says:

> the very process of learning to speak is recast in terms of forming shared experiences of reestablishing the "personal order," of creating a new type of "being with" between adult and child. Just as the being with experiences of intersubjective relatedness required the sense of two subjectivities in alignment—a sharing of inner experience of states—so too, at this new level of verbal relatedness, the infant and mother created a being with experience using verbal symbols—a sharing of mutually created meanings about personal experience. [p. 172]

Stern further makes the point that language provides the infant with words for which he has thought or knowledge already in mind, ready to be linked up with the word.

> The word is given to the infant from the outside, by mother, but there exists a thought for it to be given to. In this sense the word as a transitional phenomenon does not truly belong to the self, nor does it truly belong to the other. It occupies a midway position between the infant's subjectivity and the mother's objectivity. [p. 172]

This conceptualization applies well to interactions between a therapist and a language-delayed child: the therapist provides the child with words for nonverbally conveyed needs, desires, and feelings.

Separation-individuation theory provides us with the ability to understand behaviors in terms of intrapsychic processes and a map for expectable sequences in development (Mahler et al. 1975). This intimate knowledge of the first three years of life is very helpful in understanding children with severe delays and disturbances in object relations (Bergman 1971, 1983, 1985, Kupfermann 1971). The analysis of characteristic nonverbal play between mothers and infants (Bergman and Lefcourt 1993) has proven to be instrumental in understanding what the play of language-delayed children communicates about significant emotional events, such as separations and reunions.

The work of infant researchers has provided us with important further understanding of the complexity of the development of the self (Stern 1985) and about the specific influences of the caretaking partner (Emde 1988a,b). The children in our center who had suffered important developmental delays and environmental failures demonstrated to us a heterogeneity that made them vary considerably in their developmental achievements, such as personal agency, empathy, affect tolerance, exploration, and attachment. We have to recognize that their capacities in these different areas are unstable and shifting. Stern (1985) and Lichtenberg (1989) have shown us that it is in fact the relationships between these different dimensions that constitute what we now think of as the self. As we think of these different dimensions, it is often helpful to use the more advanced capacities as the basis for forming a therapeutic alliance. For example, in discussing a particular child, we came to realize that she was very deficient in her sense of core self but quite advanced in a sense of intersubjective self. Because she was so deficient in her sense of core self she was seen as functioning on a very low developmental level. However, our realization of her ability to connect empathetically with others provided us with a new perspective, which helped us support her sense of agency. Understanding each child not only from the point of view of sequential stages but also by appreciating the complex and highly individual developmental process of each child at any given moment helped us to make richer interpretations and more accurate interventions.[4]

The Program

The majority of the children at the City University Child Center came from Hispanic and African-American inner-city families with varied family constellations. In a given year, our program typically served six children, between the ages of 3 and 5 years, who came to the center every day to a therapeutic classroom staffed by a teacher, an assistant teacher, and university student helpers. Doctoral students

---

4. Lichtenberg (1989) provides a particularly helpful framework for assessing and correcting the uneven development of the children.

acted as therapists. The co-director[5] was a psychologist responsible for the day-to-day functioning and coordination of the entire program, including meeting the requirements of the funding agency.

The Physical Setting

The physical setting of the child center turned out to be of great importance. Adjoining the classroom was a room for water play and an office for the teaching staff. Across the hallway was a large gym room with big action toys: a play house, a slide, a jungle gym, and a fleet of tricycles and small cars. We saw children behave entirely differently in the two rooms. For example, one little boy who was always withdrawn and quiet in the classroom became lively and even boisterous as he jumped and climbed in the gym room, interacting with the other boys in the group. The classroom was located on the seventh floor of a large, modern building with many windows, escalators, elevators, corridors, classrooms, offices, computer rooms, and so on. Therapy and speech therapy rooms were located on another floor. All of the different parts of the building were at times explored by the children and their therapists. Whether a child would walk along with the therapist holding hands, walk ahead, or follow behind took on particular meaning in the unfolding of the therapeutic process. The children characteristically formed intense attachments to their teachers, to each other, and especially to their therapists. Transitions from home to classroom, classroom to therapy, and therapy to home were intense experiences and were worked on in various play situations. Therapists used the concept of *self–other action play* (Bergman and Lefcourt 1993) in the working through of these difficult transitions, separations, and reunions.

Therapy took place in corridors, on escalators and elevators—as well as in therapy rooms—because the building lent itself to exploration, to testing of separateness and autonomy under the eye of the protecting therapist. This can be compared to what happens in nor-

---

5. I would like to thank Sally Moskowitz, Elizabeth Sharples, and Junie Mayes, who acted as important co-directors.

mal development when, during practicing and rapprochement, the optimal distance between mother and toddler is worked out by both of them, mother following her toddler in his exploration of the world outside. We know the children we saw in our center had not had the opportunity to work on these issues of attachment, separation, separateness, and autonomy in their families where mothers were often overburdened and unavailable because of the difficulties in their own lives. Through the explorations of the building the children also got to know many other people, such as maintenance workers, secretaries, students, and professors.

The Treatment Design

Treatment consisted of three distinct modalities: the classroom, individual therapy, and therapeutic companions. The coordination of these modalities took place in a weekly case conference attended by the full staff. In addition, each student-therapist was assigned a supervisor. During the weekly conference cases were presented, often illustrated by videotapes of therapy sessions,[6] and were discussed from both a clinical and theoretical perspective. In this conference everyone who had any knowledge of the child contributed their particular experience. In this way each case became like a mosaic put together in the conference: the group created meaning with the therapist like the therapist created meaning with the child. The assurance that seemingly incomprehensible behaviors of the child were in fact meaningful and that often intuitive reactions on the part of the therapist were also meaningful was essential to our approach. The group process that developed during these case conferences provided excitement, stimulation, food-for-thought, and emotional support, all of which are essential for working with difficult cases. In addition, the case conference served to familiarize all participants with all the cases in treatment, making it possible to learn from comparing cases as well as following each case over time.

---

6. I would like to thank Irena Milentijevic for her conscientious contribution of videotaping therapy sessions.

The Classroom

The classroom consisted of two teachers, one Ph.D. student as teacher's assistant, and a group of volunteers who worked in the classroom at least once a week, many of whom were students on a master's level, some of whom were undergraduates, and some of whom were professionals in the field with a special interest in child development.

In the beginning we focused much of our attention on creating a classroom that combined the availability of one-on-one attention to children with the opportunity for them to develop a beginning sense of being with each other. We had hoped we would be able to use tripartite treatment design in which the mother is actually present in treatment sessions. As it turned out, the parents in the population we were serving were really not available because their own lives were too disrupted by economic and other deprivations. Often the children did not have a reliable home base to which they could become attached and from which they could separate. We had to accept the reality of the life circumstances of the families our center served and realize that sometimes what we saw as an offer of help was for these families, already overwhelmed, an additional burden. Thus, the therapeutic classroom took on a mothering function and became a kind of home base to which each child could become attached and from which each child could then separate and individuate through intensive individual psychotherapy. (See Appendix A, "The Classroom-as-Mother.") The classroom in our setting seemed to have been able to take on some of the role that an actual mother ideally plays in facilitating both attachment and separation in healthy development.

The curriculum we designed was meant first to encourage each child's unfolding sense of self, beginning by working with the body ego. We focused on the most basic activities such as eating, dressing, and moving through space. The emphasis in the group went beyond each individual, in that it offered constant opportunity for interaction and comparison. We found that at least some of the children began to watch and imitate each other. It seemed a natural step to go from the body ego, the core of each child's individuality, to the child in his or her particular environment. Class trips to each child's home were a very important first step in the process of socialization. We found these class trips formed an important bond between the children and teachers and gave the children the opportunity to experience first hand differences in each family's lifestyle: Where does everyone sleep? Where do they eat? What is the feel, smell, and space in each home? With the security provided by classmates and teachers we found the children were able to absorb and become interested in the differences in each family. It was of special interest to us that these class trips to each other's homes were the first shared experience that the children talked about and remembered. A store of shared memories was of great help in expanding the initial sense of self based on sensory experiences in the classroom. Thus, these trips were an important step in the development from the body to the mind. Once the children had been in each other's homes they could begin to work on concepts of the family different for each, yet shared by all.

We found music to be the best medium through which to introduce structured experiences into the classroom. Creating songs for different times of the day—a good morning song, a goodbye song, a song to rest by—made it more possible for all the children to accept group structures, which so often they resisted strenuously. Even those children who would not join the group at these times were helped to internalize a regulating principle. By repeating the same songs day after day some of the children learned to sing them and act them out and to have favorites to which they could look forward. Thus, they learned to anticipate and accept a piece of the outside world, a big step for those children who seemed to have been entirely inner-directed, trying to ignore what was offered to them from the outside.

Therapy

Each child was seen in individual therapy by a clinical psychology student two or three times a week. (See Appendices B, C, D and E for detailed examples of how student therapists worked at different phases of treatment.) A parent was included in sessions if at all possible. When tripartite treatment was not possible, the therapist attempted to maintain a close relationship with the family by being helpful in very practical ways, such as finding the right doctor or dentist and accompanying mother and child for physical check-ups.

Therapists saw the children at least twice weekly for two to three years in individual sessions and were in close contact with the families. The student-therapists' commitment to their child patients was perhaps most clearly reflected by the large number of therapists who continued to work with their individual patients for many years after the children had to leave our center and even after they themselves had left the Ph.D. program for an internship.

Therapeutic Companions[7]

In addition to the classroom and the therapy, some children were also seen by a therapeutic companion. We assigned therapeutic companions to those children who we felt would benefit by spending part of the day exploring the world outside the classroom. Our location in a university setting was of great help in this respect because many students volunteered to be therapeutic companions.

The role of the therapeutic companion at this center was two-fold: (1) The therapeutic companion made a bridge to the home of the children, often by making home visits, by taking the children home at the end of the day, and by sometimes sharing meals with the family. (2) The therapeutic companion made a bridge for the child to the demands and potential of the outside world by providing the necessary supportive containment for the child to be able to exercise and develop autonomous ego capacities and encounter new experiences. These experiences could be as simple as going to the grocery store and choosing what one might want to buy, going on a ride on the bus or the subway, or going to a playground or park. Therapeutic companionship provided an opportunity for the children to confront fears in vivo, for example, fear of the dark, fear of crossing the street, fear of strangers, and so on. The work with the therapeutic companion was meant to counteract the tendency for severely disturbed children to live in a very restricted world dictated by their fears and bizarre behaviors.

Therapeutic companions did not interpret feelings, nor did the relationship become the focus of therapeutic attention. Thus, the

---

7. I first developed the idea of therapeutic companions during my own work with autistic and psychotic children. For further discussion, see Chapter 13, "From Psychological Birth to Motherhood" and Chapter 17, "The Oral Deadlock."

child's relationship to the therapeutic companion tended to be more conflict-free than the relationship to the therapist. Companions often became beloved friends to the children. Many students who began their work with us as therapeutic companions eventually went on to Ph.D. programs, and several of them eventually became supervisors in our program, providing a sense of continuity and conviction.

Summary

In this chapter I have described a multidimensional treatment center located in a university setting that was in existence for fifteen years and had in the course of this period developed a treatment approach to severely disturbed children and families, based on understandings of normal development. Though we served multiple problem families we found that children—and sometimes mothers—developed strong object relationships to the center. It was our goal that children be able to use the therapeutic process to further their development and that mothers be able to use the support offered to provide a better environment for their children. Systematic follow-up studies would be of great importance, because such studies would help us to evaluate whether the internal structures we attempted to help the children develop were durable and flexible enough to withstand the separation from the therapeutic environment.

We made every attempt to be consistent about the use of the developmental approach by applying it not only in therapy but in the classroom and the therapeutic companionship. Attempting to understand what each child's particular difficulties in the developmental process had been and what the main problems were at the time they were referred, we then tried to provide a facilitating environment for the children and their families. Many times we had to take on actual caretaking responsibilities; thus, in some ways we functioned as an extended family. The process of supervision and discussion in our case conferences was another aspect of the extended family model. As we offered support to these children and their families, we needed to receive nurturing and support from working together as a group. It was our goal to help children with serious difficulties to be able to use what their families were able to offer. Just as the normal infant is an active partner in the mother–infant dyad, so we attempted to help our child patients become more active partners in eliciting caretaking from their own families. We were often surprised by the extent to which even very disturbed children in very disturbed environments could learn to receive what the environment could give rather than to make impossible demands upon it. Though we found that the tripartite treatment design was often unsuitable to the families with whom we worked and that individual treatment for parents also was usually unfeasible, we nevertheless found that at times we were able to help mothers to become more emotionally available to their children, as we helped them deal with some of their own conflicts toward their families of origin. In families where grandparents lived in the home, child care was often relegated to them, and the mothers—though relieved by the help—suffered a sense of loss of which they usually were not aware. Rather than confront that sense of loss, they sometimes turned further away from their children. Thus while a mother may not have been in formal treatment, the relationship she formed with her child's therapist could be helpful in giving her permission to take more responsibility for the care of her child and to be less emotionally dependent on her own mother. At times this may have created space for new mother–child relationships.

Appendix A

The Classroom-as-Mother

Katherine Tobias

The therapeutic nursery functions as the "classroom-mother": its basic tasks—feeding, washing, comforting, motivating, limit-setting, and soothing—can be compared to the basic activities of the mother–child relationship. The therapeutic classroom is the daily "stage" from which the children seek emotional sustenance for their efforts at physical and psychological survival and further development. Since each child seeks something different, the classroom must be flexible enough to provide differently for each child. Just as the "good enough mother" responds to her child's individual signals and needs (Winnicott 1965), so the classroom-mother must respond to each child's needs by providing the appropriate experiences. Like a baby with a mother, each child in the therapeutic classroom was an active partner in the child–classroom relationship, eliciting responses from the classroom-mother. The availability of many adults in the classroom gave each child the opportunity to choose a particular adult to become especially attached to. Many of the children who came into our program lacked specific attachment within their families: they showed absolutely no separation reactions when they first left home to come to the center. We observed that after a time, the children began to show separation reactions in relation to the classroom. For example, even though they knew their therapists well, they were at times anxious about leaving the classroom for therapy and eager to return to it. We saw these separation reactions as positive developments. The forming of attachments to the classroom may have been comparable to what happens in normal development as early as 8 to 9 months and often quite strongly during the period of rapprochement (1½ to 2½ years). Often the children became attached to the classroom first and only later to their therapists. We felt most encouraged when the children began to show that they missed their families when they were with us, evidence that the capacity for specific attachment had spread to their own families.

Like an actual mother, the classroom-mother helped to establish routines. A basic schedule was followed including time in the classroom, time in the playground, time to go to the bathroom, time to have snack and lunch, time to rest, and finally time to go home. Ideally the classroom-mother would provide the children with a consistent, responsive, and stable environment. Thus, as the mother contains the infant (Winnicott 1960) so the classroom-mother contained each child. As the children came to know they were within the protective container or holding environment of the classroom-mother, they were freed to explore the environment. When exploring, each child could depend on the safety and protection of the classroom-mother, and when experiencing distress, each could depend on it for comfort and nurturing. Furthermore, when children left the classroom-mother they could be certain that it would remain there while they were gone and would be there when they returned. This was helpful for the process of building an internal representation of a stable, care-giving environment for children in whose lives such an environment was usually not available.

Going to and returning from the classroom to the therapy room became an important journey that the children, together with their therapists, structured in their own ways. For example, one little boy who had no language when he entered our program and who lived in a very disorganized household went from the classroom to his therapy sessions in a toy pedal car. The trip from classroom to therapy room and back took up a good part of his therapy sessions because he moved very slowly in his little car. Staying in the little car seemed to help him take the classroom with him when he went to therapy. Furthermore, the little car—which he could control—probably represented a safe place in which to live, a safety he did not experience in his real life. He and the toy car were as one and could not be separated from each other. For a long while, he would not get out of the car during his therapy sessions.

Other children also had special ways of going to their therapy rooms with their therapists. Some insisted on carrying the key to the therapy room; some wouldn't go directly but had to take detours that they determined. At times they wanted to be carried; at other times they wanted to go by themselves and keep their therapist at some distance behind them as they independently navigated from one place to another. All of these choices were important clues about the way in which a child's representational world was developing and the way in which his or her ability to use the object was unfolding. From the point of view of separation-individuation, it was important that the classroom-mother served as a safe base for the children to move from and return to, much the same way an actual mother provides a home base for the exploring child (Mahler et al. 1975).

The following section provides four examples of individual children and their relationships to the classroom-mother.

Daniel

Daniel started school when he was 3 years old. He had very little expressive language, often seemed not to understand what others said, and had severe negative reactions to all transitions. Moving from one room to another provoked a tantrum. He became terrified at each move and would open his eyes very wide and cry and scream. Over time, as he grew to feel more confident about what the next place would bring and about returning to the place he was leaving, he became less upset by the transitions. Transitions continued to be difficult for him, especially the most stressful transition of all—leaving school at the end of the day. Daniel's reaction to transitions was so extreme that it seemed to us that it might be motivated by annihilation anxiety. Leaving one room to go to another seemed to threaten him with losing the ability to "go on being" (Winnicott 1965).

Over time the classroom appeared to become a surrogate love object for Daniel: the physical space, people, toys, activities, and routines provided a matrix for his going-on-being. Any changes in the classroom—in staff or schedule, for example—threatened his sense of continuity and cohesion. The terror induced by separations threw him into a panic and he acted out by hitting or kicking others, behaving like he was going to vomit, or crying and screaming and throwing himself onto the floor. These reactions suggested to us one way we could begin to understand Daniel's difficulties with transitions. Until he discovered a way to connect each person and activity to his surrogate classroom-mother, his sense of continuity would be threatened.

Although Daniel's sense of continuity appeared to be bolstered by the regularity of the classroom, finding his own role or place in it was a struggle for him. Daniel began to seek repair through copying the other children as if by being more like them he could be part of them and the group.

Sammy

Sammy, another 3-year-old boy, was more advanced in his capacity for object relating than Daniel. He had fairly good language ability and the capacity to initiate play with others. He was also able to invent games that were enjoyable to him and enticing to others. He was able to communicate his feelings easily and could show concern and care for others. In spite of these abilities, he had considerable difficulty regulating his physiological and affective states. We speculated that he had experienced difficulty early on in relation to the self-regulating other.

Sammy required a great deal of help with the regulation of basic physiological functions, such as eating and toileting, and also required a great deal of soothing. The regularity of classroom meals and toileting times seemed to be helpful to him. Classroom eating times were pleasant social occasions during which jumping up and running around were not permitted. Without an adult near him he became easily distracted, so an adult would sit next to him during meal times to help him maintain interest in his food. In this way the classroom-mother helped regulate his physiological functions.

Sammy was very sensitive to nonverbal cues from the adults around him. For example, the way they moved, talked to him, or touched him could help him maintain control. Whenever he sensed anxiety in another person he almost immediately became anxious as well. Sammy was also very sensitive to the space surrounding him. When the boundaries of his play area were not clear, he seemed to lose track of where he was and what he was doing. The adults in the classroom were very aware that they had to function in the role of the self-regulating other by providing soothing nonverbal communication as well as verbal encouragement. For example, they found that putting an arm on his chair helped provide enough of a boundary for Sammy to focus on a task.

The schedule of the classroom was itself helpful to Sammy and contributed to his ability to learn to regulate himself. He began to say things like "Now we have lunch; then we have story and rest." He also began to say encouraging things to himself such as "That's good. Try again."

Jeannie

Jeannie was referred when she was 3 years old with the diagnosis of autism. She had almost no language, was oblivious to her surroundings, and behaved as if nothing existed outside of herself unless it directly affected her. Any change in schedule left her feeling disoriented and any refusal to comply with her demands left her feeling frustrated and angry. She used others as an extension of herself, for example, to reach things she could not. If an adult refused, she screamed out in anger. Schedule and routine were of primary importance. One observer noted, "It is as if she has an internal clock that is preset for the day. If there is a change her whole world is so disturbed that it can throw her off and change her mood for the remainder of the day."

Jeannie treated the classroom as an extension of herself. She did not appear to notice anything unless it came within her orbit. She began to make occasional contact with others. For example, she might pull an adult over to see something she was doing or was interested in. She would look up at the adult and then back to the toy and seemed to enjoy the moment of sharing. This seemed suggestive of the way a young child shares new discoveries and achievements with mother and in this way imbues these activities with the warmth and sustenance of the love relationship. Like a toddler, Jeannie used her classroom-mother to enhance her pleasure with the world.

In the classroom, where Jeannie was allowed to be in control of the level of intimacy that she could bear, she began to seek out brief moments of closeness. The classroom-mother provided the opportunity for Jeannie to make connections in her own time and in her own way; it was available for Jeannie to make beginning attempts to connect and relate without intruding into her world. Eventually her world and the world of the classroom could begin to join together, thereby slowly expanding Jeannie's world.

Suzy

Suzy was a child of extremes. She was either very subdued and barely communicative or very boisterous and loud. At times she was sad, withdrawn, and petulant, at other times overly cheerful, active, and lively. Suzy moved between these extremes quickly and with little warning. It took a long time before the adults in the classroom could begin to see what triggered her shifts in mood. The classroom-mother served to contain all of Suzy's moods and ways of being. It reflected her moods back to her and in this way allowed her to try out new ways of being. Both the sad little girl and the cheerful little girl were fully acknowledged and responded to, and slowly Suzy developed the ability to be at times just a little sad, or a little happy, or a little excited, or a little scared. By containing all of who and how she was in the classroom, she could begin to see herself as more whole and less disconnected. The classroom-mother was the mother that allowed expression of anger, sadness, grief, fear, revenge, and neediness. We thought the acceptance of her negative affects would help her become less dissociated when feeling bad and allow her range of expression to expand and her affective experience to become more complex and modulated.

Eventually the classroom became a safer place for Suzy, allowing her to let go a little. For example, at the beginning she was not able to rest during rest time. She would sit on her cot with her shoes on, back stiff and erect, head up and eyes staring straight ahead. None of the usual techniques such as story telling, holding, or quiet talking helped her rest. One day she took off her own shoes and continued to sit in the same way, now with her shoes off. A few days later she lay down on top of her blanket and kept her shoes on. Then one day she took her shoes off, got under the blanket, played with her resting toy, but did not let herself fall asleep. Finally one day she fell asleep and slept well during rest time from then on.

Appendix B

Separation and Loss:
A Key Area of Conflict for Tania

Mara Silverman

Background

Tania was the daughter of a drug-addicted mother who was reported to be an inconsistent mother. While at times she showered Tania with love and affection, at other times the responsibility of having children became so overwhelming that she was unable to provide the physical and emotional nurturing Tania needed. Tania had a 1-year-old and a 10-year-old sister. Her father, who lived with the family during Tania's early years, struggled with drug and alcohol addiction, further contributing to a neglectful home environment. When she was 4 years old, Tania was removed from her parents' home by the Bureau of Child Welfare. She lived for two weeks in a foster care home after which she was placed with her maternal grandfather and his spouse of fourteen years, Tania's godmother. She had remained in this home ever since.

Since she was removed from her mother's home, Tania's contact with her mother was inconsistent. Sometimes her mother would come to visit several times per week; other times she would not call or come for months at a time. Tania's inability to count on her mother had an impact on her other relationships as well. She felt that people could not be trusted to be there when she needed them. Thus, separation was quite painful for her and a major focus of the beginning of her therapy, particularly in the ending of sessions.

Working Through Conflicts of Separation and Loss:
Transitions to and from Therapy

At the end of a therapy hour, Tania would refuse to leave the room and begin to struggle with feelings of anger, sadness, and resentment. She would often stand at the back of the playroom, telling me how much she hated me and calling me names. On occasion she would try to hurt me physically by throwing something at me or biting me.

At such times it seemed she was only able to use anger to display her fears about separating. During such an episode, the only way I was able to get Tania back to the classroom was by carrying her. Often she was able to enjoy being carried. She would settle down quickly, put her head on my shoulder, and coo. At other times she was unable to tolerate the contact and would frantically struggle to get out of my arms, insisting that she would walk by herself. When I would put her down, she would run away from me, leaving me no choice but to pick her up and carry her against her will. In my arms, she would often kick me and yell out for her teachers or godmother. Once we reached the classroom, she would turn her back on me and refuse to say goodbye.

On occasion, her reaction to separating became so intense that I was unable to penetrate her hysterical crying and screaming to soothe her. At times she seemed to be struggling with primitive feelings and anxiety about being abandoned, unable to separate her feelings for me from those for her mother. While in the throes of such undifferentiated confusion and panic, Tania was unable to accept comfort from anyone, but she was able to calm herself by vomiting. Once she had vomited, her screams would turn to whimpers and she would be able to integrate effectively with the other children in the classroom, suggesting that vomiting was a way for her to dispel the bad introjects from her system and provide herself with comfort and control.

After about six months of therapy, Tania was periodically able to leave the playroom without becoming enraged. My explicit attempts at helping her build ego strength seemed to help. The more we talked about her difficulties in separating, the easier it was for her to make the transition. In particular, the more confidence I showed in her—"I know you can leave the playroom without becoming so upset"—the easier it was for her to be confident in herself—"I'm a big girl, right?" or "I'm not going to get angry today." She usually still insisted that I carry her back to the classroom and would instruct me not to say anything. At such times, she seemed to derive great comfort in the silence and safety of my arms. Once in the classroom she was able to say goodbye without turning her back.

Our separation during spring break, which was prolonged by a student strike, turned out to be very disruptive for Tania. I attempted to maintain contact with her over the telephone. Although she did not refuse to speak to me, Tania seemed unable to make a real connection. When I tried to talk to her about the reasons we were not meeting, she would ignore me and begin to sing. The uncertainty of when we would see each other again—likely reminiscent of her mother's erratic visits—seemed intolerable. The night before I was to see her again, I called her to relay this information. As soon as she heard the news she began to share a variety of concerns with me—"Grand Daddy got mad at me"; "I'm angry at Flora (her older sister)"; "I want to go play with you." It seemed the knowledge that we would be seeing each other again dissolved some of her anger and allowed me to reenter her world.

The next day I met Tania's class at the Museum of Natural History. I arrived two minutes after the school bus and was greeted by Tania saying: "You lied to me; you said you were going to see me this morning." While she ignored me for the first half hour, she was willing to spend some special time with me afterwards. She quickly became very upset and started screaming out for her teacher. It seemed that being with me in this strange place was completely disorienting and made her feel vulnerable and scared. She seemed unable to tolerate being with me without the safety and familiarity of the playroom.

With the student strike still in progress, Tania and I met in a room adjacent to the temporary classroom. Although she had little difficulty coming with me and playing, the content of her play suggested that the separation and continued displacement had stirred up many frightening fantasies and memories. A number of dangerous images appeared: she drew pictures of sharks with large teeth who killed people in their path and talked about and imitated a man with shark teeth, who she claimed lived in her building. She also expressed her fear and anxiety about separations directly by telling me she thought I had left her and that she was angry with me. She wondered if the man using our room the previous week had been killed. She wondered if the woman she lived with for two weeks in foster care was dead. I understood Tania's fear that people die when they disappear to be connected to her fear about her mother, who would disappear for months at a time.

When we finally could return to the playroom for therapy, Tania seemed very excited to be back and spent the whole first session playing at the sink, a favorite activity. The end of our session, however, was particularly hard. She angrily refused to leave the room and then once in the hallway she ran away from me. In the stairwell she spat all over the floor and walls and refused to walk down the stairs. When I encouraged her to go with me she called me a "stupid mother-fucker" and ran in the opposite direction. I had no choice but to pick her up and carry her. Kicking and screaming, she eventually allowed me to take her back to the classroom, where she began to throw pillows and yell at the other children. The severity of Tania's reaction suggested that the month away from the playroom was not only extremely frightening and disorienting but also weakened her ego functioning and intensified the transference.

After a few weeks, there was a noticeable shift in Tania's behavior at the end of sessions. Although many still ended with yelling and spitting, she became able to leave the room and say "goodbye" without becoming enraged. While she had shown signs of this ability before the separation from me and the playroom, it now occurred more frequently and did not rely on my ego-supporting comments. We established an ending routine that helped the transitions: five minutes before the session was about to end, I would tell Tania how much time was left and encourage her to finish playing. When the five minutes were up, she inevitably would tell me she was not ready yet and would continue to play. I would get up, turn the light off, and stand by the door. Within the next minute, Tania would be able to finish playing and leave the room with me. While she still insisted that I carry her to the classroom, once we arrived she was able to integrate with the other children and say goodbye to me. It seemed that by taking some control of her departure—playing for an extra minute and putting her own closure on her play—she was able to contain her aggression and better tolerate the separation. It also seemed that she was beginning to trust that I would not disappear if she said goodbye to me.

Appendix C

Ain't Nothing Like the Real Thing: Identification Takes Hold in Frances

Nancy Tuttle Siegel

From the moment she stepped off the school bus my feelings for this particular 4-year-old have swung widely. I had unwittingly imagined myself working with neurotic children—children who needed my help but had some capacity for self expression through gestures, play, or words. I had not imagined myself working with an impermeable, unattached child, who could not play and did not care about relating and being understood. In many ways it seemed there was so little to hang onto with Frances. She didn't invite me in with words, feelings, or play. So, I found myself working with what was there—sounds she made, sights we saw together, surprises we encountered in the environment, textures of things we touched on our travels.

As I accompanied Frances about the building, I tried to engage her in the world by making the journey interesting. When she stumbled or fell I tried to articulate and experience the emotions she could not. When she showed the slightest interest in a toy, I encouraged her by elaborating on her small bit of behavior. When she would motor about chaotically, I protected her. When she turned the music way up loud, or the water on very hard, I regulated her environment. I was certainly conscious of treating her like a much younger child and occasionally wondered if I was doing the right thing.

Our early sessions contained not a hint of what was to come. Never did I imagine that this child, so unreachable and mysterious, would develop into an appealing little girl with a strong attachment to many people in her school environment.

When I met Frances she immediately struck me as odd. She moved awkwardly, with no sense of her body in space. She related poorly. In fact, there was no way to reach Frances if she did not want to be reached. Even touch, the primitive and most literal method of reaching, was often powerless. Her ability to hear language was apparently intact, but you would never know it from being with her. But she was exciting. She wanted to go everywhere and did so with her apparently boundless energy. For several months I followed her lead. Literally, she led me around the building. Though her self presentation was energetic, it was peculiarly joyless. I related to her through attuning to the few feelings she expressed. But more often, I attuned to her physical behavior. For example if she made a gurgling sound in solo water play or shuddered as cold water ran up her forearm, I responded to her as though these were communications. I tried to absorb their nature and reflect them back to her. When my response captured some aspect of her experience—a feeling she had, a sound she made, a sensation she experienced—I felt we were relating. In keeping with Stern's thoughts about attunement, I tried to render not the physical behavior itself, but the feeling behind the behavior. I hoped this would introduce her to the idea that emotions, as well as activities, can be shared.

The next phase of the treatment arose out of changes in both Frances and me. While she initially seemed like a girl in a bubble, she was beginning, periodically, to let me into her world. She began to respond, occasionally with words, but more often with a gesture of willingness, to some of my persistent efforts to join her. She would sometimes turn and request my presence with a hand gesture, give me things to carry, or make simple requests, like "turn on the light." At about this time I began to tire of the public nature of our treatment: the elevator, the escalator, and the public corridors had become our playroom. I hoped we had gotten about all we could out of our roaming treatment, decided to confine the therapy to two floors of the building, and set firm limits on elevator riding.

Initially, the limit setting was very difficult. Frances would run squarely into me—not in a defiant manner, but in a way that disregarded the fact that either of us had bodies. She wanted to get on that elevator. I relied a great deal on physical restraint during this time. She had her own physical response to the limit setting. She would fall to the floor like a sack of potatoes saying "I tired." Gradually the limit itself became grounds for experimentation. She began to test my firmness by running circles around me at the elevator doors. She would periodically take a flying leap at the doors, particularly when they were tantalizingly open. More often than not she would end up tangled in my arms or on my shoulder. This was further transformed into a way for Frances to experiment with connection at a distance. She began to make fleeting eye contact, to challenge me with a "fake out" step toward the forbidden area, and generally to enjoy our negotiating the limit.

As Frances began to transition from a physical connection with me to a more psychic connection, I was becoming aware of a subtle difference in her. I remember the precise moment I realized we were on the road to identification. In her efforts to flee the treatment room she went to many places. One of these was the bathroom. When she had finished urinating she would flush the toilet several times while sticking her head way down into the bowl. As I was worried about both her safety and her sense of privacy I inquired, "Are you okay in there? Tell me if you need some help." One day Frances was urinating, and as I quietly held the door she said with great pride, "Nancy, I'm okay." With this appeared a flurry of behaviors which I recognized as imitative of my own. She began to prepare herself for water play by rolling up her sleeves, as I had long done, saying very seriously to me "my sleeves."

Gradually her imitative efforts evolved into behaviors that seemed more like identification: there was a gradual move from imitation of my verbal scripts to an identification with certain features of my person. This phase was characterized by an utter fascination with my book bag. For months it had lain on the floor of our therapy room. In a single day it was the new favored object—and quite obviously a proxy for me. Every session for two months featured some form of bag play. She would lose interest in an activity and would suddenly say "ah, my bag." She would remove each item, one at a time, and absolutely savor it. She would look inside, select an item, and withdraw it with a big smile, direct eye contact, and a deliciously drawn out "N-a-n-c-y, for me?" She was particularly fond of my "merican express card," removed it, and placed it in her doctor's kit.

She gradually became curious about the more personal items in the bag, like pictures in my wallet and my makeup. When she found my driver's license she pointed to my picture and said with great confidence "me." I worried when she became interested in a picture of me and my siblings: What would this mean to her? She answered by showing me the picture and saying "my friends." She began to apply makeup in the session. She would smear lipstick all over her face, look in the hand-held mirror, and say she looked "better." I attempted to substitute my bag with one created just for her, but she clearly told me, in her own way, "accept no substitutes— it's your bag I want." She seemed more willing to endure the separation from my things rather than accept a substitute for them.

At times her behavior looked like she was trying to incorporate what was mine, and perhaps me with it. She brought a bag from home one day and filled it to the brim with most of my belongings. She parted with these items reluctantly and with great pain. One day she fancied my checkbook, and as we boarded the elevator at the end of the session, she alternately ate the graham crackers in her hand and gnawed on the edge of my similarly shaped checkbook.

With identification of me as a person, she became more interested in her body and in herself as a girl. Before delving into my bag she would lean all the way over and quite deliberately exhibit her rear end to me. I learned from her grandfather that she had begun expressing a great deal of interest in what she wore, favoring dresses and jeans over sweatsuits and t-shirts. She arrived at school in a dress one day and began to wear her hair in frilly ways. The hairdos were certainly arranged by someone else, but if Frances had not wanted her hair done to that degree, I have no doubt that she would have made it impossible. She also became interested in self–other action play (Bergman and Lefcourt 1993) where we would alternate roles: "you be mommy, I baby," and "I mommy, you baby."

As the relationship with me took hold, it was astonishing to see the way in which Frances's overall functioning developed. Everyone who came into contact with her noticed some aspect of her many developmental gains. She was more appealing, more adorable. She was more of a girl, less rambunctious and softer in her way of going. She was more verbal. What was initially bizarre self-talk was gradually replaced with fairly confused, but undeniably communicative speech. She spoke incessantly, often about aspects of her life—experiences with her grandfather, trouble with peers, and practices of her teachers. With words and enactment, she brought concerns about eating, "doodooing," and finally flushing into her session. She began to care about whether her words were understood. She often repeated the same phrase three or four times till I "got it."

Frances's emerging self called for a different type of therapist and engendered a different countertransference. My way of being with her was changing rapidly. I used physical contact only occasionally. The fact that there was a person in there, a person who cared about being understood and relating, carved out more room for words in our interaction. She began to respond to questions and interpretations about her behavior and her world, and she began to indicate if my interpretations were on or off target. As for countertransference, Frances's fierce attachment to me was filled with joy and pain for both of us. Sessions ended miserably. She would most often slink into the classroom without looking back at me. Seconds later she would bellow loudly and inconsolably, "What happened to Nancy?" She would frequently convince classroom volunteers to search for me. No corridor was safe from her roamings, and I frequently bumped into her and was forced to start the whole process of parting again.

For the first month of Frances's identification play, I withheld most interpretations. I wanted this process of engaging with me and with the world to flower as much as it could. When our separations became too difficult I started interpreting both the positive and negative sides of letting someone into her bubble. It was very painful for me to hear her cries. Yet it was rewarding to see that she could attach, and also that she could make some healthy restitution of her equilibrium when given the time. I witnessed this when she banged on my office door for several minutes crying, "Nancy, please!" She was finally taken to the gym by her teachers, and after an hour of play returned to my door singing a song from the classroom sweetly and joyfully, "I love you, you love me, we're a great big family." It is hard to hear a youngster in such pain, especially when you are in no position to alleviate it. Yet, I also recognized that without the ability to attach and relate—for all the joy and all the pain involved—Frances would not thrive.

In retrospect it is easy to see the many processes of development that have occurred. In no way was I able to see them at the time. I simply tried to *be with* Frances as she seemed to need me to be. When I first met Frances she was the girl in the bubble; she grew to share her bubble with me as I persistently knocked on the door, and she began to emerge from the bubble as a self, a little girl, an interested and curious child. The stage in the treatment I hope we will enter now is that Frances and I, together, will create a place to be with each other and a place to play with each other.

Appendix D
Getting To Know David:
The Introductory Phase of Treatment
Annelie H. Hartman

Background

David first came to the center when he was 4½ years old. My initial impression of him was of a quiet, passive child with an endearing disposition. His affect was typically bland and noncommunicative: he did not send forth the usual affective signals that let other people know what he was intending to do or what he was feeling. Similarly, he approached the world of human relatedness with caution, typically needing to be drawn into social interaction rather than spontaneously initiating contact with others.

David lived with his mother, three much older brothers from a different father, and an aunt and her teenage daughter. David's father lived with him until David was 6 months old, during which time there was a lot of fighting at home. Addicted to crack for several years, David's father was no longer in contact with the family and had been in and out of treatment programs without success.

David reportedly achieved all age-appropriate developmental milestones with the exception of language development. He had a history of chronic ear infections, and a hearing test showed some significant conductive hearing loss. At the time David came to the center, his mother had begun working at a job that demanded long hours, marking a significant change in the amount of time she was able to spend with her son. It was my sense from the beginning that David's mother was a well-intentioned mother who cared deeply about her son's well-being. However, the day-to-day demands of her life circumstances, which were oriented to basic survival needs and attending to immediate crises, did not allow her the time and energy required to care for David fully or to participate in his treatment.

Beginning Play Therapy: The Theme of Monster Heads

From the beginning David formed an attachment to the He Man figures, which he called the "monsterheads," and would immediately look for them by the window sill and bring them over to the table. At first he manipulated the figures on his own, making them engage and disengage, and intertwine in various positions, without any accompanying affect or verbalizations. Apart from being very invested in this play, the actions were not imbued with any consistent kind of identifying vitality (i.e., they did not have either an aggressive, playful, or affectionate feel to them). Rather, it seemed as if the actions took place within a kind of suspended play space without clear form or content. This left me feeling as if I were watching a silent, slow motion picture, and since I had minimal "context" information at my disposal to help me begin to understand the possible meaning(s) of this play, I could do little more than offer a running commentary about what I observed David doing with the dolls. In doing so, I refrained from using affect words or drawing conclusions about what the figures might be doing (e.g., the monster heads seem angry and are fighting) to avoid imposing my own agenda on David and prematurely satisfying my own need as a beginning therapist to make interpretations and deduce the "underlying" meaning of this play. My comments remained purely descriptive, such as "You are holding the monster heads and making them jump up and down," as a way of communicating my ongoing interest and desire to learn about David in whichever way he chose to make himself known to me. Only later did I realize the important function my mirroring responses served in helping David to begin to narrate his play and introduce more complex and differentiated play themes within the context of our developing relationship.

Over time David began to include me as a partner in his play by giving me one of the monster heads to hold and manipulate. Even though the figures were now clearly designated as "yours" and "mine," their identities were still undifferentiated. Mine copied everything his was doing, much to David's delight. At times I would wait before imitating, in response to which David would invite, even command me to "do it" too. Thus my mirroring behavior extended beyond verbalizations and affect attunements to include action sequences enacted in the wider range of play space. For example, the monster heads were now jumping on the floor and visiting other parts of the playroom. Consistent with the mirroring aspects of this play, the monster heads appeared to have equal status. There was no clear winner or loser, aggressor or victim. However, the type of play became increasing varied and invested with affect; at times the monster heads playfully engaged in rough and tumble play, at other times the actions were more forceful and aggressive, enabling me to comment on a broader range of action play (e.g., first the monster heads are moving around gently, now they are really pouncing on each other, etc.). As this play continued it began to take on qualities of a reciprocal interaction—you do to me what I did to you and turn taking. More frequently his monster head emerged as the "winner," and soon mine was relegated to a passive role. David would insist that I stand my monster head at the edge of the table and then let go, so that he could knock mine down to the floor as I watched, temporarily disengaged from giving my monster head a life of his own. Both monster heads repeatedly landed on the floor and my job was to pick them both up and restore them, intact, to their original positions.

Even though the themes became increasingly varied and differentiated, the overall tone of this activity was extremely playful, making it difficult for me to find connections between what David was doing with the dolls and what he might be feeling himself. It became clear to me that it was not so much the play themes that had become meaningful but rather the relational context in which they occurred. David relished my attention and interest and would gleefully burst into laughter as I followed his lead, becoming both the witness and validator of his experience. At times I noticed his excitement escalate and tailored my responses so that I would not introduce additional stimulation. It seemed to me that this type of mutually responsive self–other experience was novel for David and I did not want him to become overstimulated and lose his capacity to self-regulate and integrate these experiences into his developing sense of self and other. The monster head games began to include new dimensions of self–other action play organized around themes of separations and reunions. David would hide his monster head under the table, calling for me to find him. This hide-and-seek would continue until at last I found him again. In later sessions David would initiate this game by saying, "Where are you?" signaling me to hide my monster head so that he could now enact the role of seeker. At other times his monster head would run away and call for help, waiting for me to bring him to safety again.

Toward the end of the third month of treatment, the monster heads moved to the sink, where aggressive play continued. David repeatedly rammed his doll with full force into mine, causing them both to bounce off the adjacent wall and fall into the sink. However, new elements of gentle caretaking and using the dolls to begin to talk about and explore body parts became incorporated in this play. David would interrupt the fighting sequences to wash his monster head. He would pour the liquid soap over the doll and in a careful, soothing manner work the slimy substance into a rich lather before rinsing it off with water and starting over again. As he did this David would comment about various body parts (e.g., his butt is dirty, his legs, his face, his hair, his "pont," which is David's word for penis). Additionally David gave his monster head feelings as he made him cry because soap had gotten into his eyes or roar with anger and initiate a fight—"He's angry; he's going to knock you down."

David's increased ability to use language spontaneously to describe both what he and the monster heads were doing and feeling coincided with two important events that took place during the sessions. On one occasion, David repeatedly threw his monster head over a chair near the wall by the one-way mirror. Accidentally, the monster head landed with great force against the mirror. This happened twice, after which I intervened and stated that David could throw the monster head but needed to be careful not to throw it against the mirror because the mirror could break. In response to my words, David stopped all activity, covered his face with his arms, and put his head down on the table. He sat this way, in complete silence with no overt displays of affect for what felt to me like a very long time. It was as if he had completely shut down and withdrawn within himself. During this time I felt very helpless and wondered about how David had experienced my limit setting: Did he think he had done something wrong?, Did he think I was prohibiting this kind of play despite my reassurances that it could continue? Was he angry with me for interrupting the momentum of his activity? Many possibilities ran through my mind as I struggled to understand and ultimately help David understand what had happened. I was also torn between wanting to comfort him and observing what course this behavior would take without intervention. How long would it last? How would David emerge from this state? Would he turn to me for help or rely on his own resources? What would our following interactions be like? Since I did not specifically know what he was feeling, I again resorted to describing the events that had taken place (e.g., "After I said to be careful, you stopped playing and are now lying there very silently"). I told David that I wondered what he might be feeling and thinking and encouraged him to use words because it was my job to try to understand him and his experiences. David remained silent as I spoke, then slowly lifted his head and began to look around the playroom, avoiding eye contact with me the entire time. He then stood up and walked over to the sink, turning around once a certain distance had been established to signal me to "come on" and join him. Interactive play resumed as if nothing had happened, indicating that David was able to move himself out of this state of withdrawal and upset, and "regroup" in a manner that enabled him to return to play and restore the relationship. Despite my feelings of helplessness in the moment, this incident offered me an opportunity to begin to define my role as therapist and show David through continued interest and concern that I was both willing and able to tolerate the various forms his upset might take. In retrospect, I realized that this incident may have marked the first time that David experienced me as a separate person with an agenda of my own. His sudden withdrawal and retreat from interaction may have accompanied feelings of loss and fear that I was no longer a magical extension of himself as I had previously come to be known to him through my mirroring behaviors. Perhaps the importance of this event was not so much my ability to tolerate and respond to his upset but rather David's ability to tolerate awareness of my separateness.

Coinciding with this incident, I consciously began to use more affect language when describing his play. For example, I commented that the monster heads did a lot of different things in the playroom. Sometimes they seemed to be playing and having a good time; sometimes they seemed to be angry and would fight a lot; sometimes they seemed to be scared and called out for help; other times they would be teasing each other or playing the hiding game where they would be apart, then find each other again. Sometimes the monster heads seemed happy and laughed; other times they seemed upset and cried, needing to be comforted; sometimes they were hungry and needed to be fed. I also told him that all those kinds of feelings were OK to have in the playroom and that the monster heads and David could be any way they wanted to be, and that it was my job to try to understand what was happening and keep things safe.

After these occurrences, David increasingly made use of language to narrate his play and communicate his experiences to me. Thus the therapy sessions became a time during which "meaning" could be created, experienced, and shared within the context of a relationship. The continuity and constancy of my responsiveness as our relationship evolved—beginning with an extended period during which self and other were not yet clearly differentiated and moving toward increased awareness of separateness—enabled David to form an attachment to me that facilitated his willingness to explore both himself and the environment. My feeling that our time together had taken on a special meaning for David was confirmed by reports from the classroom staff, who noticed that David would often ask for me or insist that it was "time for Annelie to play with me." On one occasion David saw me in the hall, 45 minutes before our session and became very upset, thinking that I wouldn't come to see him that day. According to his teachers he displayed his "shutting down" behavior and did not accept their reassurances that I would be there as usual at 10:00. When I arrived, he was very excited and relieved as well as more talkative than usual as we made our way up to the playroom. Another time I arrived to find David standing outside the classroom with one of his teachers, still in his coat and visibly distressed. He would not budge and didn't respond to the teacher's attempts to discover what may have happened. Together we went into the classroom where David said he didn't want to go to the bathroom with the other children and did not want to go up to 8. I told him that was OK and that we could spend our time together in the classroom instead. I acknowledged his upset and encouraged him to tell me about it. Initially he was very quiet and brought over a puzzle to work on by the table. I told him that he didn't have to talk about what happened if he didn't want to but that how he was feeling really mattered to me, and I wanted him to know that words could really work in helping me to understand him better. As he worked on the puzzle David mumbled something about the bus driver and slowly I was able to piece together that David was upset because Mr. B. had taken a slip of paper away from him on the bus that morning. I praised him by saying, "You used your words and now I understand what happened." David then began to lead me around the classroom to show me his art work displayed on the wall and pointed out his name as well as those of his peers. Suddenly David turned to me and said he wanted to "go to 8." I explained that we could go there but I wanted him to know that our time in the room would be shorter by twenty minutes since we had already spent some of it together in the classroom. Our playroom activities began with feeding the baby dolls, briefly playing monster head games, and shooting a round of baskets, and ended with a game of Monopoly where David lined up all the houses to make a train and sang the choo-choo train song that he had learned at circle time in the classroom. More than anything his wish to go to 8 indicated to me that the playroom had taken on a special meaning for David, as had our relationship.

Appendix E

The Building of the Self in Therapy:
The Case of Tomas

Anne Adelman

Tomas was born when his mother was in her early forties and had two daughters grown and living away from home. She had divorced her first husband, the father of her daughters, and lived with Tomas's father for twenty years. Her pregnancy with Tomas was unplanned. Mother described that she had an extremely close and intense relationship with Tomas during his first year of life. As Tomas entered early toddlerhood the relationship became more difficult, marred by his screaming, which Mother found increasingly distressing and inappropriate. He did not acquire any language until the age of 2. It appeared that he did not communicate well nonverbally and that Mother was not always able to read his communications. For example, she told a story about having bought him a new pair of shoes that were a little big for him. One must have fallen off, but Mother didn't notice until they arrived at a restaurant and she realized that he had only one shoe on and that he must have been walking with just one shoe. After reporting this incident, she said "He couldn't even tell me."

At the time they entered our program the relationship between this mother and child was stormy, with constant battles, often centering on food. Tomas would only eat two or three favorite foods and his mother, in frustration and desperation, acquiesced to his demands. Nightly battles occurred around bedtime, and tantrums often occurred in public places, especially on shopping expeditions. It seemed that after the pleasurable early phase, the mother experienced traumatic disappointment and guilt about his difficulties. She vacillated between minimizing the extent of his problems and fiercely fighting with doctors and psychologists to make sure he received the best possible attention. She approached our center and especially the play therapy with the same initial suspicion, but eventually was able to develop a fairly trusting relationship with me, though she was not willing to be present during therapy sessions beyond the first three. At first she requested that she be included in the therapy. When I met her request with an invitation to participate freely and regularly, she declined, stating that she had looked forward to having free time while Tomas was in school. Thus she enacted her own ambivalent rapprochement with me but was eventually willing to meet with me on a somewhat regular basis. Her attendance at the early play sessions proved invaluable because it gave me the opportunity to observe the mother–child relationship.

The mother's careful and protective mothering created a safe and secure base for Tomas, from which he could gather a sense of initiative, curiosity, and joyful exploration of the world. At the same time, it became apparent that mother's grief over her son's impairment, which was neither fully acknowledged nor resolved, created a traumatic disjunction in their relationship. When she experienced him as failing or flawed, she withdrew from him. He came to experience her as misattuned and absent. He felt he had lost her, and the ensuing anger, anxiety, and despair he experienced then interfered with his capacity to be related, responsive, and focused on task. For example, in one session Tomas was playing with Legos, examining pieces in what appeared to be an aimless fashion and then tossing them down to find new ones. In an effort to engage him, his mother began to build a house and showed it to him, asking him to build one too. He looked away from her and continued his random play. She responded by telling him that if he did not want to play with her she would play by herself and continued building a complex house while he turned away and aimlessly explored a Lego window frame. When she was finished building she showed him her house. Tomas reacted in a rage, grabbed it from her, and broke it apart. She cried out, "Don't do that! That's mine!" This incident recreated the fundamental disjunction between this mother and her child: in the face of his frequent inaccessibility and unresponsiveness the mother experienced grief and anger, dismay and frustration that interfered with her capacity for affective attunement and empathic understanding.

At the beginning of therapy when Tomas was 4 years old, he spoke in one- or two-word phrases and often whispered unintelligibly. He did not respond when spoken to. He displayed a wide variety of bizarre behaviors, and his limited speech included the repetition of television commercials. He was often quiet and withdrawn, apart from his classroom group, unable to make a connection to the other children or the adults around him.

The first playful interaction between us was the game of peek-a-boo, which was played by Tomas climbing into a large toy chest while I sat in a nearby chair and watched. Contact between us was established nonverbally by smiling. After a while Tomas would say "bye-bye" and disappear into the toy chest, closing the cover over himself. I would wait a moment, knock on the lid and say, "Where's Tomas?" In response Tomas would throw open the lid in delight, smile, and then vanish into the toy chest again. It is important that in this game, Tomas maintained control over disappearance and reunion and that the game focused on his leaving me, not being left by me.

Early on in the treatment certain phrases, expression, or words I used were repeated in a ritualized manner by Tomas to express his dawning awareness of the world that was being formed in the playroom out of the fabric of the therapeutic relationship. For example, in an early session Tomas was manipulating a strip of formica that had become separated from the table. I remarked that "the table was broken," a phrase that became an important signal communication. Hardly a session would go by without Tomas pointing to the table and remarking, "That's the broken table." The joint recognition of the broken table early in therapy can be seen as Tomas's ability to express that something felt broken in him and that he wished his therapist to know about it. His early use of language in therapy seemed to serve the function of establishing, maintaining, and reaffirming the tie between us. The gradual development of a significant therapeutic relationship by way of shared language provided the framework for the development of an internal sense of self by encouraging the co-creation of a narrative known to us both.

A new significant play sequence emerged that involved Tomas turning on and off the light switch. He would turn off the light, lie down on a rest mat, and request that I lie down also. He would not allow me to speak. What seemed important was that he created darkness and light as a way of creating disappearance and reunion. The darkness may have represented in part his worry that he would in fact disappear if he could not be seen. Thus, the darkness Tomas created was essential in working through this facet of his separation fear, as he was able to use the symbolic absence and real presence of the therapist to integrate the frightening aspects of aloneness with the growing capacity to internally represent the comforting aspects of togetherness.

Another important game involved a giant blue ball that was rolled back and forth between Tomas and me, sitting at opposite ends of the long playroom. As the game advanced he would roll the ball to me and then run and hide, waiting for me to roll the ball back before jumping out of his hiding place to catch it. In this play sequence my function was to serve as an affirming partner for his increasingly independent actions. As I supported his wishes to direct and control the game and affirmed his growing sense of competence and mastery, his affect became increasingly joyful and his play increasingly expansive. His enjoyment and daring reflected the important developmental strides in the areas of relatedness and integration of self–other representations. The play was predictable, safe, and gratifying and permitted both an experience of himself as continuous and sustained and a gradual internalization of the relationships as consistent and reliable. The game seemed to have important undertones of a practicing subphase of separation-individuation during which infants become enthralled with the world around them and with their own rapidly developing physical abilities. It seemed that for Tomas the giant blue ball came to represent the invisible thread by which he could remain in contact with me. He regulated the distance, increasing it symbolically by hiding, yet controlling it by verbally commanding the ball-therapist to return to him. My responsiveness to Tomas's strivings toward agency and mastery provided a stepping stone toward a more consolidated sense of self, which permitted a dawning recognition of me as a whole person separate from him, yet connected by way of a mutually shared history of reliable and pleasurable exchanges.

Tomas's capacity to relate to me as a whole person became evident, initially by way of his dramatic and sudden interest in my physical presence and appearance. He began to initiate more physical contact, especially after a genuine connection had been made, such as by playing the ball game. His readiness to establish a closer and more differentiated relationship was shown by the way in which he became observant of my clothing or hairstyle, particularly of any changes. He would note at each meeting "Boots today" or "No boots today, shoes today." While becoming more aware of me as a separate person, he gradually began to examine himself in the mirror, making faces, watching himself as he walked by, and stopping short when he could no longer see his reflection. The changes taking place in his relationship to me seemed to correspond to his reworking of early object relationships with structural shifts in the development of internal representations and self differentiation. This led the way to the unfolding of themes relating to body integrity and bodily functions and control.

A play sequence emerged and became central to the therapy for several weeks. On Tomas's birthday I brought in a new toy, a dump truck, which consisted of a cab and dumpster connected by a movable joint. In the session following his birthday Tomas noticed me taking the truck out of the file cabinet that was used to store toys in the therapy room. The truck and file cabinet became an integral part of the therapy for several sessions. When entering the playroom Tomas would pick up the truck and put it into the drawer in the cabinet. He began to explore the drawers of the file cabinet, examining and naming their contents and carefully replacing anything he had removed. When he discovered that the bottom drawer of the cabinet was empty, it became his to fill upon entering the play room in the morning. He carefully put his lunch box, hat, mittens, jacket, and snow pants into the drawer. One day after spending several minutes playing with the drawer he finally climbed into the drawer himself and curled up on his jacket. Eventually he began to use the file cabinet as a receptacle for his productions, putting away drawings he had made at the end of one session and retrieving them at the start of the next. Thus, it seemed that the special truck and the file cabinet became symbols of his relationship to me and of his emerging awareness of interior spaces such as his body and mind and the mind and body of his therapist. I understood this as an indication of the progressive development of an *intersubjective self* (Stern 1985). Tomas became able to grasp that he had an interior self and that others, like his therapist, did as well. Tomas had first used the filing cabinet to explore interior spaces and began to understand that they could contain his possessions when he was not using them. One might speculate that this discovery of interior holding spaces could be related to the growing realization that he could hold in his mind the image of his therapist and that I could hold him in mind as well. Furthermore, it is interesting to consider that I had given the dump truck to him on his birthday. I recognized his birth with a toy truck with two parts linked together yet separable, perhaps symbolic of my attempt to repair his notion of psychological birth as a catastrophic event of separateness without an available other.

16

From Command to Request

The Development of Language in the Treatment of a Symbiotic-Psychotic Child

written in collaboration with
Margaret Chernack

Martin came to treatment at the age of 4, a symbiotic-psychotic child with only the most rudimentary use of symbolic function. This child emerged from a rigid, symbiotic relationship with his mother—which did not allow him to develop further along the lines of separation-individuation—and moved toward the establishment of a firmer, more differentiated and integrated sense of self and other. His development along the lines of separation-individuation is presented through a description of the development of his use of language as it emerged in the therapeutic process.

The choice of this method of presentation is based on several assumptions. First, it is assumed that the nature of one's self-concept and the level and quality of one's self–object differentiation are manifest in one's linguistic style. According to Winnicott (1967), cultural experience, play, creative activity, and the beginning of symbolization arise in a "transitional" or "potential space" that is neither inside/subjective nor outside/objective, but intermediate between subject and object. If one assumes that language develops in this transitional space, that is, at the interface of self and other, then it becomes useful to regard language as indicative of previous and present successes and failures at the interface of self and other. That is, it becomes useful to regard language as indicative of the nature of self-object differentiation. Beratis and colleagues (1982), by suggesting that early vocalizations function as transitional objects, enrich the notion of the transitional object. They recognize that there are significant differences between "blanket and babbling," and stress that such "qualitative differences in the nature of transitional objects are crucial in relationship to their significance for development" (p. 580). Thus the differences between *types* of transitional objects reflect different "levels of self–object differentiation" and "lend themselves to different aspects of emerging ego-functions" (p. 580). However, it is suggested here that *language itself* is paradigmatic of the paradox that Winnicott sees as belonging to the transitional space; it "both joins and separates" (Winnicott 1967, p. 372) at the same time. Without some recognition of separateness there would be no need for language. The development of language already implies the recognition of an other. And language is the means par excellence with which we understand, are understood, communicate, and join with the other. The development of language (which includes preverbal communication) thus embodies the paradox of oneness and separateness and provides an avenue toward understanding the development and nature of self and object representations. Thus, the description of the development of Martin's use of language also describes the construction of his self as it developed in therapy.

The Therapeutic Setting

Martin was seen in a day treatment program as part of a research project to study the relationship of cognition and object relations in psychotic children according to the theories of Margaret S. Mahler and Jean Piaget. The therapeutic program[1] employed three treatment modalities: (1) therapy; (2) therapeutic companionship; (3) classroom.

---

1. The Center was originally supported by HEW Grant #02907. It continues to be supported by the New Land Foundation, by the Plumstock Foundation, and by a number of private donors. The project is directed by Anni Bergman and Professor Gilbert Voyat.

In this setting each mother–child pair is seen by the therapist four times a week. Individual treatment sessions are conducted according to the model outlined by Mahler (1968) in her book *On Human Symbiosis and the Vicissitudes of Individuation*, in the chapter on treatment techniques. The therapist begins treatment by acting as a bridge between child and mother, bringing them closer together in a healthy symbiotic relationship by helping the mother understand the distorted communications of the child and by helping the child respond to the caretaking of the mother. During later stages in treatment, once the child has emerged as a more separate individual, the mother is no longer required to be present in all therapy sessions. The therapist of the mother–child pair also sees the mother in individual treatment sessions. Giving support to the mother in her mothering is a very important ingredient of therapy.

In addition to treatment with the therapist, the child is also seen in individual sessions by a therapeutic companion. While the therapist attempts to make a bridge between the mother and child, the therapeutic companion attempts to make a bridge for the child to the outside world. Psychotic children are not able to approach the outside world on their own, and the actual presence of the companion in everyday life situations with the child is a very important part of treatment.

The therapeutic classroom is geared to attend to the cognitive and social development of the children to the extent that they are capable of developing in these areas. The approach is development, based on the unfolding of cognitive stages as described by Piaget (1962).

The Mother–Child Pair

When Martin and his mother arrived at the Center, they were truly a symbiotic pair. Martin, at the age of 4, could not separate from his mother, and his mother seemed to accept totally his absolute dependence upon her. Martin was incapable of functioning as a separate self. He was unable to dress himself, he drank from a bottle, when he went to the bathroom he stood passively by while his mother held his penis. In bodily contact with his mother he seemed to try to establish a total union with her by melting into her, placing his face directly up against hers, putting his fingers into her eye, placing his mouth over hers. When not joined with his mother in physical contact, he would engage in repetitive, autistic-like activities such as moving cars to and fro at eye level and putting them in and taking them out of containers. Mother impassively and helplessly tolerated Martin's assaults on her body. She engaged actively with him only when he expressed a direct need of her. When he was able to maintain himself at some distance from her, she returned to an impassive, depressive stance with sporadic and intrusive attempts to lead him back into the only engagement with her of which he was capable.

The mother's active engagement with Martin when she was directly needed, and her emotional absence when he was playing at some distance from her, gave one the impression that the mother's own feeling of being alive was dependent upon Martin's interaction with her. However, it is important to add that the availability of this mother for treatment, her unfailing concern for her son's growth, her level-headedness—in short, her strengths—were a major variable in the success of Martin's treatment.

Martin is the first and only child of a young, unmarried, West Indian woman. Pregnancy and delivery were uncomplicated and motor milestones were within normal limits. His mother claims that Martin said his first word at 6 months and had names for family members at 1 year. At 18 months, language dropped out and was replaced with pointing. Martin is reported to have been a healthy and playful baby. His only significant illness was a chronic middle ear infection that was discovered and treated at 3 years. Martin has always lived with his mother, his mother's older sister, and his maternal grandmother. Martin's father has maintained inconsistent contact with the family throughout the years, with periods of regular visits alternating with periods of sporadic phone contact.

Normal Symbiotic Phase
and Symbiotic Psychosis

The theory of symbiotic psychosis, as originally conceptualized by Mahler, compares the nonhatched state of the psychotic child to the nonhatched state of the normal baby during the symbiotic stage of development.

In the symbiotic psychotic syndrome, self-differentiation from the
mother during the separation-individuation phase has failed and the
illusion of symbiotic omnipotent fusion with the mother is still being
maintained. [Mahler 1968, p. 74]

Since the time when Mahler formulated her theory of symbiotic
psychosis as well as the theory of the normal stages of development,
revolutionary advances in infant research have taken place. Researchers such as Brazelton (1981a), Stern (1980), and others have shown
that infants, even in the earliest stages of development, are capable
of complex perceptual functions and affective discriminations.
Furthermore, they have described the intricacy of early mother–child
interaction. While Mahler and her co-workers, in their research on
normal development, concentrated on the process of separation
and individuation rather than on the study of the autistic and symbiotic phases that precede it, it is nevertheless clear from the point
of view of their research that complex developments take place
during that period. The infant, in a short span of four to five
months, changes from existing in a twilight state, attuned to inner
rather than outer stimuli, to outward directedness and, in particular,
a state of specific attachment to the mothering partner. The symbiotic stage of development is the phase during which the infant develops a dialogue with his or her caretaker (Spitz 1965). Through
mirroring and mutual cueing, mother and infant become a symbiotic
dual unit.

Brazelton (1981a) describes the impact of the infant on the
caregiving of the mother. The infant's molding, nestling, turning the
head to her voice, are all powerful messages that elicit the mother's
tenderness and caregiving. Brazelton further suggests that from the
beginning, the infant has a need to alternate looking and not looking at mother—to have some control over the amount of stimulation
he or she receives.

A mother must respect her infant's needs for regulation or she will
overload his immature psycho-physiological system, and he will need
to protect himself by turning her off completely. Thus, she learns his
capacity for attention, non-attention, early in order to maintain his
attention to her. Within this rhythmic, coherent configuration, she
and he can introduce the mutable elements of communication. Smiles,
vocalizations, postures, tactile signals, all are such elements. They
can be interchanged at will as long as they are based on the rhyth-

mic structure. The individual differences of the baby's needs for such structure set the limits on it. [Brazelton 1981a, p. 18]

Brazelton continues: As one looks at the richness of such a homeostatic model, providing each participant with an opportunity to turn off or on at any time in the interaction, it demonstrates the fine tuning available and necessary to each partner of the dyad for learning about "the other" (p. 20).

It seems quite clear from this description that Martin and his mother had failed at this basic process. Both approach and withdrawal behaviors were coercive and abrupt. They lacked pleasure and playfulness. The rhythmic feedback system that provides the basis for all communication had not become established in this mother–child pair.

Brazelton describes the infant's reaction to a still-faced mother, the infant's attempts to bring the mother back, and his eventual withdrawal:

If the system is violated by a partner's non-reciprocity, the infant will respond in an appropriate manner which indicates how powerfully he is affected by the disturbance. [Brazelton 1981a, pp. 21–22]

He delineates four stages of regulation and learning within the system of social interaction between mother and infant during the first four months, that is, during the symbiotic phase. He uses the apt term *envelope of reciprocal interaction*, in which communication between infant and caregiver takes place. In the case of Martin it was in the first stages of therapy that the therapist attempted to establish such communication with him and simultaneously encouraged it between him and his mother.

The symbiotic stage in normal development is not a fixed state of nondifferentiation and nonintegration. It is the paradox of the symbiotic phase of development that at this stage, when there is the greatest degree of attunement and thus oneness between self and other, the very fact of attunement as manifested in the preverbal dialogue between mother and baby—the "dance" described by Stern (1977)— implies the existence of the beginning of differentiation. The normal symbiotic phase, the stage of dual unity, is a stage on the way toward differentiation and separation-individuation. By contrast, pathological symbiosis is a fixed state, closed to the possibility of preverbal dialogue or "dance," and thus closed to the development of true communication.

Treatment

For the purpose of this chapter, the word "request" is used to signify object-directed communications such as questions, answers, descriptions, and conversations. This serves to distinguish these from nondialogic utterances, termed "commands"—neologisms, immediate echolalia, the patient's nonsense language, and his early use of word names. This distinction is consonant with the intention of suggesting that there is a continuum of language development, a dialogic continuum. One end of this continuum is marked by linguistic phenomena that can be understood as indicative of a lack of self–object differentiation—the "command," the ideational equivalent of which is the hallucinatory wish-fulfillment. The other pole of the continuum is marked by linguistic phenomena that are indicative of self–object differentiation—the "request," the ideational equivalent of which is recognition of the other and the presence of ego functions, in particular the capacity for delay.

The Command

When Martin first came to treatment, his speech was composed largely of a babbling that had all the music, the intonation, and the cadence of a language but that at this early point contained no words. He echoed words from television (e.g., "Arrid Extra Dry," "Reggie Jackson") and had a few idiosyncratic word names (e.g., "taka taka" meant "Captain America"). Martin's object-directed communications were limited to pointing and a few word names, such as "truck," "baseball," and "Batman." The gesture, or nominative word, was used solely to indicate that he wanted an object. The expectation that his desire would be fulfilled was absolute. When he pointed to, or named and pointed to an object, and the therapist or mother got the object for him, this did not seem to be experienced as a response to a request, but rather as part and parcel of the naming or pointing. Thus it is perhaps more accurate to regard even the apparently object-directed

communications with which he began treatment as closer to omnipotent wish-fulfillments than to even very primitive forms of dialogue.
The therapist's first task thus became the reinstitution of the earliest forms of dialogue. In other words, the therapist's goal was to
become a need-satisfying object, to be included in the symbiotic relationship in which Martin and his mother were frozen, and thus to
reopen the path toward separation-individuation.

From the first day, a baseball game was initiated. It was a three-
way game. At that early point Martin was batting in his mother's
arms. The therapist said, "Mommy and Martin at bat, Meg throws,"
at which point the therapist pitched and they tried to hit the ball.
As Martin began to move from this clinging position, the ball game
had its own development. "Mommy at bat, Meg throws," and Martin
would run bases, run "home to Mommy," "safe with Mommy." When
he tentatively ran home to the therapist as well, the litany expanded
to "safe with Meg," "safe in the playroom." As he began practicing,
the ball game became "Mommy at bat, Meg throws, Martin goes," and
Martin would leave the playroom and then return to find us "still
there," "still the same," "still playing ball." As time went on the ball
game became further elaborated: "Mommy at bat, Meg throws, Martin goes," at which point Martin would invent a movement-gesture
that the therapist would imitate; the ball game would then continue.
As his movements became more elaborate, this gestural dialogue became richer. In the course of this baseball game, which developed over
the first year of treatment, the therapist slowly came to be included
within the symbiotic duo.

The previous discussion of the mother–child pair distinguished the
pathological symbiotic state from the normal symbiotic stage. The
therapist becomes the facilitator of the development of a more normal symbiotic relation between mother and child by becoming included
in what was a rigidly defensive symbiotic state, and thus the therapist is also the catalyst for the development of a dialogue between
them. In this way the path toward differentiation begins to be re-
opened. It is interesting to note that for Martin this ball game eventually became a stable structure into which he could integrate new
experiences. For example, when Martin first ventured to play with
water he next had mother and therapist play baseball, and the litany

went, "Mommy at bat, Meg throws, Martin goes," at which point Martin shouted out the word "water."

In an attempt to enter into however primitive a form of interaction/dialogue with the patient, the therapist would echo Martin's many bizarre sounds. At first this could be tolerated only if they were exact echoes of his sounds. As time went on he was able to tolerate the therapist's changing the sounds somewhat, turning them eventually from harsh noises into songs.

Martin's omnipotent naming of objects provided another vehicle for the early institution of dialogue. When Martin said, for example, "truck," the therapist brought him the object, saying, "Martin wants Meg to get the truck." While satisfying the demand, the therapist puts the demand into words. While remaining at the level of a need-satisfying object, the therapist attempts further differentiation by making small and gradual changes, staying however minute a step ahead of the level from which the patient acted or spoke. This is similar to what mothers do spontaneously with their infants, always putting into words what is happening between them. Dialogue necessitates a distance between the speaker and the responder, however minute this distance may be at first. Thus even the most primitive object relation, even the symbiotic, already implies some beginning of differentiation and thus some form of dialogue.

These interventions could be successful only because the seed of development, the precursor of dialogue, is present in even the most primitive of behaviors. When Martin used word names omnipotently, this demand or order that the need be satisfied (get the truck), was also a beginning attempt at creating order in his world (that's a truck, there's a truck). The primitive sounds and simple movements called for a response that, if directed at the child's present level of development in the context of a stable and safe "holding environment," could in turn be responded to. As Ekstein (1966) notes, "The imitative aspects of [echolalia and echopraxia] can be considered a forerunner of identificatory processes" (pp. 238–239).

In its earliest phases the therapeutic dialogue generally took the form of the therapist's slightly modified echoing of the patient (Ekstein's 1966 "quasi echopraxia and echolalia," p. 246). The patient's echoing of the therapist, while seen as defensive—a denial of self–object differentiation—was also regarded as a sign of a beginning attempt at, or a precursor of, identification with the therapist (e.g., Bergman 1971). After a time, Martin's immediate echolalia evolved into a delayed echoing of the therapist's approval of the smallest of his independent actions. Martin soon came to applaud himself and to say "good boy" when he succeeded at something. For a long time Martin made it clear that the therapist must echo his echo of the therapist and say in agreement, "Yes, good boy." As the identification became more stable and the internalization more possible, this became correlatively less necessary to Martin. The therapist's voice, its specific quality, as well as the words spoken, were quite important in the development of internalization and the resultant development in ego functions and self–object differentiation.

One day, toward the end of the first year in treatment, Martin began the session by looking through a set of blocks that had the names of important persons and television characters written on them. He began naming each one in a striking imitation of the therapist's voice. He came to a block that had the name of a staff member who had left the Center some weeks before and immediately put it behind his back. He stopped, thought, took the block out of hiding, and for the first time spontaneously said, "Jean went bye-bye." He then did the same with each of the blocks that represented someone whom he no longer saw. For Martin, at this point in his development, the ability to maintain this level of self–object differentiation in the face of object loss seemed directly correlated with his use of the therapist's voice. Martin's use of the quality of the therapist's voice was different than—and an advance over—his echoing of the therapist's words. In his echolalic repetition of the therapist's words, Martin repeated what the therapist said. In his imitation of the therapist's voice, Martin repeated what the therapist is. An affective component, represented by the quality of the voice, had been added.

Martin's language can usefully be regarded as a defensive maintenance of the earliest forms of object relations as well as an attempt at and difficulty with internalization. In the beginning phases of treatment, Martin would often talk with his mouth closed. He was unable to repeat a demand for something if it was not immediately understood and responded to. He would never ask or answer questions, and he tended to repeat words (and actions) over and over as if he would thus be able to drain them of all meaning. These phenomena were mainstays of the first year, and especially of the first six months, of treatment. They can be understood as attempts to maintain a lack of self–object differentiation, as primitive attempts to defend against separation. If the therapist or mother did not understand Martin's spoken demands, this signified that they were separate persons, incapable of mindreading and incapable of omnipotent fulfillment of his omnipotent demands. To repeat himself would be a recognition, on some level, of this state of affairs. Martin's speaking with his mouth closed seemed to have a similar anxiety-reducing effect for him, as recrossing the threshold of the playroom with his eyes closed when it was time to leave. Both were attempts to deny separation. Martin's closing his eyes at the threshold and reopening them outside the playroom had the additional significance of regaining him omnipotent control, since it was he who made the therapist disappear. The mouth-closing had the additional significance of trying to discover the therapist to be omnipotently able to know what he wished without his having to speak it out loud, without his having to ask.

In sum, the level of Martin's self–object differentiation, as reflected by his use of language in the early phases of treatment, is well exemplified by his early use of the single word "yes." An important variation of the baseball game went as follows: "Mommy at bat, Meg throws, Martin goes," at which point Martin shouted out the word "yes" a number of times and indicated that the therapist should repeat "yes." This joyful proclamation was sometimes accompanied by jumping or twirling motions and sometimes announced a cappella. This use of *yes* preceded the development and use of *no* and was, it seemed, of a different order than the use of *yes* as a response—the *yes* that Spitz (1957) describes as developmentally following the *no*. In this case, the use of *yes* as a *response* occurred quite late in the treatment and followed the emergence of *no*. First of all to emerge, however, was the use of *yes* as proclamation and command. This is not the *yes* said to others in response to a request, but the *yes* that Martin wished others to say to him, the *yes* that represented the absence of any possible *no*, the absence of any possible boundary, limit, or difference between himself and the world, between the self and the other.

Transition

The phase in Martin's treatment that was transitional between the early command language of omnipotence, of the undifferentiated self–object, and the communicative language of self to object that is predicated upon the development of more stable internalizations and resultant self and object representations, is described through what led up to and what followed from the point in Martin's treatment at which he first came to name himself.

About six months after the start of treatment, Martin began to create situations in which he was bound to experience the loss of objects and persons. Martin, who always carried with him pictures from magazines or comic books, began having his mother cut out all the individual people in the group pictures separately. He would carry these little pieces around, inevitably losing one or another of them, at which point he would himself fall to pieces. This was understood as a dramatic repetition of a fact of life that he was first beginning to experience: that loss and separation go hand in hand. Soon, however, he seemed to be purposely creating such situations. For example, he would order his mother to throw a picture away; several hours after he saw that she had taken the garbage out, he would demand the picture again and fall to pieces when she could not supply it. He would intentionally leave an object at home when he came to therapy sessions, and then fall to pieces when it was not in the therapy room.

This is similar to the behavior of a normal toddler during the rapprochement subphase. One such little boy would ask his mother to cook some food for him. The moment the food was in the pot cooking, he demanded to have it uncooked. When he was offered the same food uncooked, he was not satisfied. He broke down into a tantrum, demanding the same food that he had asked his mother to cook now to be given to him uncooked.

This phase of manufacturing tragic losses was regarded as a transitional phase in Martin's development toward object constancy during which he attempted to recapture his now waning omnipotence. He commanded the toy or picture to disappear, to stay home, to be thrown away. He then attempted to command its reappearance and, when wishing did not make it so, he was devastated. That he needed to try, to wish, to make this happen clearly signified his increasing individuation and decreasing omnipotence. Previously, he would not have needed to try or to wish that others would return since, in an important sense, he never would have experienced them as having left in the first place. Previously, when he had made the therapist disappear by turning off the light, or had made a toy disappear by closing the door or leaving the session, and then turned on the light or opened the door or returned for his next session, it is unlikely that he experienced this as the person or the object still being where he left it. Rather, he commanded its reappearance, he made it present by being present again himself.

However, with the beginning of self–object differentiation, when objects and persons had begun to have an existence apart from him, when his omnipotence was no longer absolute, he desperately attempted to recapture the old state of affairs. This phase was truly transitional, progressive as well as regressive; for by setting up the situations of inevitable loss he was also attempting to master the dawning realization that others did in fact exist apart from him, in his absence. At the height of this he came to a session in an intense panic searching for one of his blocks that he had taken home with him from the playroom some days before. His mother explained that before he left he began to take the block with him, thought better of it, and put it down in his room saying, "Captain Kirk block stay." The therapist spoke to Martin about this recurrent behavior, adding that he was so afraid of losing his mommy, since then he became afraid he would lose himself too. Martin stood up quietly in the middle of the room, and after a moment announced, "Captain Kirk block home." He then indicated that he wanted to paint, and after the therapist had, as usual, signed Martin's name to his painting, Martin patted his tummy and said, "Martin, Martin, Martin."

In the months that followed there was a considerable surge of development in language as well as an advance in and consolidation of ego functions. His language progressed beyond the nominative function, as if there were finally a subject to which he could attach predicates. In addition to naming objects, he now spoke of states of affairs— "put it away," "paper all gone," "paper fall down," "try again," "that's enough," "come on," "where's the boat? There it is." His body language, too, became more differentiated. He shrugged when he could not find something he wanted, put his hands in his pockets, began swinging his arms as he walked in imitation of a favorite male teacher, and began purposefully experimenting with turning in circles, walking backwards, falling down. His vocalizations became more varied, as he began speaking in a squeaky little girl's voice as he played with a doll, and a gruff, rough voice as he played Batman and Robin. He began joyfully experimenting with saying a word or phrase in numerous pitches, intonations, and cadences. The correlative development of his language and self representation was further demonstrated in his increased use of the mirror—watching himself cry, play, and rage as he had done so many times before but without awareness—and in his beginning to take pride and comfort in ownership during this period of increased language development.

As he began to become aware of objects as belonging to him, he began to take over some of the valuing of his products that had previously been left to the therapist. The therapist had always hung up or saved Martin's pictures despite Martin's apparent lack of interest in his own productions. Now Martin began admiring them, repeating the therapist's words, "They're Martin's," and began showing them to other people. He was able to take comfort in ownership. For example, under the pressure of an upcoming vacation, Martin wanted something that belonged to another child. When he couldn't have it he panicked. After calming down, he angrily banged on the floor and proceeded to enact in his play the other child taking his toys away. When the therapist commented that the other child certainly couldn't have his toys because they were his, Martin responded, "Martin's, Martin's," and was much comforted.

During this period in his treatment, the "yes" proclamation dropped out altogether and the "no" emerged. It is no surprise that, with the waning of omnipotence and the development of self-object differentiation, the "yes" as an omnipotent, absolute affirmation of perfect union should disappear. It is equally unsurprising that, with the beginning of self-awareness, the "no" should arise. As Spitz (1957) has shown, "The acquisition of the 'No' is the indicator of a new level of autonomy, of the awareness of the 'other' and of the awareness of the self" (p. 129). "The child's headshaking 'no' is the visible proof of his identification with the grownup; at the same time it initiates the era of allocentric communication" (p. 59). In the case of Martin, however, "yes" as a response to a request did not follow fast on the heels of the semantic "no." In fact, for almost a year Martin went to some lengths to avoid speaking the word "yes." If he attempted to indicate that he wanted something—and it should be noted that he could not yet frequently ask for something with a question—for example, by saying "go Pepsi," and the therapist asked, "Do you want to go to the store to get Pepsi, Martin?" Martin would not respond "yes," but instead would echo the therapist's words, "go to store," and add "okay," as if the idea had been the other's wish and not his own, but something with which he would go along.

By this point in his treatment Martin evinced some degree of self–object differentiation, internalization of the mothering principle, and the beginning development of self and object representations. The differentiation, the internalization, and the representations were not stable, however, and conflicts over separations were still of intense proportions. In saying "no" he indicated that he was able to separate himself from the other, but in being able *only* to say "no" he indicated that he could do so only if he alone commanded it. The self–object differentiation was uncertain, not stable and sure. To say "yes" at this point would threaten Martin with reengulfment. Further, it is suggested that the saying of *yes* involves a qualitatively different level of self–object differentiation than the saying of "no." To say "no" is to separate one's self from the other, so to speak, with one's back turned. To say "yes" is to do so face to face in a simultaneous, mutual recognition of each member of the dialogue's mutual separateness from the other. If Martin's original "yes" is, for the moment, regarded as a representation of sameness, and his "no" as a representation of difference, then the "yes" that was not yet available to him would be a recognition of similarity in the context of, or on the background of, difference. This last and more advanced capacity is a condition not only for saying yes, but also for asking and answering questions and for that advanced form of dialogue, the conversation.

The Request

In some of the developments in Martin's language during the second year of his treatment, one can see the dawnings of the language of "request," linguistic phenomena that are manifestations of a differentiation of self and other.

During his second year of treatment the word "yes" reemerged for the first time since the beginning of therapy. Along with the reemergence of *yes* came the ability and willingness to ask and answer questions. He began to attempt to describe to the therapist and his mother what had occurred to him when they were not with him. If the therapist asked what happened in school that day, he might answer in a burst, "Helen and Gary, and no coat and run." Such a response to a question is clearly predicated on the recognition that the therapist, the questioner, the other, did not and could not know what Martin, the questioned, the self, knew because the other was not the self. Similarly, to ask a question involves the ability to recognize that the other does not know what the self wants without being told, and that the other might not satisfy the request, might say "no." Further, as suggested above, a response to a question indicates that there is an ability to reach toward the other, to join with the other to a degree, but not absolutely. To answer a question indicates an ability to join with the other at the same time as, and on the basis of, the recognition that the other is not the self. This is language as communication.

In Martin's case, three phases in the development of his communicative use of language were distinguished. These phases seem to correspond, progressively, to the degree of internalization and articulation of object and self representations. At first Martin would repeat both sides of a conversation. For example, Martin asked the therapist, "Where's Carla?" The therapist responded, "I don't know. Let's look for her." Martin says, "Okay." As they walked in search of Carla, Martin said aloud to himself, "Where's Carla? I don't know. Let's look. Okay." Somewhat later, Martin began holding conversations as if with two or more parts of himself, at which point he would say, for example, "Martin, move chair. Okay. Move it. Good." Finally he was able to hold conversations with actual others, asking and answering questions and describing events.

This section closes with some recent examples of Martin's use of language, taken from the beginning of his third year in treatment:

Martin: Meg, look you got a new table.
Therapist: Yes, I did. You noticed, and then you told me, too.

Martin: Get the toys.

Martin: [looking out the window] Look, the trees, it's windy.
Therapist: [later that session] Are you looking at the trees, Martin?
Martin: Yes, and the cars.

Martin: I'm hungry.
Therapist: Would you like something to eat?
Martin: Yes.
Therapist: Would you like toast?
Martin: Yes.
Therapist: With butter or jelly?
Martin: This, this, have to choose. . . . I have jelly and you have butter.

Martin: It's night, where the sun go?

Developments of Communication in a Normal Infant

The use of language as communication as it progressed in the tripartite treatment of a symbiotic-psychotic boy from the age of 4 to the age of 6 has been described. Martin posed a strange dilemma, but also a special opportunity. He had words at his disposal, as was fitting for his chronological age; however, he used these words not as a normal child of his age would, nor even as a child much younger, first learning to talk. Rather, he seemed to use words in the way that a normal infant and junior toddler might use various forms of vocal and gestural communication. In other words, as is typical of a symbiotic-psychotic child, maturational advances could not be used in the service of his development. Rather, in the lack of appropriate object relationships, these maturational advances become a threat rather than an asset. Some examples of interchanges with an infant during the first year of his life, interchanges that illustrate communications and thus the forerunners of verbal language, may prove illuminating; without this kind of solid base in nonverbal communication, words seem to become encoded in bizarre, idiosyncratic, and repetitive patterns.

As an infant, Peter was sung to by both his parents, especially when they put him to sleep. Since Peter was a baby who did not fall asleep easily, his parents usually held him while sitting on a rocking chair and singing to him until he would fall asleep. Peter had favorite tunes beginning at an early age. These were not the usual lullabies. Rather, they were work songs that both parents enjoyed and liked to sing to him. After two to three months, when Peter's sounds were beginning to be more varied, they were clearly responsive to different situations. Cooing was the sound for intimate interchanges. A very distinctive screech denoted excitement. Finally, Peter would sing a "song" when he was ready to go to sleep. This song was quite different from his other sounds, a kind of hum on a two- or three-note scale, which was a very distinct signal. As soon as Peter started to sing his song his parents knew that he wanted to go to sleep. They would begin to sing to him and rock him, and Peter would quickly drop off to sleep. The "song" used in this way by baby Peter is comparable to what has been called command-type communications in Martin. The communications ceased as soon as the wish was fulfilled and Peter was helped to go to sleep. Some months later the song began to be used in a new way. Now Peter sang his song not only when he wanted to go to sleep, but also when he wanted to be sung to. When his request was met and he was sung to, he stopped singing, but started again when the song was finished and asked for another. One might say that the command (for the lullaby) had become a request, and that a dialogue ensued. Some months later still, Peter would request a song or music of any sort by bouncing up and down, looking smilingly and expectantly at the caregiver.

When Peter was 9 to 10 months old, now in the midst of the early practicing subphase, he discovered a new form of gestural communication in keeping with his now more mature perceptual and locomotor functions. From early on Peter's mother had enjoyed showing him pictures in books and naming objects for him. Now Peter began to point at objects and people, wishing—or rather, "commanding"—that they be named. He derived great pleasure from being carried about while he pointed at different objects, waiting for his mother to give him the name. Similarly, when he discovered objects on his own explorations, he would bring them back and show them, again wishing them to be named, acknowledged. If anyone tried to take an object that Peter brought to them, he made it clear that he did not wish to give it, that he just wanted to show it and have it named. About a month later Peter's pointing began to be accompanied by the sound "ah." Now one had to listen to Peter's sounds to begin to understand what seemed to have moved on from the command to the request. Peter no longer wanted merely to have objects named, one now had to begin to distinguish whether he wanted something done—for example, the radio turned on, or the light switch turned on and off—or whether he wanted to have something said to him. But even what he wanted to have said was no longer simply naming. Rather, it required slightly more complex statements or explanations. By this time Peter was 1 year old and capable of understanding quite well what was said to him.

Peter's early screeching sounds also had a further development. They reappeared toward the end of his first year in a form that his mother said was his "love call." This love call was meant to draw attention to himself, often from strangers who were not looking at him. This could happen in the street, in a store, in a restaurant, and so on. If he succeeded in drawing attention to himself in this way, he was jubilant. Peter's screech was comparable to Martin's "yes," a verbal communication requesting affirmation.

It is clear from the description of Peter's early "language development" that words, once they would appear—once he would maturationally be able to form them—would easily fit into an already existing, complex communication system. Martin had words to use at the time when he was developing, at a much later age, the interpersonal base for communication. On the one hand, listening to and understanding Martin's language development sensitized the present authors to a better understanding of the development of communicative powers in a normal infant. On the other hand, it is the understanding of the progress of normal development that helped decipher Martin's often strange and seemingly incomprehensible communications.

Discussion

In this chapter we have discussed the development of a psychotic boy over the course of a two-year period. We have shown how the development of his language during that time serves as an important indicator of his progress along the lines of separation-individuation toward beginning object constancy and self–object differentiation. We have speculated about some of the intrapsychic developments that we have deduced from his use of language: "from command to request." By way of comparison and contrast, we have also offered a brief vignette, based on observations of a normal child and his parents during the preverbal period of development, that is, during the first year of life, which, from the point of view of object relations development, would cover the symbiotic phase and extend into the practicing subphase of the separation-individuation process.

Symbiotic psychosis occurs in vulnerable children when the separation-individuation process cannot be successfully negotiated. The rapprochement crisis, in such cases, does not end in resolution with beginning object constancy and symbolic process. Instead, rigid restitutive mechanisms appear. "In the symbiotic infantile psychosis reality testing remains fixated at, or regresses to, the omnipotent, delusional stage of the symbiotic mother–infant relationship. The boundaries of the self and the nonself are blurred" (Mahler 1979, vol. I, pp. 139–140).

Bruner (1983) has discussed how preverbal forms of communication eventually lead to the acquisition of verbal language. He says:

> The prelinguistic communicative framework established in their dialogue by mother and child provides the setting for the child's acquisition of this language function. His problem-solving in acquiring the deitic function is a *social* task: to find the procedure that will produce results, just as his prelinguistic communicative effort produced results, and the results needed can be interpreted in relation to role interactions. [pp. 48–49]

It is this innate preparation for language, based on the earlier development of communication, that seems to be missing in the psychotic child. Even in those psychotic children who have seemed to develop normally to a certain point and then regressed, we must assume that the early mother–infant relationship was burdened by a constitutional difficulty in the infant in utilizing the mother's care, or that the mother's care was grossly lacking in the kind of attunement that infant observers can demonstrate in normal development.

Beratis and colleagues (1982) discuss the difficulty of the psychotic child in the intermediate area of experience which includes transitional objects and the development of language. In the case of Martin communicative language development was preceded by his creation of a transitional world, inhabited by all the people who became important to him. This transitional world of block people was the way that he stayed in contact with all of the people—adults and children—who became important to him in our treatment setting. The fact that all these people came and went and were not always available to him was extremely difficult for him to accept. By creating the transitional world, he would manipulate and control what in reality he could not. Eventually, he had to create losses in this transitional world before he could accept a measure of separateness, which inevitably entails loss of the symbiotic mother before separation. This is very different from the kind of practicing of separation that a normal infant or toddler will do in his peekaboo games or in his darting away, wishing to be caught up in mother's arms. In these normal games, reunion always follows a loss. In contrast, the toy that Martin had decided to leave at home was then not at his disposal. The people in Martin's transitional world were not truly symbolic as they would have been in a normal child's play. They were something in between a transitional object, a psychotic fetish (Furer 1964), or autistic object (Tustin 1981), and symbolic play. They had qualities of all these, yet were also different from all of them. They were used by Martin to replay and attempt to master the absences of people, which to him were so traumatic. Yet he couldn't use this play to help himself understand and accept people's comings and goings as a normal child his age would have been able to do. He experienced the losses he himself created in his play as if they were the same real losses of people that upset him. This seems to be a deficiency in the symbolic function that is characteristic of psychotic children. The space in which later symbolic play and communicative language can occur (Winnicott 1953, 1967) is missing. Therefore, separation is experienced as total and catastrophic—a gaping hole or wound (Tustin 1981). Repetitive play and language, which later may develop into obsessional activities and ideation, are meant to fill the hole created by every separation.

Why was it that all the people with whom Martin came into contact seemed to be of almost equal value or importance to him? He was like a collector of people. The loss of anyone seemed to threaten his whole existence. This is reminiscent of a 7-month-old normal in-

fant who, for the period of a few days, was observed to cry whenever
anyone walked out of his visual field without first stopping to talk to
him. It was as if he were realizing for the first time that people could
walk away from him. Did he displace a fear that his mother could
leave onto everybody? Or was a loss of anybody, at this particular
point, a narcissistic blow to his omnipotence, as it suddenly confronted
him with frightening empty space?

The same question could be asked about Martin. It would seem
that Martin's need for the symbiotic partner was beginning to be extended from mother to the world outside, as this world opened itself
up to him. Maybe this was similar to a normal 7-month-old who
seemed to be upset by the realization that the people who inhabited
the outside world could walk away from him. In the normal infant,
the advent of independent locomotion, accompanied by the affect of
elation, is a powerful antidote to the distress of being left. It is at
this time that every new accomplishment of the infant is applauded
and admired by the outside world and the infant begins to realize
that his accomplishments are admired. Thus, the feeling of pleasure
and affirmation arises for the infant from an inner source—being able
to move and explore—as well as from an outer source—being admired.
Martin, we surmised, did not experience this affirmation of his autonomous self during the important time of practicing. He could not
use the maturational advent of independent locomotion for practicing and exploration, and had to first have such experiences within the
responsive environment created in his therapy. We believe that
Martin's use of the word "yes," as it developed in his therapy, was
the way he expressed his beginning pleasure and autonomy and wish
for admiration and affirmation. Similarly, Weich (1978) points to the
leap from one to two word utterance occurring at 16–19 months as a
phase in which language as a transitional phenomenon occurs.

This period was followed in Martin by a kind of rapprochement
crisis, in which he actively attempted to come to terms with the fact
of loss. In creating and then mourning and protesting situations of
loss, he tried to master the loss entailed in greater realization of separateness. It was only after this had been accomplished that he began
to use his name and develop a sense of ownership and agency. And
it was only after that point in development that communicative language could appear. By communicative language we mean here lan-

guage that needed (or at least could allow for) a response from the other. Enough separateness had been established so that language could be used as a bridge from self to other. This we believe was a crucial point in his development, comparable to what we observe in normal development at the point of realization of separateness. It was only then that command language, in which the answer is part of the question and the other is part of the self, could yield to request language, in which the risk can be taken that the answer will not be part of the question, in which a true response from an outside other can be considered. The change described here is a structural one, denoting real progress toward object and self constancy. Nevertheless, the disturbance in the symbolic process that we described remains a characteristic of the psychotic self.

17

The Oral Deadlock

Treatment of a Psychotic Child [1]

written in collaboration with
Michael Schwartzman, Phyllis Sloate, and Arnold Wilson

In this chapter we shall describe a critical period in the therapy of a psychotic child. The treatment was psychoanalytically informed. Psychoanalysis would not have been appropriate as a treatment technique in a child as seriously disturbed as the one we are about to describe. We feel, however, that valuable psychoanalytic insights could be gained by studying the interaction of a psychotic mother–child pair and by describing how treatment helped the child to free himself from a pathological symbiotic relationship with his mother.

This child was being seen in a university-based treatment center for

1. HEW Grant #02907. A Model for the Development of a Professional Training Program to Educate Severely Emotionally Handicapped Children from a Psychoeducational Approach. Principal investigator: Gilbert Voyat; Co-Investigators: Anni Bergman, Linda Gunsberg.

The authors thank the staff of the psychoeducational grant for their helpful comments and support; John B. McDevitt, for his discussion at a meeting sponsored by the psychoeducational grant, Summer, 1978; the Margaret Mahler Research Foundation; and the New Land Foundation for their generous support of the work on which this chapter is based.

emotionally disturbed children.[2] The treatment design employs three modalities: (1) psychoanalytically oriented psychotherapy that uses a tripartite[3] approach, that is, mother and child seen by a therapist in joint treatment sessions; (2) a small therapeutic classroom with an individualized program for each child; and (3) individual sessions with a therapeutic companion. Therapist, teacher, and therapeutic companion work closely together as a team, planning and coordinating the total treatment approach under the supervision of a child analyst.

We shall attempt to show how the teamwork allowed us to observe an impasse that had been reached in the child's treatment, how it emerged in each modality, and how, subsequent to an intervention with the mother, a new period in the child's development unfolded. We show how the intervention at this particular point helped both mother and child to relinquish the outgrown symbiosis, which at this moment in development had become suffocating for the child and impeded his further growth. The child was in intense conflict between staying within the symbiotic orbit and daring to step out and follow his strivings toward autonomy and individuation.

In normal development, toward the end of the early practicing subphase of separation-individuation, the mother provides a "gentle push" to the fledgling, which demonstrates her confidence in his ability to sustain himself at some physical and psychological distance from her. If the gentle push is not forthcoming, the toddler's confidence in his independent functioning is undermined (Mahler et al. 1975). The "good-enough-mother" (Winnicott 1960) in normal development knows empathically when to provide the gentle push. In the treatment of psychotic mother–child pairs, the therapeutic team becomes the "good-enough-mother," and understands at what point providing a gentle push will facilitate growth. The tripartite treatment design attempts to recreate a healthier symbiotic tie between mother and child and create a facilitating environment from which individuation may occur (Bergman 1971).

---

2. Anni Bergman, the senior author, supervised this case. The co-authors carried out the treatment.
3. This design was originated by Margaret Mahler and Manuel Furer, and is described in *On Human Symbiosis and the Vicissitudes of Individuation* (Mahler 1968).

The therapeutic team is involved in the relationship of the mother and child along many lines. The therapist attempts to understand and interpret the dynamics of the interaction between mother and child and the intrapsychic conflicts of each. The therapeutic companion observes the child's interactions in the outside world. The teacher observes the child in a setting where he has to cope with the specific demands imposed by being with others in a group.

While the intervention we shall describe was formulated as a directive to the mother, it was in fact much more than that. It was an interpretation directed to the child's needs and ability to be more autonomous and the mother's capacity to allow this. For both, these capacities had been developed in the therapeutic process to this point. The interpretation elicited further memories and associations in the mother referring back to her own childhood.

The particular problem during the period we are about to discuss revolved around rigid controls the mother exerted in many areas of the child's life, and the child's compliance with them. A situation emerged that we came to understand as the *oral deadlock*. Behaviors around food became the paradigm for the ongoing situation between mother and child, as well as a metaphoric expression of their mutual difficulties in individuation. The mother constructed rules about eating that the child was to carry with him into every aspect of his life. These rules were extraordinarily severe and, amazingly, were adhered to by this otherwise very rebellious and provocative boy. Although the theme of control was of long standing, the oral deadlock, that is, the acute crisis, was reached as a consequence of the threat to symbiosis that ensued from Anthony's increasingly independent functioning both in school and companionship. Mother's heightened need to control and Anthony's masochistic surrender were an attempt on both their parts to maintain the parasitic quality of their relationship.

Presenting Problem

Anthony had originally been referred for treatment at the age of 3½.[4] At that time he was living with his mother, stepfather-to-be, and

---

4. This case was initially seen in the Therapeutic Nursery of the Albert Einstein College of Medicine, under the direction of Eleanor Galenson.

grandfather. His mother had left his biological father shortly before Anthony was born, returning to her parental home. At the beginning of treatment, Anthony's contact with the external world was tenuous at best. He was experiencing intermittent hallucinations; during more related moments, he manifested an anxious hyperawareness of others. This hyperalert state would frequently shift within seconds to frenzied, aggressive outbursts. While his attacks were usually directed at whomever Anthony perceived as the bad object, most of the time there had been no discernible provocation. During several instances of extreme fury, Anthony severed all connection with the external world, running blindly into furniture and people. His spontaneous language at that time consisted largely of disconnected, associative verbalizations, interspersed with quasi-adult phrases imitative of mother (McDevitt 1979), and some fleeting instances of more appropriate communication.

His mother's complaint was his general unmanageability, occasional soiling and wetting, and nightly waking and entering her bed. Anthony was seen in tripartite treatment sessions (Mahler 1968) three times per week. Observations of the mother–child interaction suggested a maternal style that was extraordinarily controlling and intrusive, and characterized by alternations between engulfment and emotional abandonment. The mother's engulfment of Anthony took the form of either a highly eroticized holding or a verbal interchange wherein the mother actively encouraged and took visible pleasure in her child's more bizarre fantasies. Unless the pair was intensely engaged with each other, the mother would withdraw into her own activities, ignoring the child's bizarre behaviors, seemingly unaware of what he was saying and doing.

During the period to be described, the mother's parasitic needs continued to be intense and took the form of rigid control of Anthony's food intake. Anthony was no longer as chaotic in his behaviors. While still prone to aggressive outbursts, he was capable of expressing himself verbally and through symbolic play. He had formed specific object relationships with his teacher, therapeutic companion, and therapist. He had reached a point in his relationship to his mother where he clearly wanted her love and approval, yet could only gain this by surrendering to her demands that he consider the world beyond her a dangerous and unreliable place, and that he accept only her nurturing. As the therapeutic team stood for the idea that the outside world, which included other-than-mother, could be trusted and enjoyed, he became increasingly conflicted whenever he allowed himself the experience of pleasure away from his mother. A change in the balance of forces that restrained him, we thought, would be facilitated by a change in the mother's pattern of restriction.

Mother's style of controlling Anthony had coalesced in the form of an overwhelming concern around his food intake. She rationalized this on the grounds that the child was becoming fat, would be made fun of at school, and would not have any friends. The mother had been rather lonely in her own childhood, overweight, and indeed had herself been ridiculed and humiliated by her peers. She was currently gaining weight, while being overly concerned with Anthony's weight. Thus her control of his food intake, especially the forbidding of sweets, was a narcissistic identification (Kernberg 1975) expressing her own need to come to terms with some of these same issues.

The mother was very much invested in remaining the sole feeder. Despite her concern over the child's weight, his lunchbox was filled each day with peanut butter and jelly sandwiches and cupcakes for dessert. It was as if, magically, her food in the lunchbox would not make him fat because it was intended to sustain him during her absence. Anthony, in turn, accepted her fantasy that all food in New York City was poisonous, and that only her food was safe. She spoke at great length with each team member of her wish for Anthony to have friends, yet the control of his food intake had the effect of maintaining his oneness with her and his suspiciousness of others. Anyone who would not fit into this scheme of oneness was considered an enemy to be attacked or avoided. Inadvertently, then, mother was encouraging in her child problems identical to those she herself was still struggling with. She managed to keep her child closely tied to her, protecting herself from those feelings of loss that are unavoidable for the mother who allows her child to become a separate individual. At the same time, she deprived herself of the pleasures of her child's growth that normally aid the mother in overcoming her feelings of loss. Thus Anthony was both the lonely, friendless child she herself had been and the friend to finally fill the emptiness of her own loneliness.

Observations of the Oral Deadlock

In the classroom,[5] the teacher had a daily opportunity to observe Anthony's conflicted feelings about food. While eating was a common source of enjoyment for most of the children, Anthony could not participate in the enjoyment and could not share food with anyone. It soon became apparent that the lunchbox was a means of magical communication with his mother during the day. He approached the lunchbox with great anticipation, expecting it to contain the same food every day. On those rare occasions when something was missing or different, he became very upset, screamed out abuses about his mother, and lapsed into an extremely unhappy state. If another child touched anything his mother had sent for him to eat, he would refuse it and fly into a rage at whoever had disturbed his magical communion with mother.

The children in the school were given juice and cookies each day. Anthony experienced any change in this menu as anxiety-provoking. Food that was cleared with mother was acceptable, but anything he had not told her about in advance was suspect. When there was food in the classroom in addition to the usual snack, for example, when a child had a birthday party, Anthony refused to eat what was offered and suffered for not having it, or alternately ate and then compensated by not eating something else.

A real crisis arose when a person administering Piagetian tasks came to the classroom, bringing with her jelly beans, which were materials used in the administration of the tasks, and eventually eaten by all the children. Anthony enjoyed and looked forward to the jelly beans. However, when he ate a jelly bean, he then deprived himself of dessert or left his lunch untouched. He rejected any attempt on the part of the teacher to get him to sit down and eat lunch with the rest of the group, saying he would eat later.

The therapeutic companion, who regularly made home visits and spent much time both at home and "in the world" with Anthony, was in a unique position to observe the food behaviors with and without

---

5. We are indebted to Edith Paul, the Head Teacher, for her sensitive observations of Anthony.

the presence of the mother. Here, aspects of the suffocating symbiosis, as well as the belated, clumsy, early attempts at individuation, came sharply into focus.

Anthony's mother had told him that all food in the New York City area was unclean, poisonous, and endangered his health. On trips to the Museum of Natural History, which was one of Anthony's favorite outings, he gazed longingly at the hot-dog vendor. At those times he was bogged down by conflict, wanting a hot dog but not daring to ask for it. He finally overcame the inhibition and, although anxious, ordered one and enjoyed it. From then on Anthony demanded food at the beginning of each session with the companion. If food was not immediately available, he expressed the fear that there would be none that day. This fear would then spoil his pleasure in the activities he had just begun to cherish with the companion. Anthony's eating during these sessions conveyed a quality of defiance and bravado. It seemed that overcoming the inhibition of eating away from home helped him to feel strong and manly, for it was with the companion that he achieved this greater freedom from the sadomasochistic compliance with his mother's demands.

At home, in the presence of the mother and the companion, the oral deadlock took on a special form. Mother would compete with Anthony for the companion's attention and care by offering him the foods she enjoyed, which Anthony was denied. A peculiar ritual regularly occurred after Anthony's return from companionship. He anxiously dashed in through the door and announced hysterically what he had eaten that day, anticipating some form of punishment. The mother then scolded him, and her disapproval contained an element of glee as she enforced her dietary restrictions. Anthony's own separateness achieved with the companion emerged as a threat when he was confronted by her undermining. Yet Anthony persisted in eating with the companion away from mother. The more he became autonomous, the stricter became the maternal injunctions around food. Anthony's "menu of the day" reports to mother continued, along with her sadistic comments in a sarcastic tone on how fat Anthony was becoming. This became the cue for Anthony to agitate for additional food, preferably sweets, which were consistently denied him. The mother would offer yogurt, skim milk, or cottage cheese. Anthony would then throw a tantrum, abuse his mother directly, and then settle down greedily to devour whatever she provided for him. Concurrently he began describing himself in fantasy as a "whale," a "beachball," and a "fat man at the circus," terms that imply both body image distortion and negative self-images.

The situation reached a climax when the mother offered the therapeutic companion the very foods she had just refused Anthony in his presence. Her offer served to humiliate and diminish Anthony, leaving him with a sense of profound rejection in the presence of his beloved companion. It was also a replication of the nightly scene around the dinner table. There, all of Anthony's food was prescribed and controlled by mother, while she and her husband ate what they pleased. The therapeutic companion intervened, explaining to the mother that he would eat only the food that Anthony was permitted in his presence. Thus he realigned himself with Anthony, creating a tangible counterforce to the mother's behavior.

The severity of the problem between Anthony and his mother crystallized in the therapeutic relationship as well. During a session in which he arrived in the playroom without having eaten his lunch, Anthony was able to tell the therapist that he could not possibly eat lunch as he had consumed two jelly beans in school that morning. Anthony then retreated into a toy cabinet in the playroom, slammed the doors shut, and kicked at the door panels, shrieking with rage. When he finally emerged, he assumed the pose of an orchestra conductor furiously conducting a group of imaginary musicians. Later in that same session, after Anthony managed to eat part of his lunch, he crushed the remnants in their aluminum foil wrapper into the shape of a spear with which he repeatedly hit himself in the head. No sooner had he eaten something than he felt compelled to punish himself for this transgression.

In a session that followed shortly after the one just described, Anthony entered the playroom with a big grin on his face, smacking his lips. The therapist said it looked as though he just had something good to eat in school. He said, "Potatoes," and the therapist said, "French fries?" Anthony replied, "Yes, they were divine, divine, divine." With each "divine," the words became more emphatic and the tone more bizarre. The therapist said that though it seemed he had enjoyed the french fries, it also seemed there was something about eating them that was upsetting to him. Anthony finally replied that now he could not have pretzels with his therapeutic companion. With those words he again retreated into the toy cabinet, screaming, "Trapped, I'm trapped! Let me out!" over and over. The therapist commented on Anthony's feelings of being trapped by having eaten the french fries and now feeling he had to give up the pretzels, since he had eaten something his mother would not have wanted him to have, and how worried he seemed to be about her potential anger with him—perhaps Anthony would like to decide what kind of food he ate and how much. With that, the doors of the toy cabinet opened a little, and Anthony, menacingly pointing a stick covered with red paint at the therapist, said, "You will be the first victim," repeating this several times. The therapist said Anthony seemed very angry with his mommy, and this was a scary feeling to have. Perhaps he worried she might feel as angry with him as he did with her, and punish him. Perhaps he even worried she would not love him anymore. With that, Anthony emerged from the toy cabinet and began humming the Jupiter Symphony, again pretending he was conducting an imaginary orchestra. Music had always been an important avenue for affective communication. This play metaphor conveyed to the therapist Anthony's longing for the symbiotic mother, as well as his wish to be powerful. The therapist said she understood his wish to be in control of the food he ate. With that, Anthony calmed down, and went to the dollhouse, sitting down quietly to play. In a somewhat sad and thoughtful tone he remarked, "Maybe you think I'm stupid, but I don't like to see Arnold [his therapeutic companion]. Well, I do like to see him, but I don't because when I see him I have to say goodbye." It was with the therapeutic companion that Anthony had first felt free enough to eat food not approved by mother, a relationship that represented freedom from the oral deadlock.

In subsequent sessions Anthony became more and more controlling of the therapist, which climaxed with his demand that she neither move nor speak without his express permission. Any inadvertent deviation on the part of the therapist would elicit screams of fury, with Anthony yelling, "Don't move, don't you talk, you moved your head! Don't do that! I'll kill you! Stay there, you stupid dummy! Not a word!" The therapist's interpretations were to no avail, and she felt trapped, frustrated, impotent, and enraged; she was suffering as she felt Anthony to be suffering under the yoke of the oral deadlock.

At this point the team decided to take up the issue with the mother. The therapist had two sessions, one week apart, with her. She told the mother quite directly that it was time to give Anthony more freedom about the food he ate, that this was an important aspect of growing up. At the same time, the therapist attempted to address the mother's feelings of loss arising from this moment of individuation on the part of her son. The therapist stressed that it had been very important for mother to be involved for many years in all aspects of Anthony's development. However, that time was passing and she could best serve his changing needs by relinquishing control and allowing him to be the growing boy he so desperately needed to be. Mother's initial response was the fantasy that Anthony would then be totally out of control, insatiably gorging himself and endlessly demanding food from the refrigerator. This fantasy was reminiscent of her perception of Anthony as an infant, for she had described him as then being voracious and almost insatiable. During this initial session with mother, her very realistic fear of Anthony's frequently bizarre and unpredictable responses to almost any given situation was also discussed. The therapist agreed with her that, indeed, if she did relinquish control, there was no certainty as to how Anthony would respond. Despite all her misgivings, the mother complied with the therapist's request. That evening, for the first time in his entire life, Anthony helped himself to his own dinner portions of meat, vegetables, and potatoes. To his mother's surprise, he took more meat than she would have given him and finished it all, ate almost all the potatoes he had taken, and then even swallowed a few teaspoons of vegetables, just to please her.

Suddenly, with the relinquishing of mother's oral control, various ego capacities previously inhibited by her injunctions emerged. The following day he was given permission to ride his bicycle around the neighborhood rather than having to remain directly in front of the house, constantly within mother's view. By the end of the week, Anthony began to play with other children. He increasingly explored the new world of the neighborhood and his friends' homes, excitedly describing the discoveries he was making to his mother when he returned home. In all, his mood during this period seemed to express some of the sense of exuberance frequently seen in the practicing toddler.

The following week he allowed his new-found friends to help him remove the training wheels from his bicycle, then rode off triumphantly with them. Anthony continued to explore the neighborhood with other children, and then felt sufficiently confident in his own abilities to ride a friend's five-speed bicycle. He asked mother for a new bike, one for a big boy, stating quite truthfully that his bicycle was far too small for him. His joy with the bicycle was reminiscent of the normal toddler's joy in his first wheeled possessions (Bergman 1978).

As Anthony individuated, so did his mother. In her sessions with the therapist she began to speak increasingly about herself and her own past, something she had great difficulty in doing over all the previous years of treatment. Along with other unhappy memories of her childhood and adolescence, she recalled that her own parents had never eaten dinner together. A rather poignant memory was elicited by Anthony's successfully learning how to toast bagels. Following her description of his mastery of this task, she spoke rather movingly of preparing scrambled eggs and coffee as a young child for her own mother, and then being asked to bring the food upstairs where her mother was waiting in bed. Anthony's oral mastery thus evoked a memory of her submission to her own mother.

In the classroom Anthony initiated party times as he grew more independent. He would demand at certain times of the day that he either have jelly beans, ice cream, or certain favorite types of cookies. Simultaneously, he became more amenable to assisting in the preparation of food the class was going to eat together. It was apparent that he had never eaten many foods and had no idea of how they tasted. Anthony and his teacher spent one entire school day making eggs and bacon. This and similar cooking experiences in the classroom helped Anthony to master some of his previous fears related to mother's prior prohibitions. Here, as in companionship, Anthony was able to experience the pleasures of practicing and mastery, whereas in therapy he continued to play out fantasies associated with the more painful aspects of the oral deadlock.

Developing his abilities facilitated independent functioning, but for Anthony this was not enough. Rather, he had to tolerate the fear of mother's reaction to his success and the fear of his loss of her love, which had previously been so emotionally overwhelming as to restrict him in his efforts to grow. The school experience helped Anthony consolidate the means by which he could construct and pursue a way of being for himself, while at the same time endure the ever-present fear of being by himself (Winnicott 1958a).

Despite the apparent success of the intervention, the struggle continued. The mother, who was previously incapable of letting go, relinquished her interest along with her control, which rekindled Anthony's fear of abandonment. Anthony, on his part, continued to test the mother. One day the therapeutic companion observed Anthony as he came rushing into the house, provocatively reporting on the food he had consumed during the day. He was dismayed when his mother told him he was now a grown boy and did not have to report to her. Anthony punched himself in the head and screamed, "Ma, you're killing me!" Nevertheless, it was at this time that Anthony's emotional growth accelerated. He became obsessed with knowing whether decisions had to be made by him or by the therapeutic companion, and was increasingly concerned with understanding the criteria by which either was justified in making a decision that concerned his fate. He was now willing to assume new responsibilities, and was prepared to face situations in the outer world that in the past he had feared and that frequently played into certain phobias he had. Anthony spoke of being grownup, of no longer being a child. He began tasting different foods, exploring the domain of the taste sensations that had previously been denied him. Simultaneously, he developed the ability to share his food with the companion without fear that he was being starved or poisoned. Although the mother experienced pronounced difficulties with the child's new-found autonomy and his reluctance to accept nourishment solely from her, she did not significantly interfere with this aspect of the child's individuation.

Reconstruction

In the treatment of the psychotic child, an essential point has to be stressed, namely that such a child does not develop differentiated internal self and object representations. He is intrapsychically merged with mother. The treatment task in the beginning stage is development of self–object distinctions. To achieve this, therapy begins with

the mother–child unit and proceeds through the gradual disengagement between them (Mahler 1968). In the classical psychoanalytic
approach, it is taken for granted that sufficient structure formation
has occurred to support the lens of retrospective (adult) or concur-
rent (child) analysis. In contrast, our approach allows for the failure
of structure formation that occurs in psychotic children, permitting
the gathering of preverbal data that must be attained through
mother–child observation. This data supplements and enhances our
understanding of the unfolding of both preoedipal and prestructural
development.

Mahler's theory of separation-individuation has allowed us a fuller
exploration of early development, particularly from the viewpoint of
engagement and disengagement. This is being investigated at present
by infancy researchers who hypothesize a relation between the engagement–disengagement behaviors of mother and infant and the construction of internal psychic structure (Beebe and Stern 1977, Pine
1977). In Anthony's case, we had inferred that his difficulties originated during differentiation and came to a head during the practicing subphase, when the mother confined him physically when she
could not tolerate his beginning individuation. This confinement continued taking different forms in spite of the fact that Anthony's maturation proceeded, and culminated in the impasse we have described.
By way of treatment, an imbalance arose in which the child could
not develop further without facilitation by the mother. A renunciation
of the symbiotic investment in the child by the mother had to be
accomplished before he could move on to a new level of object relations.

The modifications in treatment techniques based on an understanding of the separation-individuation process made it possible to
treat this mother–child pair. Interpretation of conflict had to be
supplemented by providing a therapeutic environment in keeping
with the developmental status of the child. This is an essential difference from classical technique, which is based on the assumption
that the child's development has proceeded to a point of intrapsychic
structuralization through which change can be effected by means of
therapeutic work with the child alone.

During normal separation-individuation, the baby separates as he
emerges from the symbiotic dual unity. Independent locomation, the

ability to move away physically, is the vehicle of the baby's early forays into the world, although it is preceded by a differentiation process that begins at the height of symbiosis. The mother, in turn, has
to relinquish her symbiotic needs and provide the space, both physical and psychological (Bergman 1978), for the optimal unfolding of
the separation-individuation process. This mother's inappropriate intrusion effectively limited the child's emerging autonomy, and culminated in what we have called the *oral deadlock*. This was a situation consequent to his treatment in which mother could not allow
Anthony to experience the pleasure and confidence in his emerging
separateness appropriate to his developmental status. As some of
these pleasures became possible they were most clearly enjoyed in
his sessions with the therapeutic companion and teacher. This experience of oral deadlock, in which mother could not allow Anthony's
development of separateness, was a repetition in treatment of a crucial time in his separation-individuation process, as we were able to
reconstruct it from the tripartite treatment sessions and individual
sessions with the mother.

We became convinced that during the symbiotic phase there must
have already been difficulty between the two. Anthony had been an
unwanted child, and in the first two months was left in the care of
the maternal grandmother. Not only was the baby unwanted, but he
reminded mother of the baby's father, from whom she had separated
in her ninth month of pregnancy. The mother's early experience of
Anthony had been as a voracious baby whose hunger she could never
satisfy. Anthony developed severe eczema beginning at the age of 2
months, when the mother was forced to take care of her own child
due to the grandmother's failing health. At the height of Anthony's
symbiotic phase, and at the beginning of his differentiation, mother
became very depressed due to the death of her own mother. She temporarily consoled herself with a very passionate love affair, describing the man as her "knight in shining armor."[6] This love affair ended
abruptly when Anthony was between 8 and 9 months old, and the

---

6. Greenacre (1960) has commented on the role of the father, the "knight in shining
armor," as rescuing the child from the symbiosis with mother. In Mrs. A.'s case, a
man helped her let go of the mother who had died.

mother lapsed into a severe depression, mourning the loss of both her mother and her lover.

Thus, during this period of symbiosis and differentiation, the mother was largely emotionally unavailable to Anthony. A real crisis in their relationship developed when Anthony was a year old, and she responded to what she perceived as his excessive demandingness by confining him to his crib. By so doing she inflicted a traumatic frustration. Anthony was prevented from exercising his newly maturing autonomous ego functions, particularly motility in service of the exploration of the world. Mother was unavailable, and Anthony was not permitted the opportunity to use his own emerging resources to cope with her depressive withdrawal.

The trauma experienced in the practicing period was repeatedly symbolized by Anthony during his therapy sessions, most frequently taking the form of a "mummy" game or a robot fantasy. The mummy, a persecutory mommy, both deanimated yet frighteningly alive, concretely depicted the essence of the struggle between Anthony and his mother. The game would begin with Anthony taping one of the small male dolls in the playroom to resemble a mummy, then building an elaborate block structure. As various male dolls set out to explore the block structure, the mummy awoke and entombed the explorers. When the men struggled against the mummy, they annihilated one another. During one particularly painful session, following the destruction of both the men who wished to go exploring and the evil mummy, Anthony unwrapped the mummy doll. He stared at it, then stated sadly, "Anthony, it was you all the time." We would understand this game to represent, on the one hand, Anthony's realization of mother's interference with his autonomy. On the other hand, it also represents an identification with the aggressor, as he turns the mother into a "mummy." On a deeper level the game also symbolizes the lack of self–object differentiation in that both the male dolls and the mummy suffer the same fate, namely not being able to move freely. In this manner Anthony repeatedly played out not only his fear of maternal retaliation for his more autonomous strivings, but also the fantasy that his potential competence and activity in the real world equaled or necessitated the "murder" of his primary object.

Anthony's long-standing fantasy of himself as a robot was a poignant counterpoint to the "mummy" game. While the mummy exists without life and is incapable of providing nurturance, the robot, similarly alive yet quite deanimated, needs no nurturance. This robot fantasy was also an expression of the manipulative, controlling aspects of mother's relationship with Anthony, as well as her communication to him that the world beyond her was not to be trusted. His frustration and rage, as well as his suspiciousness and fear, were summed up during one tripartite session in which he repeatedly asked his mother whether they could visit the home of a favorite cousin. There Anthony would be free to explore the neighborhood and play as he wished. His mother responded ambivalently, neither confirming nor denying his requests. Anthony flew into a rage, then transformed himself into a robot under the absolute control of either mother or his therapist.

Benedek (1956), describing the relationship between a depressed mother and her child, notes that the mother's frustration at being unable to satisfy the child promotes a regression that stirs up the reexperiencing of her own oral-dependent phase. The unresolved internal difficulties lead the mother to simultaneous identifications with her own mother and with her child. Thus the mother becomes the delivering and the receiving part of the symbiosis. As she fails to give successfully to her infant, she becomes the bad mother of her child as well as the bad child of her mother. The child, frustrated and enraged, becomes her bad self and also her own bad mother.

Anthony's mother had grown up with a mother who did not allow her to be an individual in her own right, but instead used her daughter to satisfy her own narcissistic needs. Her mother had been an opera singer who gave up her career when her first child, a son, was born. She expected her daughter, Anthony's mother, to realize her own unfulfilled potential by also becoming a singer. Anthony's mother pleased her mother in this way until she planned to tour the country in what would have seemed to be a successful realization of her mother's wishes. At that point, her mother refused to allow her to leave and insisted she attend a college close to home. The similarity between Anthony's grandmother's refusal to allow her daughter to explore the world and Anthony's mother's confining him to his crib at the beginning of the practicing period is striking.

In Anthony we believe that the most serious defects in identify formation took place as a result of the disruption of the differentiation and early practicing period. It was at this point in his development that his mother became severely depressed and broke off a very important love relationship. We speculate that this crisis in the mother's life was at least in part precipitated by Anthony's moving away from her as an infant naturally would at that age. Because of his mother's depression and confinement of him, Anthony did not experience the "love affair with the world," and was deprived of that blissful moment in development when one can move away from mother and yet feel at one with her. Thus we must assume he entered rapprochement without having had a chance to enjoy positive feelings of omnipotence and to consolidate feelings of pleasure and mastery that would have prepared him for the ensuing stresses and strains. He had to become separate without being ready for it. His following dilemma of entrapment and struggle to free himself during therapy from the stultifying symbiosis reached crisis proportions. We see in what we have described as the oral deadlock a continuation of Anthony's mother's refusal to allow him to exercise his growing autonomy and trust the outside world. In spite of the tripartite treatment to this point, the mother and child had not resolved separation-individuation conflicts that had begun during Anthony's differentiation and practicing subphase.

Discussion

The sources of the mother's favorable response to our intervention are to be found in many aspects of the total treatment situation: the "holding" provided by the entire team, the nature of her identifications with the therapist, and the coincidence of the intervention with an impending structural change within the child. The team understood that while the oral deadlock reflected a hopeless impasse between Anthony and his mother and the actual relinquishing of controls might come as a relief, it would also elicit feelings of loss for both. Furthermore, we realized that although the intervention was designed to alter an existing pathological relationship, it would substantially upset their way of being together.

The intervention occurred in a positive climate, as Anthony's mother had developed a sense of trust and confidence in her therapist over the years they had worked together. The mother was encouraged to express her many fears and misgivings during her individual sessions. Moreover, the therapist was sensitive to her difficulty in perceiving Anthony as separate, and to her susceptibility to narcissistic injury. The quality of the therapeutic relationship enabled the therapist to present herself as a model for identification as she conveyed the necessity for the mother to assume the role of facilitator and assist her child in his attempts to move out into the world.

Although Anthony's mother is not in analysis, she has spoken at length of her tendency to initially overvalue the current love object while denying his less desirable attributes, her deeply held feelings of inferiority, and extreme fluctuations in her self-esteem that she has described as "highs and crashes," the latter accompanied by feelings of despair. Moreover, her tendency to confuse her own needs, feelings, and wishes with Anthony's has been a constant throughout the treatment. We have inferred that, in part, her compliance with the therapist's request may have been an omnipotent participation through a process of magical identification with a parental figure (Reich 1940b). By acceding to the therapist's request, the mother not only acted in accord with her more positive maternal strivings, but also defended against her unconscious fear of abandonment by mother and loss of self-esteem, that is the potential disapproval of her therapist. The tripartite treatment design encourages and makes use of this need for magical identifications in a mother with a narcissistic personality organization. As this mother could carry within her the magical identifications with the therapist, it was possible for her to let go of her child.

A parallel aspect of the "holding" during the intervention was provided by the therapeutic companion. His presence in the home during this time supported the mother's efforts to permit Anthony to individuate. Given the nature of her pathology, it was extremely difficult for her to appreciate the emerging phallic qualities in her child. The companion aligned himself with the child's strivings directed toward the world of real people and things (Abelin 1971). While indicating to mother his respect for Anthony's changing needs, he invited her to identify and participate in his enjoyment of the child.

Contributing factors in the successful outcome of the intervention were the internal structural shifts as yet *in statu nascendi* within Anthony. During the oral deadlock, and subsequent to our intervention, we observed that he was moving away from his long-term symbiotic relationship with his mother as more clearly oedipal determinants emerged in all three modalities of the treatment design. A month before we intervened, Anthony's therapy sessions had begun to shift away from the realm of action toward greater verbalization, while his play was significantly less fragmented. Gradually his almost continuous rage toward the therapist abated as he seemed to be assessing her anew, this time as a potentially good object.

Anthony became interested in playing board games with his therapist. Oedipal elements were clearly present in his wish to capture her "men," while prior to weekend separations he frequently fantasized about her family, expressing his jealousy and feelings of exclusion and rejection. Anthony had created the game board they played on. He soon requested that the therapist save the game as it was until their next session. In this manner Anthony showed us his emerging sense of self-worth. He attempted concretely to establish a firmer notion of a world of permanent objects and relationships that extend into the future, while expressing his wish for continuity of the good relationship with the therapist. Indeed, it was at the very moment of Anthony's most extreme fury over the oral deadlock that his new observing ego capacity became evident for the first time.

As his ability to observe himself and have some symbolic distance developed, along with a core of good self-feelings, the libidinization of relationships with all team members and peers increased. His newfound autonomy allowed Anthony to become very concerned with thinking through the reasons behind his actions. As he no longer needed to believe in his total omnipotent control of the world, nor perceived himself as an utterly inferior robotlike being, he was open to listening to another's ideas and suggestions. His long-standing need to define others by where they stood in relation to his omnipotence diminished greatly. Rather than being constantly preoccupied with the struggle for control and feelings of being attacked and overwhelmed, he was more capable of attending to the realities occurring between himself and another. These developments allowed for a sharing of ideas, a greater tolerance of frustration, the ability to compromise, and a capacity for mutual understanding. Thus, while Anthony was rapidly broadening his social abilities and forming friendships in the outside world, he was simultaneously deepening his long-established relationships with important adults. This is reminiscent of normal development, when the child's growing capacity to distance from mother also permits him to see her anew each time he returns. We all observed his increased sense of trust, his confidence in his own competence, a more varied range of affect, and a new ability to enjoy the subtler aspects of human relationships.

With these affective changes his cognitive abilities were in many ways released, for now he could take another's ideas and suggestions, a step previously too emotionally conflicted for him, and look at them as advice rather than as a series of externally imposed demands. Within two months of our intervention, Anthony had consolidated his new individuation and sense of self sufficiently to represent them in a drawing made during a therapy hour. He drew two faces, labeled one "good," the other "bad," and then, in rather small, tentative letters, wrote "me" next to the "good" face.

18

A Model for the Day Treatment of Severely Disturbed Children

written in collaboration with
Arnold Wilson

In this chapter, we shall present the model of a comprehensive center that we have evolved over the last ten years in order to treat the manifold clinical issues involving autistic and symbiotic psychotic children. An illustrative case will be discussed. Our center is based on principles of psychoanalytic and cognitive developmental psychology, and was founded by Professors Anni Bergman and Gilbert Voyat. In our center, first, individual therapy with the child based on Mahler's tripartite model is provided. The therapist sees the child and mother together three times a week for one hour and fifteen minutes. He focuses his understanding upon the child, the mother, and upon the interaction between the child and the mother. In addition, weekly meetings with the parents around family and marital issues make the individual therapist also a family therapist of sorts. The therapist seeks to minimize marital and family stresses associated with having an autistic child, as well as any others that might interfere with the clinical work. We seek to create an optimal working alliance with the parents. Second, therapeutic companions meet with the child alone for five to six sessions per week, and at times make home visits. The role of the therapeutic companion is that of a bridge to the outside world, providing the necessary supportive containment so that the child can exercise and develop autonomous ego functions and encounter new experiential vistas that had hitherto been inaccessible. Third, a therapeutic classroom is in operation, which the children attend five days per week. The classroom attends equally to cognitive and social issues, and operates according to Piagetian principles of psychoeducation and Mahler's separation-individuation theory, with special emphasis on prestages of academic competence. The classroom addresses peer socialization processes as well as academic competence. We have found that, with these children, learning occurs in the presence of the supportive containment of a teacher. Although designed as three separate modalities, in essence the treatment team comprises a larger overall unit that intermeshes through the exchange of information and team supervision. The teams are closely supervised by established clinicians with a special interest in and experience with severely disturbed children and their families.

Over the last decade, we have had positive therapeutic results with many of the children we have treated. A few are mainstreamed in normal schools, while others have made more limited progress and remain in special programs. The case described is presently in treatment, is one we have high hopes for, and is intended as an example of the type of work we do. The B. family consisted of four members, Mr. B., Mrs. B., Eric (the patient), aged 7½, and David, aged 4½. The family was upwardly socially mobile, and of the upper middle class. Eric was brought into our treatment facility at age 6 because Mrs. B., who had been aware of his difficulties for some time, had not been able to find a program that met her high standards, and had read a paper describing our program. Eric was hyperaggressive, displayed autistic and symbiotic defenses and modes of behavior, and was moody, hyperactive, and at times physically abusive. Early developmental milestones were delayed, and it was reported that Eric showed neither stranger nor separation anxiety earlier than 2 years of age. Toilet training began around 22 months of age, and was never successfully completed, although Eric did have temporary periods of continence. When Eric was 2½ years old, Mrs. B. saw that he did not initiate social speech, tended to look at rather than manipulate objects, and had prolonged periods of disattention from social relationships. When his brother David was born, Eric was 3½, and there seemed to be a dramatic worsening of his symptoms. Bowel and urinary control deteriorated, and eye contact significantly diminished. This began a regressive spiral which continued until referral to our center.

Until 5½ years, Eric continued to show diminishing eye contact, little spontaneous social speech, and had general characteristics of withdrawal. He had difficulty with transitions, used personal pronouns incorrectly, began speaking to himself, and stared fixedly at his hands and bootlaces. At 4½ years of age, Eric was evaluated at a local hospital and diagnosed as autistic, a diagnosis that two years later was revised to psychotic with primary autistic features. At age 5½, Eric was placed in a special kindergarten within a public school system, where his classmates were severely learning disabled but socially well functioning. At this time, Eric became far less compliant and far more hyperactive and violent than had previously been the case. As the year progressed, his hyperactivity diminished slightly as did his negativism, although fear of strangers, telephones, and cartoons emerged. His language remained functionally retarded. Although his speech was quite complex in structure and vocabulary was varied, he had a great deal of difficulty narrating past events and could make no simple statements concerning the future. He also tended to employ neologisms and other unusual verbalizations. He did begin to use personal pronouns more correctly, although this remained a functional deficit. It was noted at this time that he was unusually insensitive to physical pain. At the age of 6, Eric was referred to our treatment facility. Mrs. B. was an educationally accomplished person, a dean at a university, while Mr. B. was a somewhat successful businessman.

Early aspects of the treatment were largely involved with establishing modes of relatedness with Eric. His mother took to our approach with a great deal of relief and felicity, finding for the first time a clinical setting that was willing to treat her child through an intensive relationship-based paradigm. Her benevolent intentions were evident from the start, as was her awkwardness in mothering. She tended to be rigid, controlling, and intrusive. Her attachment to the therapist was immediate and profound, and she greatly idealized him. The team sensed quite early that this idealization was necessary in order for the mother to ward off deep-seated depressive and guilty feelings concerning her defective child. Eric functioned largely in a regressed sensorimotor mode, preferring action to language, communicating via enactments if at all, and only providing hints of a latent intellectual potential that was later to become clearer in the treatment.

It has been described how one primary task of a mother is to capture, through her own developmental identifications, those aspects of thought and action that enable her to empathically maintain a clear sense of what her child may be feeling and thinking. This view, however, is predicated on the assumption that normal development proceeded in a heterogeneous and epigenetic fashion, so that there is some structural compatibility between the mother's and the child's developmental phasic patternings. Particular problems arise, however, in the psychotic child whose psychological orientation does not correspond to the average expectable normative thrust of human development. Thus, early in the treatment, Eric presented his mother with insurmountable problems in her capacity to empathize with and thus understand him. She was called upon to attune herself to a child who would momentarily be organized at a sensorimotor level and at the next moment present evidence of much higher psychological potential. Their difficulties in attunement coalesced into a pattern of passive-aggressive and regressive provocative style on the part of Eric, and an over-controlling and insensitive style on the part of the mother. This dilemma corresponded to our early impression that Eric's level of organization fluctuated wildly, that he was psychologically organized hierarchically at a bewildering array of levels. Three-person conflicts were superimposed upon archaic fears of annihilation and loss of selfhood, oedipal fantasies coexisted and were shaped by the fears of a child without libidinal object constancy and autonomous ego functions. In the case of Eric, a major reason his clinical status deteriorated as he aged was the growth of the disparity between his age-appropriate abilities and capacities with the archaic abilities and capacities that were not maturing but remained fixed in its most primitive mode. The havoc this wrought extended to the mother, who "became bad" because of the stress and confusion about how to respond to her child. The mother appeared less agitated when the child was in a regressed state. Some team members thought that this represented an unconscious wish to sabotage the treatment, that is, the family systems interpretation concerning a need to have the child sick. When Eric was regressed, she would express concern and despair, but would remain in synchronization with the treatment and quite available to the child. While there was increased comfort, we realized that this should not be seen as representing a wish on her part for the child to remain abnormal. Rather, the relief and empathy reflected the increased ease with which she could understand him, tend to him, and be available to him without distress and confusion. The mother lost affective and empathic contact with her child when he was in his highest mode of functioning, which made the disappointment in him and difficulty of being with him more acute and painful. This would lead her to display a constellation of reactions and behaviors that frankly endangered the treatment. It awakened hope in her, and led her to increase her pressure on Eric to function as a normal child. The therapy team is accepting and understanding of these problems in the mother, thus providing a holding environment for her and her child. The goal is to realign her relationship with Eric so that the two can break their difficult pattern of relating. Eric is improving symptomatically quite rapidly, and we are presently seeing a far more adaptive reality orientation, along with spurts of constructive aggression and psychosexual development, including bodily integrity issues (castration anxiety). His performance in school has markedly improved, he is more competitive with peers, and at present we regard his verbal skills and willingness to approach cognitive problems as some of his strengths.

Recently, two major developments have occurred. First, Eric had begun to demonstrate coherent threads of symbolic play and symbolic productions, rather than isolated and fragmented bursts of play. Second, we have had to deal with a major regression, replete with a return to provocative fecal incontinence, periodic autistic reverie states, and hyperaggression. It is felt that this regression developed in response to an incremental step in the construction of a self. As boundaries became more resilient and an increased self-observational capacity appeared, Eric has become acutely aware that there is something seriously wrong with him, that he is different and apart from other children. Within his family, the sibling rivalry has become a lost cause, as his brother, now 6 years old, has surpassed him in mul-

tiple accomplishments. This recognition of defectiveness has generated a strong regressive pull, for the normal *joie de vivre* of the competent child mastering the world does not at present exist for him.
There is more pleasure in isolation—object relating and seeking leads
to emotional pain. It is not surprising that we now see simultaneously
a new depressive potential, as social comparisons cause him acute
sensations of inferiority. This brief vignette also demonstrate an
important clinical point when doing long-term psychodynamic treat-
ments of such children, which is that progress is not linear and is
not so easily gauged behaviorally. We need to have a high degree of
tolerance for regression and periods of difficulty, for many therapeutic gains also seem to be precipitants of regression. This is not to say
that we support or sponsor regression, but rather that we tolerate it
as a natural byproduct of clinical progress. Our same tolerance, inci-
dentally, extends to the parents, who must also weather highs and
lows as their child races the clock to regain a mooring in a normative developmental process.

Interestingly, as supervisors, we have noticed that we must also
have unusual tolerance for the highs and lows of the therapeutic
team. The clinical work described in this paper is unusually taxing,
and yields few satisfactions over the short-term course in terms of
observable therapeutic gains. As a result, when clinical crises develop,
as they invariably do, team members tend to feel that they must rush
into an impetuous course of action, to make a drastic change in the
conduct of the case. We have learned to recognize these moments and
actively discouraged major deviations from the prescribed therapeutic plan unless the problem persists for an extended period of time.
The clinical evidence must be compelling before we change courses
in midstream. The momentum of the therapy is very strong, and
many problems are temporary short-lived ones that resolve in the
natural flow of events.

Our center also provides us with a natural laboratory for studying crucial aspects of childhood psychosis and the extended caregiver–
child interaction. From the first, "self–other complementing" suggests
that in the mother–child attunement each member provides the
needed and necessary actions so as to complete or fulfill the interpersonal experiences necessary for mutual fulfillment and growth.
What happens when the infant is incapable of such complementary

activity? Daniel Stern (1971), the researcher who has conceptualized these distinctions, goes on to discuss what he calls *state sharing* and *state transforming* as other ways of mother and infant to "be together." In state sharing, the infant or mother provides for the other a similar state of psychological experience. Here, the focus is on similarity of experience that each is having. By contrast, in state transforming the relationship focuses on changes in states of consciousness or awareness that occur by virtue of the action of the other. One member of the dyad leads the other by the hand into a new and hitherto undiscovered element of experiencing. Such a framework of interindividuality at such a young age boggles the imagination, yet experimental evidence suggests that it is indeed the case.

What are the implications of these research findings for the development of psychic structure in the developing psychotic child? Can a failure in mother–child attunement later be undone by psychotherapeutic ministrations? What are sequelae of failed attunements? To what extent are cognitive capacities or the level of internalized object relational structures dependent upon the mother–child attunement? These are all questions that have yet to be answered. We feel that the clinical implications offer much hope for the treatment of the psychotic child, with his lack of attunement, psychic structure formation, and miscoordinated mother–child interaction. For these reasons, we believe that our center has great potential as a research base to help us examine and answer crucial questions about the possibility for repair of the development of attunement and intersubjectivity. Mahler spoke about the "corrective symbiotic relationship." We feel that the findings of infant research provides tools to bring this about.

The mind and the brain are one. Cortical capacities set upper limits and lower limits on the functioning of psychological life. In recent years, there has amassed an overwhelming amount of research that has shown that not everyone's brain is the same. In the case of the psychotic child, what previously had been thought to be psychological manifestations of a primary disorder of attachment have, upon closer scrutiny, at times turned out to be psychological manifestations of such neurobiological events as perceptual disorders, attention deficit disorders, developmental aphasias, or hyperkinetic (epileptic) activity of the brain. The fact that such biologically determined founda-

tions exist in no way undermines the necessity of psychological interventions for such individuals. Rather, as in all psychodiagnostic
practice, the more refined the understanding and etiology of a particular disorder, the more fine-tuned and broadly based a treatment
strategy can be mobilized. As a consequence, the territory psychoanalytic theory must encompass includes the psychological manifestations of particular neurological and biological deficits. It is an of-
ten-heard truism that there is no such thing as a deficit without a
conflict. Thus, even if psychoanalysis is defined as a theory of the
mind-in-conflict, the terrain must include the deficits responsible for
the form and manifestation of conflictual impulses. This is why our
treatment program is psychodynamically informed but is also more.
We employ the knowledge gained by family therapists to help us work
with families who are in crisis because their children are ill. We respect the biological domain of functioning, and so within the facili-
ties of our center provide neurological evaluations for our children and,
when called for, medicative consultations. Guided by psychodynamic
principles of treatment, we intervene on many levels on what has recently in American psychiatry come to be known as the biopsychosocial
environment. Here, I might add parenthetically that the practical implications of much of the basic science research described has not yet
surfaced to be of great help to the front-line clinicians. A referral for
Eric for a medication consult resulted in the recommendation of no
intervention. A referral for neuropsychological examination to further
understand the functional implications of any deficits resulted in a
thick document that concluded that there was no discernible
neuropsychological impairment. We eagerly await further refinements
from the life sciences in order to better assist children such as Eric.
As academic members of a university-based clinical community, it is
also part of our intellectual responsibility to develop and export models of clinical treatment. Hopefully, this will indeed be the case, and
we will see more attention paid to the intensive psychotherapeutic
needs of these severely handicapped children.

19

To Be or Not To Be Separate

The Meaning of Hide-and-Seek in Forming Internal Representations [1]

Suddenly I come out from my hiding place. I do him the favor of being born. He sees me, joins in the game, changes expression, and raises his arms to heaven: I fill him to overflowing with my presence. In a word, I give myself.

—Jean-Paul Sartre[2]

Hide-and-seek is a universal childhood game that I hope to show serves an important function in the task of every human being to create an internal world with a variety of self and object representations. In a paper entitled "Self–Other Action Play" (Bergman and Lefcourt 1993) Ilene Lefcourt and I describe the earliest play experiences between mother and baby that promote the baby's most rudimentary sense of self and other. These games of early infancy create

1. I would like to thank Maria Fahey for her help in formulating the ideas in this chapter.
2. I would like to thank David Abrams for drawing my attention to Sartre's description of emerging from his hiding place in *The Words*.

a mutually regulated action dialogue between mother and infant, which in turn provides the foundation for what we call self–other action play. This is play in which themes of self, other, and self-with-other predominate and in which the formation, transformation, and interrelatedness of self and object representations take place. We believe that such play contributes to the formation and integration of self and object representations in a unique way. Self-other action play eventually leads to the capacity for role play, which requires at least rudimentary ability to take the perspective of an other.

Hiding and being found are exciting and pleasurable activities, which begin with the earliest peekaboo games and last in ever more highly elaborated forms throughout early childhood and beyond. Even in adulthood one may, consciously or unconsciously, hide one's true self from another and experience a very special joy when one is discovered and recognized. Babies and toddlers never seem to tire of hiding and being found by their mothers, a game played idiosyncratically by each mother–child pair. One little boy in the separation-individuation studies (Mahler et al. 1975), Peter, used to duck down behind a partition separating the mother's area from the children's play area and wait for his mother to say, "Where's Peter?" at which point he would jump up joyously and together they would exclaim, "There he is!" The particular form of his game, ducking down and popping up, was connected with his mother's way of comforting him when he was being weaned from breast-feeding by bouncing him up and down on her lap.[3] Thus Peter internalized his mother's way of comforting him and made it into an active game in which he controlled the pleasurable movement by bouncing up and ducking down in his particular version of a very early hide-and-seek game, actually a game on the border between peekaboo and hide-and-seek. Peekaboo, originated by the mother and later taken over by the baby, is a game of appearance and disappearance. McDevitt (1975) observes that at 15 months a child will initiate a game of peekaboo in anticipation of mother leaving the room. This indicates that the baby has some rudimentary knowledge of what is about to happen, namely that mother will leave and then come back.

---

3. Observation by Manuel Furer, M.D.

Peekaboo is a self–other action play originating in the differentiation subphase in which the external self–other action often changes as mother and baby interchange roles of hiding and finding (Bergman and Lefcourt 1993). Characteristic of these games that deal directly with disappearance and appearance (i.e., peekaboo and I-throw-it-away, you-pick-it-up) is the fact that they are accompanied by crescendos and decrescendos of excitement. The increase and decrease of arousal is mutually regulated and results in an experience of fluctuating, moment-to-moment state sharing (Stern 1985). The reappearance after brief disappearance evokes the joy of refinding, that is, rediscovering mother. Furthermore, the experience of "making" mother retrieve the lost object enhances feelings of the self as agent. At a time when babies are increasingly confronted with feelings of loss and separateness and are just on the brink of becoming capable of more independent activities, in particular locomotion, the emergent experience of self as agent and highlighted experiences of state sharing, that is, attunement (Stern 1985), may be particularly exciting.

As these first peekaboo games develop into ever more elaborate games of hiding and finding, certain characteristics remain constant. These are the need to repeat the game over and over again, the excitement with which the game is played, the manageable amount of anxiety about being found and not being found or about finding and not finding, the surprise that exists even if the result is well known and repeated over and over again, and finally, the joy of reunion. These games in normal development are played to master the object loss that is entailed in the process of separation-individuation and the achievement of self-object differentiation. However, these games continue throughout childhood and maybe throughout life. We might ask what other purpose is served in continuing to play hide-and-seek?

With the achievement of a measure of object constancy (which we assume to be achieved as the rapprochement crisis is negotiated at the age of about 2½ to 3 years), the child begins to be able to take the perspective of the other—one of the hallmarks of the achievement of object constancy (McDevitt 1975). Hide-and-seek games further the establishment of self–other differentiation, but at the same time they can only be played after the relationship to the mother has become securely enough established so that her return after a separation can be anticipated. In the case studies that follow we see that hide-and-seek games serve the purpose of mastering separations (Frankiel 1993), but that they could only begin to be played at a point in treatment at which the holding environment with the therapist had been securely enough established to form a home base from which the child could leave and to which he or she could return. It is interesting that even if these games are played by older children who have achieved self–object differentiation, certain characteristics of the game as it is first played seem to remain intact. One of these characteristics is that the games are repeated over and over, often with the child hiding in the same place again and again, waiting to be found even if the child knows that the hiding place is known to the seeker. In this way it seems that the child temporarily and voluntarily gives up the ability of taking the perspective of the other and accepts the seeker's searching for him or her as genuine, which makes possible the excitement, surprise, anxiety, and joy at being found. We might wonder what the meaning of this could be. It has been quite accepted that hide-and-seek games serve the purpose of mastering the loss inherent in every child's growing up and becoming more independent. It would seem that the giving up of an already achieved ability serves yet another purpose and that hide-and-seek games stand on the border of separateness and union with the loved one. The child gives up the knowledge that the other already knows where she is in order to reexperience a state of not having to recognize the other as so separate. And yet the other has to be separate enough to play along with the illusion that the child is hidden and has to be found. This duality is demonstrated by a 4-year-old boy in therapy who, when playing and replaying his hiding game, would occasionally become so overwhelmed with the joy of refinding his therapist that he would jump out of the box in which he was hiding and run to his therapist for a hug before being able to continue the game. This goes along with the notion that emotional object constancy is never fully achieved, but is a lifelong task that is always resisted by that part of the self that would like to preserve forever the bliss of being fully at one with another.

Developmentally, hide-and-seek becomes possible only when a certain amount of separateness has been achieved. The achievement of the sense of self separate from the other rests on the sense of security achieved earlier, during the symbiotic phase in which the child living in reasonably nurturing circumstances learns to know the primary caretaker as being different from all others—the one who can he relied on to fulfill both physical and emotional needs. To risk playing hide-and-seek one has to be able to take for granted that the reunion will occur and will be pleasurable.

Hide-and-Seek in Therapy: Clinical Examples

Having understood hide-and-seek in terms of self–other action play as it occurs during the separation-individuation process, I would like to give some examples of hide-and-seek in the therapy situation in cases where the separation-individuation process could not proceed in a normal fashion. One of these was my child patient at the Masters Children's Center, one of a group of symbiotic, psychotic, and autistic children. The other children described are selected from a group of children referred to the City University Child Center for severe language delays.

Rachel

Rachel, a symbiotic psychotic child, came to the Masters Children's Center in the early sixties where she was part of a research project studying the natural history of childhood psychosis under the direction of Margaret Mahler and Manuel Furer (Bergman 1971). The psychotic children in this study received intensive treatment four times a week and at the beginning were seen together with their mothers using the tripartite treatment design (Mahler 1968).

Rachel was 4 years old when she was brought to the Masters Children's Center. She presented a typical picture of the symbiotic psychotic child. She clung desperately to her mother, seemingly in an attempt to coerce her to serve only the function of fulfilling her needs. There was no pleasure in closeness for either mother or child. Rachel was rigid and panic-stricken, breaking into piercing screams at the slightest frustration. She could not tolerate her mother to converse with anyone, either in person or on the telephone. Rachel showed a mixture of symbiotic and autistic defenses. She never used language for direct communication but rather quoted from books, records, songs, and television commercials. Since everything she said was merely an echo, the reversal of personal pronouns was a natural consequence. She used quotations as a way of conveying her feelings with astonishing accuracy. When angry with her mother she might say "the poisoned apple" or "she's dead, of course," taking the words from fairly tales and folk songs. Rachel was a pretty child, clean and neatly dressed, her face set in a tight smilelike grimace. She had the broad gait of a toddler and walked cautiously with small steps, climbing steps one at a time like a 2-year-old. She would never run and was unable to climb, swing, throw a ball, or use her hands at any manipulative play. She was always either bouncing from foot to foot or jumping and waving her arms. She showed no interest in toys except as objects to chew on. When given a doll, she would undress it and then throw it away. She spent many hours listening to records or looking at a particular book that caught her fancy. When she was unsuccessful in her attempts to shut out the world, she reacted with anger and fear. If anyone tried to interest her in a new toy, she would ignore it. If not allowed to ignore it, she would knock it down, drop it, and break into loud shrieks. She refused to look at a new book, listen to a new record, or wear new clothes. Her mother had found only one activity that interested Rachel: the spelling of words usually had a soothing effect. Rachel had innumerable fears: of strangeness and strangers, of children, of riding in cars, of any kind of household machine (mixer, blender, vacuum cleaner, washing machine). She tried to climb on her mother, tearing at her body, seeming to clamor for something that the mother could not provide. Mother said that Rachel had never accepted warmth or closeness, even as a baby. Mother herself was stiff and proper, perplexed and desperate, trying to make her child behave in a more normal manner and keeping her at a distance because she was not able to interpret Rachel's distorted behavior as a need for closeness. Mother and daughter lived alone together, the parents having separated when Rachel was 2½ years old. However, the father was involved with Rachel and eventually came to therapy sessions regularly.

Rachel had been seen at several treatment centers but would not separate from her mother as these centers required. Both Rachel and her mother responded well to the demands of the intensive treatment design. They were in sessions four times a week for one-and-a-half to two-hour sessions. Both responded rapidly to the initial phase of therapy, the creation of the symbiotic milieu. Angry shrieking stopped within the first few weeks and was quickly replaced by pleasure and physical closeness and the simple games one might play with an infant. She loved to be held, fondled, rubbed, carried about, and covered up, which she called "making cozy." She also liked to play in the water with all her clothes off and then to be wrapped in a towel or sheet. All this surprised Rachel's mother, who said that Rachel had never liked being held. As we understood it, symbiotic closeness with her mother meant to Rachel being overwhelmed. Although the wish for symbiosis created a state of panic in Rachel, it became less threatening in the tripartite treatment setting. Rachel's symbiotic needs were met while the symbiotic demands placed on her by her mother were reduced. The symbiosis was diluted by the introduction of a third person, the therapist. Much of the early treatment consisted of introducing slowly and abundantly the kinds of experiences that happen naturally and almost imperceptibly in normal development, paving the way for the gradual discovery of self and other. Before the separation-individuation process could begin, a pleasurable, gratifying symbiotic relationship had to be established. This meant that experiences of mutuality could begin to take place.

After this atmosphere of safety had become established, Rachel spontaneously began to initiate games of hide-and-seek. Usually she hid in a closet, and enjoyed my elaborate attempts to find her and eventually the reunion upon being found.

The City University Child Center[4]

The children referred to the City University Child Center for severe language delays, mostly from inner-city backgrounds, have suffered major deprivations and trauma. They show severe disturbances in attachment. For example, most of them come to the all-day program showing no reactions to separation from their families, no fear of strangers. The therapeutic classroom, as well as the individual therapy, are geared to promoting attachment, and to helping the children achieve self–object differentiation and the capacity to express

---

4. I thank my students and their supervisors for the work they have done and for allowing me to use their clinical accounts. In particular, I have drawn on the work of Anne Adelman, Ines de Costa Esteves, Shelley Hooe, and Mara Silverman.

their needs for love and nurturing. Primary attention is given to affective interchange and expression based on the conviction that these are necessary for any meaningful learning to take place. Many children who come almost without language become linguistically fluent in less than a year. Others remain language-delayed but nevertheless progress in the capacity to play and the capacity to form meaningful attachments (Bergman 1992).

We have found that many of these children go through a period in which various forms of self–other action play became an important avenue of communication and interaction between themselves and their therapists. These games are an important way they learn to form internal representations of a caretaking other and of separations and reunions over which, at least in play, they can have a measure of control, even though in their lives they rarely have the opportunity to be in control or even to have reliable love objects available for identification and internalization.

Often the classroom serves as "home base" that the children must leave with their therapists and return to after their therapy sessions. Sometimes the negotiation of this journey is as important as the therapy session itself.

What many of these children have in common is a mother who cannot allow the child to gradually separate and become a person in his or her own right. Often the mother has intense symbiotic needs of her own and will experience the child's inherent need for distancing and the unavoidable periods of back-and-forth movement as traumatic abandonment, which probably replicates abandonment that they themselves have experienced as children in their own families. Such mothers respond to their individuating toddlers unpredictably and often by retaliating against the child for the child's beginning moves at becoming separate, which the mothers experience as catastrophic abandonment.

Tomas

Tomas's therapist reported that at the beginning of therapy, when he was 4 years old, he spoke in one- or two-word phrases and often whispered unintelligibly. He did not respond when spoken to. He displayed a wide variety of bizarre behaviors and his limited speech included the repetition of television commercials. He was often quiet and withdrawn, apart from his classroom group, and unable to make a connection to the other children or the adults around him.

The first playful interaction between Tomas and his therapist was the game of peekaboo, which Tomas played by climbing into a large toy chest while the therapist sat in a nearby chair and watched. Contact between them was established nonverbally by smiling. After a while Tomas would say "bye-bye" and disappear into the toy chest, closing the cover over himself. Therapist waited a moment, knocked on the lid, and said, "Where's Tomas?" In response, Tomas would throw open the lid in delight, smile, and then vanish into the toy chest again. It is important that in this game Tomas maintained control over disappearance and reunion and that the game focused on his leaving the therapist, not being left by her.

A new significant play sequence emerged that involved Tomas turning on and off the light switch. He would turn off the light, lie down on a rest mat, and request that the therapist also lie down quietly. He would not allow the therapist to speak. What seemed of importance was that he created darkness and light as a way of creating disappearance and reunion. The darkness may have represented in part his worry that he would in fact disappear if he could not be seen. The therapist says:

> Thus the darkness Tomas created was essential in working through this facet of his separation fear, as he was able to use the symbolic absence and real presence of the therapist to integrate the frightening aspects of aloneness with the growing capacity to internally represent the comforting aspects of togetherness.

Another important game involved a giant blue ball that was rolled back and forth between Tomas and the therapist, who sat at opposite ends of the long playroom. As the game advanced, he would roll the ball to the therapist, then run and hide, waiting for the therapist to roll the ball back before jumping out of his hiding place to catch it. In this play sequence the therapist's function was to serve as an affirming partner for his increasingly independent actions.

As the therapist supported his wishes to direct and control the game and affirmed his growing sense of competence and mastery, his affect became increasingly joyful and his play increasingly expansive.

His joy and daringness reflected the important developmental strides in the areas of relatedness and integration of self–other representations. The play was predictable, safe, and gratifying, and this permitted both an experience of himself as continuous and sustained and a gradual internalization of the relationships as consistent and reliable. The game seemed to have important undertones of a practicing subphase of separation-individuation during which infants become enthralled with the world around them and with their own rapidly developing physical abilities. It seemed that for Tomas the giant blue ball came to represent the invisible thread by which he could remain in contact with the therapist. He regulated the distance, increasing it symbolically by hiding, yet controlling it by verbally commanding the ball-therapist to return to him. The therapist's responsiveness to Tomas's striving toward agency and mastery provided a stepping-stone toward a more consolidated sense of self, which permitted a dawning recognition of the therapist as a whole person separate from Tomas yet connected by way of a mutually shared history of reliable and pleasurable exchanges. Tomas's capacity to relate to the therapist as a whole person became evident initially by way of his dramatic and sudden interest in her physical presence and appearance. He began to initiate more physical contact, especially after a genuine connection had been made, such as by playing the ball game.

A play sequence emerged and became central to the therapy for several weeks. On the day of Tomas's birthday the therapist brought in a new toy, a dump truck. Together they decided to keep the dump truck in the drawer of a file cabinet. The truck and file cabinet became an integral part of the therapy for several sessions. When entering the playroom Tomas would look for the truck in the cabinet. He then discovered that the bottom drawer of the cabinet was empty: it became his to fill upon entering the play room in the morning. He carefully put his lunch box, hat, mittens, jacket, and snow pants into the drawer. One day after playing with the drawer, he decided to hide in the drawer himself, curled up on his jacket.

Blossom

The therapist described Blossom as a tiny, well-proportioned little girl, striking in her ability to play alone for significantly long periods of

time. While playing alone she conveyed such a sense of self-contain-
ment that others tended to leave her to herself. She attached herself
to adults in a rather indiscriminating way reminiscent of autistic
children, engaging them in playing with her and following her nonverbal directions. Blossom first came to life in the gym room, which
is filled with action toys and climbing equipment. There she demonstrated an extraordinary energy level and good gross motor abilities,
as well as an ability to get other children to follow her lead in riding
bicycles and racing around the room. In play therapy the dominant
theme at the beginning was the dumping of toys and, in particular,
the dumping of a little baby doll out of its crib. During her first semester at our center, she never missed a day even though she was
often ill and sometimes slept through the morning. During the second semester, when she had become well adjusted to the therapeutic
nursery and indicated that she loved to be there, her mother kept
her home a good deal of the time, very possibly as punishment for
what she considered bad behavior.

An early gain in therapy was Blossom's ability to express her feelings about being left by her mother, both directly and indirectly. Toward the end of a session she began to cry and call for her "Mommy."
Soon after that she cried through a whole session and was unable to
play. She was able to express these feelings of sadness when she had
developed enough trust in her therapist to know that she could be
comforted. She showed her need for comforting by putting her head
on the therapist's lap. When her mother came to a play session Blossom was very clingy and seemed wary of the therapist. The session
following her mother's visit, Blossom did not want to leave the classroom with her therapist. Her therapist says:

> I sort of kidnapped her onto the elevator. She was clearly disap-
> pointed, angry, and upset about being separated from the other kids.
> When I acknowledged the feelings she was having, she cried and
> wanted me to carry her to the playroom. Blossom's play took a shift
> after this incident in which I acknowledged her feelings.

The therapist reports that after this session Blossom became much
more animated and began to initiate new play, namely many variations of peekaboo and games in which she invited the therapist to
mirror her excitement and enthusiasm. The therapist also describes

that after this her play became generally more elaborated, that she stopped dumping the baby out of its crib, and that she started to fingerpaint. Hiding and being found became an important part of each session, along with being able to play more constructively, for example, with blocks. She handed blocks one by one to the therapist. The therapist built a tower, and Blossom had great pleasure in knocking it down and repeating the game all over. Two sessions later she put the baby doll on a chair at a table and put other family figures around. Then during the last session before a holiday she played a new variation of hiding and being found. Blossom hid under the table. This time instead of wanting to be found by her therapist, she invited the therapist to hide with her. Blossom indicated that they were to be extremely quiet. She then emerged from the hiding place, took all the toys from the window sill and piled them up in front of the door, thus indicating that she did not want the session to end; she did not want to be left by her therapist. Finally, she became very low-key and asked her therapist to carry her from the playroom back to the classroom. The therapist says:

> This was the last session before the break. Her behavior suggests to a remarkable degree that she was aware that we would not be meeting for a while and that she wished we could stay together.

Tania

Tania's therapist remarked that when she first met her, Tania took her hand and went instantly with her to the therapy room. The therapist felt she was a child who craved attention and was willing to have her needs met by anyone who showed interest in her. After a few weeks there was a shift and Tania refused to go with her therapist, wouldn't make eye contact with her, and turned away from her. On the way to the therapy room she cried and called out for Mommy. Following this, Tania began to show signs of growing attachment and reluctance to separate at the end of sessions. As the attachment to her therapist grew, she began to be able to express her fears about being left. She started to have great difficulty in leaving the play-room and began to show feelings of anger, sadness, and resentment. Leaving therapy sessions became more and more difficult with each passing session. Finally, she just refused to leave and was able to show her therapist that she was afraid that she would not see her again. The therapist says:

> The only way I was able to get her to leave the playroom was by carrying her. Initially once in my arms she no longer seemed angry and hateful. On the contrary, she acted like a placated child who expressed her satisfaction by settling into my arms, nuzzling her head into my shoulder, and cooing.

During this time Tania began to play hide-and-seek games with her therapist. She asked to be put down and then would run away and hide. When she was found she had a big smile on her face. The therapist felt that this game was very reparative for Tania. It allowed her to control the separation and to be found and resettle in the arms of her therapist, who would then carry her the rest of the way to the classroom.

Discussion

All the cases described have certain important characteristics in common, though each child finds a unique way to play the game and has a unique moment in which the game begins. The common element seems to be that before the game begins, the child has to establish a unique attachment to the therapist and to feel safe. Feeling safe means knowing that the self that wants to be out in the world away from the therapist will be accepted and that the therapist will be an affirming partner for the child's independent actions. Feeling safe also means that the therapist's arms will be open to welcome the child back into the closeness of the holding environment. Leaving the nest does not mean that the nest will be threatened; it does not mean that the nest will collapse or disappear when the child wishes to return to it. Thus, Rachel only begins to hide in the closet after a pleasurable relationship to her therapist has been established. Both Blossom and Tania begin to play after pain of separation has been acknowledged and they allow themselves to be carried in the therapist's arms. Tania begins therapy a very needy little girl who hungers for attention from anyone who will give it. Only as she gets attached to her therapist can she then fully experience longings for her mother and begin to experience separations from her therapist, now a beloved and reliable person, with pain and resentment. She will leave the playroom only when carried in her therapist's arms, and only then can she begin pleasurably to play hiding games.

Another theme in these hide-and-seek games is that the hiding place is usually an enclosure, a claustrum of some kind, which is different from hiding behind an object or another person, as in the example of Peter hiding behind the partition. Rachel hides in the closet, Tomas hides in the file drawer, and Blossom hides under the table. In the case of Tomas, there is a clear connection between the truck given to him by his therapist on his birthday that he keeps in a filing cabinet drawer and himself eventually curling up beside his truck in the same drawer. This makes the hiding place very suggestive of a womb from which he emerges to be "born" and wishes to be welcomed by his therapist.

Blossom begins to be able to express feelings about separation from her mother as she becomes attached to her therapist. Later she does not want to leave the classroom, which may symbolize the mother. The words the therapist uses to describe what happens are interesting: "I kidnapped her into the elevator and acknowledged her feelings." Blossom then asks her therapist to carry her. Was it significant that the event took place in the elevator? As a claustrum par excellence, the elevator perhaps signifies the therapist's womb, thus the therapist's full acceptance of her as a baby. After this incident, in which the safety of closeness seems to become established because her feelings are fully acknowledged, she spontaneously begins to play peekaboo and hiding games. Her favorite hiding place is under the table, a claustrum with a full view of the outside world from which she can be born and reborn to the delight of her therapist.

What seems to be universal is the appearance of the hiding games after a close, safe relationship has been established, which gives the child, possibly for the first time, a therapist-mother who can be fully absorbed with the child and provide a safe holding environment. It is interesting to contemplate that the child leaves this holding environment and runs to find a hiding place that is often a womblike place, a claustrum. Thus, on the one hand the child runs from the therapist's arms to show his or her independence, which is to be enjoyed by the therapist. On the other hand, the child leaves the therapist to hide and enact a symbolic birth experience—a fantasy of being back inside the mother's body and then emerging, the birth to be celebrated by the mother-therapist.

References

Abelin, E. (1971). The role of the father in the separation-individuation process. In *Separation-Individuation*, ed. J. McDevitt and C. Settlage, pp. 229–252. New York: International Universities Press.

——— (1975). Some further observations and comments on the earliest role of the father. *International Journal of Psycho-Analysis* 56:293–302.

——— (1980). Triangulation, the role of the father and the origins of core gender identity during the rapprochement subphase. In *Rapprochement*, ed. R. Lax, A. Burland, and S. Bach, pp. 151–169. New York: Jason Aronson.

Ainsworth, M. D. S., Blehard, M. C., Waters, E., and Wall, S. (1978). *Patterns of Attachment*. Mahwah, NJ: Lawrence Erlbaum.

Arlow, J. (1982). Problems of the superego concept. *Psychoanalytic Study of the Child* 37:229–244. New Haven: Yale University Press.

Asch, S. S. (1966). Claustrophobia and depression. *Journal of the American Psychoanalytic Association* 14:711–729.

Bachrach, H. M. (1976). Empathy. *Archives of General Psychiatry* 33:35–48.

Balint, M. (1959). *Thrills and Regressions*. London: Hogarth.

Beebe, B., and Lachmann, F. (1988). The contribution of mother–infant mutual influence to the origins of self and object representations. *Psychoanalytic Psychology* 5:305–337.

Beebe, B., and Stern, D. (1977). Engagement–disengagement and early object experiences. In *Communicative Structures and Psychic Structures*, ed. N. Freedman and S. Grand. New York: Plenum.

Benedek, T. (1938). Adaptation to reality in early infancy. *Psychoanalytic Quarterly* 7:200–214.

——— (1956). Toward the biology of the depressive constellation. *Journal of the American Psychoanalytic Association* 4:389–427.

——— (1970). The family as psychological field. In *Parenthood: Its Psychology and Psychopathology*, ed. E. J. Anthony and T. Benedek. Boston: Little, Brown.

Benjamin, J. (1991). Father and daughter: identification with difference— a contribution to gender heterodoxy. *Psychoanalytic Dialogues* 1:277–299.

Beratis, S., Miller, R., and Galenson, E. (1982). Separation-individuation and transitional objects in a four-year-old psychotic child. *International Journal of Psychoanalytic Psychotherapy* 9:561–582.

Beres, D. (1968). The role of empathy in psychotherapy and psychoanalysis. *Journal of Hillside Hospital* 17:362–369.

Beres, D., and Arlow, J. (1974). Fantasy and identification in empathy. *Psychoanalytic Quarterly* 43:26–50.

Bergman, A. (1971). "I and you": the separation-individuation process in the treatment of a symbiotic child. In *Separation-Individuation: Essays in Honor of Margaret S. Mahler*, ed. J. B. McDevitt and C. F. Settlage, pp. 325–356. New York: International Universities Press.

——— (1978). From mother to the world outside: the use of space during the separation-individuation phase. In *Between Reality and Fantasy*, ed. S. Grolnick and L. Barkin, pp. 147–165. New York: Jason Aronson.

——— (1981). Ours, yours, mine. In *Rapprochement: The Critical Subphase of Separation-Individuation*, ed. R. F. Lax, S. Bach, and J. A. Burland, pp. 199–216. New York: Jason Aronson.

——— (1982). Considerations about the development of the girl during the separation-individuation process. In *Early Female Development: Current Psychoanalytic Views*, ed. D. Mendell. New York: Spectrum.

——— (1985). From psychological birth to motherhood: the treatment of an autistic child with follow-up into her adult life as a mother. In *Parental Influences in Health and Disease*, ed. E. J. Anthony and G. H. Pollock, pp. 91–121. Boston: Little, Brown.

——— (1987). On the development of female identity: issues of mother–daughter interaction during the separation-individuation process. *Psychoanalytic Inquiry* 7:381–396.

———— (1992). Using insights from observational research of mothers and babies in the therapy of preschool children: the City University Child Center. In *Models and Techniques of Psychotherapeutic Interventions in the First Years of Life*, ed. D. Stern. Milan: Raffaelo Cortina Editore.

Bergman, A., and Chernack, M. (1982). From command to request: the development of language in the treatment of a symbiotic psychotic child. *International Journal of Psychoanalytic Psychotherapy* 9:583–602.

Bergman, A., and Ellman, S. (1985). Margaret S. Mahler: symbiosis and separation-individuation. In *Beyond Freud*, ed. J. Reppen, pp. 231–256. Hillsdale, NJ: Analytic Press.

Bergman, A., et al. (1976). *The Separation-Individuation Process*. A film in three parts produced through the Margaret S. Mahler Research Foundation.

Bergman, A., and Lefcourt, I. (1993). Self-other action play: a window into the representational world of the infant. In *Modes of Meaning: Clinical and Developmental Approaches to the Study of Symbolic Play*, ed. A. Slade. New York: Oxford University Press.

Bergman, A., Schwarzman, M., Sloate, P., and Wilson, A. (1983). The oral deadlock: treatment of a psychotic child. *Journal of the American Psychoanalytic Association* 31:443–465.

Bettelheim, B. (1976). *The Uses of Enchantment: The Meaning and Importance of Fairy Tales*. New York: Knopf.

Bion, W. R. (1962). *Learning from Experience*. New York: Basic Books.

———— (1967). *Second Thoughts*. London: Heinemann.

Blos, P. (1967). The second individuation process of adolescence. *Psychoanalytic Study of the Child* 22:162–186. New York: International Universities Press.

Blum, H. (1976). Masochism, the ego ideal, and the psychology of women. *Journal of the American Psychoanalytic Association Supplement* 24:157–192.

Bornstein, 'B. (1945). Clinical notes on child analysis. *Psychoanalytic Study of the Child* 1:151–166. New York: International Universities Press.

Bowlby, J. (1961). Separation anxiety: a critical review of the literature. *Journal of Child Psychology and Psychiatry* 1:251–269.

Brazelton, T. B. (1981a). The first developmental stages in parent and infant attachment. In *Emotion: Theory, Research, and Experience*, vol. 2., ed. R. Pluchik and H. Kellerman. New York: Academic Press.

———— (1981b). Neonatal assessment. In *The Course of Life: Psychoanalytic Contributions toward Understanding Human Development*, vol. 1, ed. S. I. Greenspan and G. H. Pollock, pp. 203–233. Washington, DC: U.S. Government Printing Office.

Brazelton, T. B., and Als, H. (1979). Four early steps in the development of mother–infant interaction. *Psychoanalytic Study of the Child* 34:349–369. New Haven: Yale University Press.

Brazelton, T. B., and Cramer, B. (1990). *The Earliest Relationship: Parents, Infants, and the Drama of Early Attachment.* Reading, MA: Addison-Wesley.

Brazelton, T. B., Koslowski, B., and Main, M. (1974). The origins of reciprocity: the early mother–infant interaction. In *The Effect of the Infant on Its Caregiver,* ed. M. Lewis and L. Rosenblum, pp. 49–76. New York: Wiley.

Brazelton, T. B., Tronick, E., Adamson, L., et al. (1975). Early mother–infant reciprocity. In *Parent–Infant Interaction,* Ciba Foundation Symposium 33, pp. 137–154. Amsterdam: Elsevier.

Bretherton, I. (1984). Representing the social world in symbolic play: reality and fantasy. In *Symbolic Play: The Development of Social Understanding,* ed. I. Bretherton, pp. 3–41. Orlando, FL: Academic Press.

Brody, S., and Axelrod, S. (1970). *Anxiety and Ego Formation in Infancy.* New York: International Universities Press.

Bruner, J. S., and Sherwood, V. (1976). Peekaboo and the learning of rule structures. In *Play, Its Role in Development and Evolution,* ed. J. S. Bruner, pp. 277–285. New York: Basic Books.

——— (1983). Thought, language, and in interaction in infancy In *Frontiers of Infant Psychiatry,* ed. J. Call, E. Galenson, and R. Tyson, pp. 38–52. New York: Basic Books.

Buie, D. (1981). Empathy: its nature and limitations. *Journal of the American Psychoanalytic Association* 29:281–307.

Cath, S., Gurwitt, A., and Gunsberg, L. (1989). *Fathers and Their Families.* Hillsdale, NJ: Analytic Press.

Cath, S., Gurwitt, A., and Ross, J. (1982). *Father and Child.* Hillsdale, NJ: Analytic Press.

Despert, J. L. (1940). A comparative study of thinking in schizophrenic children and in children of preschool age. *American Journal of Psychiatry* 97:189–213.

Drucker, J. (1979). The affective context and psychodynamics of first symbolization. In *Symbolic Functioning in Childhood,* ed. N. R. Smith and M. B. Franklin, pp. 27–41. Hillsdale, NJ: Lawrence Erlbaum.

Ekstein, R. (1966). *Children of Time and Space, of Action and Impulse.* New York: Appleton-Century-Crofts.

Eliot, T. S. (1943). *Four Quartets.* New York: Harcourt, Brace.

Elkisch, P. (1956). The struggle for ego boundaries in a psychotic child. *American Journal of Psychotherapy* 10:578–602.

Emde, R. (1980a). Emotional availability: a reciprocal reward system for infants and parents with implications for prevention of psychosocial disorders. In *Parent–Infant Relationships*, ed. P. Taylor, pp. 87–115. Orlando, FL: Grune & Stratton.

——— (1980b). Toward a psychoanalytic theory of affect. II. Emerging models of emotional development in infancy. In *The Course of Life, Vol. 1, Infancy and Early Childhood*, pp. 85–112. Adelphi, MD: National Institute of Mental Health.

——— (1983). The prepresentational self and its affective core. *Psychoanalytic Study of the Child* 38:165–192. New Haven: Yale University Press.

——— (1988a). Development terminable and interminable: I. Innate and motivational factors from infancy. *International Journal of Psycho-Analysis* 69(Part 1):23–42.

——— (1988b). Development terminable and interminable: II. Recent psychoanalytic theory and therapeutic considerations. *International Journal of Psycho-Analysis* 69(Part II):283–297.

Emde, R., Gaensbauer, T., and Harmon, R. (1976). *Emotional Expression in Infancy: A Biobehavioral Study* [Psychological Issues Monograph 37]. New York: International Universities Press.

Erikson, E. H. (1959). *Identity and the Life Cycle* [Psychological Issues Monograph 1]. New York: International Universities Press.

Fast, I. (1979). Developments in gender identity: gender differentiation in girls. *International Journal of Psycho-Analysis* 60:443–453.

Fenichel, O. (1945). *The Psychoanalytic Theory of Neuroses*. New York: Norton.

Ferreira, A. J. (1961). Empathy and the bridge function of the ego. *Journal of the American Psychoanalytic Association* 9:91–105.

Fliess, R. (1942). The metapsychology of the analyst. *Psychoanalytic Quarterly* 11:211–227.

Fonagy, P., and Target, M. (1998). Mentalization and the changing aims of child psychoanalysis. *Psychoanalytic Dialogues* 8(1):87–114.

Fraiberg, S., Adelson, E., and Shapiro, V. (1975). Ghosts in the nursery: a psychoanalytic approach to the problems of impaired infant–mother relationships. *Journal of the American Psychoanalytic Association* 14:387–421.

Frankiel, R. (1993). Hide and seek in the playroom: on object loss and transference in child treatment. *Psychoanalytic Review* 80:341–359.

Freud, A. (1963). The concept of developmental lines. *Psychoanalytic Study of the Child* 18:245–266. New York: International Universities Press.

——— (1965). *Normality and Pathology in Childhood. Assessments of Development*. New York: International Universities Press.

Freud, S. (1921). Group psychology and the analysis of the ego. *Standard Edition* 18:69–143.

——— (1931). Female sexuality. *Standard Edition* 21:223–243.

——— (1933). The dissection of the psychical personality. *Standard Edition* 22:57–80.

——— (1957). Mourning and melancholia. *Standard Edition* 14:243–258.

Furer, M. (1964). The development of a preschool symbiotic boy. *Psychoanalytic Study of the Child* 16:332–351. New York: International Universities Press.

——— (1967). Some developmental aspects of the superego. *International Journal of Psycho-Analysis* 48:277–280.

——— (1974). *The psychoanalytic process, the therapeutic alliance and child observation*. Paper presented at the Midwinter meeting of the American Psychoanalytic Association, New York, December.

Gaddini, E. (1969). On imitation. *International Journal of Psycho-Analysis* 50:475–484.

Gaddini, R., and Gaddini, E. (1970). Transitional objects and the process of individuation: a study of three different social groups. *Journal of the American Academy of Child Psychiatry* 9:347–365.

Galenson, E. (1971). A consideration of the nature of thought in childhood play. In *Separation-Individuation: Essays in Honor of Margaret S. Mahler*, ed. J. B. McDevitt and C. F. Settlage, pp. 41–59. New York: International Universities Press.

——— (1974). The emergence of genital awareness during the second year of life. In *Sex Differences in Behavior*, ed. R. C. Friedman, R. M. Richart, and R. J. Van de Wiele, pp. 223–231. New York: Wiley.

——— (1976). Some suggested revisions concerning early female development. *Journal of the American Psychoanalytic Association* 24:29–57.

Galenson, E., and Roiphe, H. (1971). The impact of early sexual discovery on mood defensive organization and symbolization. *Psychoanalytic Study of the Child* 26:195–216. New York International Universities Press.

——— (1974). The emergence of genital awareness during the second year of life. In *Sex Differences in Behavior*, ed. R. C. Friedman, R. M. Richart, and R. J. Van de Wiele, pp. 223–231. New York: Wiley.

——— (1976). Some suggested revisions concerning female development. *Journal of the American Psychoanalytic Association* 24:29–57.

Garvey, C. (1977). *Play*. Boston: Harvard University Press.

Geleerd, E. R. (1958). Borderline states in childhood and adolescence. *Psychoanalytic Study of the Child* 13:279–295. New York: International Universities Press.

Gergely, G. (1997). Mahler's work as reflected in the mirror of modern developmental psychology. In *Der Beobachtete und der Rekonstruierte Saügling*, ed. W. Burian, *Psychoanalytische Blätter* Band 10, pp. 91–118. Göttingen: Vandenhoeck & Ruprecht.

Green, A. (1975). The analyst, symbolization and absence in the analytic setting. *International Journal of Psycho-Analysis* 56:1–22.

Greenacre, P. (1957). The childhood of the artist: libidinal phase development and giftedness. *Psychoanalytic Study of the Child* 12:27–72. New York: International Universities Press.

——— (1960). On the nature of the parent–infant relationship. *International Journal of Psycho-Analysis* 41:571–584.

Greenson, R. R. (1954). The struggle against identification. *Journal of the American Psychoanalytic Association* 2:200–217.

——— (1960). Empathy and its vicissitudes. *International Journal of Psycho-Analysis* 41:418–424.

Grossman, W. I., and Stewart, W. A. (1976). Penis envy: from childhood wish to developmental metaphor. *Journal of the American Psychoanalytic Association* 24:193–212.

Harlow, H. F., and Harlow, M. K. (1965). The affectional systems. In *Behavior of Nonhuman Primates*, vol 2, ed. A. M. Schrier, H. F. Harlow, and F. Stollnitz. New York: Academic Press.

Hermann, I. (1936). Clinging-going-in-search: a contrasting part of instincts and their relation to sadism and masochism. *Psychoanalytic Quarterly* 45(1976):5–36.

Hoffman, M. L. (1978). Toward a theory of empathic arousal and development. In *The Development of Affect*, ed. M. Lewis and L. A. Rosenblum, pp. 227–256. New York: Plenum.

Holland, N. N. (1978). What can a concept of identity add to psycholinguistics? In *Psychoanalysis and Language*, ed. J. H. Smith, pp. 171–234. New Haven: Yale University Press.

Jacobson, E. (1957). On normal and pathological moods: their nature and functions. *Psychoanalytic Study of the Child* 13:279–295. New York: International Universities Press.

——— (1964). *The Self and the Object World*. New York: International Universities Press.

Kernberg, O. (1975). *Borderline Conditions and Pathological Narcissism*. New York: Jason Aronson.

Khan, M. M. R. (1973). The role of illusion in the analytic space and process. *Annual of Psychoanalysis* 1:231–246.

Kleeman, J. A. (1976). Freud's view on early female sexuality in the light of direct child observation. *Journal of the American Psychoanalytic Association* 24:3–27.

Kramer, S. (1979). The technical significance and application of Mahler's separation-individuation theory. *Journal of the American Psychoanalytic Association* 27(Supplement):141–163.

Kupfermann, K. (1971). The development and treatment of a psychotic child. In *Separation-Individuation*, ed. J. McDevitt and C. Settlage, pp. 441–470. New York: International Universities Press.

Lax, R., ed. (1986). *Self and Object Constancy: Clinical and Theoretical Perspectives*. New York: Guilford.

Lax, R., Bach, S., and Burland, J., eds. (1980). *Rapprochement: The Critical Subphase of Separation-Individuation*. New York: Jason Aronson.

Levy-Warren, M. (1996). *The Adolescent Journey: Development, Identity Formation, and Psychotherapy*. Northvale, NJ: Jason Aronson.

Lewin, B. D. (1935). Claustrophobia. *Psychoanalytic Quarterly* 4:227–233.

Lewis, M., and Rosenblum, L. A., eds. (1974). *The Effect of the Infant on Its Caregiver*. New York: Wiley.

Lichtenberg, J. (1989). *Psychoanalysis and Motivation*. Hillsdale, NJ: Analytic Press.

Lichtenstein, H. (1961). Identity and sexuality: a study of their interrelationship in man. *Journal of the American Psychoanalytic Association* 9:179–260.

Loewald, H. (1978). Instinct theory, object relations, and psychic-structure formation. *Journal of the American Psychoanalytic Association* 26:463–506.

——— (1980). Instinct theory, object relations, and psychic structure formation. In *Rapprochement: The Critical Subphase of Separation-Individuation*, pp. 65–76. New York: Jason Aronson.

Mahler, M. S. (1942). Pseudoimbecility: a magic cap of invisibility. In *Selected Papers*, vol. 1, pp. 3–16. New York: Jason Aronson, 1980.

——— (1958). Autism and symbiosis: two extreme disturbances of identity. *International Journal of Psycho-Analysis* 39:77–83.

——— (1961). On sadness and grief in infancy and childhood: loss and restoration of the symbiotic love object. *Psychoanalytic Study of the Child* 16:332–351. New York: International Universities Press.

——— (1963). Thoughts about development and individuation. *Psychoanalytic Study of the Child* 18:307–324. New York: International Universities Press.

——— (1965a). Thoughts about development and individuation. *Psychoanalytic Study of the Child* 18:307–324. New York: International Universities Press.

——— (1965b). On the significance of the normal separation-individuation phase: with reference to research in symbiotic child psychosis. In

Drives, Affects, Behavior, vol. 2, ed. M. Schur, pp. 161–169. New York: International Universities Press.

—— (1966). Notes on the development of basic moods: the depressive affect. In *Psychoanalysis: A General Psychology: Essays in Honor of Heinz Hartmann*, ed. R. M. Loewenstein, L. M. Newman, M. Schur, and A. J. Solnit, pp. 152–168. New York: International Universities Press.

—— (1968). *On Human Symbiosis and the Vicissitudes of Individuation: Infantile Psychosis*. Madison, CT: International Universities Press.

—— (1971). A study of the separation-individuation process and its possible application to borderline phenomena in the psychoanalytic situation. *Psychoanalytic Study of the Child* 26:403–424. New Haven: Yale University Press.

—— (1972a). On the first three subphases of the separation-individuation process. *International Journal of Psycho-Analysis* 53:333–338.

—— (1972b). Rapprochement subphase of the separation-individuation process. *Psychoanalytic Quarterly* 41:487–506.

—— (1979). *The Selected Papers of Margaret S. Mahler, Vols. I and II*. New York: Jason Aronson.

—— (1983). The meaning of developmental research of earliest infancy as related to the study of separation-individuation. In *Frontiers of Infant Psychiatry*, ed. J. Call, E. Galenson, and R. Tyson, pp. 3–6. New York: Basic Books.

Mahler, M. S., and Furer, M. (1960). Observations on research regarding the "symbiotic syndrome" of infantile psychosis. *Psychoanalytic Quarterly* 29:317–327.

—— (1963). Certain aspects of the separation-individuation phase. *Psychoanalytic Quarterly* 32:1–14.

Mahler, M. S., and LaPerriere, K. (1965). Mother–child interaction during separation-individuation. *Psychoanalytic Quarterly* 34:483–498.

Mahler, M. S., Pine, F., and Bergman, A. (1970). The mother's reaction to her toddler's drive for individuation. In *Parenthood: Its Psychology and Psychopathology*, ed. E. J. Anthony and T. Benedek, pp. 257–274. Boston: Little, Brown.

—— (1975). *The Psychological Birth of the Human Infant*. New York: Basic Books.

Mahler, M. S., Pine, F., Bergman, A., and Smith, J. (1982). *On the Phenomena Indicative of the Emergence of the Sense of Self*. A film produced through the Margaret S. Mahler Research Foundation.

Main, M., Kaplan, N., and Cassidy, J. (1989). Security in infancy, childhood, and adulthood: a move to the level of representation. In *Growing Points in Attachment Theory and Research*, ed. I. Bretherton and E. Waters. Monographs of the Society for Research in Child Development 50:66–106.

McDevitt, J. B. (1975). Separation-individuation and object constancy. *Journal of the American Psychoanalytic Association* 23:713–742.

——— (1979). The role of the internalization process in the development of object relations during the separation-individuation phase. *Journal of the American Psychoanalytic Association* 27:327–343.

——— (1981). The role of internalization in the development of object relations during the separation-individuation phase. In *Rapprochement: The Critical Subphase of Separation-Individuation*, ed. R. L. Lax, S. Bach, and J. A. Burland, pp. 135–149. New York: Jason Aronson.

——— (1983). The emergence of hostile aggression and its defensive and adaptive modifications during the separation-individuation process. *Journal of the American Psychoanalytic Association* 31:273–300.

——— (1985). *Preoedipal determinants of an infantile gender disorder.* Paper presented at the International Margaret S. Mahler Symposium, Paris.

——— (1988). *The origin of intrapsychic conflict during the separation-individuation process.* Paper presented at the Margaret Mahler Symposium, Medical College of Pennsylvania, Philadelphia, PA, May.

——— (1997). The continuity of conflict and compromise formation from infancy to childhood: a 25-year follow-up study. *Journal of the American Psychoanalytic Association* 45:105–126.

McDevitt, J., and Settlage, C., eds. (1971). *Separation-Individuation: Essays in Honor of Margaret Mahler.* New York: International Universities Press.

Meissner, W. W. (1970). Notes on identification, I: Origins in Freud. *Psychoanalytic Quarterly* 39:563–589.

——— (1971). Notes on identification, II: Clarification of related concepts. *Psychoanalytic Quarterly* 40:277–302.

——— (1972). Notes on identification, III: The concept of identification. *Psychoanalytic Quarterly* 41:224–260.

Modell, A. (1990). *Other Times, Other Realities: Toward a Theory of Psychoanalytic Treatment.* Cambridge: Harvard University Press.

Nachman, P. (1991). The material representation: a comparison of caregiver- and mother-reared toddlers. *Psychoanalytic Study of the Child* 46:69–90. New Haven: Yale University Press.

Nelson, K., and Gruendel, J. (1981). Generalized event representation: basic building blocks of cognitive development. In *Advances in Development and Psychology*, vol. 1, ed. A. Brown and M. Lamb, pp. 131–158. Hillsdale NJ: Lawrence Erlbaum.

Norman, E. (1948). The play of a psychotic child. *British Journal of Medical Psychology* 21:155–170.

—— (1954). Reality relationships of schizophrenic children. *British Journal of Medical Psychology* 27:126–142.

Olden, C. (1958). Notes on the development of empathy. *Psychoanalytic Study of the Child* 13:505–518. New York: International Universities Press.

Olesker, W. (1984). Sex differences in 2- and 3-year-olds: mother–child relations, peer relations, and peer play. *Psychoanalytic Psychology* 1(4):269–288.

—— (1990). Sex differences during the early separation-individuation process: implications for gender identity formation. *Journal of the American Psychoanalytic Association* 38:325–346.

Parens, H., et al. (1976). On the girl's entry into the Oedipus complex. *Journal of the American Psychoanalytic Association* 24(5):79.

Piaget, J. (1962). *Play, Dreams, and Imitation in Childhood.* New York: Norton.

Pine, F. (1971). On the separation process: universal trends and individual differences. In *Separation-individuation: Essays in Honor of Margaret S. Mahler,* ed. J. B. McDevitt and C. F. Settlage, pp. 113–130. New York: International Universities Press.

—— (1977). Early object experiences in the development of communicative structures: issues posed. In *Communicative Structures and Psychic Structures,* ed. N. Freedman and S. Grand. New York: Plenum.

—— (1979). On the pathology of the separation-individuation process as manifested in later clinical work: an attempt at delineation. *International Journal of Psycho-Analysis* 60:225–242.

—— (1981). In the beginning: contributions to a psychoanalytic developmental psychology. *International Review of Psycho-Analysis* 8:15–33.

—— (1985). Pathology of the separation-individuation process. In *Developmental Theory and Clinical Process,* pp. 227–247. New Haven: Yale University Press.

—— (1990). *Drive, Ego, Object and Self.* New York: Basic Books.

—— (1994). The era of separation-individuation. *Psychoanalytic Inquiry* 14:2–24.

Reich, A. (1940a). A contribution to the psychoanalysis of extreme submissiveness in women. In *Annie Reich: Psychoanalytic Contributions,* pp. 85–98. New York: International Universities Press, 1973.

—— (1940b). Narcissistic object choice in women. In *Annie Reich: Psychoanalytic Contributions,* pp. 179–208. New York: International Universities Press, 1973.

Resch, R. (1979). Hatching and the human infant as the beginning of separation-individuation: what it is and what it looks like. *Psychoanalytic
Study of the Child* 34:421. New Haven: Yale University Press.

Roiphe, H. (1968). On an early genital phase: with an addendum on genesis. *Psychoanalytic Study of the Child* 23:348–365. New York: International Universities Press.

——— (1991). The tormentor and the victim in the nursery. *Psychoanalytic
Quarterly* 60:450–466.

Roiphe, H., and Galenson, E. (1981). *Infantile Origins of Sexual Identity*.
New York: International Universities Press.

Sander, L. W. (1976). Issues in early mother–child interactions. In *Infant
Psychiatry: A New Synthesis*, ed. E. M. Rexford, L. W. Sander, and T.
S. Shapiro. New Haven: Yale University Press.

——— (1977). Regulation of exchange in the infant–caretaker system: a viewpoint on the ontogeny of "structures." In *Communicative Structures
and Psychic Structures*, ed. N. Freedman and S. Grand. New York: Plenum.

——— (1983). Polarity, paradox, and the organizing process in development.
In *Frontiers of Infant Psychiatry*, ed. J. Call, E. Galenson, and R. Tyson,
pp. 333–346. New York: Basic Books.

Schafer, R. (1959). Generative empathy in the treatment situation. *Psychoanalytic Quarterly* 28:342–373.

——— (1968). *Aspects of Internalization*. New York: International Universities Press.

——— (1974). Problems in Freud's psychology of women. *Journal of the
American Psychoanalytic Association* 22:459–487.

Schore, A. (1994). *Affect Regulation and the Origin of the Self: The Neuro-
biology of Emotional Development*. Hillsdale, NJ: Lawrence Erlbaum.

Searles, H. F. (1960). *The Nonhuman Environment in Normal Development
and in Schizophrenia*. New York: International Universities Press.

——— (1973). Concerning therapeutic symbiosis. *Annual of Psychoanalysis*
1:247–262.

Settlage, C., et al. (1990). An exploratory study of mother–child interaction
during the second year of life. *Journal of the American Psychoanalytic
Association* 38:705–732.

Shapiro, T. (1974). The development and distortions of empathy. *Psychoanalytic Quarterly* 43:4–25.

Shapiro, W. (1987). One went right: woes from Wall Street to the Gulf—
but a happy ending in Texas. *Time* 130:30.

Shopper, M. (1978). The role of audition in early psychic development with
special reference to the use of the pull toy in the separation-individu-

ation phase. *Journal of the American Psychoanalytic Association* 26:283–310.

Slade, A. (1986). Symbolic play and separation-individuation. *Bulletin of the Menninger Clinic* 50:541–563.

——— (1987a). A longitudinal study of maternal involvement and symbolic play during the toddler period. *Child Development* 58:367–375.

——— (1987b). Quality of attachment and early symbolic play. *Developmental Psychology* 23:78–85.

Slade, A., and Bergman, A. (1988). The clinical assessment of toddlers. In *The Assessment of Children and Adolescents*, ed. J. Sours and M. Mahler. New York: Jason Aronson.

Sroufe, L. A. (1979). The coherence of individual development: early care, attachment and subsequent development issues. *American Psychologist* 34:834–841.

Spitz, R. A. (1957). *No and Yes: On the Genesis of Human Communication*. New York: International Universities Press.

——— (1965). *The First Year of Life*. New York: International Universities Press.

Steinbeck, J. (1972). *Travels with Charley*. New York: Bantam.

Steiner, J. (1992). The equilibrium between the paranoid-schizoid and the depressive positions. In *Clinical Lectures on Klein and Bion*, ed. R. Anderson, pp. 46–58. London: Tavistock/Routledge.

Stepansky, P., ed. (1988). *The Memoirs of Margaret S. Mahler*. New York: Free Press.

Stern, D. (1971). A micro-analysis of mother–infant interaction. *Journal of the American Academy of Child Psychiatry* 10:501–517.

——— (1974). The goal and structure of mother–infant play. *Journal of the American Academy of Child Psychiatry* 13:402–421.

——— (1977). *The First Relationship: Mother and Infant*. Cambridge: Harvard University Press.

——— (1980). *The early development of schemas of self, of other, and the various experiences of self and other*. Paper presented at the symposium on Reflections on Self Psychology, the Boston Psychoanalytic Society and Institute.

——— (1982). *Implications of infancy research for clinical theory and practice*. Paper presented at the 13th Annual Margaret S. Mahler Symposium.

——— (1983). The early differentiation of self and other. In *Reflections on Self Psychology*, ed. S. Kaplan and J. D. Lichtenberg. Hillsdale, NJ: Analytic Press.

——— (1985). *The Interpersonal World of the Human Infant*. New York: Basic Books.

——— (1992). Pre-narrative envelope: an alternative view of "unconscious fantasy" in infancy. *Bulletin of the Anna Freud Centre* 15:291–318.

——— (1995). *The Motherhood Constellation: A Unified View of Parent–Infant Psychotherapy.* New York: Basic Books.

Stern, D. N., Barnett, R. K., and Spieker, S. (1980). *Early transmission of affect: some research issues.* Paper presented at the First World Congress on Infant Psychiatry, Portugal, April.

Stoller, R. J. (1976). Primary femininity. *Journal of the American Psychoanalytic Association* 24:59–78.

Tustin, F. (1981). *Autistic States in Children.* Boston: Routledge and Kegan Paul.

Tyson, P. (1982). A developmental line of gender identity, gender role, and choice of love object. *Journal of the American Psychoanalytic Association* 30:61–86.

Voyat, G. (1978). Cognitive and social development: a new perspective. In *The Development of Social Understanding*, ed. J. Glick and A. Clarke-Stewart. New York: Gardner Press.

——— (1980). Piaget on schizophrenia. *Journal of the American Academy of Psychoanalysis* 8:93–113.

Weich, M. (1978). Transitional language. In *Between Reality and Fantasy: Transitional Objects and Phenomena*, ed. S. A. Grolnick and L. Barkin, pp. 411–423. New York: Jason Aronson.

Winnicott, D. W. (1953). Transitional objects and transitional phenomena: a study of the first not-me possession. *International Journal of Psycho-Analysis* 34:89–97.

——— (1956a). *D. W. Winnicott: Collected Papers.* London: Tavistock.

——— (1956b). Primary maternal preoccupation. In *Collected Papers*, pp. 300–305. London: Tavistock, 1958.

——— (1958a). The capacity to be alone. In *The Maturational Processes and the Facilitating Environment*, pp. 29–36. New York: International Universities Press, 1965.

——— (1958b). Anxiety associated with insecurity. In *Collected Papers*, pp. 97–100. London: Tavistock.

——— (1960). Ego distortion in terms of true and false self. In *The Maturational Processes and the Facilitating Environment*, pp. 140–157. New York: International Universities Press, 1965.

——— (1963). The development of the capacity for concern. In *The Maturational Processes and the Facilitating Environment*, pp. 73–82. New York: International Universities Press, 1965.

——— (1964). *The Child, the Family, and the Outside World.* London: Penguin.

——— (1965). *The Maturational Processes and the Facilitating Environment.* New York: International Universities Press.

——— (1967). Location of cultural experience. *International Journal of Psycho-Analysis* 48:368–372.

——— (1970). The mother–infant experience of mutuality. In *Parenthood: Its Psychology and Psychopathology,* ed. E. J. Anthony and T. Benedek. Boston: Little, Brown.

——— (1971). *Playing and Reality.* New York: Basic Books.

Credits

The author gratefully acknowledges permission to reprint material from the following sources:

Chapter 1: Parts of this chapter originally appeared in "Margaret Mahler's Theory of Separation-Individuation" in *Handbook of Child and Adolescent Psychiatry*, edited by J. Noshpitz. Copyright © 1996 HarperCollins.

Chapter 2: In *Between Reality and Fantasy*, edited by S. Grolnick and L. Barkin. Copyright © 1978 Jason Aronson Inc.

Chapter 3: In *Rapprochement: The Critical Subphase of Separation-Individuation*, edited by R. Lax, S. Bach, and J. A. Burland. Copyright © 1980 Jason Aronson Inc.

Chapter 4: In *New Ideas in Psychology*, vol. 1, no. 2. Copyright © 1983 Elsevier Science.

Chapter 5: In *Early Female Development: Current Psychoanalytic Views*, edited by D. Mendell. Copyright © 1982 Spectrum Books.

Chapter 6: In *Empathy II.* Copyright © 1984 Analytic Press.

Chapter 7: In *Parental Influences in Health and Disease,* edited by E. J. Anthony. Copyright © 1985 Little, Brown and Company.

Chapter 8: In *Psychoanalytic Inquiry,* vol. 7. Copyright © Analytic Press.

Chapter 9: In *Children at Play: Clinical and Developmental Approaches to Meaning and Representation,* ed. A. Slade and D. P. Wolf. Copyright © 1994 Oxford University Press.

Chapter 10: In *Journal of the American Psychoanalytic Association.* Copyright © 1996 International Universities Press.

Chapter 11: In *The Seasons of Life,* edited by S. Akhtar and S. Kramer. Copyright © 1997 Jason Aronson Inc.

Chapter 12: In *Issues in Psychoanalytic* Psychology, vol. 19, no. 2. Copyright © *Issues in Psychoanalytic Psychology.*

Chapter 13: In *Parental Influences in Health and Disease,* edited by E. J. Anthony. Copyright © 1985 Little, Brown and Company.

Chapter 14: In *Separation-Individuation: Festschrift in Honor of Margaret Mahler.* Copyright © 1971 International Universities Press.

Chapter 15: Parts of this chapter originally appeared in *Models and Techniques of Psychotherapeutic Interventions in the First Year of Life,* ed. D. Stern and G. Fava. Copyright © 1992 Raffaello Cortina Editore.

Chapter 16: In *International Journal of Psychoanalytic Psychotherapy,* vol. 9. Copyright © 1982 Jason Aronson Inc.

Chapter 17: In *Journal of the American Psychoanalytic Association,* vol. 31. Copyright © 1983 International Universities Press.

Chapter 18: In *Infantile Autism,* vol. 146. Copyright © 1987 *Infantile Autism.*

Chapter 19: In *The Psychoanalytic Review,* vol. 80. Copyright © 1993 Guilford Publications.

Index